Florida in the
Popular Imagination

ALSO BY STEVE GLASSMAN

*Florida Crime Writers: 24 Interviews*
(McFarland, 2008)

# Florida in the Popular Imagination

Essays on the
Cultural Landscape of
the Sunshine State

*Edited by* STEVE GLASSMAN

McFarland & Company, Inc., Publishers
*Jefferson, North Carolina, and London*

Thanks to Embry-Riddle Aeronautical University
and especially Provost Richard Heist
for the sabbatical that made this book possible.

LIBRARY OF CONGRESS CATALOGUING-IN-PUBLICATION DATA

Florida in the popular imagination : essays on the cultural landscape
of the Sunshine State / edited by Steve Glassman.
    p.    cm.
Includes bibliographical references and index.

ISBN 978-0-7864-3964-5
softcover : 50# alkaline paper ∞

1. Florida — Social life and customs.  2. Florida — In popular
culture.  I. Glassman, Steve.
F311.5.F616  2009
306.09759 — dc22
                                        2009009460

British Library cataloguing data are available

©2009 Steve Glassman. All rights reserved

*No part of this book may be reproduced or transmitted in any form
or by any means, electronic or mechanical, including photocopying
or recording, or by any information storage and retrieval system,
without permission in writing from the publisher.*

Cover images ©2009 Shutterstock

Manufactured in the United States of America

*McFarland & Company, Inc., Publishers*
  *Box 611, Jefferson, North Carolina 28640*
    *www.mcfarlandpub.com*

For Stuart McIver,
who contributed greatly to the popular culture
and history of the state of Florida

# Table of Contents

PREFACE     1

Mickey, Mammals, Movies, and More: A Theme Park Extravaganza
 *(Joy M. Banks)* . . . . . . . . . . . . . . . . . . . . . . . 5
Before the Mouse: From Glass-Bottom Boats to Gatorland
 *(Keith L. Huneycutt)* . . . . . . . . . . . . . . . . . . . 19
Where Being Gay Isn't a Drag *(Margaret Mishoe and Michael Perez)* . . 33
The Architecture of Dreams *(Jeff Morgan)* . . . . . . . . . . . . 46
Weathering the Climate *(Steve Glassman)* . . . . . . . . . . . . 57
Taking to the Water *(Duncan H. Haynes)* . . . . . . . . . . . . 77
Sunsets, Sunglasses, and Celebrities on the Small Screen
 *(Valerie E. Kasper)* . . . . . . . . . . . . . . . . . . . . 98
Dangerous Game: Snakes, Gators and One-Ton Sharks
 *(Steve Glassman)* . . . . . . . . . . . . . . . . . . . . 117
Hollywood East *(Linda B. Moore)* . . . . . . . . . . . . . . . 138
"'If you don't like this town get out and stay out'":
 Ernest Hemingway's Key West *(E. Stone Shiflet and
 James H. Meredith)* . . . . . . . . . . . . . . . . . . . 147
The Space Coast: Where Dreams Meet Possibilities
 *(Tammy Powley)* . . . . . . . . . . . . . . . . . . . . 159
Cuban Miami: Manufacturing Casablanca *(Rafael Miguel Montes)* . . . 172
The Highwaymen and Other Black Icons *(Edmondson Asgill)* . . . . . 185
The Dazzling Lure of Treasure Hunting *(Kathleen Robinson)* . . . . . 201
Snowbirds Seek Solar Solace *(Steven Knapp and
 Sarah M. Mallonee)* . . . . . . . . . . . . . . . . . . . 217
Spring Break *(Jeff Morgan and Salena Coller)* . . . . . . . . . . 231

Motorsports Rev Up the Economy *(Alan Pratt)* . . . . . . . . . . . . 236
Peculiar Presidential Politics Among the Palm Trees
*(Steve Glassman)* . . . . . . . . . . . . . . . . . . . . . . . . . . 252

ABOUT THE CONTRIBUTORS   265

INDEX   267

# *Preface*

One of the first things I did on moving permanently to Florida many decades ago was head down to the local branch library and check out a history of the state. Every school kid knew Florida was the first part of the continental United States discovered by Europeans. And just about everyone knew that it was from Florida that human explorers blasted off for the moon. To add a little sauce to that, some scholars believe that Ponce de León first made landfall in the Sunshine State just a stone's throw from the very spot at Cape Canaveral from which the Apollo missions were launched. I figured with bookends like those, the history in between had to be spellbinding.

As far as I was concerned, Florida oozed fascination. I can thank Uncle Sam (and the Westinghouse Corporation) for my introduction to the Sunshine State some years earlier. As a raw youth, I had been sent to Key West and Miami for Peace Corps training. Later in the South Pacific where I was posted, my friends tell me I talked about Florida incessantly. And why not? Florida seemed so much more tropical. There were miles of beaches and palm trees everywhere in the Sunshine State, neither of which, beaches or palm trees, were easy to find in the islands I was in — or many other islands — in the South Pacific. Even those bugbears of the tropics, hurricanes (or typhoons or willy willies, as you please), were more common in Florida than where I was stationed because of the lack of the Coriolis effect (which provides the spin needed to get tropical cyclones going) near the equator. So it was no surprise to find me back in Florida.

But what I found in that book written by a professor who was touted as the grand old man of Florida history was surprising: hardly anything of interest ever occurred in the Sunshine State. His was easily the most boring history I have ever read. I put that book down and picked up the *Miami Herald*. Flipping through that paper, I was amused and occasionally horrified but almost always fascinated by the environmental investigations of Carl Hiaasen, the humor of Dave Barry, and the crime reporting of Edna Buchanan as well as stories of the general carryings on in Miami and the rest of the Sunshine State. Maybe historical things of note had not happened in Florida, but things were hopping here at present. Some such as the Mariel Boatlift, which along with the Iran hostage crisis put a period on Jimmy Carter's presidency, attracted national attention. But many more, such as the doings of local gangster Monkey Morales, were parochial affairs. Otherwise, Florida both pleased and astonished me. The flora in south Florida — like almost everything else in south Florida — was altogether

1

different from the flora of any place in the continental U.S. And when I moved to central Florida some years later and found seemingly northern plants such as maple trees commonplace, the way they were growing knee-deep in the swamps was hardly like back home in the Midwest. Their foliage might have changed colors like good maple trees, going vibrantly red, but that happened late in December or even January. I have rarely heard anyone remark on the fall colors in central Florida because even though there is pretty good color in patches here and there, there isn't really an autumn to go with it.

In short, Florida was strange from the point of view of the Upper 48. I became aware of that fact when I was watching a year-end wrapup of the cable news/entertainment show *Countdown with Keith Olbermann*. Keith's program mines the wire services and the Internet for oddball carryings on, and at the end of the year he recounts the oddest of the odd. Olbermann crowned Florida as the weirdest of the 50 states and concluded the program with a rundown of its most outlandish activities. He was impressed with the number of creatures in the Sunshine State that could (and occasionally did) devour or otherwise kill humans: gators, sharks, panthers, black bears, pythons, wild hogs, rattlesnakes. He even cited manatees and dolphins, which harm no one. In particular, he seemed obsessed with the python that tried to swallow an alligator in the Everglades. Likewise, the ingenuity (read stupidity) of Florida criminals was celebrated, and also remarked upon were the Teri Schiavo case and, years before, the TV personality who committed suicide on live TV. Behind Olbermann's poking fun at my adopted state may have been the man's well-known tilt to the political left. He may have felt a bit of lingering peevishness at Florida's puzzling performance in the 2000 presidential election.

All this got me to thinking. Perhaps Florida was not one of those places where important battles were fought or where men in clean linen speaking fine phrases swapped colonies and redirected the lives of millions as if they were checkers on a board. But it is equally clear the Sunshine State has developed a popular culture that has entranced (and sometimes repelled) vast hordes in other parts of the United States and to a lesser extent the world. So why not, I asked myself, contact a group of qualified scholars to do an examination of our popular culture? That I have done and what you have here is the fruit of that effort.

Anyone can write about popular culture; it is, after all, popular. The contributors to this volume, however, are all professional scholars. Most hold Ph.D.s and all have been published previously. Readers should not think the essays are over their heads. Because we are writing about popular culture, I asked the contributors to avoid academic language and write in straightforward, informal American English. Here and there a couple of them took refuge in academic habits but by and large each essay in this collection can be read with profit by anyone. The works cited lists will clue readers into the amount of research and complexity of ideas contained in the essays. Most contributors cite a substantial number of sources, and all consult a full range of scholarly and popular material. The scholars writing in this book are almost all native Floridians, and by "native Floridian" I mean someone like me who moved to Florida from elsewhere several decades ago. There are even a few of that real oddity, Floridian by birth. My point is that the contributors have lived the culture of the Sunshine State as well as having studied it.

Seventy million people — impressive by any standard — pass through the portals of Florida theme parks annually, so we start our investigation with a discussion of Mickey and Shamu and the crew. Joy M. Banks of nearby Lakeland directs us in our search, and her colleague at Florida Southern College, Keith Huneycutt, describes the tourist attractions enjoyed by tin-can campers in the days before the megaparks elbowed out the more organically Florida parks (Huneycutt himself was a latter-day tin-can camper). We then head south with my colleagues at Embry-Riddle, Margaret Mishoe and Michael Perez, as they discuss the development of "gay" Florida, including the development of South Beach and the deconstruction of Key West. Jeff Morgan of Lynn University talks about the distinctive architecture of central and south Florida.

No book on Florida popular culture would be complete without an essay on hurricanes and the various other meteorological events Florida is famous for. I tackle those topics, and the equally integral topic of Florida boat culture is dealt with by Duncan H. Haynes, a man of many vocations and avocations. Haynes is a retired research scientist from the University of Miami, but I came to know him by the pen name of Dirk Wyle as the author of a series of mystery novels set in south Florida. Valerie E. Kasper of St. Leo University discusses the television shows filmed and set in Florida, and I give the lowdown on the dangerous creatures in Florida, of which there are a fair number. Linda B. Moore of the University of West Florida, our lone representative from the panhandle, provides a rundown of the films set and filmed in the state.

The first of the individual subjects up for consideration is, not surprisingly, Papa Hemingway. Hemingway lived in our state just a few years and none of his major works is set here; nevertheless, his memory lives on in the popular imagination thanks to the annual look-alike contest in the Keys and, more important, his towering figure in popular culture. E. Stone Shiflet of Capella University and James H. Meredith of the Air Force Academy direct our investigation of him. Our next two topics are also absolutely essential to any venture into Florida popular culture. Tammy Powley of Indian River Community College tells us about the development of NASA and the moon shot from the Florida shores, and Rafael Miguel Montes of Saint Thomas University discusses the Cuban experience in Miami by critiquing several popular travel books on his hometown. Edmondson Asgill of Behune Cookman University expounds on several themes of the African American experience in Florida. (If you have not yet heard of the Highwaymen school of landscape painters, his essay will prove instructive and maybe profitable, should you happen to find one of the Highwaymen's paintings tucked away in the attic.) Kathleen Robinson of Eckerd College gives us the scoop on Florida treasure hunting. Almost everyone is familiar with Mel Fisher's stupendous finds, but Kathleen tells us what earlier treasure seekers and "wreckers" went through as well. Steven Knapp and Sarah M. Mallonee of Indian River Community College discuss the so-called snowbirds or temporary winter residents of the state. Jeff Morgan and Salena Coller of American InterContinental University talk about another Florida iconic institution, spring break. They tell us when it started, just prior to World War II, and how it spun off after a fashion from baseball's spring training. Yet another vernal rite that developed in the Sunshine State is NASCAR's premier event, the Daytona 500. My colleague at ERAU, Alan Pratt, no stranger to motorsports, examines how this Florida motorsport event came to eclipse the older Indy-style race events in the national consciousness. Pratt also pays attention to a more specialized, though considerably larger event attendance-wise, Bike Week. Finally, I close out the book with a discussion of the 2000 presidential election.

This book is addressed to the student of Florida popular culture. That student may be in high school, an undergraduate at a community college, or a graduate student at an Ivy League university considering a topic for a dissertation in the humanities. That student may be an elderhostel denizen who hasn't cracked a book for a while but thinks it's high time to learn about one of the more interesting areas of the country. Florida is a big state with much going on and to date not nearly enough has been written about it. Read this book, get some ideas, fire up your computer and draft an article for Wikipedia — or my next effort on a topic of Florida popular culture and history.

# Mickey, Mammals, Movies, and More: A Theme Park Extravaganza
*Joy M. Banks*

Florida. Some readers may see the word; think of the state; and then think of things like beaches, orange trees, and alligators. Then there are others who see the word; think of Orlando; and think of theme parks, roller coasters, and tourists. I should confess now that I am a Florida native. I did not grow up in Orlando, but I was always keenly aware of the impact of tourists on my hometown. My parents seemed to be tenser while driving in the winter months. We always had to leave more time to get places, and inevitably when we got wherever we were going, it was crowded. Summer was the season of bliss. The roads weren't full, the restaurants weren't that crowded, and it was so hot that no out-of-state person would dare venture to Florida. Even in my own child mind, I realized that Florida was a state that, for whatever reason, wanted to cater to all of these strangers, and that it had been doing this since long before Disney. My great-grandfather from Baltimore drove busloads of people to the state just for the oranges after World War II. My grandparents from Vermont would drive down U.S. 1, in the days before I-95, with their camper behind them to visit the Sunshine State. Tourism is not new to Florida; however, my task is not to talk about the industry as it was in Florida. In fact, discussion of the industry as a whole will only be a by-product of a closer look at the modern-day theme parks and attractions in the state and their perception in popular culture. In his book *Land of Sunshine, State of Dreams: A Social History of Modern Florida*, Gary Mormino offers this staggering statistic:

> Remarkably, five of America's top seven mega-theme parks are located in Orlando, annually bringing crowds who purchase nearly 50 million tickets and spend $17 Billion. To put such numbers in perspective, consider that on the eve of the Magic Kingdom's opening in 1971 about 3.5 million tourists visited Central Florida annually [104–105].

Keep in mind that these numbers are from 2002. The 2007 numbers for park attendance released by the Themed Entertainment Association (TEA) and Economics Research Associates (ERA) are even more astonishing. Estimated figures for the Walt Disney World, Universal Orlando, and SeaWorld resorts, including their related water parks, show that nearly 70 million people visited, clearly illustrating why so many non–Floridians consider the state to be one giant theme park. This chapter will give a better understanding of modern theme park history and development in Florida, the various audiences the parks hope to attract to their sites, and the impact the big three — Disney World, SeaWorld, and Universal Orlando — have on their communities. Since these three corporations are not the only theme-park investors in the state, there will also be a brief discussion of three other modern theme parks in the Sunshine State.

Of the big three parks, Disney World arrived first in central Florida. Much has been written on this pet project of Walt Disney, but most folks may not know what drew Disney to such an odd location in the first place. According to Allen Morris in the 1963–1964 *Florida Handbook*, Orlando had just over 88,000 inhabitants (263) and Miami had over 290,000 residents (261) in 1960. Why choose such a desolate location? One reason may have been that Disney's family actually had a history in central Florida dating back to the 1880s. In *200 Quick Looks at Florida History* (2000), James Clark explains that Disney's grandfather (Kepple), father (Elias), and mother (Flora) failed miserably in Florida. Elias tried his hand at producing oranges, but unfortunately, his crop was destroyed by a freeze after less than a year. Elias and Flora promptly left Florida and never returned. The land purchased by Walt in the mid–1960s was only a few miles away from the homestead his father tried to farm (93). While sentimentality may have initially attracted Disney to the central region of the state, practicality eventually won him over to the city of Orlando. In a discussion about Disney's selection process, Mormino states that no other location in Florida "could match Orlando's winning combination of climate, cheap land with plenty of room for expansion, and a large nonunion workforce to meet the park's needs" (102). How could a businessman resist such a prospect? Disney's ability to strike a deal with the state allowed his park the luxury to develop and expand free from interference from the state or local governments. The park essentially acts "as a county within a county, a private corporation with the power and autonomy to construct and manage an amusement park" (Mormino 103). Perhaps the most visible example of Disney's power today is the Mickey Mouse-shaped electrical pole along the side of I-4 near Lake Buena Vista. Most natives probably see the irony in the iconic symbol as part of the power company's infrastructure, but tourists get a kick out of it.

Construction on Disney World, a park slated to be much larger than its sister in California, began in 1969, three years after the designer's death (Mormino 103). In the tradition of the Disneyland park in California, the Magic Kingdom at Walt Disney World (and the other parks designed later) was not engineered or designed but rather "Imagineered." Karal Ann Marling, in "Imagineering the Disney Theme Parks," explains that the term Imagineering is "Walt's own term: imagination + engineering = 'Imagineering'" (30). The entire idea of Walt Disney World was based on the notion of capturing the imagination and making it a reality, ultimately creating a unique escape from the mundane world. This idea works. Mormino notes that "the opening of the Magic Kingdom instantly changed the dynamics of Florida and American tourism. Never in the history of the Sunshine State had the opening of a single business so altered the course of an industry" (104).

The Magic Kingdom was only the beginning of the Walt Disney World dream for Orlando. The people in the Imagineering Department created River Country (1976), the first water park opened by Disney, which closed in 2001; Epcot (1982), the last original Walt Disney-conceived idea; Disney-MGM (1989), now called Disney's Hollywood Studios; Typhoon Lagoon (1989), the second Disney water park; Blizzard Beach (1995), an attempt to create a frozen land in the Florida sun and relieve overcrowding at Typhoon Lagoon; and finally Disney's Animal Kingdom (1998), the most recent addition to the Disney family in Florida (Ridgway 153, 120, 147, 155, 181). Resorts from the rustic (Fort Wilderness) to the elegant (The Grand Floridian) and activities like Downtown Disney complete the Disney experience for visitors. In fact, visitors who stay in a resort can completely avoid Orlando traffic and those pesky other distractions (like the other theme parks in the city). In the Lonely Planet guide to Florida, Kim Grant describes the airport-to-resort shuttle services that Disney provides its guests in addition to the seamless transportation network linking all of the various Disney parks (295–96). Staying in a resort also offers other perks:

> Not only can it save you shelling out for theme park parking, a rental car and gas, but the best perk is the "extra magic hours" available to resort guests only. This allows you to either enter early or stay up to three hours later than when the parks open/close to the public [295].

By providing these kinds of services to guests, Disney's dream of creating a magical world for his guests, removed from the banality of real life, is realized.

The construction of Walt Disney World opened the floodgates for tourism to enter central Florida. Parks such as Busch Gardens, established in 1959 as an actual garden to complement the Anheuser-Busch brewery in Tampa felt pressure to expand and compete (Mormino 108–109). Other, older parks, like those discussed elsewhere in this book, felt the squeeze of Disney's popularity and were forced to close. Disney's success, however, did not prevent others from coming to town but rather fostered their development. Encouraged by Disney World's success in Orlando, the owners and developers of SeaWorld decided to try their hand at Florida. *Florida*, part of the Eyewitness Travel series, explains that SeaWorld opened in 1976 and "is a match for any of Orlando's other theme parks" (176). In fact, many travel books boast of SeaWorld's accessibility and likability. The *Mobile Travel Guide: Florida* says, "SeaWorld Adventure Park, Orlando, offers the absolute best of all the theme park worlds" (153) and *Lonely Planet* adds that while "sometimes overlooked in the shadow of those giant mouse ears, SeaWorld and its sister park, Discovery Cove, are two parks that more than hold their own in this thrill-packed city" (Grant 268). SeaWorld has always been my favorite park. I remember visiting as a child and being amazed at the animal shows: dolphins swimming and jumping, orcas making big splashes, and seals and sea lions doing a comedy act. The marketing team at SeaWorld did its job because as a child, and even into my teen years, I always referred to any orcas as "Shamu." SeaWorld offered the spectacle of real animals rather than the fantasy of cartoon characters. The only concession to fantasy the marketing team seemed to make was naming the various characters of their live shows— Clyde and Seymore the Sea Lions are still my favorite — and providing mass-produced souvenirs to purchase in park gift shops. Until just recently, I still had a deck of cards I bought as a child that had all of the various SeaWorld characters printed on them. In her book *Spectacular Nature: Corporate Culture and the SeaWorld Experience*, Susan G. Davis notes that while most other major theme parks in the world rely heavily on fantasy creatures and cartoons, "The SeaWorld chain discovered the charisma of marine mammals and the benefits of specializing in marine nature and wildlife" (25). While "Clyde and Seymour" still perform at the daily shows, SeaWorld seems more confident in relying on this strength — its real animals— rather than concocting an imaginary world of cartoons.

In 1977, SeaWorld branched out into the water park business, building Wet'n'Wild (*Eyewitness* 186). This addition occurred about the same time as Harcourt Brace Jovanovich (HBJ) purchased the SeaWorld chain from its original developers. According to Davis, HBJ had high hopes of successfully integrating the marketing of the marine park into its other educational endeavors (26). Some readers may even remember a series of children's books that HBJ developed that were labeled "A SeaWorld book for young readers," books that may still be in some public libraries today. The publishing house's efforts were not as profitable as they imagined, however, and in 1989 the parks were purchased by Anheuser-Busch, a company familiar with the theme park industry and with one park already in Florida (26). Anheuser-Busch's control of the park brought revitalization to SeaWorld as it embraced the essence of animals as the main attraction.

In 1998, Wet'n'Wild was sold to the Universal Orlando Resort, but SeaWorld was not done with the water park business (Rose). In "What's Doing in Orlando," Sara Kennedy highlights the July 2000 opening of a new kind of park: Discovery Cove. Discovery Cove is unique in that it offers visitors the chance to actually swim with marine wildlife, most notably the dolphins. Mike Beirne described the new concept in his pre-opening article, "Into the Swim": "The 35-acre amalgam of white sand beaches, lagoons, tropical aviary and waterfalls will be unlike most crowded theme parks by limiting admission to about 1,000 reserved places daily" (5). The exclusivity of the park does not come cheap, however, with current pricing to swim with the dolphins ranging from $269 to $289 per person depending on the season. After the unveiling of Discovery Cove, Anheuser-Busch launched a new marketing campaign for SeaWorld, once again emphasizing visitors' ability to "connect with nature" (Beirne, "Unexpected" 9). SeaWorld's attitude towards Walt Disney World also changed with this new campaign: "Unlike previous strategy which used discounts and deals to lure Disney patrons for a day or two visit, the Anheuser-Busch unit is trying to get vacationers to make a Busch park their travel destination" ("Unexpected" 9). Further updates to the SeaWorld park in 2006 and the addition of the new water park Aquatica in the summer of 2008 place the SeaWorld Orlando resort in an excellent position; however, park attendance numbers will probably never surpass those of the Disney parks. The Disney parks in Orlando hold four of the top eight positions for theme park attendance in 2007 (the other four are various Disney parks around the world) (Rubin 7). SeaWorld aims to create experiences that Disney cannot, mainly interaction with aquatic animals. Daniel Keller offers a rather poetic view of SeaWorld's mission in "Creating a New Reality: Reinventing SeaWorld Orlando's Legendary Waterfront":

> The park's animals are more than just entertainment — they are its raison d'etre, a living lesson of friendship, caring, and conservation, with a devoted staff of trainers, scientists, and environmentalists nurturing the park's flora, fauna, and aquatic surroundings around the clock, whether ore [sic] not there are visitors [77].

SeaWorld has moved far beyond children's books and playing cards to create this memorable interaction with aquatic life in a city about fifty miles away from the nearest Atlantic beach.

The development of major theme parks did not end with SeaWorld. The final major contender for the tourist dollar in Orlando planned to meet Disney head-on. From the very beginning, Universal had an eye on Disney's attendees. In "Riding the Movies" (1991), B. D. Johnson describes the initial impetus for the Universal park in Orlando:

> In the early 1980s, MCA assembled a 444-acre tract of land just 15 km [9 miles] from Disney World. Hoping to take a King Kong-sized bite out of Disney's business, the company explored the possibility of building a studio park with Paramount Pictures, which [Michael] Eisner then headed. That deal fell through, and Eisner moved to Disney in 1984. Then, beating Universal to the punch, Eisner went ahead with Disney-MGM Studios at Disney World [49].

Johnson describes the Universal executives as "enraged" by Eisner's actions and includes some rather colorful exchanges between Eisner and Jay Stein, an MCA executive (49). While MCA's plans for the park were big, the road to success has been a bumpy one. Johnson describes the malfunctioning of three different rides in the park shortly after its opening in 1990 (50). In fact, broken rides are what I remember most about Universal Studios in the days before Islands of Adventure and City Walk. While Disney probably has its fair share of broken rides (Thunder Mountain was undergoing some "Imagineering" work the last time I was at Disney), Universal seemed to lack Disney's ability to disguise malfunctions.

But a bumpy start did not deter development for Universal. The park continued to push the envelope with technology, developing more advanced rides, retiring rides from older movies, and continually pumping money into the park. Faye Bowers's "When E.T. Elbows Mickey: Florida's Clash of the Theme Parks" discusses huge projects by the new owner, Seagram Company, including "a $2.5 billion expansion project." You read correctly; that's billion with a "b," and it seems even more impressive when you take into consideration that project took place over ten years ago. Frank Rose describes what he saw on a special tour with Edgar Bronfman Jr., "the Seagram heir":

> Islands of Adventure ... is one cool park. The existing park — Universal Studios Florida, with its "Ride the Movies" theme — is an invitation to step inside the big screen.... The new one uses the movies as an elaborate excuse to shoot you through the air, dump you into the water, toss you upside down, and otherwise subject you to the rigors of extreme fun.

"Extreme" only begins to describe the various rides in Islands of Adventure. The Incredible Hulk roller coaster was the first roller coaster I ever rode. I was in college, and peer pressure worked its dirty magic on my mind. For those of you who have been on this particular coaster, you will realize my mistake at making this my virgin coaster ride. From the Universal Orlando Web site, we learn that the ride goes from "zero to 40 mph in two seconds flat," the coaster "launches riders upward 150 ft. and reaches top speeds of 67 mph." This was no spin on the magical teacups at Disney, and Branford and the other Islands developers did not want it to be. Rose offers a quote from Branford on the subject: "'What is Disney? Disney is family, it's fun, it's warm, it's safe. We're not. And that means we're going to skew to a slightly older audience. North of 8, north of 9 — that's who we're going after, plus parents.'" With rides like the Incredible Hulk and the Amazing Adventures of Spider-Man, I think they've succeeded in attracting their target audience. The *Lonely Planet* description of Universal is my favorite: "Universal Orlando Resort is like Disney's punky little sister. It does its own thing, runs with a slightly different crowd and throws the best parties that last until the sun comes up" (297). The addition of hotels, restaurants, and City Walk created a real contender for Disney's market. The park's marketing, much like SeaWorld's, also centers on turning "Universal into a destination, instead of a place to go after you've done everything at Disney World" (Rose). This notion is emphasized on the park's Web site, openly inviting visitors to compare Universal experiences directly with those at Disney. This "Compare to Disney" link is visible not only on the Universal Orlando Resort homepage, but almost every subsequent page in the Web site. While the chart offers a somewhat honest comparison between the two resorts, there is an obvious bias towards Universal, including such comparisons as "Today's Hottest Entertainment" versus "Yesterday's Classic Fairytale." Universal's direct battle approach appears to be working. Whereas SeaWorld may never reach Disney's extraordinary attendance numbers, the parks of Universal are making a good show. The TEA/ERA report estimates that approximately 13 million visitors passed through the gates of Universal Studios, Islands of Adventure, and Wet'n'Wild in 2007. This is about twenty-five percent of the nearly 51 million visitors of the six Walt Disney World parks in Orlando.

While the history of their development provides a wonderful background for the analysis of each of these parks, nothing can compare to the personal experiences and opinions of park attendees. I often wonder at the fanaticism with which some attendees approach a day (or multiple days) at a park. Keep in mind, again, that I am a Florida native. My attitude towards theme parks is much like my attitude towards the beach. I grew up in a house that was less than five miles away from the beach. We went to the beach just about every Saturday of my childhood. I don't need to go to the beach anymore. The same thing goes for Florida theme parks. While I have not been to them as often as I have been to the beach, I have been to all the parks at least twice in my life, some more times. I really do not need to go again (unless someone offers me free tickets). My sentiment towards these parks, however, is not common, as shown by the multi-billion dollar tourism industry in Florida. There are some people in this world that could go to one of these theme parks all day, every day and still never be satisfied.

I will offer a few examples. During my brief time living in Pennsylvania, I met many wonderful people. They were fascinated that a Florida native would move to their state; I was fascinated by their perception of my home state. Most belonged to the set of people mentioned in the introduction who, when thinking of Florida, thought of Orlando and theme parks, with a few alligators thrown in for excitement. One individual that I met while working was obsessed with Disney. She and her family would travel annually to the park for an entire week. They would go to all the parks, stay in one of the resorts on site, and spend lots of money. She was a shoe-in for the Disney Dollar program, basically a dollar-for-dollar currency exchange that provides visitors money with various Disney characters on it. *Lonely Planet: Florida* explains that "the dollars won't net you any additional savings, and are more of a novelty to wide-eyed youngsters who want to purchase a souvenir with Mickey money" (276). My co-worker kept some of this money in her wallet as a souvenir of the trip. When she wasn't at Disney, she was thinking about Disney, looking at Disney merchandise catalogs, selecting Disney memorabilia to purchase, and talking about her next Disney trip. I was amazed, especially since there were so many other theme parks closer to where she lived. Obviously, her excitement was about more than just a few fun rides, and she is not alone. My sister-in-law in Florida has a close friend who often takes her children to the park. The friend says that every visit to Disney World is like another birthday for her children: they get to do whatever, whenever they want. As I understand it, if that means her child wants ice cream for every meal, the wish is granted. That seems to take Disney's latest campaign — the "Year of a Million Dreams" — to an entirely different level.

Please don't think me a cynic. I understand the wonder that a place like the Magic Kingdom can hold. I remember meeting the various characters as a young child. I have wonderful memories with my dad of spinning as fast as we could on the teacups and covering my eyes as we nearly crashed through walls in Mr. Toad's Wild Ride (a ride that runs no more). I even danced with Minnie Mouse. I see my three nieces enamored with the Disney princesses and talking excitedly about eating breakfast with some of the characters during their first trip to Disney (although the breakfast with Cinderella was already sold out). Disney has that kind of memorable brand. Fred Wiersema, a business strategist, acknowledges the success of Disney branding:

> I would be hard-pressed to come up with more than a handful of remote locales where the name Walt Disney doesn't evoke at least minimal recognition. If not the Disney name, then certainly the Disney characters are bound to bring a knowing smile to faces of children and adults from Burbank to Beijing, Honolulu to Helsinki [ix].

Disney's advantage with the recognition of its characters is most certainly why it consistently has the highest attendance rates at its parks around the world. If my experience living in Pennsylvania was culture shock, imagine my surprise when I was in France studying for a month during 2003 and discovered that Mickey Mouse was being used to represent my entire country. During one lesson, we were given a worksheet entitled "De quelle nationalité sont ces poules?" ("What nationality are these hens?") Nine hens are dressed in various garb representing different countries. The French hen has a beret and a baguette, the British hen has an umbrella and a bowler hat, and the American hen has the head of Mickey Mouse. More than one of my American classmates protested the representation. Move over, Uncle Sam, here comes Mickey!

With Disney's strong presence in the world, why would other theme parks even try to compete with the Disney machine? Apart from the obvious response of money, I think that developers at SeaWorld and Universal realize that the childhood attraction of Disney World's Magic Kingdom has a tendency to fade. Disney probably even realized this, adding EPCOT, Disney's Hollywood Studios, and Disney's Animal Kingdom. I still declare that SeaWorld is by far my favorite modern Florida theme park. Who can beat the penguin exhibit and the splash zone at the dolphin show? Many of my friends in the 20- to 30-ish age range agree with me, too. While a quick survey of a handful of Floridians is hardly scientific, SeaWorld seems to have the ability to capture the imagination and spirit of an older crowd. My most recent trip to the park is several years removed at this point, but a few of my close friends who have insider access were able to go to Aquatica before it opened to the public. Once again, SeaWorld found a way to immerse visitors in an interactive experience with sea mammals. Take, for example, the Dolphin Plunge ride: "Two side-by-side enclosed tube slides send you racing through an underwater world that is home to a playful pod of beautiful black-and-white Commerson's Dolphins" ("Dolphin Plunge"). As if one underwater experience isn't enough, Aquatica also offers guests the opportunity to experience aquarium life at a more leisurely pace. Loggerhead Lane takes the lazy river concept to a new level by transporting riders "through an underwater world colored by exotic tropical fish" ("Loggerhead Lane"). My friends had nothing but positive things to say about this new water park, declaring that it truly was unlike anything they had ever experienced. This seems to be a concession to those of us who may not be able to afford over two hundred dollars per person to actually swim with the dolphins over at Discovery Cove. While SeaWorld may not have the same type of fanatic following as Disney, the wonder created in the three aquatic parks still attracts a devoted crowd.

So with dreamers and sea lovers out of the way, what audience remains? Everyone else, and Universal has welcomed the challenge of meeting the needs of those that are left. In addition to the Incredible Hulk and the Amazing Adventures of Spider-Man features, the Universal theme parks seem to cater directly to adolescent boys and their older counterparts with areas dedicated to Marvel Comics and Jurassic Park, and rides featuring the Simpsons, various aliens, and skin-crawling themes. Where Disney fulfills every girl's dream of meeting a "real" princess, Universal allows boys to meet "real" superheroes. The *Lonely Planet* guide admits that "the two parks are more directed toward teens and adults than the Walt Disney World parks" (297). Universal made the assumption that all children must grow up at some point, much to the chagrin of Peter Pan, and has successfully created two environments for this more "mature" crowd.

The cultural impact of these mega-parks goes beyond simply the tourists. A huge infrastructure exists in Orlando to support the day-to-day functioning of each of these parks. Remember, one of the key factors that attracted Walt Disney to Orlando in the first place was its large population of non-union workers. That workforce continues today. In 1999, shortly before Islands of Adventure was to open, thousands of employees in the music industry were looking for work "even as 6,000 Floridians line up to staff a new theme park in Orlando" (Rose). Upon moving to Lakeland (about an hour west of Orlando) from south Florida to attend college in 2001, I began to realize what a huge impact the big three had on high school- and college-age students. Not only had these parks impacted the landscape of central Florida, but their arrival changed the very economic structure of the entire county and surrounding areas. Most of the people I knew from high school that attended the University of Central Florida (UCF) in Orlando got jobs at one of the major theme parks. Of all the parks, Islands of Adventure was perhaps the favorite since it was so new. Sometimes the only appeal of working at a park is free admission. One former employee of City Walk, part of the Universal Orlando Resort, said, "I needed money and wanted a job that would be fun. Also, I enjoyed the idea of going in the parks for free." I enjoyed having friends who worked at the parks and could get me into them for free. Why do they have a disproportionate number of high school and college age employees? She believes it is the pay. Few adults are willing to work irregular hours for minimum wage. A former Disney employee shared similar feelings. She worked at the park during high school in the late 1990s: "As a student and under 18, I would say that working for Disney was great. If I needed a weekend off for school activities they gave it to me no questions asked." Of course, after she turned 18 and no longer was protected by child labor laws, the park's attitude changed; her employers were not quite as flexible. When she was denied vacation time to go on a family trip, she simply quit her job. I believe this is a pattern. Young workers apply for jobs, work the set period of time to earn free tickets, use their tickets, and quit their jobs, perhaps moving on to another park to do the same thing. There is probably little company loyalty. It's just another after-school job with some pretty awesome perks. With almost fifty thousand students enrolled at UCF, the parks have a nearly endless supply of willing park workers, no matter their level of loyalty.

The attitudes of the corporate sector are a bit different. The parks are all known for recruiting individuals directly from colleges and universities. They all have internship programs. The Disney employee quoted above also worked as a summer college intern at Universal Orlando Resort in landscape maintenance. Whereas her experience at Disney was merely "a paycheck and a fun atmosphere," her work as an intern was directly related to her field of study. My favorite stories about her work at Universal during this time included when she dived behind bushes when guests were coming to give the illusion of a maintenance-free landscape or when she made drastic landscaping changes overnight before park guests arrived. Her stories provided an interesting perspective into all that goes into maintaining these fantasy worlds.

Apart from providing employment, the Big Three support a huge hospitality industry. A SeaWorld employee, who started as an intern at one of the Disney resorts, shared what attracted her to the company: "It was my deep love for animals and nature that really made me connect with the park. Everything was real, no animatronics." She did not have the same feeling at Disney. Much like she knew that the Mickey Mouse wandering around in the park was merely an employee in costume, she often felt that corporate employees also wore a sort of Disney-fied mask rather than presenting their true nature. After changing her internship to SeaWorld, she realized that she had found a corporate home where even the "VP of Marketing for all 10 [Anheuser-Busch] parks knows my name, my NFL team, and my professional strengths [and] weaknesses." Hopefully this atmosphere will remain with the sale of Anheuser-Busch to Belgium's InBev; the fate of the Busch family of parks is still uncertain (Foust 52–53). Regardless of the future of the park, this employee has gained invaluable experience that she feels she would never have received while working at a park like Disney that does not necessarily allow its younger managers to explore other areas of work. The most important thing to remember about park employment, according to this source, is that "theme parks have more career opportunities than people realize. It's not just about ride operations; it's culinary and banquets, it's marketing and sales, it's events, it's entertainment and concerts, it's engineering, it's finance." And all the parks are willing to train young, eager employees to do it the Disney or Universal or SeaWorld way.

Since this chapter includes all of Florida's modern theme parks, not just the successful ones, I would be remiss if I ended without mention of a few lesser-known parks. The first of these parks opened in 1993 and had the regal name Florida Splendid China. But don't plan a trip there — this park closed its doors in December 2003. According to Robert H. Brown's *Florida's Lost Tourist Attractions* Web site, Florida Splendid China was built as a sister park to one in Shenzhen China. Unfortunately, "Americans never embraced Florida Splendid China." The park did create some controversy with the public. Protesters would picket outside the gates, claiming the park "was a tool for propaganda rather than entertainment" and pushing to stop visits from area schools. I have at least one memory of this park. When I was in eighth grade, the sixth graders at my school were able to travel to Orlando to visit Splendid China as a supplement to their social studies class. That is probably the first and last time I heard of anyone going to the park. Perhaps this had something to do with the protesters.

The next attempt at creating a faraway land came in 2001, when the Holy Land Experience opened its doors (Pinsky 101). This endeavor seemed to have a better market than Florida Splendid China. In "'Six Flags Over Israel,'" Mark Pinsky notes that "central Florida is a hospitable environment for evangelical Christianity, and local pastors have hailed the attraction as an asset" (101). Holy Land has sparked its own controversies, most of which come from the Jewish community's distaste for the park's greater purpose: "sharing the gospel with Jews in the United States and Israel" (Pinsky 103). The park's owner, Marvin Rosenthal, insisted in 2001 that "Holy Land does not intend to single out Jews, or to lure them to the park under false pretenses" (Pinsky 103). The park continues to survive through the controversy, attracting groups of amateur Biblical scholars hoping to see the true dimensions of Solomon's temple and the details of the Israelite's desert tabernacle; families looking for something less commercial to do in Orlando; and curious locals who have always wondered just what the park involves. With ticket prices around half the cost of the other major theme parks, this seems like a bargain trip. Where else can you go to shake hands and have your picture taken with Noah and Jesus in the same day? I have heard from various visitors that the Holy Land Experience truly is unique, whether you go for the spiritual nature of the park or the sometimes kitschy nature of things like the camel-shaped benches.

Not all of the modern theme parks in Florida follow the Disney/SeaWorld/Universal model. At least one has tried a new sort of experience in addition to an entirely different location. Wannado City, opened in 2004, is geared almost exclusively toward children between 4 and 11 years old. In an *Advertising Age* article, Laurel Wentz explains that "Wannado City is billed as a 'real-play' park that lets kids try out different jobs and make their own decisions" (12). Unlike the Big Three, with their discrete domains, Wannado City is located in the Sawgrass Mills Mall in the greater Ft. Lauderdale area of south Florida. Sawgrass Mills Mall is an attraction in and of itself, billed on its Web site as "Florida's largest retail & entertainment center," featuring "more than 350 name-brand stores and outlets." For CIE, a Latin-American amusement park company, to open a new park in a mall like this seems ingenious. According to the parents' page on the Wannado Web site, children over the age of eight can be left alone in the park, where trained staff will monitor their participation in the park activities. As far as I know, none of the Orlando parks let visitors do that. Even if parents choose to participate with their children, they always have the option of retreating to the "Eagle's Nest" where adults can "enjoy free high-speed Internet access and digital cable television, or relax with a gourmet coffee, pastry or dessert." My eleven-year-old sister recently traveled to this park with her Girl Scout troop, and all of the girls had a fantastic time. The park offers over 200 different job experiences that visitors can try. In one day, participants can realistically sample five to six different occupations such as veterinarian (my sister's favorite), firefighter, actress, newspaper photographer, landscaper, and archaeologist. Children are able to dress in the clothes of the professions, use tools of the trade, and interact with one another to create a realistic experience. Rather than children going to a theme park to meet a particular character, Wannado City allows children, or "kidizens" as the park calls them, to become any character they wish. This sort of environment might be a better place, or at least a more educational place, to let a child's every dream come true.

Undoubtedly, these three small parks will never garner the attention that the other three have gained. Their attendance numbers will probably never appear on the *TEA/ERA Attraction Attendance* reports. But their existence shows just how important and widespread tourism is in Florida. It's nearly impossible to travel to a part of the state that isn't affected in some way by tourism. Dave Barry, a former columnist for the *Miami Herald*, offers a humorous explanation of how to find Disney World:

> Once you get to Florida, you can't miss Disney World, because the Disney corporation owns the entire center of the state. Just get on any major highway, and eventually it will dead-end in a Disney parking area large enough to have its own climate, populated by large nomadic families who have been trying to find their cars since the Carter administration. Be sure to note carefully where you leave *your* car, because later on you may want to sell it so you can pay for your admission tickets [54].

While Barry takes some creative license with his Disney experience, remember that the park does have its own governing body, and Florida only has a handful of major highways so most of them really do lead to the park in some way or another. If a road does not lead to Disney, it takes you to some other tourist destination in the state.

Florida, Orlando, and, more specifically, the people living there have forever been changed by the presence of these theme parks. Every time I drive through Orlando, I see something new: a new hotel, a new shopping mall, a new restaurant. The landscape is forever changing, and it does not include many orange trees or swamps. Perhaps the next big theme park in the state will be a two-hundred-acre park with man-made beaches, landscape-designed orange groves, and carefully maintained swamps. Disney can help with the Imagineering, Universal can produce a nice film to show, and SeaWorld can donate some alligators. I can see the advertisements now. Florida: The Theme Park. Experience the entire state in eight hours or less without leaving the park. Opening Summer of 2020. Watch out for mosquitoes.

## WORKS CITED

Barry, Dave. *Dave Barry's Only Travel Guide You'll Ever Need*. New York: Fawcett Columbine, 1991.
Beirne, Mike. "After Unexpected Attendance Surge, Busch Tends to Gardens, SeaWorld." *Brandweek* 18 Feb. 2002: 9.
_____. "Into the Swim." *Brandweek* 6 Dec. 1999: 5.
Bowers, Faye. "E.T. Elbows Mickey in Florida's Clash of the Theme-Park Titans." *Christian Science Monitor* 4 Dec. 1996. http://www.csmonitor.com/1996/1204/120496.us.us.1. html.
Brown, Robert H. "Florida Splendid China." Florida's Lost Tourist Attractions. http://www.lostparks.com/china.html.
Capodagli, Bill and Lynn Jackson. *The Disney Way: Harnessing the Management Secrets of Disney in Your Company*. Foreword by Fred Wiersema. New York: McGraw-Hill, 1999. ix–x.
Clark, James C. *200 Quick Looks at Florida History*. Sarasota, Fla.: Pineapple Press, 2000.
"Compare to Disney." Universal Orlando Resort. Universal Studios. http://www.universalorlando.com/disney_comparision.html.
Davis, Susan G. *Spectacular Nature: Corporate Culture and the SeaWorld Experience*. Berkeley: University of California Press, 1997.
"De quelle nationalité sont ces poules?" Course handout. Cours de Conversation, Dixième Étage. Centre International d'Études Françaises. Université Catholique de L'Ouest, Angers. May 2003.
"Dolphin Plunge." Aquatica: SeaWorld's Water Park. Busch Entertainment Corporation.http://www.aquaticabyseaworld.com. Path: Explore Aquatica; Catch a Wave; Dolphin Plunge.
*Eyewitness Travel: Florida*. New York: DK Pub, 2006.
"Facts at a Glance." University of Central Florida Office of Institutional Research. http://www.iroffice.ucf.edu/character/current.html.
Foust, Dean, Jack Ewing, and Geri Smith. "Looks Like a Beer Brawl." *Business Week* 28 July 2008: 52–53.
Grant, Kim, et al. *Lonely Planet: Florida*. Oakland, Calif.: Lonely Planet, 2006.
*The Holy Land Experience*. Trinity Broadcasting Network. http://www.theholylandexperience.com/index.html.
"The Incredible Hulk Coaster." Universal Orlando Resort. Universal Studios. http://www.universalorlando.com. Path: Theme Parks; Islands of Adventure; Attractions; Incredible Hulk Roller Coaster.
Johnson, B.D. "Riding the Movies." *Maclean's* 11 March 1991: 48–51.
Keller, Daniel. "Creating a New Reality: Reinventing SeaWorld Orlando's Legendary Waterfront." *Sound & Video Contractor* 24.2 (2006): 76–83.
Kennedy, Sara. "What's Doing in Orlando." *New York Times* 23 July 2000: TR14.
"Loggerhead Lane." Aquatica: SeaWorld's Water Park. Busch Entertainment Corporation. http://www.aquaticabyseaworld.com. Path: Explore Aquatica; Catch a Wave; Loggerhead Lane.
Marling, Karal Ann. "Imagineering the Disney Theme Parks." In *Designing Disney's Theme Parks: The Architecture of Reassurance*. Edited by Karal Ann Marling. Paris: Flammarion, 1997. 29–177.
*Mobile Travel Guide: Florida*. Lincolnwood, Ill.: ExonMobil Travel Publications, 2007.
Mormino, Gary G. *Land of Sunshine, State of Dreams: A Social History of Modern Florida*. Gainesville: University Press of Florida, 2005.
Morris, Allen. *The Florida Handbook: 1963–1964*. Tallahassee, Fla.: Peninsular Publishing, 1963.
Pinsky, Mark I. "'Six Flags Over Israel': An Evangelical Alternative to Disney World Makes a Stormy Debut in Central Florida." *Christianity Today* 5 March 2001: 101–103.

"Plan Your Visit." Wannado City. Wannado Entertainment. http://www.wannadocity.com/grown_ups/planvisit.php.

Powers, Scott. "Attendance at Theme Parks Continues to Skyrocket." OrlandoSentinel. com. 14 March 2008. http://www.orlandosentinel.com/news/local/orange/orl-parks1408mar14,0,5698343.story.

Ridgway, Charles. *Spinning Disney's World: Memories of a Magic Kingdom Press Agent.* Branford, Conn.: Intrepid Traveler, 2007.

Rose, Frank. "Edgar Bronfman Actually Has a Strategy — With a Twist." *Fortune* 1 March 1999. http://money.cnn.com/magazines/fortune/fortune_archive/1999/03/01/255800/ index.htm.

Rubin, Judy, ed. *TEA/ERA Attraction Attendance 2007: Themed Entertainment Association/Economics Research Associates' Attraction Attendance Report.* Burbank, Calif.: Themed Entertainment Association, 2008. http://www.themeit.com/attendance_report 2007.pdf.

"Sawgrass Mills: A Simon Company." Simon Property Group. http://www.simon.com/mall/default.aspx?ID=1262.

"SeaWorld Adventure Parks Orlando." Busch Entertainment Corporation. http://www.seaworld.com/orlando/default.aspx.

"Universal Orlando Resort." Universal Studios. www.universalorlando.com.

"Walt Disney World." Disney. http://disneyworld.disney.go.com/wdw/index.

"Wannado City." Wannado Entertainment. http://www.wannadocity.com/.

Wentz, Laurel. "CIE to Open First U.S. Park." *Advertising Age* 9 Feb. 2004: 12.

# Before the Mouse: From Glass-Bottom Boats to Gatorland

*Keith L. Huneycutt*

Fishing, hunting, golf, beaches, abundant sunshine — there was much to capture the popular imagination and bring visitors from northern states to Florida following World War II. Tourism had at first suffered a downturn with the changes brought about by the war, but the war brought many military personnel and associated civilian workers to Florida. As David J. Coles explains, "Dozens of military installations were activated before and during the war" (1). Memories of these warm places and nearby intriguing sights no doubt lured numerous veterans and civilian workers to return to enjoy the pleasures of Florida with their families in happier times. Many other factors brought hordes of families like mine — and many quite unlike mine — to the Sunshine State. In the later years of the war, Florida tourism received a boost from well-paid civilian workers taking a "furlough" (Coles 1). In postwar years, the tourist trade flourished. In his *Land of Sunshine, State of Dreams*, historian Gary Mormino identifies additional reasons for the boom in Florida's popularity:

> In history's most spectacular burst of economic expansion and upward mobility, millions of European immigrants and their children, industrial laborers, and displaced farmers acquired middle-class status and comforts unimaginable a generation earlier. World War II, the GI Bill, a resurgent labor movement, technological advances, a buoyant economy lifted by housing, automobiles, and durable goods purchases, a Cold War, and an activist federal government salvaged and redeemed capitalism. A vacation in Florida signified both a democratic right and a republican virtue.... Identified by what they thought, and defined by what they bought, Americans' postwar dream list included a house, a car, and a vacation.... Postwar affluence, gleaming new cars, and paved roads made Florida vacations attainable for large numbers of Americans [77–78].

When people follow their imaginations to explore places away from home, they become tourists. The imaginations of many travelers to the state were filled with images of an exotic land to which they could escape from their colder and less exciting home states and provinces. Scores of roadside attractions and theme parks, small by today's standards, had a key place in this vacation fantasy, planted there by word of mouth, personal memories, memories of past journeys shared by families and friends—and heavy marketing. According to Ken Breslauer, "A common unifying characteristic of commercial Florida tourist attractions is the promotional methods they utilized ... colorful roadside signage, mass-distributed brochures and a plethora of souvenirs to promote themselves" (10).

My family was one of those lured back by heavy advertising that stimulated our imaginations, and by the older generation's memories formed in Florida during the war. Though my earliest winter tours of Florida in the 1960s included exciting motel stays along the way, my family's later journeys—reflecting the growing national prosperity into the seventies—were in a more refined style as we towed first a modest Shasta trailer and later a twenty-nine-foot Holiday Rambler. Beginning in Charlotte, North Carolina, a typical trip meant following the Airstream (actually, a series of increasingly longer models) towed by my Uncle Ben, a good-natured, Canadian-born B-17 turret-gunner who had trained in Lakeland, down U.S. 301, with our first stop coming near Ocala at Silver Springs. The vacation plan varied from year to year so that sometimes we followed U.S. 41 and U.S. 19 (later I-75) down the gulf coast to St. Petersburg and some years the Tamiami trail to Miami, where, early in World War II, my father had been stationed, my mother joining him until he was shipped off for duty in England. The return journey up U.S. 1 and A1A took us to Marineland, which showcased marvels of the sea long before SeaWorld. Many years included a trip up or down Highway 27 and west on U.S. 92 to witness the ski shows and floral displays of Cypress Gardens.

Today, many of the old attractions we saw still have their places in the popular imagination, but many are gone, and most of the survivors have been forced to change. The focus of this essay will be on four themed, open-air attractions that capitalized on an aspect of Florida's natural attributes and managed to survive in some form: Silver Springs, the most splendid example of fresh-water spring parks; Gatorland, the most famous of the parks exploiting Florida's native wildlife; Marineland, the oldest park taking advantage of Florida's proximity to salt water and sea creatures; and Cypress Gardens, which made good use of Florida's friendly climate for botanical growth and water sports.[1]

Some of the theme parks that survived the rise of Disney and similar I-4 vacation giants retain a small but perhaps secure place in the imagination of many contemporary Americans and even some Europeans that the super parks can never displace. The most resilient attractions are centered around a feature that isn't quite Disneyfiable. For instance, Silver Springs, which was often my family's first stop when our wheels caught up with our imaginations, has expanded in different directions over the years but is still based upon a natural feature that can not be assembled or transplanted. Florida's freshwater springs have long captured the imagination of those who saw them and even those who only heard about them. Florida boasts "the deepest and largest known springs in the world" (Stamm 11).[2] These stunning places appeal to the human imagination through their natural beauty, needing no artificial enhancement. According to Doug Stamm, "Florida's Paleo-Indians ... believed these springs held sacred waters with magical properties capable of curing their sick and healing their wounded" (10). Later, Florida's springs probably played a role in perpetuating the Fountain of Youth myth that reached Europe.[3] In the 1770s, Philadelphia native William Bartram described the astonishing Florida springs in his *Travels* (published in 1791), stimulating the curiosity and creativity of many readers, American and European alike, and even inspiring the "mighty fountain" (line 19) feeding "Alph, the sacred river" (line 3) of Samuel Taylor Coleridge's *Kubla Khan* (written in 1787-88 and published in 1816), a poem often considered emblematic of the poetic imagination. Later, former president Ulysses S. Grant exclaimed, "This is the greatest wonder I have ever seen!" (Mormino 86). During his 1884 journey to Florida from his residence in New Orleans, where he worked as a journalist, Lafcadio Hearn, the son of an Irish surgeon and a Greek woman, traveled by the riverboat *Osceola* to behold "those subterranean rivers, those marvelous volcanic springs haunted by dim traditions of the Fountain of Youth, and by the memory of the good gray knight who sought its waters in vain" (162). Hearn describes the eight-mile-long Silver River leading to its source in the springs as "a flood of fluid crystal, — a river of molten diamond, — a current of liquid light" (165). When his boat reaches the main spring, Hearn observes: "Down, down, deep, there is a mighty quivering visible; but the surface remains unmoved; the giant gush expends its strength far beneath us. From what unilluminated caverns, — what subterranean lakes, — burst this prodigious flow? Go ask the gnomes! Man may never answer" (165).

In order for these natural wonders to reach the minds of the multitudes, they needed to be promoted and made easily accessible to the public. Silver Springs was the first of them to captivate the fancy of large crowds, and undoubtedly the most successful. The first round of mass tourism to the springs followed the Civil War, when many visitors, including authors Harriet Beecher Stowe and Sidney Lanier, reached this destination by steamboat via the Oklawaha River. The invention of the glass-bottomed boat, apparently coming at the end of the nineteenth century, and improvements to the Silver Springs fleet in the 1920s and 1930s brought numerous visitors who came to stare through the undistorted window into the clear water (Hollis 7–10). According to Wendy Adams King, "The relative transparency of the Silver River's waters coupled with the glass bottom of the boat promised Silver Springs tourists beauty, motion, and spectacle while also offering them a scientific education, a sense of national pride, and a sense of cultural progress" (2). Owners and entrepreneurs William Carl Ray and W. C. Davidson, who had acquired the property surrounding the springs in 1924, continued to develop and publicize this attraction for four decades. One of their best business moves was to hire Ross Allen, who in 1930 established the Ross Allen Reptile Institute at Silver Springs and in 1935 added a replica Seminole village staffed by Everglades Seminoles (Hollis 11–12). Allen, who worked at Silver Springs for nearly five decades, did much to help popularize the site.

Making appearances on television, in movies, and even in Marjorie Kinnan Rawlings's 1942 classic *Cross Creek*, Ross Allen appealed to his audience with a charismatic personality and contagious fascination with the creatures that he introduced to the public. Today, he is remembered at Silver Springs at Ross Allen Island, which displays Florida and non-native animals and an exhibit in his honor.[4]

Prior to World War II, Silver Springs had expanded into a theme park with the Reptile Institute, the Jungle Cruise, the Seminole Indian village, and an African American storyteller. The film industry added to the popularity of Silver Springs as underwater scenes for various films were shot there, including scenes from the 1939 film *Tarzan Finds a Son*.[5] After the war, Silver Springs became an even more popular film location, with much of *The Yearling* (1949) being shot there. The famous underwater scenes for the 1953 feature *The Creature from the Black Lagoon* were filmed at Wakulla Springs, with sometime Silver Springs underwater actors Ricou Browning starring as the creature and Ginger Stanley Hallowell performing the female lead's stunt swimming. The 1955 sequel, *The Revenge of the Creature*, was shot mostly at Silver Springs with these with same two underwater performers. *The Creature Walks Among Us* (1956) "split its underwater filming between Silver Springs and Wakulla Springs" (Hollis 20–22).[6] To this day, the captains of the glass-bottom boats proudly point out the creature's cave to awed passengers. Television likewise spread the fame of Silver Springs. Perhaps the most famous television series to make extensive use of Silver Springs for underwater scenes was *Sea Hunt* starring Lloyd Bridges, which aired from 1958 to 1961. This aquatic adventure show was primarily filmed in California locations but many scenes were shot at Silver Springs and Florida's Marineland and Cypress Gardens parks. Tim Hollis explains that "former 'Creature from the Black Lagoon' Ricou Browning stood in for the villains" in underwater scenes at Silver Springs (30–31).[7] Over the years, Silver Springs has provided the underwater setting for twenty-six films and twenty-seven major television shows, specials, and commercials, exposure that has assisted the Silver Springs publicity department in assuring that Silver Springs remains in the public eye ("Learn").

Publicity of various kinds, from travel narratives to poems, has in fact helped turn people's attention to the idea of Florida's springs ever since their discovery by Europeans. Like other theme parks and roadside attractions, Silver Springs suffered during World War II, but it made a remarkable comeback largely due to heavy promotion during the post-war era of economic expansion and increased travel. According to Tim Hollis, "Silver Springs brochures were printed in quantities of seven million at one time; its postcards were printed not only in English, but also in German, Portuguese, and Spanish"; the Silver Springs marketing department erected billboards all over the northern states and distributed "photo features to major magazines and newspaper wire services" (17–19). My family's car joined thousands of other vehicles carrying "Don't Miss Florida's Silver Springs" bumper stickers back north. Peripheral enhancements, such as the addition of Tommy Bartlett's International Deer Ranch in 1954, brought larger crowds. However, as Gary Mormino explains, "The area's inaccessibility limited the appeal of Silver Springs," but "aggressive advertising and highway construction made Silver Springs a popular destination, and by the early 1950's it was annually attracting a million visitors" (86–87). Even as many old-time attractions such as the closely related and once-famous Weeki-Wachee Springs[8] suffered from the rise of the Orlando giants and the construction of the interstate highway system in Florida, Silver Springs "remained hale and hearty" (Hollis 33).[9]

Today, Silver Springs has no doubt diminished in the popular imagination, apparently little known outside of the state. Those who do hear about the springs find that they must make the journey through an increasingly congested Ocala, and many tourists consider that effort too much. Many of the peripherals—rock, pop and country concerts, an adjacent water park, giraffes and other exotic species on display, etc.—have little or nothing to do with the distinct qualities of Florida's springs, and yet the attraction of the Silver Springs itself will always appeal to visitors determined to see for themselves a unique natural attraction.

Cypress Gardens, founded in 1936, was a regular stop on my family's yearly pilgrimages. Unlike Silver Springs and other springs attractions, which built up parks around a natural feature, Cypress Gardens was almost entirely a designed attraction, but it nevertheless captured the nation's imagination as a required destination for a taste of the good life. Gary Mormino comments on the success of this invented necessity: "Arguably the best-known Florida attraction between the 1950s and the opening of Disney World in 1971 ... Cypress Gardens lacked a spectacular natural setting or a busy highway funneling tourists north and south" (88). Despite these obstacles, Cypress Gardens in its prime captured public attention through a combination of promotional strategies devised by its founder, Dick Pope, and his family.[10] Mormino explains that "throughout the 1950s, publicity about the park saturated the media; photographs appeared in hundreds of newspapers each day" (89). Frequent feature appearances on television shows and in successful Hollywood films helped to keep Cypress Gardens in the public's mind. Esther Williams starred in *On an Island with You* (1948) and *Easy to Love* (1953) while Betty Grable starred in *Moon over Miami* (1941).[11]

What exactly were the features that Pope so skillfully presented to the world? The park's name suggests much. Although the park certainly displays many impressive specimens of the native cypress trees evoked by its name, more memorable to visitors are the flowers. My mother and aunt anticipated these floral displays year-round, especially as we planned our annual trips. Since the park's early days and into the present era, extravagant and creative flower gardens have been a trademark of Cypress Gardens—effectively relating the park to a natural attribute of the state that has long been in the minds of foreign visitors. According to Charleton Tebeau, when Ponce de León first stepped ashore in April of 1513, he called the place Florida "after *Pascua florida*, the Feast of Flowers at Easter time" (21). No doubt the native springtime blooms impressed the explorer also. Since then, multitudes of travelers have been drawn to Florida's botanical beauty, associating the state with flowers and luxurious plants. Florida's plant life has inspired numerous tributes, as in the following description of a Lake George island by William Bartram, observed from a naturalist's perspective during the trip he took in the 1770s through Florida:

> This delightful spot, planted by nature, is almost an entire grove of palms, with a few pyramidal magnolias, live oaks, golden orange, and the animating zanthoxylon. What a beautiful retreat is here! Blessed unviolated spot of earth, rising from the limpid waters of the lake: its fragrant groves and blooming lawns invested and protected by encircling ranks of the yucca gloriosa. A fascinating atmosphere surrounds this blissful garden; the balmy Lantana, ambrosial citra, perfumed crinum, perspiring their mingled odours, wafted through zanthoxylon groves [*Travels* 143].

Most visitors who come to Florida for the botanical experience are drawn not to the trees and flowers of the woods and fields but to organized displays. Sarasota Jungle Gardens, Miami's Parrot Jungle, and Mountain Lake Sanctuary in Lake Wales, with its famous Bok Tower, are among the surviving small attractions built around designed landscapes.[12]

Cypress Gardens has kept the public's attention for so long not only by taking advantage of Florida's ideal climate for lush gardens, but also by exploiting its ideal setting for water sports, featuring motorboat racing and above all, water skiing.[13] As with many young spectators since the first ski shows in 1947, the Cypress Gardens skiers inspired my own determination to return home and take up the sport. In addition, the elements of pageants, celebrity appearances, and an invented southern-belle tradition appealed to the popular imagination and brought visitors to Winter Haven by the millions during the park's best years.[14] As Gary Mormino explains, "Cypress Gardens succeeded because it offered something for everyone. To ... midwesterners, it supplied clean-cut family entertainment; to the middle classes who could not afford Paris ... it was America's Versailles Gardens; to a public not yet saturated by cable television and cynical about packaged entertainment, Dick Pope created something beautiful and entertained crowds with thrilling water sports..." (90).

In recent years, Cypress Gardens has joined parks such as Silver Springs and Busch Gardens in further diversifying its offerings to appeal to a wider variety of visitors, and it retains its core of imaginatively landscaped grounds and unforgettable water ski shows. Cypress Gardens has added over forty rides (including large roller coasters), rock and country music concerts, and various indoor shows, such as a fairy-tale-themed ice-skating show performed by Russian skaters—not exactly a Florida-themed attraction, but memorable anyway. Despite these efforts, it has struggled to maintain a favored place in the popular imagination. Sadly, Cypress Gardens has changed ownership multiple times and in 2003 actually closed.[15] With the assistance of state and local governments and new private ownership, Cypress Gardens was reinvented in November 2004 as Cypress Gardens Adventure Park. According to the park's Web site,

Now, guests will find an exhilarating world of thrilling rides, Splash Island water park, dazzling entertainment, historic gardens, animals, the famed Southern Belles and world-famous water ski show, as well as Jubilee Junction, an old-fashioned village chock-full of exceptional shopping and fabulous food. Approximately 1.4 million guests sampled the delights of the newly refurbished park in 2005, one of the highest attendance counts at Cypress Gardens in the history of the park and the trend continued into 2006 ["Park History"].

Despite the optimistic tone of the web site, Cypress Gardens again struggled during the summer of 2008. Its management intends to have the park open only on weekends during September 2008 and plans to determine if other measures are necessary (Maready). As several online commentators to the Lakeland *Ledger*'s article on this development have pointed out, Cypress Gardens appears to be losing its appeal for most people besides local residents. This oldest Florida theme park, like a few other surviving old parks, has attempted to stay in the mind of the public by accumulating entertainment features that diverge far from its original Florida-related roots, but for Cypress Gardens, this strategy may have failed.

Why my family always passed up Gatorland I do not know, but perhaps the adults were satisfied by the smaller alligator exhibits at other stops such as the Jacksonville Zoo, or perhaps they thought that this attraction was too rough for young children. Gatorland Zoo remains one of the very few old parks that have managed to maintain their popular favor, with few alterations to their original conceptions. Gatorland's appeal lies almost exclusively in alligators and crocodiles, though a few other reptiles, a handful of birds, and some deer add a little variety. Unlike the creatures at the obviously African-themed Lion Country Safari located near West Palm Beach, nearly everything at Gatorland is either native to Florida or seems as if it could be (iguanas, Australian emus, Galapagos giant tortoises, and Nile crocodiles are among the exotics). Clearly, however, alligators are the thing. Florida's alligators have long captured the imagination of travelers, including that of the French painter Jacques Le Moyne de Morgues, who joined the second French expedition to Florida in 1564 and made a series of drawings of Timucuan Indian life, including a drawing of the natives capturing and killing huge alligators.[16] Years later, one of the peninsula's most famous guests, William Bartram, depicts the Florida beasts in romanticized terms:

> Behold him rushing forth from the flags and reeds. His enormous body swells. His plaited tail brandished high floats upon the lake. The waters like a cataract descend from his opening jaws. Clouds of smoke issue from his dilated nostrils. The earth trembles with his thunder ... immediately from the opposite coast of the lagoon emerges from the deep his rival champion. They suddenly dart upon each other. The boiling surface of the lake marks their rapid courses and a terrific conflict commences.... The proud victor returns to the place of action. The shores and forests resound his dreadful roar, together with the triumphing shouts of the plaited tribes around, witnesses of the horrid combat [Bartram 115].

Contemporary visitors to the state can, of course, find plenty of alligators at places besides Gatorland, including Okalee Village, where Seminoles and other trained (and brave) people handle alligators; most zoos; the venerable St. Augustine Alligator Farm Zoological Park; Silver Springs; Palmdale's Gatorama,[17] and most lakes, streams, rivers, and nearly every other unenclosed body of water.[18] However, Gatorland offers a combination of ways to celebrate alligators (including at the charming Pearl's Patio Smokehouse) that would be hard to improve upon. In addition, without necessarily being aware that they were seeing Gatorland, viewers from across the U.S and the world have been exposed to the creatures and grounds of Gatorland. According to the attraction's Web site,

> Over the years, Gatorland has provided the film and television industries with a unique location to capture incredible footage of alligators, crocodiles and the natural Florida environment. Hundreds of programs have been filmed at Gatorland, from the alligator scenes in the blockbuster movie *Indiana Jones and the Temple of Doom*, to documentaries from National Geographic, the Discovery Channel, and the BBC, even television series such as *American Choppers*, *The Pet Psychic*, and *Swamp Thing* [Gatorland.com].

Gatorland entertains a respectable 400,000 visitors per year, quite a crowd for a small, old-fashioned, slightly sinister attraction in the Orlando happy park neighborhood. A recent search on youtube.com turned up over one hundred film clips taken at Gatorland. Perhaps part of its appeal lies in the landmark entrance, a famous giant alligator mouth appearing in thousands of photographs, including the one on the front of the dust jacket of Charlie Carlson's *Weird Florida*.[19] When this distinctive Florida icon was damaged by fire in November 2006, it caught the attention of the national news media, including *The New York Times* and *Desert News* (Salt Lake City). If the entrance and the many images of it capture the imagination, the alligators themselves are what hold it. Gatorland has more than two hundred crocodiles of various species and over a thousand alligators, including specimens over fourteen feet long.

Entertaining and surprisingly educational, Gatorland's wrestling show remains a major part of the appeal of this park. Unfortunately for future visitors to the Sunshine State, the art of handling alligators may be in decline. A 1998 *New York Times* article on alligator wrestlers offered these observations on the sport's history:

> Most shows are a far cry from the ones contrived in the 1920s, when white entrepreneurs, sensing a potential gold mine, sought to attract tourists to the state by promoting two of Florida's distinctive assets, Seminole Indians and alligators. Soon, the trade flourished, as roadside shows featuring young Seminoles wrestling alligators dotted major highways as well as areas that are now part of downtown Miami. Today, it is estimated that only two dozen people still wrestle alligators on a regular basis. "Alligator wrestling is dying out, short of people who have a true love for it," said Tim Williams, the director of public relations and entertainment at Gatorland, an animal park in central Florida ["From Alligator Wrestlers"].[20]

The Gator Jumperoo is the feature perhaps most responsible for Gatorland's distinctive reputation. *RoadsideAmerica.com* describes the show as follows:

Gator Jumperoo works like this: A dinner bell is rung next to the big pond, and a pack of 20 or so ten-footers swim over in anticipation. The pond is surrounded by a covered boardwalk, lined with tourists, camcorders at the ready. Signs warn everybody not to lean out over the water. Music blares over loudspeakers as chicken carcasses are hung on a kind of Swiss sky ride cable-and-pulley system, then run out over the pond. The gators jockey for position, rocket out of the water — sometimes nearly five feet straight up — grab the meat, and then fall back with a mighty splash [Kirby].

This well-kept, generally pleasant little attraction makes the best use of one of Florida's best-known natural attributes, alligators, giving visitors a close up look and some basic information about the big reptiles that non-residents (especially college sports fans) associate with the state.

Gatorland continues to hold its special place in the popular imagination, not just in the United States, but in Europe as well, as demonstrated by the glowing write-up in the *Irish Times Box Office* web site, which declares that the Gatorland Jumperoo is "a must see for the entire family!" Similarly, an article in *the Belfast* (Northern Ireland) *News Letter* declares that "a visit to Gatorland is a fascinating part of the entire Florida experience, and an essential visit on any trip to Orlando" (Neillands 2). During my own recent visit to the park, a show-of-hands poll conducted by a surprisingly eloquent alligator wrestler revealed that many visitors were from other states and a few were from other countries. Gatorland's corner in the popular imagination — and in the Orlando tourism world — seems secure.

For my family, Marineland was the last important destination on the way home — or the first destination on the way down. Like many other visitors, we went to nearby St. Augustine to take in a few different attractions each trip, sometimes even stumbling upon a bit of history as a bonus— the ancient Castillo de San Marcos, the Old Jail, Potter's Wax Museum, and Ripley's Believe it or Not (real history or not) all appeared on our flexible itineraries, but Marineland remained a mandatory stop for years. Marineland was the first of the old theme parks to take full advantage of Florida's association in the minds of many with the seas adjoining Florida's 1,146 miles of shoreline. It originated "in 1938 as an effort to duplicate the variety of marine life as it exists in the wild for the purpose of filming.... Parts of the Tarzan films starring Johnny Weismueller [and] *The Revenge of the Creature*" were among the popular movies with underwater scenes shot there (*Marineland: History*). According to Gary Mormino, "Marineland illustrated the connection between nature and spectacle. One of Florida's most popular tourist attractions, Marineland enjoyed success built upon location, promotion, and dolphins. By the early 1950s Marine Studios and its acclaimed oceanarium were drawing a half million customers annually" (90–91). Mormino points out that "when the partners discovered that blue bottlenose dolphins ... could be trained to perform tricks above water, [it] became primarily a tourist attraction" (91). Nothing in my own imagination could have matched the spectacle of the acrobatic performances of these athletic dolphins. Today's shows at similar parks, despite the additional element of trained humans in colorful costumes diving off platforms, swinging on ropes, and swimming with the dolphins and their relatives, are tame in comparison, though no doubt they are less strenuous for the animals. These creatures, though apparently smiling and happy to show off, may indeed have endured unjustifiable stress while performing their stunts, and animal-rights observers have been correct to keep an eye on animal performances; nonetheless, crowds of people were drawn from far away to witness their feats. They were amazing.

The Miami Seaquarium followed Marineland in 1955, but its distant location diminished its competitive threat to Marineland. Marineland was the first big theme park that motorists on U.S. 1 and A1A encountered, and a natural place to stop. The Seaquarium never competed with Marineland in the way that the much closer Orlando parks did later; in particular, the larger and even more spectacular SeaWorld overshadowed its older rival soon after its opening in 1973. The completion of I-4 in 1971 had already begun to ease the way for motorists to drive past Marineland to Orlando; likewise, the gradual opening of I-95 to Miami by 1987 drew many travelers farther down the state. The Seaquarium was less affected by the forces that diminished the popularity of Marineland, and it benefited from I-95. Today, the Seaquarium thrives with over 600,000 visitors yearly; it "is recognized as South Florida's most popular 'gated' attraction" (miamiseaquarium.com).[21]

In contrast, Marineland serves as an example of an old theme park that has failed to compete successfully with the newcomer Orlando goliaths and to adapt successfully to the altered traffic patterns caused by the expanded interstate system. Marineland's appeal to the imagination was eclipsed by that of the much larger SeaWorld, which repeated Marineland offerings such as aquariums and dolphin shows and added much, including the hard-to-top trained killer whales—all strategically within sight of I-4. After closing in 2004, Marineland reopened in 2006 in a barely recognizable form. Marineland still has its dolphins, including Nellie—at 55, the world's oldest dolphin in captivity—and some of its original modernistic structures, but much of it is gone, including the oceanarium filled with sea animals, and most importantly, its aquatic stadiums. Now Marineland maintains and breeds dolphins for research and offers up-close, in-the-water encounters similar to those available at Orlando's Discovery Cove, but only a handful of visitors pay the nominal fee for watching the graceful mammals swim, toss beach balls, and occasionally jump.

The beginning of the end for many small parks like Marineland may have been the growing success and expansion of Tampa's Busch Gardens. Ken Breslauer claims that "Busch Gardens must be credited with setting a new standard for Florida tourist attractions, but at the same time it directly contributed to the demise of many smaller roadside attractions" (40). Busch Gardens, which has long appealed to American and foreign visitors with its lush gardens and hospitality house, has perhaps best challenged the Disney empire on its own terms. Opening in 1959 as a free-admission refuge for visitors to Tampa's Anheuser-

Busch brewery, Busch Gardens gradually added exotic birds and African animals viewed from a monorail.[22] The park has survived in Disney times by retaining its core, while matching the Orlando sites in some areas such as entertainment and beating them in others, notably with its impressive collection of thrill rides. Busch Gardens has thereby assured itself a fair share of the youth and young adult market while it draws older members of the family with its traditional features.

The opening of the Magic Kingdom in October 1971 and subsequently of SeaWorld and Universal Studios was largely responsible for the demise of many small theme parks, and many other factors such as the construction of super highways that bypassed the smaller attractions, contributed to the change in tourism patterns.[23] Although theme park owners such as Dick Pope, the founder of Cypress Gardens, welcomed the arrival of Disney World as a boost for the tourist industry, as Mormino explains, "The new era of the mega-theme park doomed the old world of roadside attractions" (105–106). Among the many attractions that disappeared are Six Gun Territory near Silver Springs, Sarasota's Floridaland, and Clearwater's Sea-Orama.[24] In contrast, a number of attractions have been taken over by state or city governments and preserved in one form or another. For example, the state government rescued Rainbow Springs, a natural attraction that had once been expanded into a theme park complete with glass-bottom boats, a riverboat, a monorail, an aviary, and other embellishments (Hollis 75–90). Today, the springs are protected in an attractive state park with the usual swimming and canoeing facilities. A few traces remain of the theme park, notably the concession stand, the artificial waterfall, and an empty aviary, and some fine gardens that were maintained in part by local volunteers when the commercial enterprise closed in 1974. Similarly, the city of St. Petersburg in 1999 stepped in to preserve the Sunken Gardens. Many of the surviving old parks have lost their large place in the popular imagination: the idea of the family road trip to Florida to sample several small attractions during a vacation has been replaced by the prepackaged dream deal to Orlando. Yet these sites still provide recreation for local residents and a few non-residents who seek them out as a quieter alternative to the one-stop vacation.

By the time Walt Disney World opened, bringing a new era of tourism to Florida, my family's interest had turned away from the themed attractions to other Florida pleasures, concentrating on lakes, beaches, and trailer campgrounds. Walt Disney World and the other huge Orlando entertainment parks never found their way into my family's idea of Florida. Though we continued to visit Florida until the early seventies, I never saw Disney World until I returned to Florida as an adult to work and live, lured back in part by Florida's remaining wonders from an earlier era, which had captured my imagination many years before.

## Notes

1. Ken Breslauer, considering the full range of Florida's roadside tourist attractions, identifies these characteristics common to most attractions established before 1971: "[Each was] built originally to be a commercial attraction ... located adjacent to a major high-

way.... Three highways (U.S. 1, U.S. 27, and U.S. 41) account for more than half of the attractions established between 1929 and 1971.... Admission was charged.... [Each was] operated for profit and privately owned; [Each] utilized some aspect of the state's Flora and Fauna as a central theme" (9–10).

2. According to Charlton Tebeau, "The state has the country's largest number (seventeen of a total of seventy-five) of first magnitude springs, which discharge 100 cubic feet or more of water per second, and fifty second magnitude springs discharging from ten to 100 cubic feet of water per second" (6).

3. As *The Florida Reader* states, "How much the search for the magical spring motivated Ponce de León's expedition remains unclear; however, the role of that search and the way European historians like Peter Martyr d'Anghiera perpetuated the myth are critical elements in the mythology of the discovery of Florida" (22). For a discussion of the Renaissance origins of the Fountain of Youth myth associated with Florida's springs, see Ammidown, page 240. The Fountain of Youth association was pronounced, though fanciful, during the post–Civil War tourism surge at Silver Springs; as Margot Ammidown points out, "An 1874 article in *Scribner's Monthly*, entitled 'Pictures from Florida,' makes reference to the Fountain of Youth in describing the state's first popular natural attraction, Silver Springs..." (242); interestingly, a recent SouthernLiving.com travel article makes the same association in its by-line (Thomas).

4. According to the Silver Springs Web site, "The exhibit ... showcases archive photographs and information on the world famous naturalist Ross Allen. For nearly fifty years, Ross Allen owned and operated the Ross Allen Reptile Institute at Silver Springs which contained an extensive collection of snakes, crocodilians, and animals from around the world." For a concise biography of Allen, see Brown, "Ross Allen's Reptile Institute."

5. For a discussion of this film and its use of Silver Springs, see Doll and Morrow, pages 360–363.

6. Doll and Morrow discuss *The Creature* and its sequels in *Florida on Film*, 327–330.

7. According to the *SCUBA Guy's Sea Hunt Trivia Guide*, Silver Springs "was a second-unit shooting site for footage that appears in as many as 100 episodes of SEA HUNT. While tens of thousands of feet of film were shot at Silver Springs, a good portion of the film was never needed or used."

8. For a general discussion of Florida's springs accompanied by excellent photographs, see Doug Stamm, *The Springs of Florida*; also, for a discussion focused on the springs that have appealed most to tourists, see Tim Hollis, *Glass Bottom Boats and Mermaid Tails: Florida's Tourist Springs*.

9. According to Gary Mormino, "By the 1960's so popular was the mermaid show that women from five continents auditioned for the privilege" of "being a 'mermaid' at the attraction" (88). Today, Weeki-Wachee Springs, despite some problems in recent years, has managed to survive — with the help of extras such as a water park — and continues to offer its mermaid shows, though its fame has declined. For a recent account of the life of the mermaid cast at Weeki Wachee, see Schoeneman.

10. See Mormino, pages 88–90.

11. Mormino, page 89. For more on *Easy to Love*, see Doll and Morrow, *Florida on Film*, 52–55; for *Moon over Miami*, see 145–148. For an overview of Cypress Gardens in film and television, see Flekke, pages 83–94.

12. Margot Ammidown's article on small tourist attractions offers interesting insights into these and other old garden attractions in Florida, many of which made direct references to the Garden of Eden in their promotions.

13. Florida has an estimated 30,000 lakes (Tebeau 6).

14. For a discussion of the history of Cypress Gardens and numerous photographs documenting the history, see Flekke.

15. See "Theme Park In Florida Is Nothing But a Memory."

16. For a reproduction of this plate and a translation of the accompanying text, see O'Sullivan and Lane, pages 89–90.

17. Gatorama, which opened in 1957, is less famous than Gatorland, but offers a comparably fascinating reptile experience for the visitor. See Peter Genovese, "This Place Bites," in *Roadside Florida*, pages 45–52.

18. For a selection of poetic tributes to the Florida alligator, see Jones and O'Sullivan, pages 219–222.

19. Gatorland's iconic gator-jaw entrance has in recent years had to compete with other giant gator jaws and even full-body gator replicas designed to capture the motorist's attention. See Genovese, "The World's Largest Gators and other Giants along the Road," in *Roadside Florida*, especially page 119.

20. See also Rick Bragg's "Filling the Job Is Like Wrestling Alligators."

21. Along with the Seaquarium, the Miami area offered many other themed attractions, including the Monkey Jungle, the Parrot Jungle, and Riviera Tropical Gardens, all three surviving today.

22. Mormino, page 109.

23. For a discussion of the impact of Walt Disney World and other huge Central Florida themed fun parks on smaller Florida tourist destinations, see Mormino, pages 100–112. See also Breslauer, pages 19–20.

24. For more about Six Gun Territory, see Hollis, pages 47–58; for Floridaland, see Walton 103–104; for Sea-Orama, see Breslauer 70. Robert H. Brown's *Florida's Lost Tourist Attractions* Web site (http://www.lostparks.com/index.html) currently lists over 150 closed theme parks and roadside attractions and has articles on over 50.

## WORKS CITED AND CONSULTED

Ammidown, Margot. "Edens, Underworlds, and Shrines: Florida's Small Tourist Attractions." *The Journal of Decorative and Propaganda Arts* 23 (1998): 239- 259.
Bartram, William. *The Travels of William Bartram*. Ed. Mark Van Doren. New York: Dover, 1928.
Bragg, Rick. "Filling this Job is Like Wrestling Alligators." *New York Times*, September 20, 2000.
Breslauer, Ken. *Roadside Paradise: The Golden Age of Florida's Tourist Attractions 1929–71*. St. Petersburg: RetroFlorida, 2000.
Brown, Robert H. "Ross Allen's Reptile Institute." *Florida's Lost Tourist Attractions*. 1997–2006." 11 August 2008. http://www.lostparks.com/rossal.html
Coles, David J. "'Keep the Home Fires Burning': Florida's World War II Experience." In *The Florida Handbook, 2001–2002*, 28th ed., compiled by Allen Morris and Joan Perry Morris, 428–432. Tallahassee: Peninsular, 1999. Rpt. Florida Department of Veteran Affairs: Florida's World War II Memorial. 26 July 2008. http://www.floridavets.org/wwii/history4.asp
Doll, Susan, and David Morrow. *Florida on Film*. Gainesville: University Press of Florida, 2007.
"Fire Kills Animals, Chars Florida's Gatorland." *Desert News* (Salt Lake City), November 7, 2006. FindArticles.com. 28 Jun. 2008. http://findarticles.com/p/articles/mi_qn4188/is_20061107/ai_n16826232.
Flekke, Mary M., Sarah E. MacDonald, and Randall M. MacDonald. *Cypress Gardens*. Charleston, S.C.: Arcadia Publishing Images of America Series, 2006.
"From Alligator Wrestlers, an Education." *The New York Times*, August 9, 1998.
Gatorland.com. 2004. 25 June 2008. http://www.gatorland.com
Kirby, Doug, Ken Smith, and Mike Wilkins. "Gators!" *RoadsideAmerica.com* 2008. 27 June 2008. http://www.roadsideamerica.com/set/gator3.html

Genovese, Peter. *Roadside Florida: The Definitive Guide to the Kingdom of Kitsch.* Mechanicsburg, Penn.: Stackpole Books.

Hearn, Lafcadio. *Floridian Reveries.* Reprinted in *The Florida Reader*, edited by Maurice O'Sullivan and Jack C. Lane. Sarasota, Fla.: Pineapple Press, 1991. 161–165.

Hollis, Tim. *Glass-Bottom Boats and Mermaid Tails: Florida's Tourist Springs.* Mechanicsburg, Penn.: Stackpole Books, 2006.

King, Wendy Adams. "Through the Looking Glass of Silver Springs: Tourism and the Politics of Vision." *Americana: The Journal of American Popular Culture* 3.1 (Spring 2004). http://www.americanpopularculture.com/journal/articles/spring_2004/king.htm.

The *Irish Times* Box Office. http://www.keithprowse.com/tickets/slink.buy/irishtimes/eJ5R/Gatorland%C2%AE_1_Day_Ticket-Gatorland_Orlando_Florida-Orlando.html.

Jones, Bill. "The SCUBA Guy's *Sea Hunt* Trivia Guide." 2007. http://home.houston.rr.com/thescubaguy/News/SeaHuntTrivia.html#Locations

Jones, Jane Anderson, and Maurice O'Sullivan, eds. *Florida in Poetry: A History of the Imagination.* Sarasota, Fla.: Pineapple Press, 1995.

"Learn About Our Heritage." *Silver Springs.* 2008. http://www.silversprings.com/heritage.html.

Maready, Jeremy. "Cypress Gardens to Test Weekends-Only." *The Ledger*, 28 July 2008: B1.

"Marineland: History." 2008. 17 July 2008. http://www.marineland.net/history.php

Martin, Richard A. *Eternal Spring: Man's 10,000 Years of History at Florida's Silver Springs.* St. Petersburg, Fla.: Great Outdoors, 1969.

"Miami Seaquarium: Come Make Friends." 2008. http://www.miamiseaquarium.com/visitor_info/history.asp

Mormino, Gary R. *Land of Sunshine, State of Dreams: A Social History of Modern Florida.* Tampa: University Press of Florida, 2005.

———. "World War II." In *The New History of Florida*, edited by Michael Gannon. Gainesville: University Press of Florida, 1996. 323–343.

Neillands, Robin. "Book Me In, and Make it Snappy; Robin Neillands on Florida's Gatorland." *Belfast News Letter* (Northern Ireland), 6 November 1997: 24.

O'Sullivan, Maurice, and Jack C. Lane, eds. *The Florida Reader.* Sarasota, Fla.: Pineapple Press, 1991.

"Park History." Cypress Gardens. 2008. http://www.cypressgardens.com/parkHistory.php

Savage, Carol. "Oh, My! See Exotic Birds, Reptiles, Mammals at St. Augustine Alligator Farm Zoological Park." *The Ledger.com*, March 16, 2008. http://www.theledger.com/article/20080316/NEWS/803160483/1326.

Schoeneman, Deborah. "Mermaids Past and Present Keep Things Real." *The New York Times*, January 6, 2008:10.

Stamm, Doug. *The Springs of Florida.* Sarasota, Fla.: Pineapple Press, 1994.

Tebeau, Charlton W. *A History of Florida.* Coral Gables, Fla.: University of Miami Press, 1971.

"Theme Park in Florida Is Nothing But a Memory." *New York Times*, April 14, 2003, 17. http://query.nytimes.com/gst/fullpage.html?res=950DEED7133BF937A25757C0A9659C8B63.

Thomas, Les. "Fabulous Florida Springs." *SouthernLiving.com.* 2008. http://www.southernliving.com/southern/travel/outdoors/article/0,28012,1827134,00.html?cnn=yes.

"Wildlife Exhibits." Silver Springs. 2008. http://www.silversprings.com/wildlife.html.

# Where Being Gay Isn't a Drag
*Margaret Mishoe* and *Michael Perez*

Florida, the state nobody wanted. When England and Spain were vying for control of the land that would be Florida, they never really fought. Push would come to shove and whoever was occupying the territory would draw back their forces and the other side would take over. After the Revolutionary War, folks thought we should come on down and fight the Indians, but they retreated into the Everglades; we couldn't find them and so we said what the hell, let them have it. Hence, the Seminoles became the only Indian tribe we never signed a peace treaty with. This worked for them because they became the only Indian tribe we never broke a peace treaty with, thus they won on two fronts.

The personal diaries of military men sent from England, Spain, France and the United States armies never say, "Wow, what a great place." They universally say, "It's hotter than Hell and the mosquitoes are trying to kill me." And, of course, "I love you, Mama."

When the Civil War broke out, no one in Florida seemed to give a damn. The state was trying to decide what side to be on and the decision proved to be largely geographic.

It was, after all, the southern-most point, so presumably Floridians thought they had to be with the South. The decision was unremarkable, as no major battles were fought here, and the state offered no particular strategic locations. Forts were established; the men in wool uniforms wrote home about the conditions (see above) and that was essentially that.

All of this goes to prove that Florida was a throw-away state, that, for the most part, no one had any real interest in. It was briefly discovered in the 1920s, when retirement became a real possibility for a small group of Americans. They believed in the brochures sent to them and they invested in Florida retirement land. They ended up owning some swamp land filled with alligators and they lost their money. This was the precursor to the Great Depression. The current housing problems, starting in Florida and continuing onward, seem to suggest that things do not change.

From this the reader may understand why Florida, a state full of people largely indifferent to what anyone else in the U.S. thinks about them, became a haven for gay and lesbian communities. This chapter will discuss the financial influence of gay and lesbian society, how local and state governments have responded, and how gay and straight people have merged in an entertainment venue that is also a tourist attraction. The chapter will include how certain communities, primarily South Beach in Miami and Key West, have become meccas for gays and lesbians.

## Drag and the Tourist's Wallet

Men dressing as women have provided entertainment for a very long time. It's claimed that the phrase "drag queen" had its origins in the train of the dresses worn by male performers (usually adolescent boys) taking women's roles in Shakespearean plays, women being forbidden to take the stage at the time because it was considered unsuitable. As, Wikipedia, the wildly popular and unpredictable collective online encyclopedia of our time, asserts, "The term *drag queen* originates in *Polari*, a subset of English slang that was popular in some gay communities in the early part of the twentieth century. Drag meant 'clothes,' and was also theatre slang for a woman's costume worn by a male actor. Queen refers to the trait of affected royalty found in many drag characters."

From Milton Berle to RuPaul — or even both at once, as a notorious MTV Awards clip still proves — people do like men as women if laughter comes with it. Assuming that Florida still has a vested interest in laughter as an active, diverse aspect of the tourism industry — and if several famous movies still hold their power as far as the revenue generated by the art of female impersonation is concerned — then Florida shows no sign of giving up the show for the folks who, on holiday, can see a man in a dress and experience the whole she-bang safely and with camera ready, and recall the whole she-bang as an odd but "funny-ha-ha" souvenir (and not so much funny the other way, to borrow a phrase from Billy Ray Thornton).

Perhaps this essay's title may recall the slapstick-yet-stock Mike Nichols movie *The Birdcage*, a gently successful 1995 remake of a late seventies French film *La Cage Aux Folles*, that itself had turned into a successful Broadway show in the mid–1980s. While watching Robin Williams teach Nathan Lane how to spread butter on toast like a man at an outdoor café on the South Beach strip where for some odd reason the passersby ogled Lane's histrionic fits as if he were a freak, or at least out of his domain, you really witnessed, with stereotypical and undeniable fun, Hollywood's idea of how tourists should interact with (as has been the trend to call them lately) "the gays."

Yet even before being "birdcaged"— perhaps much before, maybe somewhere in the late last half of the last century — Florida had gradually established itself as setting The Golden Drag Rule, the Sunshine State being the place where any tourist game enough to venture into a den of lipsticked inequity could emerge tickled, a little shocked, but with suntan and reputation intact. It appears then that Walter Disney indeed left his mark in places other than Orlando: now visitors from Missouri, Japan, or those bearing the mighty maple leaf on their car tags can expect to be titillated a bit as they crowd into a car for Mr. Female

Impersonator's Wild Ride, taking a walk on the "drag bar wild side" and coming out, so to speak, with their virtual Mouse ears intact (with apologies to Mr. Lou Reed).

Fact is, Florida has always been a haven, and not only a winter one, for drag performers. In its heyday, there was a limited but bustling Southern show bar circuit that exchanged performers for guest appearances and competitions (Miss Gay Ft. Lauderdale, Miss Gay Miami) with their Georgia counterparts (Miss Gay Atlanta, Miss Gay Georgia, and even on occasion, a Miss Gay Illinois as a Miss Gay Atlanta. The Northern wing of the Southern show bar circuit still thrives today as exemplified by Chicago's renowned show bar and now-popular venue for bachelorette parties, The Baton, which is still home of the longest running revue in the U.S. with its celebrated performer Chili Pepper, a former Miss Gay Atlanta, notorious for her 24-karat gold — or was it 14-karat diamond?— tipped fingernails).

Chicago bears a mention here for the basic migratory nature of the circuit, as the performers became peripatetic because of money, trophies, prestige, and above all, cover charges, drink minimums, and demand. A sizable minority of attendees at the clubs sponsoring the fully-choreographed revues and competitions may have been there simply because of their tour package destinations, rather than because they were part of the supportive and sharing queer communities that generated the revenue to foster such a crossover. The Baton stands today as a classic, tenacious example; but our sights are set on the Sunshine State, where boys can look good in bikinis year 'round — and mostly at night.

Florida show bars — or bars with a show — in Tallahassee, Jacksonville, Tampa or St. Pete stand today as quite a contrast to the clandestine "speakeasy" atmosphere of pre-Stonewall gay bars, which endured years of raids and abuse from local police. That is, until a fateful night in June 1969. That night, two distinct representatives of a not-yet-coalesced community made a statement that would loom larger than a Georgia boy in heels. Around midnight, a throng of bar patrons, mostly pissed-off drag queens and butch lesbians, finally fought back and rioted as they were being dragged into a paddy wagon from the Stonewall Inn to spend a night in the Greenwich Village precinct — *again*. Perhaps as a by-product of gay liberation, which careened wildly into media awareness as a result of the Stonewall raids, parents of gay and lesbian teenagers and adults, introduced to the '70s and '80s phenomenon of the gay bar with drag show ("The Locker Room Disco Showplace" in Atlanta) and then full drag bar with dance floor ("Illusions" in Midtown Atlanta), brought their families to the bar to see the show and glimpse what The Out Life entailed. This was a safer haven with familiar tunes, drink specials, fewer raids and sometimes a waitress with 5 o'clock shadow.

These parents in turn brought their friends and the tourist drag circuit was born — if indeed it ever needed to be. One might say that it didn't really come out so much as come out and *multiply*, seemingly overnight. And with multiplication comes the need for T-shirts, special events, and rides and snacks: thus,

Gay Day at Disney World came into being. If only for a day, some might say they enjoyed a Magic Queendom. But the event wouldn't exist if it didn't make money. The topic has been clearly addressed by a wildly popular international Web site on its tourism page:

> Gay Days at Disney began in 1991 as Gay Day in the Magic Kingdom when a group of local lesbian and gay computer enthusiasts publicized through word-of-mouth, the Internet and flyers an informal get-together they had scheduled at the Magic Kingdom. Thanks to the controversy generated by flyers, which used the image of Mickey Mouse, his right ear sporting a Lambda [a greek symbol appropriated by the gay and lesbian community] earring, radio shows and local newspapers provided free advertising, and more than 2,500 gay women and men flocked to the Magic Kingdom. That band of red-clad, gay Disneyphiles doubled in size to 5,000 the following year, establishing a tradition of meeting on the first Saturday of June. Since then, the crowd has grown exponentially, and Gay Day is now just shy of a gay week.
>
> The Gay Day celebration attracts over 125,000 gay women and men to Orlando for five fun- and sun-filled days of entertainment in and around Disney's Magic Kingdom. Gay Day at Disneyland (www.gayday2.com) is not as big, but draws several thousand gay women and men to Anaheim's Magic Kingdom. Although neither event is sanctioned by Disney, both receive the blessing and cooperation of Walt Disney Company, which has admirably and continually refused to yield to protests from the conservative right, which of course also makes good business sense, given the millions of dollars in revenue these events generate [Gay.com].

Thus it appears that any Gay Day (or Night, which is more like it, as everyone looks better with a little dimmed lighting) to be successful financially, or to be worth the travel time and money, needs a good, lucrative drag show, in order to pay for the lights and rent, not to mention the cast's depilatory crème bill. It must be accessible, friendly, and not reminiscent of a John Carpenter Halloween (though Halloween has unofficially become the Night When Any Man Can Wear a Dress Without Repercussions.) What the show cast doesn't really want is to frighten its customers—just to tousle, and certainly tease them *a bit*. A scared drag show tourist in Florida may be like a detour off the beaten track in a rent-a-car on I-95 just outside of Miami: they didn't want to go there, the scenery may scare them because it seems out of control when it's really only unfamiliar, and they may not exactly jump at the idea of opening their wallets there by choice. You're scared, you just want to go home, and two clicks of your heels won't make it happen. You only need a Glinda in a bubble to come and show you, if not the way home, a safe good time through a mildly freaky show. And you may go in to your show bar with a movie image or two in the back of your mind, but you'll be exiting with your ears stinging if you don't pick up on some unspoken rules.

For *The Birdcage* sanitizes some of the requisite elements in any good drag show worth its (inflated) admission price, namely, Straight People Abuse. In the film you may recall that, in order to keep their reputations intact, a U.S. senator and his wife must dress up and exit a show bar in South Beach with the regular cast—thus, abuse with awkward happiness and an undetected getaway—all singing "We Are Family," the drag show equivalent of "It's a Small World After All." Thus it appears by the finale of Nichols's film that the reach of Mickey Mouse's tail stretches longer than one might suppose: up and down the East Coast of the peninsula, with that occasional detour to Tallahassee, Jacksonville, Daytona or the Tampa Bay Area, to finally curl around the best and Southwestern-most haven for drag debauchery (and expectations), Key West, with its tip pointed back northeastward to the Mama-of-All-Respectable-Tourist-Drag Show venues—Miami.

Miami drag shows always seem to hold a touch of Jackie Gleason's Miami Beach standard. For those of us young enough to remember what a spectacle from Miami was supposed to look like from the late sixties, here were the sassy, diverse, outrageous and raucous elements: June Taylor dancing girls, "The Honeymooners," bellows and pratfalls, absurd skits, pantomimes, even a lip-sync moment or two, all led by a bug-eyed, full-figured man who brayed then went sweet on his Alice, did floppy cartwheels and was light as a feather ... *hmmm*. For if the great Mr. Gleason was anything but literally gay, he embodied true gayness in the old-school sense, and still embodies general gayness and mirth—if by *gay* you mean blurring the line where people expect you to stay within your physical, no, *biological* limits.

It might be useful to pause to ask the germane: why would anyone want to know the history of drag shows in Florida, and where to find one today? One marketable reason is that drag shows are fun, and a mild way to experience the debauchery that Las Vegas offers 24/7 while sitting down, enjoying a beverage, and wondering if what you're seeing is real in the comparatively safe company of your partner or traveling companion. This companion will want what you both see to go home with you in the form of stories. No matter how you dress them up or down, Florida tales always travel well—and will never have to stay back in Florida, ever.

There has always been a Fun Freak Show aspect to a drag show, one where another world is sideshow-glimpsed as a Magic Kingdom of Greasepaint and Mascara. What a Floridian drag show offers a tourist is an exotic experiment that resembles the let's-put-on-a-show of a High School Musical (again, see Disney), wherein the songs are familiar, the depravity grotesque but never (intentionally) scary, and the expectations are delivered: a sing-along tune, a pretty girl, a big opening and closing, and above all, boys who look like girls who will be boys that unnerve their beholders only enough to buy one more round and not talk about it too much on the tour bus the next morning.

In the rare instance you have actually seen the *original La Cage Aux Folles* and endured subtitles under the pressure of potentially bearing the title of Heterosexual Who Digs Foreign Films About Drag Queens, then you would have noticed that *le film* takes place in a sunny seaside resort, well-known for its promise to deliver the finest in Riviera indulgence—St. Tropez. Our own journey needs an extended stay itself at this point to pay tribute to the city in which Mike Nichols situated *The Birdcage*—none other than Miami Beach—and specifically South Beach—Florida. And, in good Miami Beach early-bird style, at South Beach you might even have dinner thrown in with your revue: every Friday night at a hip venue bar called Funkshion (1116 Lincoln Road) there is a dinner buffet with shows at a (reasonably) respectable hour. Funkshion's clip on YouTube shows a show montage, with a performer leading the audience in "Happy Birthday" to a skittish man (I think). Not knowing who's what for a night or a song is part of the controlled risky fun a good drag show offers: the aforementioned ride on the wild side, but with virtual safety bars.

But is South Beach a faithful translation of St. Tropez? Yes, insofar as the comparison extends to any given day when vacation season is open, which, for either city, only means a day when the sun is out. The likeness should include, for your walk on the wild side, a trip to a show bar as opposed to a gay bar catering to specific areas of the gay community—such as leather bars, women's bars, or after-hours clubs. The latter example is a place where heterosexuals and homosexuals (and for that matter, bisexuals or transgender folks) meet on common ground—a place where the phrase "you don't have to go home but you can't stay here" isn't heard until birdsong if at all, a place that a tourist with an early schedule to follow will probably not get to experience, no matter how much they'd like to. The after-hours bar is no stranger to hosting a drag show, but usually the clientele of the former is there to spend money on alcohol instead of tips for drag performers.

Now let's assume that you are a tourist with an early sightseeing tour who's never tipped a drag queen in your life—indeed you don't even know what that means, much less how to do it. What should you expect, or better, *do?* Let's make a quick list of do's and don't's, depending on how much walk you want and/or how wild the side.

1. DO arrive at the club/bar early. You're supposed to; you're a tourist. Remember: when in doubt, act your part, not your age.
2. DO order one drink more, at least, than the minimum per person. The drag bar is no place to count ones, not even if you're about to tip Miss Gay Universe herself. Go to the bathroom and count coins. Just be careful if you do it in plain sight. Someone might think you're taking on a new profession. And you thought you were on vacation!
3. DON'T say "What?" to your waitress/waiter/etc. every time they speak. Remember that Miracle Ear is practically a religion South of Orlando. If you can't hear, you're committing a blasphemy smaller than incorrect tucking. Have your honey do the ordering.
4. DON'T tip a performer with change. Ever. Change is indeed musical. It is not meant to become your sudden spray of bugle beads ... on your forehead.
5. DO walk to the edge of the stage to allow the performer time to work out how and when she will accept your tip. Bum-rushing the diva is not suggested,

unless your Citizen's Band radio is fired up in the parking lot along with your 16-wheeler. Trust me, you're gonna need to call for some back-up, good buddy.

6. Remember: a "he" is always referred to as a "she." It's just like the Army: some things you just don't question; you learn the lingo, and rise in the ranks. "*Ma'am, yes, ma'am!*"

7. Which means the Brigadier General is always the Mistress of Ceremonies, or the lady holding the mike and working the room. If you must "holla" at anyone during this show, she is not the one, private. Watch *Torch Song Trilogy* to get an idea of what happens when you talk back to the Major-(ette).

8. DO expect lip-sync, the art of mouth-music synchronization, to be taken to a sublime level of artistry. You may swear that's really Whitney Houston holding that long note. This you can also see in the Magic Kingdom, when suddenly a show appears from nowhere, and Snow White dances in front of Cinderella's castle while gently admonishing her seven small charges to whistle while they work it. This art goes by the name of pantomime in any other change of clothing; the drag show has raised it to an Olympic skill. One gold-medal challenge is as follows: if your performer seems to have lost her place momentarily, she will be mouthing the combined words "lemonjuice" (to replicate *I love you*) or "lemonjello" or even "bananamotherfu\*\*er" until she gets back to the place in the song she knows. And as far as the illusory impact of lip-synching is concerned: would children ever question whether or not that's really Snow White singing? Of course not. Kids know queens are magical.

9. Last, and never least: if you are hot and male, under NO CIRCUMSTANCES shall you sit up front. For some reason, dudes that look like dudes and *really are* (for the opposite of this see No. 10) are considered fair game for "revenge teasing." Trust me; the only consistent negative buzz ever generated by tourists at a drag show is as follows: "Some mean ole rackin'-frackin' queen done made fun of me." Indeed. You know what they say: when in Rome ... do as your Roman sisters do. Have fun and leave the debate at home or better, on the tour bus, as to Who Looked Like A Real Girl and (secretly) Whom You May Have Kinda Liked. Always end with this bit of show wisdom: a drag queen can sniff out a tense heterosexual like a vintage bottle of Chanel No. 5. See, the women all around you are whooping it up and flashing their pearlies—lighten up, big guy. And yes, you'll still be *very* manly when the lights come up ... more so for trying on for size the estrogen that's freely flowing around you.

10. One last thing: what you will be watching is a classic part of what has now been upgraded to the title of The GLBTQ Community, a work in progress; feel free to holler the word "WORK!" at a performer a time or two as you kick back and take it all in. And be on the lookout for the Floridian Drag Queen's up-and-coming equal and show-stealer, the Drag *King*. (And I'll let you ponder and work that last phrase out on your own.)

## Political Fallout for the Gay/Lesbian/Bisexual/ Transgender/Queer Communities

While most politicians will agree that gays and lesbians represent a strong commercial venue in Florida, they still have some major problems supporting them. Some of the politicians really suffer a morality distance from these societies. They honestly believe that the lifestyle itself is contrary to biblical beliefs and ethics. However, if we look closely at the habits of some politicians, we might infer that they are much more mindful of their constituents than they are worried about scripture. Not to tar a group with a single brush stroke, but the actions of a few Florida politicos indicate that many of them are not over constrained with morality. After all, it was a Floridian congressman who hung around the dorms of young pages in Washington, and when he was caught immediately went to rehab for alcohol problems so as to avoid prosecution. Apparently the strategy worked, as the matter seems to have been dropped. It was a fine Floridian who hired a blonde beauty for his secretary; he was informed that she could not write a letter and that she literally could not spell her name. The senator called the spellings variants and shouted in defiance, "She's worth her weight in gold!" At that time many Floridians giggled out loud, but then he got elected to the U.S. Congress and took her with him, so more fool we. He was almost immediately named the most corrupt congressman in office. I could go on, but you get my drift.

So when exactly did the Florida legislature decide that gays and lesbians were not welcome in Florida? It was pretty early on actually. The country was rushing along with McCarthyism, so Florida went for McCarthy with a kick. Not content to just root out communists, Florida went for a purge of homosexuals. This was started with the "Johns Committee" (and yes, everybody gets the pun). Started in 1956, the committee headed by former governor Charley Eugene Johns mandated the legislature to "Investigate all organizations whose principles or activities include a course of conduct [that would be considered] inimical to the well being and orderly pursuit of their personal and business activities by the majority of the citizens of this state." To say that is a broad and vague law is to treat it gently. Most of us would be afraid to leave home each day with this mandate fresh in our minds. But with this ready, set, go mentality, the Johns Committee was off and running. The clear agenda was to force educators out of their jobs. The committee members believed that gays could "turn" children, and that is why gays were moved to be educators. Thus teachers from kindergarten to college were targeted. The destruction of lives and livelihood are well documented. Many students were also pulled out of classes and expelled. Criticism of the Johns Committee was rampant on college campuses, but that criticism was intensified by a report called *Homosexuality and Citizenship in Florida*. The report noted that "homosexuals have an insatiable appetite for sexual activities and find special gratification in the recruitment to their ranks of youth.... We must just do everything in our power to create one thing in the minds of every homosexual and that is to keep their hands off of our children.... If we don't do something soon we will wake up one morning and find they are too big to fight. They may be already. I hope not."

This report was so vivid that when it was published, it was sold on the streets of New York as pornography. Now that's irony. In an interview in 1972, Charley Johns said that he had to find a way to stamp out homosexuality: "I don't get no love out of hurting people. But the situation in Gainesville, my Lord have mercy. I never saw nothing like it in my life. If I saved one boy from being made homosexual, it was justified." Johns apparently never went into a classroom except to pull gay teachers and students out for interrogation; perhaps he should have lingered awhile to work on his language arts.

One would like to think that Florida had progressed into the 2000s. But still related to the Johns Committee is the law that forbids gay couples from adopting. They can be foster parents, but they cannot adopt. What does this mean? Florida laws are enigmatic. Interesting is the amendment for the Florida constitution on the 2008 ballot. Amendment 2 would create a constitutional ban on gay marriage. Florida already has a law on the books that proclaims that marriage is only to be between one man and one woman. But hey, if you can have one law that disallows personal freedom on the books, why not two? We know how well 50 percent of American marriages work out. But that doesn't really matter. In the words of great politicians everywhere, "We've got to protect the children."

## An Unintended South Beach Legacy

What really seemed to put South Beach on the national map of consciousness for good — at least, as reported by Tom Brokaw's hiccup of a drone straight into the national and certainly global imagination was an incident that made 1997 memorable and sadder in several worlds: the murder of Gianni Versace by a spree killer named Andrew Cunanan. The latter was to die by his own hand several days later, having slain Versace on the front steps of his renovated Italian villa in the center of South Beach as he returned from breakfast. Cunanan's lifestyle soon became apparent, as Versace was the first of five men he murdered with no apparent connection. As more and more news outlets carried the story longer and longer, the world of fashion and international glamour became more and more stunned by the loss of its crown couture prince, ever-youthful, puckish, and tanned — and more and more Americans seemed to want the dirt on the story. *Why Versace?* It was reported in the press at the time that Cunanan turned tricks for older male clients in order to gain entrée in a world he could not claim — a world of upwardly-mobile, international gay men who knew what South Beach was becoming, and had always been: a small gay mecca. Even though *Miami Vice* and Scarface supplied our imaginations with plenty of colorful and virile images to situate Miami and Miami Beach, South Beach had always been a dorky kid sister in many ways, even during its Jackie Gleason Show heyday.

"Before *Miami Vice*" and "After *Miami Vice*" have become our common-era distinctions: now South Beach is indeed where fashion, thugs and SPF 40 commingle and prosper since the opening of Irene Marie Models in 1989 at SoBe (given that acronym way before the popular juice-sucrose beverages, without a doubt). Irene Marie was the first international full-service modeling agency in Florida, a good reason for Versace to buy in the area. Cunanan and Versace appear to have met only briefly and tragically. What the murderer accomplished opposed his victim's achievements: he gained a quick spin in the media, unearned except from another's permanently borrowed life, the ultimate knock-off made for the streets. And for a few weeks, Cunanan dragged South Beach into an incessant glare that almost outmatched its noonday rays. He has kept the area in the public zeitgeist as That Place Where Gays Play and Die, or Make A Dress. In an inhumane moment, South Beach was outed, all around the world — a status that its isolated big sister to the Southwest, strong from surviving hurricanes and Henry Flagler's folly, knew all about, albeit for happier reasons, usually related to pens, liquor and pies — and gradually, capital-S Sushi in a giant pump at midnight on New Year's Eves.

## A Key to Key West

In the 1700s and 1800s, Key West was an isolated island, home to a very few people. Hardly anyone in the country knew or cared to know about the island. It was home to nomads and local fishermen who really loved to be left alone. Those days of isolation came to an end in 1905 when the construction of the Overseas Railroad began. "Seven years later, on January 22, 1912, the first train from the mainland rolled into Key West, and an umbilical cord was formed upon which key dwellers became ever more dependent" (Viele 99). The train did not do much for the local population, but it did let word leak out that there was a beautiful, isolated island within reach. In 1917, when the move to build the Overseas Highway began, sports fishermen and yachtsmen had already been drawn to the Keys. But then the wealthy and famous began to notice the Keys. Their visits would promote more construction during the twenties and thirties. It was only a mater of time before the famous writers and artists of the time would seek out the Keys for rest and recreation.

Why would famous writers and artists seek out Key West as a primary place of residency? New York was the party town from the 1930s till the 1970s. The wealthy wanted to party with the talented. The talented people relied on the wealthy for publicity and occasionally money. It was a cannibalistic atmosphere. The parties were not so much social events as they were "wow, look who I could get to come" events. One has only to look at the description of the party scene in Truman Capote's *Breakfast at Tiffany's* to see how he viewed the New York social scene. The writers and artists needed a refuge. If you were not in town, you could not be accused of shirking your party obligations. Also, many of the most famous artists and writers were gays and lesbians. The wealthy New York crowd was aware of this, but Middle America was not. Key West was a tiny town that still observed its own rules. The islanders did not question the lifestyles of their artists. They did not question anyone else's lifestyle either. Thus, Key West, with its tiny cottages, unpaved roads and limited social life, became a refuge, once again, for people who wanted to be left alone.

Elizabeth Bishop, a noted American poet, lived in Key West for a number of years with her companion, Louise Crane. In *One Art*, a collection of her letters, she writes about her life in Key West:

> It is the rainy season and we have had the most magnificent thunderstorms almost everyday. I have taken a little room in our favorite hotel here to work in the mornings. The hotel is rather like a ship — all white paint, shutter doors, long red carpets and views of the ocean, and almost deserted this time of the year.... I am planning on staying here until I can get the things I am working on finished — probably until the middle of July [Giroux 91].

Key West from the thirties through the seventies was a little-known refuge for eccentrics and homosexuals. The streets were unpaved; tiny cottages sold for modest amounts of money, there were bathhouses and openly gay bars. Gay couples could be seen on the streets holding hands and openly kissing. It was also a place for writers and artists to gather. Hemingway's house is still a museum to the artist, although many other famous names in the arts loved the tiny island. Allison Laurie, in her book *Familiar Spirits*, states that the following artists also enjoyed winters there: "Frost and Stevens were gone, but in the '70s John Brinnin, John Ciardi, Barbara Deming, Ralph Ellison, John Hersey, Richard Wilbur and Tennessee Williams still wintered there" (125). Indeed, Tennessee Williams and Truman Capote once shared a bungalow there.

Capote was known for enjoying the nightlife that Key West offered, which was primarily a bar on every corner. He had a tumultuous affair with a young man named John O'Shea. A story told by Capote on numerous TV talk shows was about a late night encounter with a young woman who asked him for an autograph and then slipped off her shorts and presented her backside to him. He supposedly signed and then an ambitious bartender leapt over the bar and presented Capote with his penis and also asked for an autograph. According to Capote, he looked at the young man and said, "Oh dear, I don't believe I can, perhaps I could just initial it." That was his talk show joke about the event, but according to Gerald Clarke's biography *Capote*, these infamous lines were uttered by John O'Shea (456).

The stories told about the famous writers and artists who loved Key West are endless. They include Hemingway and his famous six-toed cats; the Hemingway look-alike contests continue today. Key West became a symbol for sexual freedom. The New Year's Eve parties, where gays and straights stand together in Mallory Square to watch Sushi, a famous drag queen, descend from a huge red high-heeled slipper into the new year, are still going strong and are viewed on Youtube by millions (International Herald Tribune Americas). However, the Keys are changing; Key West more than most. Wealthy people are starting to build McMansions. The salt marshes were filled in to build a landing strip. The stray chickens that once had the run of the island have been gathered up and hauled away. Even the famous cats are under attack. The rich do what the rich do. They tend to find a place that is isolated and beloved; they fall in love with it themselves, and then they move in and force change. Think of Aspen, where the entire local population was forced out because property values and taxes became prohibitive. This is the current state of Key West. While gays and lesbians still have a prominent presence in the town, that presence is diminishing. The wealthy newcomers are pushing to get rid of the tacky T-shirt stores and the bar on every corner attitude. They want a lush private paradise. They do not seem to understand that they already had it. The gay and lesbian communities will probably fade away in Key West and turn up somewhere else. People who look, for whatever reasons, to find a place to just live will usually find it. That place will have no rules about holding your lover's hand in the sunlight.

## Conclusion

While the gay and lesbian community is large and vibrant in Florida, it still has a dark side. Gays are often the victims of assault. Suicide rates are still high in the community and recently a young man was shot outside a gay bar simply for wearing women's clothes. Luckily, the old chestnut "I thought he was making a pass at me" didn't work. Everyone in the crowd said the assailant fired directly at his victim with murderous intent. What a silly excuse that is anyway. Try to consider what would happen if women started shooting men who made unwelcome passes at them.

Visitors who come to Florida should come with an open mind and take advantage of all the diverse and entertaining things to do in this state. That includes going to the drag queen shows and having some wonderful adult fun. Send the kiddies to bed, hire a sitter and go forth into the night. Have fun and spend a little money. The state of Florida may have a little trouble dealing with its gays and lesbians, but they have no trouble enjoying your money. Go to Key West and let Sushi make fun of your heterosexuality. Where in Missouri can you find a night out like that?

### Works Cited

Bishop, Elizabeth. *One Art: Elizabeth Bishop Letters*. Edited by Robert Giroux. New York: The Noonday Press, 1994.

Capote, Truman. *Breakfast At Tiffany's and Other Stories*. New York: Random House, 1951.

Clarke, Gerald. *Capote*. New York: Simon and Schuster, 1988.
"Gay Days at Disney World." Gay.com. http:www.gay.com/travel/article.html?sernum= 14260.
Lurie, Alison. *Familiar Spirits*. New York: Penguin Books, 2002.
Viele, John. *The Florida Keys: A History of the Pioneers*. Sarasota, Fla.: Pineapple Press, 2002.

# The Architecture of Dreams
*Jeff Morgan*

September 11 has had and continues to have numerous effects on America and Americans, including from an architectural standpoint. Because architecture helps define culture and ultimately ourselves, the change in the New York City skyline has changed America and Americans. Architecture definitely has its place in the popular imagination. When our family goes to Europe, most of our photos are of buildings and structures that we have seen in film, books, magazines, newspapers, and on television. We identify the places with their buildings. So a vacation to Rome means several photos of the Coliseum; to Paris, the Eiffel Tower; to London, Big Ben. In the states, we make the same associations. The Philadelphia vacation photo album has several shots of Freedom Hall; Washington, the White House; and San Antonio, the Alamo. Clearly, the identity of a place is inextricably linked with its architecture. Though a travel guide may strongly suggest that we stray from the beaten path for a road less traveled in order to genuinely experience a culture, that road would not lead us to experiencing and identifying with the popular culture of the place. From an architectural perspective, the identity of a place seems to be created by older buildings, which have had, in some cases, centuries to form in the collective unconscious. But what if we tried to better understand the identity of a place that doesn't have significantly older architecture to help create an identity in the popular imagination? Turning our gaze to Florida, the buildings and structures that rise up to form the state's identity are all rather new, comparatively speaking.

To be sure, Florida is different. That's one of the main reasons why people come here. Florida and the Fountain of Youth myth have become a part of the collective unconscious of the United States, and from this archetype flows a drive that compels many people to come to Florida in search of something different, something that will reinvigorate them, something that will regenerate them. However, Florida's exotic appeal is not limited to her beautiful sandy beaches, warm weather, or sub-tropical flora and fauna. Many come to Florida to see buildings. There is no Fountain of Youth romanticized by Spanish explorers, but visitors do come to Florida to see architecture that helps symbolize the reinvention that is at the heart of the mythology of the Fountain of Youth. They want to see Vizcaya, Worth Avenue and other marvels from Mizner, the fabulous resort hotels of Flagler and Plant, and the Art Deco of South Beach. Even if you have no intention of seeking it out, Florida architecture can lure you and take you temporarily out of yourself. This enables you to reinvent yourself, the way Florida architecture often reinvents herself, serving as a model of change and flux, though different than what you would find elsewhere in the United States. In conjunction with the other state wonders, Florida architecture holds a certain mythical, revitalizing place within the popular imagination. It is symbolic.

The image of Florida as a very different place architecturally begins in the early twentieth century with the spread of Mediterranean Revival architecture, which is generally characterized by impressive façades, multiple stories, stucco walls, tile, terra cotta, and elaborate windows and doorways. This architectural style may be found elsewhere, as in the Francis Marion Stokes Fourplex in Portland, Oregon, or the Plaza in Kansas City, but, other than in California, the style is not as prevalent in other places as it is in Florida. Moreover, the identity of these other places is created by other architectural styles. Even California, which has its fair share of Mediterranean Revival architecture, is still captured in the popular imagination more often with structures like the Golden Gate Bridge, Spanish missions built well before Mediterranean Revival, or even the Rose Bowl.

In Florida, though, the style is prevalent and, consequently, definitive of Florida architecture in the popular imagination. Virtually every building in Coral Gables is Mediterranean Revival. Additionally, the style is intertwined into Florida myth and the Fountain of Youth. Inherent in the name is the connotation of reinvention and amalgamation. The combination of Spanish, French, and Italian style transports the viewer to a more cosmopolitan than metropolitan setting more common in the industrial north of the United States. This cosmopolitan character of the architecture frees the viewer from local, provincial, and even national prejudices. Moreover, the "revival" aspect of the architecture further frees the viewer from his past, providing the space for him to revive himself. It seems almost fate that this state so associated with the Fountain of Youth myth would unfold an architecture that advances the myth beyond the days of Spanish exploration.

In time, when the railroads came bringing building materials that could take Florida architecture beyond the antebellum estate or the cracker house, Florida herself was reborn or reinvented. In describing the changing Florida of the early twentieth century and the era of Mediterranean Revival, Beth Dunlop writes, "Florida itself was an invention, a tropical wonderland built on swamp and muck by canny and imaginative entrepreneurs, and it stands to reason that the Mediterranean Revival architecture that would come to symbolize this made-up place would be made-up as well, an architecture of fabrication more than scholarship, of improvisation more than precision" (191). Dunlop's disdain for the style aside, Mediterranean Revival fits form to environment, but all the bright colors, the tile, terra cotta, terraces, archways, Venetian doorways, courtyards and vaulted ceilings aren't just designed to provide relief from the Florida heat; these details suggest an image of romance that fosters individual transcendence for the viewer of these buildings and, consequently, lines the pockets of those behind the presentation of the image.

Nothing better exemplifies the grand possibilities of transcendence than Vizcaya, an estate and gardens in the Italian palazzo style overlooking Biscayne Bay in Miami. It was built between 1914 and 1922 for James Deering, then vice president of International Harvester, the farm equipment and truck builder now known as Navistar. However, Deering's estate is not simply the result of big spending. Vizcaya is a work of art that originally encompassed 180 acres. Paul Chaflin oversaw every artistic aspect of Vizcaya, but F. Burrall Hoffman designed the buildings and Colombian Diego Suarez the gardens, and Deering stocked the rooms with centuries-old European art that he gathered from his many travels abroad. Strolling about the mansion and its extensive gardens, which are now a museum, you are removed to another time and place. Lavish salons and dining rooms wrap around an inner courtyard that was originally sans ceiling. Now there's a glass roof. Walk out the other side of the courtyard and you step out into a Venetian scene. A stone barge rests there in Biscayne Bay, just yards from the steps to the house, creating a narrow channel. Striped poles for docking lean in the waters. Go back inside and take winding stairs to the second floor that surrounds and looks down upon the courtyard and see all the guest bedrooms, Deering's own room and private bath, and an impressive kitchen and breakfast room. An elevator deposits riders at the outside pool adjacent to the house. Surrounding the house are the exquisite gardens, including mythical statuary, maze-like shrubbery, and geometric flower beds reminiscent of the Jardines de Sabatini outside the Palacio Real in Madrid or the Jardin des Tuileries outside the Musée du Louvre in Paris, further enhancing the European feel of Vizcaya. However, the estate still has a Florida stamp on it, notably with the native hardwood hammock around the western front of the estate and the impressive orchidarium, the flower stamped into the popular imagination of Florida thanks to Susan Orlean's *The Orchid Thief* and the film adaptation of her book, appropriately called *Adaptation*.

More commercial in its design but nonetheless important for its fostering of the Florida myth in the popular imagination is the Mediterranean Revival architecture of Addison Mizner. This is the architecture that Dunlop has in mind when she criticizes Florida's Mediterranean Revival; however visitors in large part identify Florida with this style. One of Mizner's most enduring symbols is Worth Avenue in Palm Beach. One of the most elegant avenues in the world, the Rodeo Drive of the East, the 300 block of Worth Avenue boasts the residence of Addison Mizner, Via Mizner; Via Parigi; and the Everglades Club, all fostering the myth of regeneration and all sights that people want to see. These buildings were built in the years just before the 1929 crash. They represent the flamboyance of the Roaring Twenties.

Mizner himself represents that same flamboyance. He was, as Catherine Orr characterizes him, "a 'social' architect" (5). Coming from a rich San Francisco family, he worked for the South Florida elite, particularly in Palm Beach, designing primarily private clubs and estates in a style no doubt influenced by his early travels in Latin America and his architectural studies in Salamanca,

Spain. After the death of his father, the financial situation of the family worsened significantly, and Mizner capitalized on the Alaska gold rush, bringing back riches, and, upon returning to Guatemala, took advantage of some instability there to bring back some lucrative relics from churches. With these riches, he was able to return to the architectural studies that took him from Honolulu to all parts of Europe. He eventually came to Florida and began the work that he is most remembered by, work that, for the most part, appears on one street, Worth Avenue in Palm Beach.

On one side of the street, with its back to the street in the tradition of Spanish plazas like the Plaza Mayor in Madrid, stands the Everglades Club, Mizner's first Florida project, built in 1918 but renovated by Mizner for several years afterwards. You can't get in without a card, but you can still see the gated archway entrance with the balcony, stained windows, the pairs of arched windows, the dome tower, the slanting tile roofs coming at you from various angles, the textured stucco, and much more. Inside are the spiral stairs, the cloisters, the loggias, the gardens, the court of oranges, the fountain in the patio, and the terraces. There's the ballroom, a long room lined by windows, with its high vaulted ceilings of wood, magnificent chandeliers, fireplace, and exquisite furnishings. Very similar to that is the dining room, sans one wall of windows but with frescoes from Achille Angeli. Also inside are individual apartments, like that of Paris Singer, heir to the Singer sewing machine fortune and the man who brought Mizner to Palm Beach in 1918. The tilework in his bathroom is especially notable in the tub area, around the sink, and on the floors. And all the windows in the apartment point to Mizner's concerns about the Florida heat and the necessity to create cross drafts in virtually every room he designed. The principle is quite evident with the Cosden House in Palm Beach, the doorway of which opens up with a view through the house to the sea. This is not unlike the Key West shotgun-style house, which not only afforded a breeze but allowed irate fathers to chase the men who sparked their daughters, shooting straight through the house at the fleeing young courter.

Across the street from the Everglades Club is the most accessible evidence of Mizner's Mediterranean Revival style. Built in 1924, Via Mizner and Via Parigi are "a stretch of Worth Avenue ... built as a single design" (Hoffstot). Within Via Mizner there's Mizner's house (in the tower), Villa Mizner, but it's the vias that touch everyone because, as Ida M. Tarbell writes in reference specifically to Via Mizner, "This little street is open to all the world" (xl). Winding within the block is a maze of loggias, terraces, quaint art and jewelry shops, and cafés. The lush vegetation of ficus and bougainvillea, the tiles against the stucco, and the slanting clay roof tiles create a blend of color that, combined with a breeze, transport you into a setting very different from what you would experience in the Midwest or Northeast. Again, Ida M. Tarbell puts it best when she writes, "You enter the little street freely and its pink, blue and cream-colored fronts, its gay little shops, its cafés, the chairs on the sidewalks, give you a real sense of what a Florida town might be if it could escape the domination of the Northern town" (xl). Mizner's Mediterranean Revival architecture makes that escape, and those who view it with an eye toward escaping need only let Mizner's work take them by the hand.

My personal favorite of Mizner's buildings, the one that takes me away every time, is the 1923 Gulfstream Golf Club on North Ocean Boulevard, A1A, in Gulfstream. The façade, set back upon an immaculate lawn dotted with palm trees, at once presents splendor and at the same time distance. I may never mount those semi-circular stairs, placed like parentheses before a grand row of columned archways. But, then again, I may, and that is the dream that Florida architecture can build. Nobody built it better than Addison Mizner.

His influence is ubiquitous in South Florida, so many housing developments copy his style. In West Palm Beach, the town that started as a home for Palm Beach servants, a recent development reeks of the Mizner style. City Place, an invented downtown for West Palm Beach, is a conglomeration of condos huddled around a bevy of shops and restaurants, with all the trappings of the Mediterranean Revival style that Mizner launched, but without the ease and with neon. There is a courtyard area in the center of City Place where people gather at tables for drinks and listen to music, but the essence comes across as the kind of fabrication that Dunlop alludes to. In fact, the most genuine site in City Place is the Harriet Himmel Theater, a one-time church that dates back to 1926. The old First United Methodist Church, which is now a cultural and performing arts center, stands in typical Mediterranean Revival style, with its open-truss, high cypress ceilings, tiered mezzanine, large pairs of windows, and textured stucco.

Still, perhaps the most obvious modern homage to Mizner is Mizner Park in Boca Raton, the same town that Mizner went to "in 1925, at the height of the Florida land boom, [to join] in a scheme to promote a large new subdivision" (Curl xvii). Again in the style of something like Madrid's Plaza Mayor, Mizner Park has its back to Federal Highway. Two one-way, cobblestone streets, separated by a grassy median with tiled fountains and geometric landscaping, are in the middle of rows of shops and restaurants in mauve stucco with terrace and courtyard dining and multiple levels to the terra cotta roofing of the apartments above the retail level. Mizner designed actual buildings in Boca Raton, but the subdivision scheme never reached fruition thanks in large part to the 1926 hurricane, the same one that prompted Miami to roof Vizcaya's courtyard. The Boca Raton subdivision scheme is indicative of Florida's association with the Fountain of Youth myth, as speculation and get-rich-quick schemes are economical ways to regenerate yourself. Fortunately, for those seeking a more spiritual transcendence, there's still the option of simply communing with, among other beautiful sights in Florida, her great architecture.

Before leaving Palm Beach, the island town that exudes the kind of opulence that many dream about, there's one more work of Mediterranean Revival architecture that deserves attention, Flagler's The Breakers. This is not the 1896 Breakers. It burned down in 1903, nor is it The Breakers built immediately in its place, for it burned down, too, in 1925. What still stands is the third reincarnation of the hotel, completed in 1926 by the Flagler machine, still operating after Henry's death in 1913. Designed by Leonard Schultze, and more Italian than Spanish in design, The Breakers is a monument to the kind of good life we all long for, a life Henry Flagler lived. Flagler worked with John D. Rockefeller and helped Rockefeller start the Standard Oil Company in 1870, before embarking on developing Florida by building railroads and hotels, the most notable of which is The Breakers. Entering The Breakers from the west, a long road leads to a centered fountain based on the one at the Palazzo Pitti in Florence (Braden 322). Rising to the sides of the fountain are the impressive, if not iconic, twin towers, the signature architectural feature of The Breakers, quite distinguishable from across the Atlantic Intracoastal Waterway and imprinted into the minds of those who have seen them. These towers dwarf the tower of Mizner's Everglades Club, but Mizner preferred his work to blend more with the environment.

The Flagler System spared no expense with The Breakers. This hotel is, after all, a flat-out ad for Flagler and Florida, which were at one time synonyms. The main lobby is "modeled on the Great Hall of the Palazzo Carega in Genoa" (Braden 326) and the interior architecture dazzles with vaulted ceilings, richly painted pendentives, and columned arches. Almost everything is covered in frescoes and tapestries. The lobby leads straight to a central patio of tropical plants, geometric flower beds and fountains. Looking east into the courtyard and through a wall of windows, you can see the Mediterranean Room, whose sky mural ceiling makes every day a beautiful day. Beyond the Mediterranean Room is the Venetian Room, whose windows face out into the Atlantic. On the south side of The Breakers is the lovely Tapestry Bar with its Mizneresque wooden beamed ceiling, and the most stunning room in the resort hotel, The Circle, a dining room whose shape fits its name, having a centered glass ceiling from which drops a gorgeous chandelier. The domed ceiling also has frescoes depicting classic Mediterranean scenes. There are more interesting sights inside The Breakers than outside; in fact, the interior character of The Breakers contrasts a bit with the exterior, which is customary for the time and particularly results from some of the additions and renovations done over the years. This is not the case with the exterior of some other hotels in the Flagler System.

From the outside, Flagler's St. Augustine hotels are more marvelous to the eye, and though they do not have the *je ne sais quoi* of The Breakers, they are sights to behold. Flagler is associated with three St. Augustine hotels, the Ponce de León, the Alcazar, and the Casa Monica. Only the latter is still a hotel, but all three still survive. Designed by Carrère and Hastings, the Ponce de León, though Moorish in some of its styling, takes on a decidedly and appropriate Spanish flavor for St. Augustine, which was settled by the Spanish before Jamestown. What first strikes the viewer is the color contrast. The gray cement walls, which were made with shells that give them that Florida touch, contrast with a red brick trim, the usual terra cotta roofing tiles, and a dash of yellow on the wooden trim of the windows. In fact, the hotel was the first major building in the Untied States constructed of poured concrete. In 1906, Carrère wrote for *The St. Augustine Evening Record*, "When you decorate a hotel so artistically that you get a man to go there for something else than to eat or sleep you have accomplished a great deal for art" (quoted in Braden). To be sure, with the Ponce de León and its Spanish towers, chimneys, arched windows, columned archways, loggias, marine theme seen in much of the detailing and so much more, once again we see Florida architecture as an inspiration, as worthy of meditation. In fact, the hotel is now the site of Flagler College, where students walk the halls, finding inspiration beyond the wise lectures given by their professors.

To enter the Ponce de León, or Flagler College, students must pass a pair of lions guarding the entrance. Inside, more grandeur awaits. Students dine in the old dining hall with Tiffany glass and pendentives of George Maynard's paintings of women, similar to the ones in the pendentives of the building's rotunda. Students can take visitors through the great rooms of the Ponce de León like the rotunda, which stretches four floors, from the eye-catching marble fireplace on the first floor to the sitting area and galleries on the second and third floors. The fourth floor is a domed ceiling, only visible from the first floor. There is space, though, above that dome — another dome that functions as a solarium. The guest rooms are now student dormitory rooms. In keeping with the marine theme, which runs almost everywhere from the terra-cotta dolphin fountains bordering what was an entrance for ladies to the terra-cotta mermaids at the main entry, the dorm room doorknobs are shaped like seashells. Students meet their professors in the service building to be advised and evaluated, and we would be advised to heed Susan Braden, who in her great book *The Architecture of Leisure* writes, "In an evaluation of the Ponce de León, it must be acknowledged that the hotel captivated the public's imagination" (177). It still does.

Flagler's other two St. Augustine hotels also captivate the imagination and further the vision of Florida as a mythical place capable of inspiring us to change our lives. As the students who attend Flagler College are changing their lives, the Alcazar has changed. The Alcazar is now, in part, the Lightner Museum; the rest is either retail space or city government offices. Like the Ponce de León, the Alcazar is made from poured concrete highlighted by red brick and terra-cotta, and it was designed by Carrère and Hastings in Mediterranean Revival with emphasis on Spanish and Moorish influence, such as in the minarets. A telling difference between the hotels is the difference in their names. Alcazar can be translated as "house of Caesar." Indeed, the Alcazar looks a bit like a fortification, especially in the baths portion of the complex, which has windows shaped like arrow slits. Coupling the old Alcazar Hotel with the eclectic collection of Chicago publisher Otto Lightner's Victoriana, which includes, among other oddities, a shrunken head, echo the multiple uses of the building in the past — part hotel, part bath, and part casino. A visit to the Alcazar complex compels you to reflect upon the change and flux in your own life, how you wear many in a lifetime, and the opportunity Florida provides for manifesting such change.

In the lifespan of the Casa Monica, we see significant change and flux. First, the Casa Monica isn't actually a Flagler-built hotel. Flagler purchased it in 1888, months after it opened, from Franklin Smith, founder of the YMCA, and renamed it the Hotel Cordova. In 1902, a bridge connected it with the Alcazar. However, its years as a hotel, like those of the previous two, were numbered. In 1962, it became the St. John's County Courthouse. Yet thirty years later, it was back as the Casa Monica and is still a hotel today. In fact, King Juan Carlos and Queen Sophia of Spain stayed at the Casa Monica in April 2001. Even the majestic seek out the majesty of inspiring Mediterranean Revival Florida hotels such as the Casa Monica. The Ponce de León, the Alcazar, and the Casa Monica, designed by Smith and more Moorish than the other two, represent more than one time and place. Your imagination can drift from medieval days on the Mediterranean to a time when northern Florida ruled in the popular imagination of the United States. However, with the railroad came South Florida hotels set in more tropical climes, and the people followed. Still, one hotel that must not be overlooked in this survey lies across the peninsula.

We have seen a decidedly increasing Moorish influence in the three St. Augustine hotels. Henry Plant's Tampa Bay Hotel, designed by John A. Wood and opened in 1891, takes Islamic Revival to a whole new level. Plant's hotel is almost entirely red brick, characteristic of Islamic Revival. It has lots of minarets. Its windows, unlike the smooth arches of the likes of Mizner, are more pointed in the center, more horseshoe shaped, very Venetian. Its onion domes have silver roofing and recall, actually, the Taj Mahal more than anything else. These influences are no doubt the result of Plant's extensive travels, afforded by the money he made in the transportation industry, both railway and steamships. His Tampa Bay Hotel exudes a cosmopolitan aura.

However, the Tampa Bay Hotel is a Florida hotel. Like the architects of the Ponce de León, Wood created his cement out of native supplies, local oyster shells and sand in this case. Braden further informs us that Wood used "Florida cypress wood for door casings and window frames" (271). Inside, that trend continues with mahogany in the dining room and doors and a solarium to take advantage of the Florida sun. There are also verandas and tropical landscaping, further providing a Florida feel. Additionally, the Tampa Bay Hotel set the precedent followed by the Ponce de León, which became Flagler College in 1967. In 1933, Plant's Tampa Bay Hotel became, in a large part, the University of Tampa. The rest became a museum, again setting a precedent to be followed by Lightner with the Alcazar. What we have here is an illustration of the change and flux that Florida personifies in its incessant reinventing of itself.

Just as Mediterranean Revival was an artistic response to an earlier style, so evolving Florida architecture responded to it. The next great phase of Florida architecture to play a role in the popular imagination of the United States was Art Deco, most notable in the South Beach area of Miami. Art Deco was modern, and as Allan T. Shulman writes, this "modernism was an important link between distant Miami and contemporary American ideas and practices" (336).

Yes, one can point to New York and the Chrysler Building or the interior of Radio City Music Hall as prime examples of the architectural style, but Miami Art Deco takes the simple geometric functionalism of northern industrialism and machinery found in the paintings of Charles Sheeler, and has fun with the lines, helping to reinforce Florida as a destination where you can play and lose yourself. Moreover, "Nowhere," as Nicholas N. Patricios writes, "is there the concentration of Art Deco hotels and apartment buildings that there is in Miami Beach" (97).

A leisurely stroll down Collins Avenue or, especially, Ocean Drive in the South Beach area of Miami Beach yields countless examples of Art Deco. One stretch on Ocean Drive between 5th and 15th presents the best illustrations of the style that has characterized the area known as America's Riviera. Pastels, vertical configurations, geometric ornamentation, friezes, rounded corners, and playful symmetry can be seen in South Beach hotels such as the Adrian (1934), Edison (1935), Cavalier (1936), Waldorf (1937), Cardozo (1939), and Avalon (1941). The dates are important. These hotels were built during the Great Depression. Patricios is again instructive when he writes, "The images of fantasy and romance in the styles were attempts to delight tourists and seasonal residents and lift their spirits" (113).

As we look at each of these hotels in order, we will begin to feel the full weight of Patricios' words. First, the Adrian delights with its pink and teal pastels, rounded awnings that are verticality accentuated by pilasters (a common use of columns in this architectural style), and geometric relief, particularly that which flanks the doorway with swirling relief rising toward a light near the top center of the configuration. Next, the Edison delights the eye with its vertical façade, yellow arches, overall yellow and green pastels, and orange signage on the right front with Art Deco lettering naming the hotel. The Cavalier, as with most of these hotels, also uses vertical influence with pilasters much like the Adrian. Enhancing the sense of rising, which symbolically reinforces the uplifting feeling you get from viewing this art and which connects with the overall emphasis on a change for the good that seems to permeate much of Florida's architecture within the popular imagination, is a mast topped with a flag and rows of three tall lean windows connected by striping. The Waldorf is an angular hotel on a corner lot with an ornamental lighthouse right at the corner and wrap-around windows at the angle and rising to the top. The Cardozo stretches its rectangular design to rounded ends, the stretching furthered by awnings that serve as stripes. Its verticality, again so prominent in Art Deco design, comes out in its flag-topped mast and lean windows. Finally, the last and the latest hotel, the Avalon, sits like an angle on a corner lot with its yellow tower right at the corner accentuated by light green rounded awnings.

Two of these hotels were designed by the same architect, one who stands out as an exemplary artist in this style, one who, like Mizner in Palm Beach, is associated with the identity of the place through his architecture. Henry Hohauser is responsible for The Edison and The Cardozo, as well as, to name a few, The Surf and Hotel Webster from 1936, The Governor, Greystone and Colony hotels from 1939, and The Neron and The New Yorker from 1940. Hohauser is also responsible for several apartments in South Beach, but I would like to focus on one more particular work of his, The Park Central from 1937. Once again, we have pastels, blue this time. Once again, we have the verticality quite present in the façade framed at the top and bottom by decorative circles and accented by centered triangles and a finial. Windows are at the extreme ends of the hotel, and the rectangular second floor windows wrap around the hotel. The Park Central can more accurately be categorized, as can some of the other hotels addressed above, as Streamline Moderne, but the resemblances with Art Deco are far more evident than the differences. Additionally, Streamline Moderne is more associated with post–World War II architecture, as in Igor B. Polevitzky's Shelbourne, built in 1954 on Collins Avenue.

Miami has been very active in preserving the Art Deco district, which was once on the brink of extinction. The city took a major step toward preserving the area with the Miami Beach Historic Preservation Ordinance. This kind of recognition actually has more weight than national recognition. Yes, the Art Deco district of Miami Beach is on the National Register of Historic Places; in fact, it is the first "area" to make the list, which had previously solely included individual buildings. Cities need to take the reins to preserve our history, for, as historian Timothy B. Tyson writes, "We are all the captives of our origins, especially when we do not fully know and understand them" (265). Tyson recognizes that we are defined by place. Now, if architecture, at least in part, defines a place, and if the most defining elements of a place are the historical buildings and those historical buildings are not preserved, our ability to understand ourselves becomes compromised. Noted South Florida architect Rick Gonzalez, president of REG Architects, puts it best when he says, "Historic buildings add great value to our communities and give us a great pride of place." Gonzalez should know. He has been instrumental in trying to save one of the historic buildings in my town.

As a resident of Boynton Beach, Florida, I am all too aware of the importance of historical preservation. Recently, we lost our 1926 Seaboard Airline Railway Station to developers who razed the structure. Then the developers fell victim to the recent economic slump and went under. This station, designed in the Mediterranean Revival style, was significant and helped define what it meant to live in Boynton Beach. Anyone in America who ate pineapple in the '30s and '40s probably ate pineapple that came out of that station. Pineapples and farming are part of our roots. The origins of Boynton Beach are firmly rooted in rural soil. Another key component of our heritage is our old high school, which is also in Mediterranean Revival style and is under assault from politicians and developers who see capital rather than community. Wayne Siegel, public affairs director for Boynton Beach, points out how buildings like the 1920s-era high school "help us learn about past generations and show the cultural influences that contributed to the development of the community." He adds that saving such buildings is "an integral part of our civic heritage." The buildings of Boynton Beach may not be part of the popular imagination, but collectively they represent a style of architecture that helps define Florida. As we lose these smaller buildings, we must cherish those that remain even more, particularly iconic ones such as those addressed in this essay. If Florida is to remain a symbol of change, a symbol of the human capacity for transcendence, Florida architecture must be preserved, as Boynton Beach Library/Museum Archivist Janet DeVries asserts "for the enrichment of present and future generations" and to remain in the popular imagination. If the buildings are not there, they cannot be a part of the popular culture. What we have right now clearly helps define Florida as a place associated with change and reinvention, in conjunction with her mythical roots in what may be her most famous architectural wonder, which only exists symbolically, the Fountain of Youth.

## Works Cited and Consulted

Braden, Susan. *The Architecture of Leisure: The Florida Resort Hotels of Henry Flagler and Henry Plant*. Gainesville: University Press of Florida, 2002.

DeVries, Janet. E-mail interview. August 11, 2008.

Dunlop, Beth. "Inventing Antiquity: The Art and Craft of Mediterranean Revival Architecture." *Journal of Decorative and Propaganda Arts* 23 (1998). 191–207.

Gonzalez, Rick. E-mail interview. August 12, 2008.

Hoffstot, Barbara D. *Landmark Architecture of Palm Beach*. Pittsburgh: Ober Park, 1974.

Mizner, Addison and Donald Curl. *Florida Architecture of Addison Mizner*. Introduction by Donald Curl. New York: Dover, 1992. xi-xxvi.

Orr, Catherine. *Addison Mizner: Architect of Dreams and Realities (1872–1933)*. West Palm Beach: Norton Gallery of Art, 1977.

Patricios, Nicholas N. *Building Marvelous Miami*. Gainesville: University Press of Florida, 1994.

Shulman, Allan T. "Igor Polevitzky's Architectural Vision for a Modern Miami." *Journal of Decorative and Propaganda Arts* 23 (1998). 335–359.

Siegel, Wayne. E-mail interview. August 11, 2008.

Tarbell, Ida M. "Addison Mizner: Appreciation of a Layman." In *Florida Architecture of Addison Mizner*. New York: Dover, 1992. xxxiii–liv.

Tyson, Timothy B. *Blood Done Sign My Name*. New York: Three Rivers, 2004.

# Weathering the Climate
## Steve Glassman

Every day for the past four decades about a thousand people crossed into Florida with the intention of calling the Sunshine State home. The engine tugging most of them inside the borders, at least early on, was the state's climate. The state has figured as a winter haven in the popular imagination from before the Civil War, when such notables as Ralph Waldo Emerson sought refuge here from New England's icy winters. One of the first talking motion pictures, the Marx Brothers' 1929 production *Cocoanuts*, featured the balmy climate of the southernmost state. In the years since, Florida's climate has figured largely in the nation's (and the world's) films, novels, and vacation plans. Was it possible for a movie about Florida in days gone by to not have a hurricane appear when a story point was required? The John Huston/Humphrey Bogart classic *Key Largo* is a case in point.

Florida has, according to *The Climate and Weather of Florida*, "The sunniest winter climate in the eastern United States, the highest average January temperature in the nation, an average annual minimum temperature exceeded only in Hawaii, the highest annual maximum temperature (tied with Hawaii), and nine of the top eleven cities in the country, as judged for having the most desirable climate" (Henry 7). The problem with this rosy assessment is that until quite recently Florida's climate was considered among the most hostile in the nation. In 1950, for instance, Florida was the least-populated state in the Deep South, and the reason for that was the "tropical" climate. From the arrival of the Pilgrim Fathers, Americans had been prepared to deal with cold. We learned to bundle up, and Ben Franklin long ago improved heating systems. But if you were excessively warm, only so many garments could be peeled off with telling effect, not to mention the affront of near naked bodies to the thinking of the post–Victorian age. Even today when the twin miracles of electricity and air conditioning—the putative fathers of both, by the way, called Florida home at least part of the year, Thomas Edison in Ft. Myers and Dr. John Gorrie in Apalachicola—the climate is looked on with a Manichaean turn of mind by many Floridians. The mad dash many northerners make from their snow-shrouded parking places through the cold to the kitchen door is matched by the slower, sweat-popping stroll many Floridians make into the air conditioning. Indeed, many residents of the Sunshine State are virtual prisoners of air conditioning from April through November or even later, and it is a rare building in the state that doesn't run its cooling system at least a few days every month of the year. But most of us focus on the mild, pleasant days when we think of Florida's climate—as proved by those thousands a day immigrating to our fair state.

The topic of this essay is weather, not climate. Although the climate, that is the general aggregate of daily weather, may have been tamed by electricity, Florida's unusual weather events are arguably the most violent in the nation. Consider these facts. The single most lethal weather event in the United States, on a year-by-year basis, is death from lightning strike. More people lose their lives, year in and year out, in Florida to lightning than in any other state; in short, our fair state has the unenviable lock on the annual record. Deadly as lightning may be, it does not command great attention in the mass media and among the public at large. For that, something much more widespread and threatening is required, and few would argue that the most dramatic weather-related event on the planet is the hurricane. Again, Florida comes in first in the rogue's gallery of states devastated by these powerful and capricious storms. Forty percent of all hurricanes that strike the U.S. hit Florida. Two of the three category five, mega-hurricanes (with winds in excess of 155 miles per hour on landfall) that have smashed into the U.S. hit Florida, and the most hurricane-related deaths were recorded, not in the Gulf after Hurricane Katrina, but long ago in the Everglades after an unnamed and almost-forgotten storm swamped the south shore of Lake Okeechobee. The only phenomenon that rivals hurricanes in their devastation and the fear they put in the hearts of those in their path are tornadoes. On a square mile, dry-land basis, Florida is struck by more tornadoes than any of the legendary states in tornado alley, Texas, Oklahoma or Kansas, and in many years Florida tops the list in the number of tornadoes recorded in the nation. In terms of the tornado's little brother, the waterspout, Florida produces more than any place on the globe.

Before taking up these and other extreme weather phenomena such as wildfires, the "ear amoeba," and the red tide, let's devote a word or two to Florida's "tropical" climate. In this state and in weather discussions generally, hardly any word is used with less consistency than "tropical." The southern limit of Florida is 24½ degrees north latitude, one full degree poleward of the Tropic of Cancer. Is it correct, then, to say that any part of Florida has a tropical climate? Many literal-minded persons seem to think not, and they eschew the term "tropical" for the climate in the warm southern portions of the peninsula in favor of the word "subtropical." Unhappily, the use of this term, rather than clarifying matters, actually muddies the waters. If the climate of southern Florida is subtropical, what then would be the climate of the central portions of the peninsula, say around Orlando, which is universally recognized as an order of a degree cooler? Can it be characterized as warm temperate, perhaps? That would be fine except for the fact that a place such as St. Louis, whose airport seems to be socked in by ice and snow on a routine basis, can also be—and frequently is—regarded as warm temperate.

As always in such matters, it is a good idea to consult the experts. In this case the experts, those who study climates, do not speak with one voice. The first person whose climate study reached a wide and accepting audience was Wladimir Köppen. He was German, with Russian roots, who refined his system in the first several decades of the twentieth century. He broke the climate of the entire world into handful of types on the basis of temperature, precipitation, and a few other meteorological factors. The first of those types he designated as tropical. Without going into needless detail, we can say, aside from a generally robust temperature regime with at least moderate rainfall, the main requirement for a tropical climate is a monthly average temperature (daily highs plus daily lows divided by two) of 64 degrees. Much of the southern quarter of the Florida peninsula meets these criteria. More specifically, the climate of the coasts from Vero Beach on the south-central Atlantic to the Ft. Myers–Punta Gorda area on the Gulf, including much of the Everglades and all of the Florida Keys, is termed tropical by the Köppen system. The area is designated in particular a tropical savannah climate, meaning the rainfall is not as heavy as an equatorial climate, where more than a hundred inches a year is required.

So what did Köppen call the climate of central and north Florida? Are you ready for this? Warm temperate. That's right. According to the Köppen system, Vero Beach is tropical but Melbourne, only thirty or so miles away, is warm temperate, the same designation used for icy-snowy St. Louis. But remember, Köppen attempted to categorize the climates of all the low-altitude, moist, inhabited areas of the globe into only three climatic regimes. For instance, in his scheme, St. Louis and Anchorage have warm temperate climates and Fairbanks is cold temperate. Even if the Köppen system with certain modifications is still generally accepted, his classifications are not always particularly helpful when trying to draw conclusions about the climates of an area as small and geographically unique as Florida.

So let's see what Herbert Riehl has to say about the climate of Florida and like regions. Riehl was professor emeritus at Colorado State University in Fort Collins when he wrote *Climate and Weather in the Tropics*. Colorado State's meteorological department, though far away from the Sunshine State, has an impressive record of predicting the number and strength of hurricanes in an upcoming season, and it was the first institution to do so. Riehl opens his book with the question, where are the limits of the tropics? After citing the dictionary definition of the tropics, he goes on to say, "Another definition would be the latitudes thirty degrees north and south, these then divide the global surface into two halves, tropics and extratropics. So bounded the tropics are the source of all momentum and most heat for the atmosphere." He further amplifies this definition on a practical basis, saying the latitudes in which the prevailing winds are from the west can be regarded as the temperate zone, and the areas with prevailing easterlies the tropics. As it happens, easterlies (known to everyone from grade school as the trade winds) are prevalent from about thirty degrees to the equator, although in winter they shift a bit south of that mark in the northern hemisphere to about twenty-eight degrees or approximately the latitude of Melbourne and Tampa. In sum then, so far as Florida goes, Riehl extends the region that can be called tropical a touch farther north. And he leaves a band of about 120 miles, between the 28th parallel in winter and the 30th (near St. Augustine) in winter in limbo, without a designation. Part of the year this area is "tropical" and part of the year the winds are variable and it is therefore not really fish nor fowl. Riehl, like Koppen, was concerned with the climates of vast regions and hence is not much help to us in coming up with the proper moniker for our little postage-stamp of geographical area.

Scientists who have been keenly aware of Florida climate, on the other hand, were the early horticulturalists and botanists who did so much to make Florida the garden spot it is. Tom Barbour, professor at Harvard but Brevard County near-native, is one. Henry Niehrling, of central and southwest Florida, and Charles Torrey Simpson of Miami are two other notable authors and experimental growers. The most famous in his time, and the best known even today would surely be David Fairchild. Fairchild worked for the U.S. Department of Agriculture as a plant explorer. He first visited Florida in the late nineteenth century. He ultimately bought an estate in south Miami and planted it with all manner of tropical trees that he imported from around the globe. Today his place, known as the Kampong, is still a research garden, and the larger and better known Fairchild Tropical Garden, also in Miami, commemorates his name and good work. As an introducer of vegetation, Fairchild was acutely aware of the various climatic requirements of plants. He and others worked out a practical rule of thumb for Florida microclimates. Tropical Florida was delimited by the area where coconut palms could grow without protection in the open — in most years. The region he and others designated as subtropical was demarcated by the sweet orange tree surviving in the open — in most years. The area north of this was called "warm temperate," and there only hardy citrus (satsuma tangerines, kumquats and the like) could survive on a regular basis.

These climate designations are idiosyncratic in terms of Florida. They may or may not make sense in other areas of the world, but they are perfectly useful in our state, both practically, in terms of knowing what will live in a front yard most winters, and generally, to give an outsider an idea of what to expect in Florida in the winters, helpful both if you want to spend a few days' vacation or settle down for good. Among the many positive features of the Fairchild system is its ability to account for unusual spells. At present, when it has been almost twenty years since a major freeze, coconut trees are frequently seen growing and producing fruit as far north as New Smyrna Beach in north-central Florida. On the other hand, during the very cold years from 1977 to 1989, few orange trees—let alone orange groves—in the New Smyrna area survived. During that period, there were only a handful — well, perhaps two handfuls — of very cold nights, but those nights devastated the semi-tender vegetation. So for the time being, New Smyrna's climate may be considered tropical (as it was in days past when coconuts also grew there) and other times in days past it was warm temperate (during the years with those deadly outbreaks of freezing cold), but on an on-going basis, according to Fairchild's scheme, it is best to call that region and most of the peninsula north of Vero and Punta Gorda to a line drawn from St. Augustine to Cedar Key subtropical. The area north of there, including the panhandle, can be designated warm temperate, but remember the term "warm temperate" is used with the special Florida meaning — a zone where hardy citrus fruits grow. Don't confuse Pensacola's or Tallahassee's climate with St. Louis.

## Lightning

According to the Web site www.lightningcapitaloftheworld, "The odds of being struck by lightning are like the odds of hitting the lottery, but if you live in Florida your odds" increase (Welcome). Unhappily, the chances are only better in the Sunshine State for being struck by a lightning bolt, not winning the big money. Those living in the parallelogram from Daytona to Tampa and Cape Canaveral to Ft. Myers can expect forty lightning strikes within a half mile of themselves in the course of an average year, and some spots in this region will endure lightning more than one hundred days a year (Henry 152). South of this zone, say in Miami, you can expect a mere 25 lightning bolts within a half mile of you and your home per year, and those to the north can expect even fewer, with a statewide average of 10 to 15 strikes within a half mile.

Anyone within earshot of the crack and boom of a lightning strike is intuitively frightened. You hardly have to know that the temperature of lightning registers four times hotter than the surface of the sun, at more than 50,000 degrees Fahrenheit, or that the bolt that just struck within 300 or so yards — if the crack is heard — is even hotter than lightning encountered elsewhere in the country. Most likely, you don't even want to know those things. You just want shelter — and to be sure the shelter is safe against those sometimes intrusive bolts.

Lightning is a by-product of thunderstorms. Therefore it follows if Florida — and particularly central Florida — is the lightning capital of the country, it is also the thunderstorm capital. Florida's pre-eminence can be accounted for, in part, by the diversity of the Florida landscape. Looking down from an airplane, you can see watery habitats of many kinds and shapes, circular sinkhole lakes, swamp strands, cypress domes, sawgrass prairies, and the occasional sizable stream such as the St. Johns River and many larger lakes such as Lake Eustis. On the spectrum of terra firma there may be patches of pine flatwoods, hardwood hammocks, dry prairie, scrub pine habitat, subdivisions and so on. The humid Florida air, once heated, rises, but the rate of heating varies with each of the patches in the mosaic landscape. As you may remember from school days, rising air cools, sometimes as dramatically as 5.6 degrees per thousand feet. Air that is 88 degrees at ground level may be 20 or more degrees cooler just four thousand feet up. Once the air reaches dew point, the water vapor condenses, and raindrops form. That rain may fall to the ground as one of the many localized showers common in the state during the rainy summer season. Or it may be caught by updrafts in towering cumulonimbus clouds. As the condensed water keeps going up, it may freeze as snow, snow pellets, or ice. When the updrafts are no longer strong enough to keep their burden aloft, down the frozen moisture goes, melting, losing heft. It is met by other upwelling drafts which shoot it aloft and freeze it again. All this coming and going — up and down, freezing and thawing — has an effect similar to a man wearing a polyester suit on a dry winter day shuffling back and forth across a nylon rug. A charge is built up, as of static electricity. When the man in the polyester suit touches a metal object, a spark will shoot off. Similarly with lightning, when the charge is right, the electricity explodes, and the creatures below and for a few miles around cringe from the fearful power unleashed.

Florida is not the only area of the world or even the United States with months of warm, moist weather. The lower of Gulf Coast of Texas is almost a mirror image of the southwest coast of Florida, and Georgia and other locales have similar humidity and warmth for part of the year. So why are they not also the lightning capital of the country? The answer is the sea breeze. Florida has two of them, one coming off the Atlantic and another off the Gulf. Their interaction produces a dynamic that creates more thunderstorms than any place in the United States, and therefore more lightning. Texas and Georgia have only one coast. Occasionally their seabreezes collide with an approaching frontal system for rip-snorting thunderstorms, but they lack the interaction on an ongoing basis. South Florida, where the breezes collide on a daily basis during the warm months, has fewer storms and therefore less lightning than central Florida, because of the Everglades. The river of grass makes for a large, open, more or less uncluttered expanse that heats uniformly and hence is less inclined to the micro-climatic interaction of the central peninsula. The panhandle, which also has fewer storms, is similar to Georgia and Texas, with only one seacoast and therefore no colliding sea breezes. Occasionally, the engine producing thunderstorms will be shut down in central Florida when something known as the subtropical high, usually centered over Bermuda in the summer months, shifts south and west and squats over the peninsula, stifling the sea breezes.

Most lightning is of the cloud-to-cloud variety, where bolts shoot from negatively charged clouds to positive ones. The mechanics of a cloud-to-ground strike run like this. Normally, the earth is negative (or ground.) But during thunderstorms, this condition reverses, and an area directly below the thunderhead becomes temporarily charged positive. As the negative force grows in a cloud, positive ions on the surface yearn toward their opposite number, utilizing tall buildings or lone up-thrusting trees and the like as conductors. When the charges collide, the lightning burst heats the air around it to more than 50,000 degrees. Enough electricity is generated to run a 100 watt bulb for a quarter of a year.

According to the National Weather Service, 3,696 people were struck dead by lightning in the United States from the late 1950s to early in the present century (Key). Four-hundred twenty five of these lived in Florida, or about 11.5 percent of the lightning fatalities. Figuring the percentage of victims poses a problem as about 6 percent of the nation's population now lives in Florida, but in earlier times the rate was much smaller. Suffice it to say that the chances of being hit in Florida are two to three times higher than average for the nation. In many years, lightning produces more deaths than tornadoes and hurricanes combined. On a year in-year out average, only flooding is more deadly than lightning. In days gone by, Florida was considered the lightning capital of the world. Then satellite monitoring came along, and we learned that tropical central Africa — owing to many of the same dynamics but on a larger scale — received many times more lightning strikes during its rainy season.

It is estimated that a square yard of Florida real estate is struck by lightning only once every 100,000 years. Using that rule of thumb, your chances seem pretty good. But that is the wrong kind of thinking about this very dangerous phenomenon. For instance, when moving into a new neighborhood, I casually mentioned to my neighbor that a friend's husband had been struck by lightning. She told me her first two husbands had both been struck and killed by it. Anyone who engages in outdoor activities in Florida, whether for employment, such as construction workers—among the most often struck, or sport, such as hikers and fishermen, need to take the danger very seriously. If less than thirty seconds elapse from the appearance of a bolt and the resulting thunder, the storm will be within six miles, and, according to the U.S. Weather Bureau, you are at risk. A car, RV or travel trailer will provide protection. Lacking that, head for low woods and, as everyone knows, avoid tall trees and banish those golf clubs, shoes with metal spikes and so on. Even couch potatoes are not completely out of harm's way. Stay away from landlines of any kind, telephonic, electrical or plumbing. Twelve percent of lightning injuries are caused by persons connected with these items during storms.

## Tornadoes

I was born and raised in the Sunflower State, in other words, Kansas, the state in which tornadoes cause the most damage on a prorated per-dollar basis. Yet it wasn't until I moved to Florida that I ever heard the freight-train roar and witnessed first hand the devastation of a tornado. Once, a dozen or so years ago, looking west out of my front door, I noticed the weather was peculiar and different. It was an overcast day and the quality of the light and the breeze had somehow become downright weird. I stepped outside to get a better look, when I heard that distant telltale roar. I ducked back inside the house. Before I could snap my fingers the door slammed shut, a panel of screen from the porch blew in, and a huge branch from a neighbor's sycamore tree crashed on my chain link fence. The twister actually passed one block to the south, and my place was probably just grazed by the fierce gusts drawn into the low pressure at the center of the tornado. Those actually hit by the funnel cloud had somewhat more damage, but it was minimal, as tornadoes go. This is not unusual among Florida funnel clouds. Though accounting for more twisters on a square-mile basis than any other state, most Florida events are of the F0 category, with circulating winds of less than 73 miles per hour. None of this, however, means Florida tornadoes should be taken lightly. The following year a more serious twister passed a few miles north of my house, devastating some homes on a street, bypassing others and thoroughly gutting a high-rise condominium. More recently, a Florida tornado hit the university where I work. In the twinkling of an eye $25 million dollars in damage occurred, and one large, two-story building was destroyed. (Fortunately, this occurred on Christmas Day, and the campus was almost totally deserted.)

Meteorologists are not satisfied that they completely understand how or why tornadoes form (Geerts). There seem to be a variety of ways these powerful twisters come about. One thing is certain — the forceful updraft-downdraft currents in thunderstorms must begin to spin horizontally. During the summer rainy season, the convergence of sea breezes can, at times, provide that spin. A sea breeze may seem a mild sort of engine. As it happens, summer tornadoes are the most plentiful of Florida tornadoes and they are also the weakest, rarely more intense than an F1. The velocity of the winds in the vortex of an F1 go less than 113 miles per hour. These funnels can tear up roofs, throw cars around, and demolish shacks but rarely cause death or massive devastation. These twisters decay quickly, frequently dissipating after only ten minutes or so. The mild nature of these summer tornadoes allows Florida to brag about ranking right up there with the big boys in Tornado Alley in terms of quantity, but when it comes to fatalities, Florida rates only about midway among the fifty states.

Fall tornadoes are frequently the spawn of hurricanes, and naturally these powerful storms cannot be gainsaid. However, the most devastating of Florida's twisters occur in the winter and very early spring. Frontal systems are responsible for them. Many of the worst smack the panhandle, part of what is called Dixie Alley, Tornado Alley's southern winter residence. As we all know from news reports, incredible devastation occurs then in the Gulf States, and occasionally Florida feels its wrath too. One notable occurrence happened during the so-called storm of the century in March 1993, when 27 tornadoes hit Florida, resulting in 26 deaths. In 1998, 42 people were killed in or near Kissimmee during a similar storm. More recently, in early February 2007, 21 people died from damage caused in an early-hour, 75-minute weather orgy in Lake County, in the north-central peninsula. Two of the three tornadoes in that supercell were rated as high-end EF3s. Each of these twisters was a quarter-mile wide and forged a wake of devastation from 15 to 22 miles. Based on the destruction, it is believed their wind currents approached 200 miles an hour.

Waterspouts are sometime considered to be tornadoes over water. There is a good reason for this supposition because when a tornado goes over water, it officially becomes known as a waterspout. And *some* waterspouts are formed in exactly the same way as tornadoes and are therefore just as deadly and powerful. But most are not.

Any certified romantic who has spent much time gazing out over Florida waters such as Tampa Bay, Mosquito Lagoon, Lake Okeechobee, or Florida Bay can be justly accused of having funnel clouds, like sugar plums, dancing in his head. Waterspouts can form in a number of ways, including, at times, from a clear sky. Waterspouts also can be found over any body of water, but generally, they are considered a tropical and subtropical phenomenon, and Florida leads the nation, and evidently the world, in the production of this interesting and, as such things go, not particularly threatening event.

Joseph Golden, who is the world's pre-eminent authority on the subject, earned his doctorate from FSU and did his research primarily in the Keys. He defines the waterspout as a "funnel which contains an intense vortex, sometimes destructive, of small horizontal extent and which occurs over a body of water" (Waterspout Climatology). A waterspout is usually associated with fair-weather cumuli, those puffy, cotton-candy-like clouds so common over Florida during much of the year. As with Florida rainy-season thunderstorms, fairly low intensity winds seem to be responsible for the formation of many of them. They occur most commonly in warm, shallow expanses of water such as Florida Bay, the various Indian River lagoons, Lake Okeechobee, and Tampa Bay. And they seem to form along or near boundaries and the intersection of boundaries. For instance, two weather-service researchers in Melbourne found that

> in the Cape Canaveral area, the shape of the coast, combined with the large intracoastal lagoons [the so-called Banana River, Mosquito Lagoon and Indian River Lagoon] and numerous islands, to produce boundaries and initiate convective cells through differential heating. Seas breezes north and south of the tip of Cape Canaveral often converge over these lagoons, providing the necessary boundaries, in coincidence with developing cells formed due to intricate differential heating.... Waterspout formation in this area is most often observed after the onset of daily heating in the late morning through early evening hours [Choy].

Meteorologists refer to waterspouts developing as "spinning up," and they designate five phases of spout development. Phase one is indicated by a dark spot on the surface of the water with a light-colored disk in its middle (Waterspout Climatology). During phase two the spot begins a twirling, spiraling development. During the third phase an "eye" develops with a twirling cascade of spray around it. The fourth phase is the mature stage of the spout, where it stretches from the surface into the overhead bank of cumulus. A "spray shell" may surround the vortex to a height of several hundred feet. Some spouts are practically motionless, but others move forward at a speed of ten miles or more per hour, and these produce a wake and "wave train." The last phase is decay. The life cycle of most waterspouts is brief, lasting ten or twenty minutes.

Waterspouts generally form in open water, are visible for a long distance, have a small circumference, possess relatively low wind currents of less than 67 miles per hour, and 70 percent of the time are not associated with lightning. For these reasons, along with the attributes that they can be spotted at a distance, are small and easy to maneuver around, and are no more threatening than a freak gust of wind make them, on balance, fairly innocuous. Many a motorist has pulled onto the shoulder of the Overseas Highway in the Florida Keys to admire one or more waterspouts twirling harmlessly in the distance. While making this observation, the driver may have basked in the sun, and numerous boaters may have continued fishing and generally going about their business. Because of its high population density, the Tampa Bay area is the only place in the state where waterspouts commonly do much damage, but sometimes it is considerable, as in October 1992. A few years ago one wandered into Miami Beach causing some damage. Fishermen whose boats have been struck by waterspouts—at least the weaker kind of waterspout—claim the main damage is the tangled gear left in their wake. Dr. Joe Golden, the waterspout expert, recommends—evidently not entirely tongue in cheek—that boaters caught unawares by a waterspout dive overboard to avoid being snarled in lines. Up to 500 waterspouts form each year in the Keys, and a lesser number develop in other watery locations in the state. Most of us would probably prefer simply to steer clear and admire the funnels from a safe distance.

## The "Ear Amoeba"

The problem with taking Dr. Golden's advice and going underwater — aside from locating your boat afterwards and getting back aboard — is avoiding the "ear amoeba," at least if you are in fresh water. Although not a weather event per se, the "ear amoeba" only is troublesome, or so it is believed, in shallow bodies of warm fresh water in the summer. Old-time Floridians frequently claim that the microbe is found only in Florida and attacks only teenage boys. Strangely enough, boys and young men in their twenties do seem to be the victims of this unusual disease, which was isolated only in the 1960s in tropical Australia after an outbreak caused the death of number of young men. Most had fever, headache, vomiting, stiff neck and hallucinations. These symptoms persisted for a couple of weeks, and when they were severe enough to require hospitalization, most victims died within twenty-four hours. None survived. Their symptoms were similar to bacterial spinal meningitis, but an examination of the spinal area found no bacteria. Autopsies of their brains, on the other hand, turned up swarms of amoebae. The creature was identified as a *Naegleria amoeba* that normally eked out a parasitic existence in the mucky bottoms of ponds and lakes, where it lived off algae blooms and similar ilk. How the one-celled creature came to infect the brains of its victims was—and remains—something of a mystery.

The term "ear" in the common name indicates the early thinking, but nowadays researchers believe water forced up the nose of victims allows the amoeba to invade the brain. Once in the mucous lining it multiplies rapidly and works its way deep inside the skull. In that incredibly rich environment, the simple parasite responds by multiplying itself exponentially — doing neither itself nor its victim any good, as both organisms are doomed to perish (Pegram). So far as is known, no human victim has ever survived a diagnosed case of primary amoebic meningoencephalitis (PAM), as it is known to health professionals. Much is still to be learned about this disease. Is roughhouse play such as diving, ducking, and wakeboarding that might ram water into the nose and which boys and young men are more likely to be engaged in the reason that age group and gender appear to be the almost sole victims of this disease? Occasionally, patients turn up with no traceable history of bathing in shallow, stagnant water. On the other hand, the *Naegleria fosterii* amoeba has been identified in the mouths of perfectly healthy people. The organism can occur in threatening quantities in any warm pool of water and has been identified as far north as South Dakota. Warm springs in the desert Southwest are another location where it frequently strikes unsuspecting victims. In 2007, six people died from PAM in the United States, one in Arizona, two in Texas and three in central Florida. Not surprisingly, health professionals advise those of any age or gender swimming in questionable waters to hold their noses while diving and to wear noseplugs.

## Red Tide

The red tide is another weather-related organic phenomenon with a much higher public profile. Though rarely life-threatening to humans, the tide can litter a beach with tons of dead fish, and manatees, dolphins and sea turtles may also fall victim to it. People coming in contact with the tide by swimming or wading develop dermatitis. Clearly, strolls on a beach adjacent to an outbreak are verboten, and not simply because of the stench of rotting fish. Even driving down a seaside highway with the windows open may yield an irritating hack and gravelly voice for several days (Florida). Though fish killed by the organism are perfectly safe to eat, shellfish contaminated by the organism will sicken people who consume them, whether eaten raw or cooked.

The creature responsible for the red tide in Florida, like the ear amoeba, is a one-celled organism. In the tide's case it is called a dinoflagellate, and is a type of algae. Specifically, the Florida culprit is called *Karenia brevis*, and it is found in concentrations of less than 1,000 units per quart of water throughout the Gulf of Mexico on an ordinary basis. The trouble begins when the organism encounters a shoal of nutrient-starved water in the open sea, generally in the high-heat phase of late summer. The population of *Karenia* starts building, and then when wind or water currents propel it into nutrient rich inshore waters, the population of these tiny plankton, like the *Naegleria* amoeba on encountering mucous tissue, explodes. The water is stained red (or brown or yellow), and its toxic byproduct takes a nasty toll. Outbreaks may last days or weeks. Cold weather usually spells the end of the tide—but not always. Sometimes it can stay in an area for as long as a year and a half.

The red tide appears to have been noted by early explorers of the Gulf, but it seems to be more common nowadays than in days gone by. Similar "tides" of toxic plankton occur in tropical and subtropical waters throughout the world. In Florida, the red tide is usually confined to the Gulf of Mexico. Now and then a *Karenia* population is swept by the Gulf Stream to the Atlantic coast of Florida for the rare outbreaks there, such as in north central Florida in the fall of 2007. It has occurred as far north as North Carolina.

Cigatera poisoning, like the red tide, is also caused by a dinoflagellate (Briggs). In this case, the tiny organisms accumulate in apex predators in tropical or subtropical waters. When a human eats a contaminated fish, a serious illness can ensue. It begins as ordinary food poisoning. With luck, it'll end there, but severe cases develop extraordinary neurological symptoms. For instance, a victim's teeth can become unusually sensitive to heat or cold or pressure, or the patient may feel as though a limb is on fire. On occasion, death can result, and for those who survive, symptoms may recur years later. The species most commonly associated with cigatera poisoning are large moray eels and barracuda over five pounds, almost always during the summer months.

## Wildfires

One morning in late May 1985, coffee cup in hand, I received the shock of my life by looking out the back window of my house in Ormond Beach. My neighbor's house had disappeared. It had been engulfed by a bank of fog-like smoke.

Heavy mist occurs everywhere now and then, and the jolt to my nervous system would not have been nearly as profound had it not been for the experience of the night previous. I had driven by backroads to DeLand, thirty miles away. In three areas close to the populated region near the coast, wildfires had been burning. In one spot a fire department crew was working to contain the blaze. In another the forest burned unmolested in a fiery red glow reminiscent of the fires of hell, and in a third location, a highway patrol officer stood by the side of the road, hands slack by his side, as the woods burned nearby. It was clear he was neither able to get help to put out the fire nor figure out how to handle the traffic that continued to zip down the highway—or in any way get control of the situation. A couple of days day before, I had noticed from my office building in western Daytona Beach a column of smoke rising from the vast swamp west of I-95. So in a matter of 60 hours or so, the situation had gone from one wildfire to more than the authorities could cope with, to smoke completely obliterating the neighbor's house. A few hours later the closer neighbor's house, less than a hundred feet west, disappeared in the smoke bank, and ash, like large puffs of snow, began falling from the heavens. All of central Florida, from my perspective, seemed to be burning. Then just when the situation seemed psychologically untenable, on Memorial Day weekend, those summer cumulonimbus clouds seemed to respond to the sympathetic invocations of the smoke clouds on the ground. A couple of gullywasher rains fell. The fires went out, and the rainy season continued on as though nothing untoward had occurred.

Wildfires are an integral part of Florida's climate and weather. A severe freeze in the January prior to the 1985 blazes set the scene for the fires in the early summer. Much vegetation had transmogrified from greenery to kindling, then a slight delay in the onset of the summer rainy season, which usually kicks in in May, heightened the tinder-dry aspect of the entire peninsula. In late May when the thunderstorms started zinging lightning bolts, the entire peninsula ignited — with the able assistance of a few human arsonists. The authorities were overwhelmed. The whole thing — including that freeze on the day of Reagan's second inauguration — had a Hollywood aspect to it, something seen in movies but not actually experienced. This, by the way, is a pretty good description of Florida's weather and climate as a whole. It is almost perfect, if you like sun and the temperatures a bit on the warm side, as you might expect the weather to be in a good Hollywood feature, but occasionally it turns dramatically. On Super Bowl Sunday in 1985, the day before Reagan's inaugural, it was sunny and pleasant in Florida. The next morning, a bucket of water had frozen solid in my front yard. In a couple of days, it was pleasant and sunny again.

But to return to the subject of wildfires, the four most common trees in Florida are the sabal palm (the state tree), the live oak, the cypress, and the pine. Each of these is the dominant species in specific Florida habitats, and all of these habitats, even cypress domes and strands, are swept occasionally by fire. (Cypress, though perfectly capable of growing in water, will only germinate on dry land, so any place cypress grows can dry out and burn.) Most of these dominant trees have some defense against fire, but the habitat with the least ability to cope is the live oak (or hardwood) hammock, and it is found in areas best situated to repel fire. The two species most able to survive an assault of flames are the pine and the palm. Palm trees, both the sabal palm and the shrubby saw palmetto, can have their fronds burned off and they grow back as though nothing untoward has occurred at all. Anyone who has made the mistake of trying to burn a green pine log knows that it is almost impossible to ignite. But when heated to a high enough flashpoint, pine trees burn in any condition — and how. Burning is just a wily evolutionary strategy of the pine family to preserve itself. The cones of the sand pine, for instance, pop open like popcorn with intense heat and only then will their seeds be released. These seeds sprout in the burned-over area, clear of competition, and give the seedling pines a head start without which they could not excel. The more valuable longleaf pines also appreciate a good fire now and then to clear out the competition from encroaching hardwoods.

The most recent major outbreak of fires in the state occurred about ten years ago. Like the mid–1980s epidemic, it started with the delay of the summer rains. For a few days the temperature seemed abnormally warm, then the temperature hit 100 degrees four days in a row. A 100-degree reading, surprising as this may sound, is very rare in peninsular Florida, and four of them consecutively had occurred only in a few places previously in the peninsula. The upshot was very dry conditions, including a desiccation of vegetation akin to the Reagan inaugural freeze. Although there was little lightning to spark blazes, the odd flashpoint here and there triggered fires that were very difficult to extinguish. Before long, the entire peninsula was smoldering. Fire crews from around the nation were called in to help. Giant helicopters swinging buckets with swimming pools of water were commonplace in the sky. I remember seeing, daily, from atop the high-rise bridge over the Intracoastal Waterway, a bank of smoke blown back by the sea breeze from a line of fires burning in the woods on the far side of I-95. For weeks those fires inched closer to settled parts. At night when the sea breeze died down a pall of smoke pushed toward the coast, irritating throats and sensitive lungs. These fires were ultimately quelled the same way as the 1980s blazes—by mother nature herself. About the Fourth of July, torrential rains drenched the peninsula, and what seemed like another Hollywood episode that was really just a natural part of the Florida ecology concluded.

Afterwards, a homeowner in an outlying area wrote the editor of a local paper to say that all pine trees near Florida subdivisions should be cut down to prevent future wildfires. His strategy might help to prevent such conflagrations, and regrettably it seems to be what is occurring more and more often in Florida. An equally sensible solution would be to keep the subdivisions out of the pine flatwoods, which are areas that will be subject to widespread burning.

## Hurricanes

Residents of Jacksonville have a one-in-100 chance of being slammed by a hurricane in any given year (Henry 197). Those in Daytona Beach have twice the chance, but still a very modest one in 50. Below the out-jutting of Cape Canaveral, the chances in the Melbourne–Vero Beach area degenerate to one in 20, whereas the probability of the Tampa Bay area being struck is one in 25. The odds of catching a hurricane in the St. Marks to Apalachicola region of the panhandle are one in 17, and in Pensacola the probability rises to one in eight, whereas the folks in extreme southeast Florida have a one in six chance of catching the big one. In short, any long-term resident of Florida, with the possible but unlikely exception of denizens of the northeast portion of the state, will suffer a hurricane during their tenure in the state.

My first Florida hurricane came in 1966 in Key West. I was holed up in a faded resort hotel with about a hundred Peace Corps trainees, right on the beachfront. The eye of Hurricane Inez passed directly over the city. During the lull, I and just about every one of those soon-to-be Peace Corps kids, contrary to instructions from the authorities, went out onto the lawn and listened to the hurricane-force winds whipping around the eyewall. It all seemed a grand lark.

The town of Key West suffered little damage and the storm surge, the supposed killer associated with these tropical storms, did not even reach the grass beyond the rocky beach (if I remember aright). All told, Inez killed a thousand people in the islands of the Caribbean and attained sustained wind speeds of 150 miles per hour, although the storm that smacked Key West was a shadow of the juggernaut that lashed the Antilles and later Mexico. In the years since, I have been involved in (or avoided) many more hurricanes and tropical storms, and even a couple of typhoons. No longer do they seem a grand lark. Nor do they seem particularly dramatic and powerful. Mostly, they are just a pain in the butt.

Hurricanes are more akin to a biblical plague of locusts than they are to tornadoes. The damage they do is often incremental but insidious. After a storm has passed you can drive down a street and the destruction may seem incidental — a few blue tarps on roofs here and some soffit ripped off there. What you might not see are the houses impregnated with water and a blossoming mold content, and the heartsickness of the inhabitants who have to deal with a myriad of small (or large) factors such as lack of electricity and loss of income from being out of work, or the high deductible in the special hurricane clause of their homeowners' policies. When multiple hurricanes smash the same area in a given year or successive years, as happens now and again in hurricane-prone Florida, the incidence of mental illness in the relevant population is not inconsequential.

Hurricanes are mega-scale rotating storms that form over oceans in the "tropical" regions of the world, or from about five degrees to thirty degrees of latitude (174). These cyclones require a laundry list of atmospheric conditions to form and sustain themselves. Table stakes are warm surface waters of 80 degrees or higher (Winsberg 132). The heat and vapor of the water provide the basic energy. The embryonic engine that taps into this power is a low-pressure system of some sort. Usually, the most devastating to Florida come off the Sahara desert in the months of July, August and September. In a normal year somewhere between fifty to seventy of these lows drift out of the desert onto the sea. Many die for lack of warm water owing to the cold current sweeping south along the African continent, the cold-water return for the Gulf Stream. But those that find a suitable source of warm water may begin to spin thanks to the steadily blowing trade winds. At this point, the tropical wave may intensify to a tropical depression and perhaps even a tropical storm when sustained winds hit 39 mph. It can intensify to a hurricane (74 mph) if a variety of other atmospheric conditions are present. Naturally, instability, allowing the warm humid air to rise forming thunderstorms, is required. Also needed is a band of humid air miles above the storm. In addition, the atmosphere has to form a sort of chimney that allows the air rushing into the tropical vortex to wick away, rather than choking or "filling" the storm.

These Saharan storms are called Cape Verde hurricanes, after the island chain off the coast of Africa, and they have given us Hurricane Andrew, a category five storm, as well as most other August and September hurricanes. From late September through October, Florida hurricanes frequently form in the Caribbean or Gulf of Mexico. These storms can be every bit as dangerous as the Cape Verde storm. Hurricane Wilma, which slammed the Yucatan in 2005 as a category five and later hit south Florida as a much reduced but still devastating hurricane, was one of these.

Much is known about hurricanes; much more is yet to be learned. For instance, in days gone by, it was taken as gospel fact that the killer force in hurricanes was the storm surge. Clearly, the surge, a wave that can be — though infrequently is — as much as twenty feet above normal sea level, is a very dangerous element. The hurricane season peaks near the autumnal solstice when abnormally high tides are in effect. A confluence of these events makes for enormous devastation. Many have been swept away. But during Hurricane Andrew, which caused $25 billion in damage mostly in suburban Miami, the effect of the storm surge was minimal. The force of the wind created most of that vast financial loss. Although the dead center of Andrew made landfall not much more than 30 miles from the national hurricane center on the campus of the University of Miami, the storm was initially cataloged as category four. Only after years of study did meteorologists reassess the impact and decide it was indeed of the most intense type, a category five. Hurricane Mitch, on the other hand, was a lowly category one hurricane when it made landfall in Central America. Nevertheless, it killed at least 12,000 people; perhaps as many as 20,000 perished owing to its slow-moving nature and extremely high rainfall, 36 inches, with unofficial reports of twice that amount in a few areas. Floods and mudslides did the damage. And that category one storm, normally considered almost innocuous, was the second most deadly in the entire history of Atlantic hurricanes. You have to go back to the eighteenth century to find a more deadly tropical cyclone. Hurricanes usually track along at ten to fifteen miles an hour, but the Long Island Hurricane of 1938, sometimes called the Long Island Express, rode the Gulf Stream north at 70 mph. It slammed into New York and lower New England with little or no warning, making it one of the most devastating — and deadly — United States hurricanes in the twentieth century. In short, hurricanes can be devastating in many different and unpredictable ways.

Not surprisingly, these powerful storms turn up at needed points in popular media such as at the climax of *Key Largo*. Strangely enough, hurricanes have also interfered at historical key points as well. In the 1560s, France attempted to make Florida a Huguenot outpost. The Spanish, getting wind of the plan, dispensed Pedro Menendez with a fleet to destroy the French. The wily French commander, Jean Ribault, who wrote the first book on Florida (oddly enough in English), arrived with his own fleet. It was superior to the Spanish fleet, and after trading insults with Ribault, the Spanish armada commander slipped his cables and retreated toward Havana. The next day Ribault sailed after him. His ships were caught in a hurricane near Cape Canaveral. All the boats were lost, and Ribault and a dispirited and bedraggled crew struggled north along the strand, where Menendez found and killed them. A similar fate was met by FDR's Bonus

Army during the Great Depression. The self-anointed Army included World War I vets who had fallen on hard times. They lobbied the government for assistance from a shanty village in Washington, D.C. To get these very visible and embarrassing demonstrators out of the way, Franklin Roosevelt sent them to a make-work project in the middle Florida Keys, where they were sheltered in tents as a Labor Day storm brewed in the Bahamas.

After a fair amount of waffling, a special train was dispatched along the Overseas Railroad to evacuate the ragtag army and local residents. The train arrived as the storm was raging toward its peak, and a seventeen foot storm surge swept the island. The wave engulfed the locomotive sitting on the tracks, and water slammed down its pipes, extinguishing the fire in the firebox. The train was literally dead in the water, as storm tides swept Lower Matecumbe Key. The hundreds now loaded aboard the cars were sitting ducks. One might expect the railroad grade, the highest point on the key, to have been among the safest refuges. Possibly, but there were no really safe havens. Weather.com, the Weather Channel Web site, estimates the sustained winds at up to 200 mph — and possibly faster — high enough to blow ten of the railroad cars clean off the tracks. They were swept away like flotsam, those inside drowning. Even the raised berm on which the rails had been laid was blown away or washed out in spots. A survivor of the storm later wrote, "Sheet metal roofs became 'flying guillotines,' decapitating several victims, amputating the limbs of others. Whirling lumber became lethal javelins, impaling victims or knocking them loose from precarious grips on poles and trees. Like exploding atoms, pounding sheets of sand sheared clothes and even the skin off victims, leaving them clad only in belts and shoes, often with their faces literally sandblasted beyond identification" (weather.com). On occasion the tempest could be helpful, as when it smashed J. E. Duane's cottage on Long Key and sledded him, like a surfer, into the fronds of a coconut tree. A hunk of flying debris knocked Duane unconscious but he clung on for dear life and awoke twenty feet above the ground. A young novelist making a reputation for himself in a Key West hideaway, Ernest Hemingway, ventured north after the storm to report that Indian Key, in the channel between the two Matecumbe Keys, "was swept absolutely clean, not a blade of grass." Part of Indian Key collapsed and is now submerged, it is believed, on account of the action of this great storm.

Nine years before the Labor Day hurricane slammed into the middle keys, in 1926, the Miami Hurricane blasted Dade County. This was at a time in the Florida land bubble when prices had begun to slacken, what analysts today like to call a good time for bargain hunters. Speculators betting on the Florida boom were to be totally disappointed because a powerful category four storm roared ashore. It demolished hundreds of houses, many constructed of nothing more substantial than chicken wire plastered over with stucco. It famously stranded boats and ships throughout areas adjacent to Biscayne Bay. John Kenneth Galbreath listed this hurricane as creating a major ripple in the financial markets and, as such, he believed it was one of the major causes of the Great Depression.

Two years later, a hurricane pasted Palm Beach then roared inland, squatting over Lake Okeechobee. Ironically, this hurricane had almost no effect on history, being almost completely forgotten. Nevertheless, it wreaked absolute havoc on the southern shore of Florida's great lake. The 1926 hurricane had sent a floodtide of water over the agricultural fields adjacent to the lake, drowning as many as 200 people. The local folk, therefore, ringed the south end of the lake with a small levee, six to nine feet high. The winds of the category four storm swept across the shallow lake bottom like a broom pushing water before it on a driveway. In a matter of a few short hours, a storm tide smashed against the levee, overtopping it in places. In other spots, the dikes gave way, and water, now deeper than the height of the levee owing to a complicated mix of hydraulics and the shifting of wind direction after the passing of the eye, flooded the houses in which families sheltered. The water rose about a foot a minute, giving those inside barely enough time to crawl into their attics (Will 21–57). Those with the forethought to bring axes cut through roofs and escaped the floodwaters that continued to rise above the rafters of many modest cottages. Those without tools—or those in houses too well built to hack through the roofs—drowned en masse. In the aftermath, search parties were dispatched in boats along the canals leading from the lake; they returned towing six to eight bodies tied by a single rope around the neck looking as though they were dragging "a bunch of grapes" (Will). The bodies were first bundled into coffins, then when the coffin supply was depleted into rude crates with a name scrawled on top. After a while they were simply sorted by race, piled up, and cremated. After a few days the skin peeled away, and race and identity were no longer observable. Crude oil and gasoline were poured on the makeshift pyres and ignited. Eventually, the Red Cross estimated about 1,800 persons died in this great tragedy. It was the third worst natural disaster ever to befall the United States after the 1900 Galveston hurricane and the Johnstown flood, and as a point of grisly interest, the body count may very well have exceeded Johnstown's 2,200 as many of the victims were seasonal laborers from the Bahamas. Because of relaxed immigration restrictions for seasonal labor, the means of keeping track in those days was very limited.

In the last hundred years or so, Florida has on ten occasions been struck by three or more hurricanes in a single season, and in four seasons, 1906, 1935, 1948, and 2004, by four hurricanes (Henry 207). Forty percent of Florida's Atlantic hurricanes and 70 percent of the Gulf hurricanes spawn tornadoes, averaging four tornadoes for Atlantic storms and eight for the Gulf ones. All usually produce these twisters well inland, starting at about fifty miles from the coast, sort of helping to equalize the odds of damage between coastal and interior populations. Storm surges of twenty or more feet are possible and have occurred in parts of Florida, as in the Labor Day hurricane of 1935. The most surge-prone hurricanes have fast, forward motion, and the most vulnerable areas in term of the storm tide are those with gently sloping and shallow offshore waters as on the Gulf coast or in bays such as Tampa and Biscayne Bay. Though

Florida is not greatly flood-prone owing to its generally level terrain and large number of swamps to absorb overflow, hurricanes are also capable of dumping as much as three feet of water in a twenty-four hour period and causing flash floods. Such an incident occurred at Yankeetown in 1950 when 38.7 inches of rain fell. More recently, Tropical Storm Fay produced thirty or more inches of precipitation in parts of Brevard County in August 2008. On a historical basis, Florida's chances of being struck by a hurricane forming in the North Atlantic are slightly less than one in five, or in other words, very high.

Florida's climate remains among the most pleasant and gentle on the globe. Droves will continue immigrating to the Sunshine State, at the rate of around a thousand a day, and more will come to visit. All, however, should be aware of the state's extreme weather and unusual conditions. In particular, you need to be very careful of hurricanes and their sometimes unpredictable and multi-faceted abilities to cause damage to property and persons. Your safety, as demonstrated by the historical Florida storms and more recently in New Orleans with Hurricane Katrina, rests in your own knowledge and judgment.

## Works Cited and Consulted

Briggs, Amy and Maija Leff. "A Comparison of Toxic Dinoflagellate Densities along a Gradient of Human Disturbance in the North Line Islands." Stanford University, 2007. http://www.Stanford.sea.edu/research/Leff_Briggs_Final_Paper.pdf

Centers for Disease Control. "Harmful Algal Blooms: Red Tide." http://www.cdc.gov/hab/redtide/#about.

Choy, Barry K. and Scott M. Spratt. "Using the WSR-88D to Predict East Central Florida Waterspouts." http://www.srh.noaa.gov/mlb/spoutpre.html.

Florida Department of Wildlife. "Looking at the Red Tide Database." http://www.florida marine.org/features/view_article.asp?id=25871.

Geerts, B. and E. Linacre. "Tornado Formation." June 1998. http://www-das.uwyo.edu/~geerts/cwx/notes/chap07/tornado_form.html.

Henry, James. A, Kenneth M. Portier, and Jan Coyne. *The Climate and Weather of Florida.* Sarasota, Fla.: Pineapple Press, 1994.

Hodanish, Stephen, Dave Sharp, Waylon Collins and Charlie Paxton. "Florida Monthly Lightning Climatology." http://www.srh.noaa.gov/mlb/waf_dos.html.

Kahn, Chris. "Brain-Eating Amoeba Kills 6 This Year." October 1, 2007. http://www.the ledger.com/article/HM/20071001/HEALTHNEWS/70930009/-1/HEALTH0203.

Pegram, Cynthia T. "City Doctor Evaluated Deadly Brain-Eating Ameba." *The News and Advance* (Lynchburg, Va.), October 6, 2007. http://www.newsadvance.com/servlet\/Satellite?pagename=LNA%2FMGArticle%2FLNA_BasicArticle&c=MGArticle&cid=11 73353025504&path=!news!archive.

Riehl, Herbert. Climate and Weather in the Tropics. London: Academic Press, 1979.

Roach, John. "Key to Lightning Deaths: Location, Location, Location." *National Geographic News,* June 22, 2004. http://news.nationalgeographic.com/news/2003/05/0522_030522_lightning.html.

Shelton, Robyn, "3rd Death in Orange Linked to Amoebas." *Orlando Sentinel,* September 8, 200, A1. http://pqasb.pqarchiver.com/orlandosentinel/access/1332483551.html?dids=1332483551:1332483551&FMT=ABS&FMTS=ABS:FT&type=current&date=Sep+8%2C+2007&author=Robyn+Shelton%2C+Sentinel+Medical+Writer&pub=Orland+Sentinel&edition=&startpage=A.1&desc=3rd+death+in+Orange+linked+to+amoe bas.

"Waterspout Climatology. " Student project in Applied and Basic Climatology at the University of Nebraska, Fall 2001.
"Welcome to the Lightning Capital of the World." http://www.lightningcapitalofthe world.com.
Will, Lawrence, E. *Okeechobee Hurricane and the Hoover Dike: 2000 Perished in One Hour in 1928.* St. Petersburg, Fla.: Great Outdoors Association, 1961.
Winsburg, Morton D., with James O'Brien, David Zierden and Melissa Griffin. *Florida Weather.* 2nd ed. Gainesville: University Press of Florida, 2003.

# Taking to the Water
## Duncan H. Haynes

With its long and friendly coastline, Florida is the most boating-intensive state in the union. Considering Florida's geography, it couldn't have turned out differently. The state occupies a long peninsula that juts out 400 miles south of the mainland with two shores— one facing the Atlantic and the other facing the Gulf of Mexico. Its panhandle extends far to the west, occupying 230-some miles of mainland coastline and blocking all of Georgia and most of Alabama from access to the Gulf. Pensacola, at the state's western extreme, is only 200 miles from New Orleans. Florida is blessed with this long coastline. But what about California? It has a long coastline. Why is Florida so special? The answer is that Florida's coastline is boater friendly. Florida's is not a rugged coastline where ocean waves roll in to crash against rocky cliffs. Most of Florida is fitted out with a triple coastline, where ocean waves roll up onto sandy beaches sitting on barrier islands. These islands are separated from the mainland by complex backwaters. Thus the barrier islands of Florida's coastline provide the boater with two layers of mangrove-lined shoreline with a generous expanse of placid water in between. Access to the ocean is afforded by numerous inlets— gaps between the oblong barrier islands. All told, Florida has over 8,000 miles of shoreline!

And that is just the peninsula and mainland. Thrown in as a bonus are the Florida Keys, a chain of islands extending southwest from Miami like a 130-mile-long string of pearls, terminating at legendary Key West.

No wonder the state has roughly 1,250 marinas and numerous fishing and diving charter operations. No wonder boating is a major part of the Florida economy, supporting a host of commercial activity such as boat building, boat dealerships, boat yards, boat repair, storage and launching operations. No wonder boating is popular in Florida. The waters are warm, friendly and accessible year round. Florida water isn't just something to look at, it is something that invites physical involvement. Florida water presents a constant invitation to throw out the anchor and jump over the side. And if you don't like salt water, Florida has plenty of fresh water.

## Florida Yacht Clubs

The Florida boating experience can be quite varied, ranging from fishing in aluminum utility boats on Lake Okeechobee to "big game fishing" in the Gulf

Stream. It can be as extensive as a thousand-mile coastal cruise in a trawler yacht or it can be as simple as a one-hour, high-speed spin on the Intracoastal Waterway on a boat that is designed for little else. Florida boating covers the whole range between purposeful and harmful or obnoxious activity. Serious Florida boating also covers a large range of cost and skill. With sailing it can range from a simple day sail to a competitive one-design small boat race to an international offshore competition with expensive, carefully engineered yachts. Since much of the serious Florida boating activity is organized by yacht clubs, it is appropriate to consider them as a subject unto themselves.

Keep in mind, of course, that the term "yacht club" is often misused to lend dignity to real estate developments that happen to be near the water. The Florida Council of Yacht Clubs lists 37 clubs that fit the true definition. These dot the coastline from Pensacola to Jacksonville. Starting our consideration in the Coconut Grove section of Miami, the Coral Reef Yacht Club has a large white clubhouse purchased from a millionaire's estate in 1955. "For almost fifty years, sailors from all over the world have entered through our stately royal palmed driveway to participate in some of the best competitions in the world of yacht racing," proclaims a club document. One of its most popular races is the Columbus Day Regatta, which launches dozens of heats of length-classified cruising boats on a zig-zag course, producing a spectacle which looks dramatic in aerial photographs—a continuous line of sailboats stretching from Dinner Key to the upper end of Elliott Key.

A few hundred yards to the south of the Coral Reef Yacht Club is the Coconut Grove Sailing Club, whose second-story terrace bar and restaurant looks out over its large mooring area and Biscayne Bay. Across the bay is the Key Biscayne Yacht Club, founded in 1955. It sponsors a full array of one-design competitions which attract teams and contestants from all over the world.

Twenty-some miles to the north along the Intracoastal Waterway, the Ft. Lauderdale Yacht Club provides its members with a rich tradition and unparalleled level of distinction (to use the club's words). The club is particularly distinguished by its involvement in the Southern Ocean Racing Conference activities and its Fort-Lauderdale-to-Charleston Ocean Yacht Race.

An older club up the coast is the Smyrna Yacht Club, established in 1928. Things are older in Florida the farther north they lie. The Florida Yacht Club, located on the St. Johns River in Jacksonville, was established in 1876! At that time Jacksonville was the southernmost venue for high-end social activities. The rich and well-heeled came to the city by rail or by private yachts to enjoy the winter season. The club was a city landmark and high-profile social destination with its ladies' card rooms, men's meeting rooms, open porches circling the building on the second floor and ballroom which hosted numerous cotillions, lady's days, and a Christmas ball. Unfortunately, in 1901 the clubhouse met the fate of many large wooden buildings. It burned to the ground. The present clubhouse was built in 1928.

The next oldest institution is the Halifax River Yacht Club, founded in 1896 in Daytona when the town was less than 20 years old. The area around the club was considered alligator territory, which made the club something of a novel venue for upholding the fine traditions of going to the sea in ships. Now, the club continues its old traditions with its "Dash" to the ancient city of St. Augustine. The club's new traditions include line dancing at social functions.

Next oldest is the Pensacola Yacht Club, founded in 1908 and located on the Florida Panhandle. The club maintains a serious schedule of local and coastal events, as does the St. Andrews Yacht Club in Panama City. Organizations on the northern part of Florida's west coast include the Davis Island and the St. Petersburg Yacht Clubs. Farther to the south, the Sarasota Yacht Club takes pride in its cruising regattas and its historic association with circus entrepreneur John Ringling. Marking the south corner of the west coast, the Marco Island Yacht Club sits proudly in the mouth of the Marco River, its two-story, white stone "Old Florida" style clubhouse gleaming in the sun.

Most of these yacht clubs have a range of dress codes, which often exclude T-shirts and cutoff jeans. Banquets and social functions often require black tie or club uniform (sometimes service dress—double breasted sack cloth of naval blue or white). Formal yacht clubs are few and farther between in the Florida Keys. There, waterfront bars and Margaritaville revelry seem to be stronger regulators of boating culture.

## Fresh-Water Boating

The Florida peninsula is a veritable reservoir of fresh water that provides the boater with 4,500 square miles of inland waterways. And this doesn't count numerous ponds, lakes and rock quarries that serve as the attractive centers of "lakefront residential communities." All told, Florida has three million acres of lakes and 12,000 miles of rivers and streams, many of them spring-fed.

Florida's southern third is dominated by the Everglades, a "river of grass" as described by its early ecologist and champion, Marjory Stoneman Douglas. This slow-flowing, shallow "river," which is almost as broad as the peninsula itself, provides a unique habitat for many interesting species of bird, reptile and edible fish. It delivers fresh water to the ocean through Florida's mangrove-lined southern coast, providing a brackish, protected breeding ground for ocean fish and an aquatic playground for explorers in kayaks, canoes and small boats. To the north of the Everglades and feeding it with fresh water is Lake Okeechobee. The lake has the distinction of being the second largest freshwater lake completely within the U.S. border.

The middle third of the state has numerous lakes of all sizes, many interconnected by rivers, streams or canals. The fishing is very good and there is nothing more romantic or just good for the soul than witnessing a Florida sunset on the water. Farther to the north are numerous lakes and an added feature — springs fed by underground water with origins hundreds of miles to the north.

The joys of freshwater boating are available to almost every Floridian willing to invest a few hundred dollars in a canoe, kayak or aluminum utility boat. Lakes, rivers and streams abound. The southern section of Everglades National Park has marked canoe trails that snake through mangrove or cypress swamps, with narrow passages connecting ponds and lakes. Everglades City is a perfect spot to launch a kayak and explore the waterways that weave in and out among the islands. But you do not have to go so far from home. The typical Floridian is never more than ten miles from a usable river or lake.

Take Greater Miami as an example. It has network of canals that interconnect with lakes, both large and small. Designed as a flood-control system to connect the Everglades with Biscayne Bay, these canals offer miles and miles of canoe and kayak trails. With a bit of local knowledge, you can put in on Biscayne Bay and paddle up the Coral Gables Waterway, going past multi-million-dollar homes. Most have sizable cabin cruisers at their docks. Working your way under concrete arch bridges and through neighborhoods, you pass chic houses with swimming pools in their back yards. The only nuisance is the barking dogs, but most of these are toy poodles. The rottweilers don't like the water and the Labrador retrievers are friendly. I was once pursued by a pair of gung-ho German shepherds, but that was in a canal system running through a rougher part of town.

A mile or so up the Coral Gables Waterway, you cross under U.S. 1. Then the waterway becomes narrower and its coral walls are lined with ferns and vines. Then you pass under quaint bridges and paddle through a golf course and past the historic Biltmore Hotel. From there, with some local knowledge you can work your way to the vast "Blue Lagoon" beside the Miami International Airport. From there, with sufficient strength, stamina and time, it is possible to paddle west to the Everglades. Alternatively, you can connect with the Miami River and paddle north, all the way to Lake Okeechobee.

Miami also offers great opportunities for small boating in salt water. After putting our canoe or kayak into Biscayne Bay, we could just as easily have paddled south past the seawall-protected front yards of multi-million-dollar homes to Matheson Hammock Park which features both a wading beach and a long stretch of mangrove-lined coast. (The park is one of many centers for kite surfing, that dynamic hybrid of surfing and sailing where the guy or gal hydroplanes at high speed, pulled along by an oblong parachute flying 30 to 60 feet in the air.) Or we could have paddled north, visiting the spoil islands and anchorages of Coconut Grove and the waterfronts of Miami and Miami Beach. For saltwater boating, Biscayne Bay is the first in its class, providing a large area suitable for boats of all sizes and convenient to a large, world-class city. We will return this topic later when we revisit Miami by yacht.

Returning to the freshwater delights of the Florida inland, we will note that the Miami River connects with the Miami Canal, which is connected to Lake

Okeechobee, several dozen miles to the north. At the time of this writing, our country's second largest body of inland water is suffering low levels due to the combined effects of a couple of years of drought, due to continued release to maintain natural flow through the Everglades, and due to the growing and incessant thirst of Palm Beach, Broward and Miami-Dade counties. While the lowering of Lake Okeechobee has been something of an ecological disaster, it has proven an archeologist's delight, revealing antique boat motors, a wealth of Indian artifacts, and an interesting collection of Florida Cracker detritus.

The Okeechobee region has an interesting Indian history, going back at least 2,000 years. This is supported by archeological evidence for a series of mounds, roads and canals around the lake, and by the discovery of gold, silver and copper ornaments. The era of Indian influence ended in the early days of our post–Revolutionary War history with the forced removal of the Indians to Oklahoma. After that a cattle industry developed, powered by enterprising individuals who rounded up and drove free-living cattle by cracking whips. This, together with hog-driving, gave rise to the term Florida Cracker.

Lake Okeechobee was and still is a fisherman's delight. From a jetliner window, it appears as an enormous oval that occupies your full field of vision. On closer inspection, you notice that its surface is etched by the wakes of small boats speeding from one side to the other. To see the lake from the ground, you have to climb the enormous earthen dikes. These were built as a Depression-era engineering project to prevent this large body of water from being swept by hurricanes to drown the surrounding agricultural community, as it did in 1926 and again in 1928. The outside of the dyke is ringed by a canal lined with fishing shacks and trailers. This residential strip is several hundred yards wide and extends for most of the lake's perimeter. The space between the structures is filled, as often as not, with a motley collection of trailerable fishing boats—everything from dull and dented aluminum utility boats to shiny blue bass boats with embedded gold flakes. The impression is that it's the world's largest freshwater fishing camp.

The lake also has the distinction of being the centerpiece of the Okeechobee Waterway, which runs 152 miles, cutting across the state from east to west and linking the two coasts for ocean-capable yachts with drafts of up to 8 feet. From an historical standpoint, the waterway is the "improvement" of two rivers, the St. Lucie, which drained the lake to the east, and the Caloosahatchee, which drained the lake to the west.

The first work on what was to become the waterway was started in 1881 by a rich man named Hamilton Disson, who dug a canal to connect to the Caloosahatchee River with Lake Okeechobee. The next important contribution came from Napoleon Broward (as in Broward County), who initiated work to connect Lake Okeechobee to the St. Lucie River. The work was taken over by the Army Corps of Engineers and completed in 1937. Improvements included diking the lake, deepening the rivers, and installing locks to control water levels in the canals.

From the standpoint of a mariner traveling from east to west, the waterway starts just inside the Atlantic coast near Stuart and runs along the St. Lucie Canal to the lake. There, the most interesting destination is Clewiston, a center for sugar cane harvesting and refining activity in the area. Exiting the lake, the waterway runs along the Caloosahatchee River to Ft. Meyers where it exits into the Gulf of Mexico near Sanibel Island. The waterway makes a convenient passage for ocean-capable motor- and sailing yachts. The adventure experienced by three young people making this transit in a sailboat was described in a half-century-old novel titled *The Lion's Paw*, by Robb White. People traveling up and down the state on the Florida Turnpike or I-95 will experience the waterway as an unexpected climb in the roadway. From a curiously tall bridge they can catch a fleeting glimpse of a winding "river."

One of the most interesting true rivers in Florida begins somewhat north of Lake Okeechobee. It is the St. Johns River, which is distinguished by its *northward* flow. Its "headwaters" start southeast of Orlando and lead to a series of interconnected lakes. In Florida's early days, steam-driven river boats plied its lower reaches, delivering goods and connecting towns along their banks. Today these waters are plied by sport fishing boats, houseboats, pontoon party boats and by a dwindling number of commercial fishermen.

Larger, ocean-going cabin cruisers become prevalent around Sanford, the half-way point. Here, the river is broad and serious navigation is aided by red and green channel markers on pilings. At its marina you can see ocean-capable yachts. But not all the serious St. Johns River navigation is done by yachts. Consider the female eel, spawned in the Sargasso Sea, who swims up the mouth of the St. Johns River (near Jacksonville) and up the river past Sanford and up through the lakes and streams to the dryer and more elevated Ocala National Forest where she spends months and years growing and maturing in spring-fed streams until it is time for the reverse migration to meet up with her male counterparts in the Sargasso Sea to mate, spawn and die! I had the pleasure of swimming with a young female in the Juniper Spring in the Ocala National Forest. It was possible to rent a canoe and ride down the narrow stream that this adolescent female swam up.

For nature lovers wanting to experience a spring-fed river in a kayak, canoe or small boat, Florida offers dozens of opportunities around the state (see Florida's *Fabulous Canoe and Kayak Trail Guide*). The clarity of the water is unsurpassed, and gliding over the bottom under the right light conditions, you have the feeling of flying through the air.

This is not to say that all the water in Florida rivers is so delightful. Spring-fed streams feed into slow-moving rivers, and sometimes the spring is in the middle of a cypress swamp. Alligators and water moccasins abound. The same can be said for much of the St. Johns River and many urban canals. Thus the majority of the popular Florida inland boating experience tends to be centered around fishing, drinking beer and other activities that do not require immersion. This is all the more true for rivers in the Florida Panhandle, which carry muddy water from Alabama and Georgia at slow speed.

## Boats for Florida Salt Water Environments

Florida offers variety and transitions to the open ocean — mangrove-lined creeks, rivers and inlets, large expanses of shallow salt water, shelves of moderate depth extending miles from shore, and coral reefs. This range of environments enables a variety of sporting activities, including fishing, snorkeling and diving. Choosing the right boat is important. Motorboats get there faster but with a sailboat, the journey itself can be just as much fun. Since much of the interesting fishing water has a depth of five feet or less, the boat's draft is a serious consideration. Typical differences in draft of a conventional sailboat and motorboat might be 4½ feet versus 3 feet. Shallow draft is a plus for visiting the mouths of rivers and making passages between barrier islands and keys. However, deeper draft is important for boat stability in the open ocean, particularly in a storm. Generally, boat stability increases with increasing length and draft. Usually a sailboat will have better "seakeeping" characteristics than a motorboat of comparable length. Some hull designs work well in high waves, others do not. As Ben Candidi, sailor and my fictional hero in *Bahamas West End Is Murder*, says, "Sure, that sleek boat would look great skimming along at 30 knots on a balanced plane in the protected waters of some bay. But caught in a winter storm in the Gulf Stream, it would be a rolling death trap."

## Troubles in Boating Paradise

Florida's delightful coastal environment — its abundance of good weather and flat and clear water — can make boat handling seem as simple as driving a car. That illusion can be quite dangerous. Every day, on every stretch of coast, hundreds of people motor out beyond the limits of their knowledge, ability and luck. As a result, dozens have to be towed, rescued or searched for. The Coast Guard has its hands full, especially on weekends.

One of the most frequent problems is running out of gas. Other frequent problems are air in fuel lines, bad electrical connections, clogged injection systems, fouled spark plugs, corroded contacts and dead batteries. It is an uncomfortable feeling, drifting and bobbing in your boat at all angles to the waves having no idea as to why the darn thing quit on you and won't start, and having no idea what to do about it. In that circumstance, the only option is to turn on a hand-held VHF radio and try to hail a towing service to come out and get you. Costs can be in the hundreds of dollars if you are not already a member.

Florida marine horror stories abound. Listen to the story a friend told me about how his friend took him on what was supposed to be a 40-mile trip from Miami to Bimini.

"The boat started sinking and the Coast Guard rescued us," he told me.

"Why did it start sinking?" I asked.

"We never found out. It just went slower and slower and we noticed it was lower in the water and my friend went below and it was filling up with water."

"What did you do?"

"He got on the radio and talked to a Polish freighter that was nearby and they called the Coast Guard."

"What did the Polish freighter do?"

"They kept circling us until the Coast Guard came."

"What did the Coast Guard boat do?"

"It wasn't a boat. It was a helicopter. They lifted us off the boat. They lifted us off the boat just before it sank."

So two guys could have died for something as simple as a hose coming off a marine toilet. Why did they almost die? Because the one who was supposed to know how to deal with these things didn't.

Well, I've seen worse — a charter boat tied up to the docks in Key West with an "open for business" sign. Looking down on the cockpit, I noticed an improvised aquarium-pump-and-hose arrangement pumping water out of an open bilge at full speed. The improvised pump was running on shore power. I wondered if the alcoholic captain thought that his regular bilge pump would be that much faster when he got under way with a load of passengers. The Key West latitude seems to bring out many changes in boating attitude.

## Five Florida Boating Regions

Although the Florida Keys define Florida boating in the popular imagination, Florida saltwater boating should really be considered in terms of five different regions—the West Coast/Gulf of Mexico; the Florida Bay; the Florida Keys; Biscayne Bay; and the East Coast. The Keys jut out from the bottom of Florida, starting at Miami Beach and extending southwest into the Gulf of Mexico. Florida Bay is the area between the Keys and the south tip of Florida, opening to the Gulf of Mexico. Biscayne Bay is a long body of water protected by Miami Beach, Key Biscayne and Elliott Key. Florida's East Coast is protected by barrier islands, in whose backwaters runs the Intracoastal Waterway. The barrier islands and waterway create the "three layers of coastline" mentioned earlier.

### West Coast and Gulf of Mexico

The west coast of Florida defines the eastern edge of the Gulf of Mexico. The continental shelf along Florida's West Coast is very wide and the water tends to be shallow and silty due to suspended sand. This makes for excellent beaches (finely pulverized white quartz) and the fishing is good. Draft is an important consideration, particularly for larger sailboats, but captains of smaller sailboats and motor craft will find many interesting possibilities outside and among the barrier islands. Snorkeling and swimming while at anchor are less interesting due to the monotonous bottom and low visibility in the water. Exceptions can be found farther out by scuba diving on wrecks.

However there is no greater pleasure than pulling into an historic town by water — seeing it as it was seen by the original explorers and settlers. The West Coast has many interesting ports of call. At the extreme west end of the state is Pensacola, an interesting city with a deep water port, a sizable bay of the same name and a famous Naval Air Station. The bay and the coastline a couple of dozen miles to the east are protected by a long barrier island, behind which runs the Gulf Intracoastal Waterway. To the west are Ft. Walton Beach and barrier-island-encrusted Apalachicola. Florida towns with the name "beach" usually sit on barrier islands. In the Florida Panhandle the towns have a deep southern flavor — a magical combination of historic and gracious architecture, slow-paced living, natural friendliness and charm.

The town of St. Marks and Apalachee Bay mark the beginning of the "Big Bend." Here the coastline curves to the south for about 140 miles, ending with Tarpon Springs. Having few barrier islands, the Big Bend does not have an intracoastal waterway. Its coast is mostly in its natural state and is largely undeveloped. It offers the shallow-draft cruiser miles and miles of virgin beach, estuaries and rivers (the Steinhatchee, the musically celebrated Suwanee, and the Crystal.)

Cruisers with greater than four-foot draft must stay 5 to 10 miles offshore and will have to use an auxiliary craft such as a hard-bottom inflatable to visit these areas. The shores and rivers of Big Bend offer good fishing and an abundance of animal life. This includes wild hogs, black bear, river otters, manatees, the usual alligators, herons, bald eagles, egrets, and wild turkeys. With its shallow water, the area supports a lot of oystering, crabbing and shrimping. The area is only lightly populated. The trees along the rivers' banks are often draped with Spanish moss, and every bend in the river can deliver a new sight.

The Big Bend ends at Tarpon Springs (an historical town famous for sponge harvesting carried out by Greek immigrants), more barrier islands and a peninsula with the cities of Dunedin, Clearwater and St. Petersburg. Behind the peninsula is Tampa Bay, accessible under its famous 149-foot-high Sunshine Skyway bridge, under which pass ocean-going vessels. Tampa Bay provides a large expanse of protected water convenient for day sailing, fishing and running around in speedboats. On the north shore of the bay lies Tampa, a major port city famous for its history of cigar making. One of its more interesting sights is the University of Tampa, housed in the once world-famous Tampa Bay Hotel, built in Moorish and Turkish style in 1891. One of the city's most interesting commercial attractions is Busch Gardens.

To the south of Tampa Bay lies Bradenton, the mouth of the Manatee River, then Longboat Key and the Sarasota Bay. The area is replete with Spanish history, which includes visits by Alvar Nuñez Cabeza de Vaca and Hernando

DeSoto. Sarasota is a charming, southern-style town which serves as a second home to lots of northeastern and midwestern "snow birds" during the winter season. The town's attractions include the John and Mable Ringling Museum of Art. Farther to the south lies Venice, which is followed by an interesting group of islands that shroud the mouth of the Peace River. The islands include the charming Sanibel, which served as the hideout of a famous pirate named Gasparilla. Close by is Captiva Island, which got its name from its use as a holding station for Gasparilla's female captives, whom he kept in untarnished condition while awaiting payment of ransom. He forbade, under pain of death, every member of his rapacious crew from setting foot on the island. Today, the island serves as a refuge for birds.

Sanibel Island was the destination of the fictional crew that embarked on an adventure on the Okeechobee Waterway. Its exit was close by — the mouth of the Caloosahatchee River. Sanibel Island is famous for the shells that can be found on its beaches, including the lion's paw.

Farther to the south are Ft. Myers Beach, Naples and Marco Island. South of that comes Everglades National Park. Everglades City, which lies somewhat inland, is a good destination for shallow-draft craft. Everything about this small town speaks of fishing, both commercial and sport. Its Rod and Gun Club offers Old-Florida-style waterfront dining. The Historic Smallwood Store Museum recreates the trading post, general store and post office that opened there in 1906. The old building is filled with turn-of-the-century relics, including hand-operated washing and wringing machines and collections of ancient products in tin cans. It is also a good place to tank up on local history, which included much lawlessness and skullduggery.

Ten Thousand Islands — a maze of mangrove islands (not quite that many, actually) divided by creeks — is an interesting area to explore with shallow-draft craft, especially for bird watching. The area is most famous for its fish, which have a ferocious appetite for baited hooks, and for its mosquito population, which has a voracious appetite for human blood. I once experienced the latter when becalmed during a nighttime passage ten full miles off shore! The sound of their wings filled the air as soon as the wind disappeared, and although we saturated ourselves and our clothes with mosquito repellant, the cursed insects kept everyone up all night.

The description has taken us to the southern tip of Florida. The mouth of the Shark River is an interesting place to visit in relatively shallow-draft boats. The river allows fishing and exploration for many miles into the Everglades. Still farther to the south is Cape Sable. Behind that is Flamingo. The stretch between is an amazingly unspoiled strip of sand beach, behind which are cypress or mangrove, pines and hardwoods on hammocks. At Flamingo, small boats can be lifted to the Wilderness Waterway, a canal going into the Everglades and north to Everglades City. Flamingo has a fish-camp atmosphere and is also a popular destination for campers and kayakers visiting by auto.

## Florida Bay

As mentioned earlier, the Florida Bay is wedged between the southern tip of Florida and the Florida Keys. East of Flamingo, the Florida Bay becomes enclosed and shallow, with seagrass-stabilized mud flats and numerous tiny mangrove islands. The area often seems more like land than water, and it can quickly become a nightmare for a small-boat operator who fails to take careful note of the twists and turns he took to get there.

The bottom is an uninteresting mix of seagrass and sponges, but the area can be heaven to a fisherman, especially one with local knowledge. Unfortunately, the area is also on the verge of ecological disaster. The shallowness of the water, the strong Florida sun and absorption of its rays by seagrass can heat the water to bathtub temperatures. This causes rapid evaporation, which tends to increase the salt concentration of the water. Due to the mangrove island and mud-flat barriers and the blocking effect of the Middle and Upper Keys, there is not much tidal current to flush out the concentrated salt water. Thus these shoals depend on fresh water from the Everglades to dilute the salt back to acceptable concentrations. Yet this flow of water is often interrupted by efforts to maintain acceptable levels in the Everglades while satisfying South Florida cities' growing thirst for fresh water. Other threats to the area are algae blooms that appear periodically and render the water as green as a mill pond. They seem to be caused by an overload of nutrients, due to their release either from the Everglades or from stirred-up bottom sediment from the bay, itself.

Due to its labyrinthine nature, this region is most conveniently reached from the northern side of the Florida Keys, which we will see is served for its entire length by a moderate-draft, marked channel.

## Piloting in the Keys

Having dispensed with the silty waters of the West Coast and the shallow water of the Florida Bay, I can assure you that the remainder of the state's coastal waters have the exceptional clarity for which Florida is known. The Florida Keys are quintessential. You can usually see the bottom and navigating is delightful. Additionally, changes in water color will tell us a lot about the water's depth. Of course the boat should have a good depth sounder and appropriate nautical charts. However some skippers find it hard to use charts when zipping along at speeds exceeding 40 miles per hour. The same can be said of map-based GPS displays. Over-reliance on charts or GPS-linked map displays can lead to problems, especially in places where shoal patches are too small to chart. As one sailing skipper asked rhetorically, "If the chart tells you to go *there* and what you see there is a bunch of long-legged birds wading and catching fish, what would you do?"

Being able to "read the depth" of the water ahead from its color is a useful skill in the Keys. In the absence of wading birds, the small-craft captain can be guided by some simple rules, which I will pass on from the Florida Keys Online Guide.

"Brown, Brown — Run Aground." Yes, it is best to stay away from that brown patch because the color comes from sea grass or shallow coral close to the surface.

"White, White — You Might" (run aground). White color indicates a sandy area or a bare patch of coral rubble, which may be quite shallow.

"Green, Green — Nice and Clean." When the water is green it is usually deep enough for shallow-draft boats. Larger yachts and sailboats should exercise caution.

"Blue, Blue — Cruise on Through." Deep water such as the Gulf Stream and the ocean side of coral reefs will appear as a light, transparent blue.

The small-craft captain needs to keep in mind that the bottom dead ahead can change very quickly when his boat is on plane, moving along at 45 miles per hour. The blue water ahead may suddenly reveal a patch of white, indicating a coral formation just below the surface. Also, a clean strip of green can suddenly turn brown and the boat's bow can turn into a plow, with sickening deceleration. An all too frequent occurrence is when the skipper doesn't run aground, but cuts a groove in the sea grass bed with his whirling propeller and digs a trench in the sand with his prop wash. This destroys habitat for the fish that live in the grass and it changes the pattern of tidal flow. A long passage of time is required for the grassy patch to repair itself.

For boaters equipped with a depth sounder and experienced in reading water color and bottom features, there is no greater joy than looking down with Polaroid sunglasses and seeing patches of sand, grass, sponges, sea fans and brain coral glide or zip below. Florida water is so clear that you have the sense of flying over this landscape.

## *Florida Keys*

As mentioned earlier, the Florida Keys jut out from the bottom of Florida, starting at Miami Beach and extending into the Gulf of Mexico. The Keys are a chain of islands which rise only a few feet above sea level. They are surrounded by shallow water, and much of the space between them is impassible to deep-draft boats.

The northern side of the Keys faces the Florida Bay, which, as mentioned earlier, is dotted with small mangrove islands and crisscrossed with shallow banks which impede navigation for all but the smallest boats. The north side of the Keys is served by a system of marked channels running its length, from which Florida Bay can be explored.

The south side of the Keys is open water, 12–20 feet in depth, which extends from shore as a shelf for about four miles. At its edge are coral reefs. The water is very clear and the reefs make good destinations for diving. Beyond the reefs, the depth increases abruptly and you encounter the blue water of the Gulf

Stream. The coast of Cuba is only 90-some miles to the south and the area between is called the Straits of Florida. The Gulf Stream moves outside the reef line and through this strait, northeastward, at about four nautical miles per hour. After passing the protected Biscayne Bay and Key Biscayne, it turns northward, passing through the strait between Florida's east coast and the Bahamas. The Gulf Stream continues for the full length of Florida's east coast and beyond. The live coral reefs stop just below Key Biscayne.

In early Florida, the Keys were islands in every sense of the word. Passing from one to the next required a boat — usually a sailboat. Key West, at the end, was an important fishing town and naval base. It was also strategically important as a waypoint for navigation between New Orleans and the East Coast.

The Keys became completely accessible by land when Henry Flagler extended his Florida East Coast Railroad to Key West in 1912. (More on him later.) A railroad going over the ocean was a great novelty. However, early publicity did not include the information that the "ocean" under the railroad was seldom deeper than about 15 feet. The over-water portion of the railroad ran on bridge-like structures of elevated track resting on concrete columns. Later, the bridges played host to automobiles, with two narrow lanes of highway fitted on a metal superstructure above the tracks. As automobile traffic waxed, rail traffic waned. Modern, multi-lane bridges now carry the automotive traffic. The remnants of the Flagler bridges are used as fishing piers. To the Florida boater, they serve as reminders of a bygone era, especially during sunsets.

As mentioned, the Keys are surrounded by shallow water on all sides. The shelf along the southern coast of the Keys extends four to six miles from shore. This expanse of water is somewhat protected from high seas in storms by the reefs lining the shelf's southern edge. Due to the high water clarity, views of the bottom and marine life are spectacular, especially in the summer. Viewing the bottom through polarized sunglasses, which cut the surface glare, give the strange feeling of hovering above a magical landscape. The water is good for sailing, fishing and diving. Past the reefs are the deep and blue waters of the Gulf Stream.

The Florida Keys are popularly divided into three regions: the Lower Keys, from Key West to Bahia Honda; the Middle Keys, from Marathon to Islamorada; and the Upper Keys, from Islamorada to Key Largo and the top of Elliott Key. We usually refer to the southern side as the "ocean side" and to the northern side as the "bay" or "Gulf" side. The ocean side has the large expanse of clear water with interesting bottom. A large swath of it is marked as Hawk Channel, which runs parallel to shore and provides the mariner with anxiety-free transit up and down the Keys. Farther out from the channel, the bottom is speckled with coral formations and the edge of the shelf is dotted with reefs, which thrive from contact with the fast-moving Gulf Stream waters from the Straits of Florida.

The "gulf" and "bay" waters north of the Keys are less than pristine. The "gulf side" designation is more appropriate for the Lower Keys, where we are speaking of the Gulf of Mexico. In the Middle Keys, it is the Florida Bay. In the Upper Keys it is the Florida Bay, or any of several "sounds" that separate the northerly Keys from the Florida mainland.

The captain of a shallow-draft boat will have a choice of numerous passages between the ocean side and bay sides. The deeper-draft captain has fewer choices, and we will plan our Florida Keys voyage from his point of view. We will pick up our journey in Key West.

Key West offers numerous docks and anchorages. Ashore there are many attractions to visit, including the Hemingway House, Sloppy Joe's (the author's favorite bar), the Mel Fisher Maritime Museum featuring sunken treasure, the Pirate Soul Museum, and the sunset celebrations at Mallory Dock.

Transit from Key West to Miami can be quite simple. You can sail out past the reefs and jump into the Gulf Stream, which is moving up the coast at a speed of four nautical miles per hour. Yachtsmen interested in local color will take Hawk Channel, which runs on the "ocean side," inside the reef line and closer to shore. At frequent intervals along our northeasterly route, live reefs are equipped with mooring buoys where you can tie up and spend hours exploring the coral with snorkel or scuba. Closer to shore, notable sites are Bahia Honda and its state park, the Seven Mile Bridge and the Moser Channel. The latter provides a crossing between the ocean and bay sides. The town of Marathon on Vaca Key is a fine jumping-off point for great diving.

Farther north are Lower Matecumbe Key and nearby Indian Key, which has an interesting historical and archeological site. Plantation Key is next, followed by Key Largo with John Pennekamp Coral Reef State Park. The park takes in a large expanse of water on the ocean side. The diving is excellent. The Florida Keys Online Guide Web site lists 13 sites. The most spectacular is Molasses Reef, which ranges from quite shallow to 50 feet deep. The most unusual dive site in Pennekamp Park features Christ of the Deep, a 9-foot-tall bronze statue which stands at a 25-foot depth amid a bed of brain coral.

Boats with draft of 4½ feet or less can go up the Keys on the bay side, following a carefully marked channel that leads through and past a collection of sounds, keys and cuts. These have interesting and descriptive names, such as Buttonwood, Lignumvitae (a Florida tree), Cowpens (where original settlers held "sea cows" or manatees for slaughter), Tarpon Basin, and Blackwater Sound. Jewfish Creek takes us under a tall bridge serving U.S. 1—the Keys' lifeline to the mainland. Jewfish Creek takes us to Barnes Sound, which is connected to Card Sound, which is connected to Biscayne Bay, leading to Miami.

As you may have guessed, "creeks" in the Keys are quite different from the usual. They are saltwater channels that cut through mangrove swamps and connect larger bodies of water. Many are subject to vigorous tidal flow.

Vessels transiting on the "outside" can duck into Angelfish Creek to Card Sound, connecting with Biscayne Bay and Miami.

## Biscayne Bay

The water of Biscayne Bay and Greater Miami's coastline are protected by Elliott Key, Key Biscayne, and the strip of dead coral reef between them. This makes Biscayne Bay an excellent area for sailing and fishing, daytime anchoring and swimming off the boat. I see pods of dolphins there almost every time I go. I often see manta rays gliding along the bottom and sea turtles paddling near the top.

Miami offers excellent transient docking facilities at Dinner Key. The latter is on the edge of the city's historic but commercialized Coconut Grove district. Once a fishing village, Coconut Grove is older than the city that overgrew it. Things that can be visited on foot include Scotty's Landing Waterfront Restaurant, the Miami City Hall (formerly the Pan American Airlines terminal for seaplanes flying to Havana), Peacock Park (on the site of the historic Peacock Tavern), and the outdoor cafés of Commodore Plaza. The latter is named for "Commodore" Ralph Middleton Munroe, an early settler, mariner and wrecker. His 1891-vintage, hand-built house, the Barnacle, is at water's edge, open for visitation as a state historical site. A mile or so to the north is the palatial, Italianate Vizcaya Museum and Garden, built in 1916 by Chicago industrialist and art patron James Deering. His mansion graces the waterfront; his bedroom window has a majestic view of the bay.

Coconut Grove was more important than Miami in the early days. In fact Miami was first known as Ft. Dallas. Miami received a major boost when Henry Flagler extended his Florida East Coast Railroad to it in 1896. Flagler started his railroad around 1890, buying up and connecting rail facilities and building hotels to serve as winter destinations. By 1912 he had extended it to Key West.

Greater Miami offers many choices for docking and many opportunities for exploring by water. Picking up on the canoe or kayak tour described earlier, you can paddle or motor past the Grove, past the high-rises of the Brickell Financial District, past the downtown, and past the port to the small islands of "inner" Biscayne Bay. This is the portion of the bay that divides Miami and an auto-accessible island named Miami Beach. Here you will encounter another type of small craft — Waverunners and Jetskis, traveling at speeds upwards of 50 miles per hour, piloted as often as not by teenagers and traveling in packs. These watercraft are available, alas, at numerous concessions on Miami Beach.

## The East Coast

While Biscayne Bay still has some of the feel of the Florida Keys, all traces are lost at the level of downtown Miami. This brings us to the fifth region, Florida's East Coast. Here, the northbound cruiser is faced with two choices: the Atlantic Ocean or the Intracoastal Waterway. From Miami all the way up to Jacksonville, the East Coast is covered with barrier islands. Their tidal backwaters are connected by the Intracoastal Waterway. Inlets between the barrier islands allow passage from the Intracoastal to the Atlantic Ocean. The distance between inlets averages a couple of dozen miles. Many have shallow and unreliable depths and are subject to considerable tidal rip.

On a sunny and calm day you can see many small boats anchored on the ocean side within swimming distance of a sandy beach. However there is no good anchoring ground out there. The waves can be high, especially in the winter. Substantial waves are the norm at latitudes north of Palm Beach where the Little Bahama Bank ends and the waves can roll in all the way from Africa. This is good for surfing but not necessarily for boating. The East Coast of Florida is good for sailing and fishing, but is less interesting for snorkeling because of its depth and the absence of reefs. It can be interesting for scuba diving, but first it is necessary to devote a few words to the ocean bottom.

Going out from the sandy shores of the barrier islands, you notice that the clear Atlantic waters get progressively deeper, with 40–70 feet being a typical depth out to two miles. Beyond that, the water depth increases precipitously. The bottom is a mixture of sand and sea weed at shallow depths, progressing to a calciferous bottom supporting a mixture of sponges and sea fans at lesser depths and small growths of live coral at greater depths. The latter are unable to grow to the size necessary for the type of live reef found in the Keys. One problem is the difficulty establishing a foothold in the underlying rock. The other problem, suggested by concerned marine scientists, is algal growth fueled by nutrients spewed out from sewage treatment plants. Their outflow pipes discharge lightly treated sewage near the edge of the shelf. Heavily populated Miami-Dade, Broward and Palm Beach counties have large outputs, and it is not clear that release at the edge of the Gulf Stream is any sort of guarantee that it will not pollute the shallower water.

In the absence of live coral reefs, the East Coast's most popular scuba diving destinations are ships which were sunk to provide artificial reefs. Most lie a couple of miles offshore in 60–90 feet of water Their metal hulls serve as frameworks for coral growth and their labyrinthine internal structures serve as fish havens and as challenges to the bold submarine explorer. Scuba divers without their own boats have a choice of many dive shops and dockside charter operations to deliver them to wrecks. The Force-E South Florida Dive Centers Web site lists 10 wrecks between Ft. Lauderdale and the Jupiter Inlet north of Palm Beach.

Between the sixteenth and eighteenth centuries, a lot of wooden ships sank on this coast. The strait between the eastern coast of Florida and the Bahamas was a route for heavily-laden treasure ships delivering Mexican and Peruvian gold to mother Spain. The strand between Miami and Palm Beach is known as the Gold Coast, because it received masses of gold from the sinking of Spanish treasure ships, notably from the sinking of a fleet in a violent storm on July 30, 1715. The stretch of coast above Palm Beach is known as the Treasure Coast. Florida's southeast coast and the nearby Bahamas have a long and rich history of piracy. Treasure ships and pirates are gone now, but the Gulf Stream reigns eternally.

## The Intracoastal Waterway of Florida's East Coast

The Intracoastal Waterway provides a channel of wave-protected water that extends up the length of the state and beyond. Linked to the waterway are the lion's share of the state's 1,250 marinas and most of them are full. On weekends when the sun is out but the Atlantic waves are high, too many of these vessels are on the Intracoastal running at high speed. Sometimes the destination is a waterfront restaurant and sometimes it is a crowded spit of sand like Sandspur Island (a.k.a. Beer Can Island) near Baker's Haulover. (The names say it all.)

A lot of interesting cities and towns can be seen on a northward cruise of the Intracoastal Waterway. Sailboat captains must get used to running on the auxiliary engine. Several miles north of downtown Miami, we come across a large collection of tall condominium buildings — the City of Aventura. Welcome to the "condo canyon." The condominiums and cities never seem to stop — Hallandale, Hollywood and Dania Beach.

Ft. Lauderdale to the north is the next reliable point to enter the ocean (via Port Everglades), and its New River provides an opportunity for a waterborne visit to the city's downtown. Ft. Lauderdale is, in places, a virtual honeycomb of canals. It has a year-round census of over 17,000 boats and an extensive collection of marinas with a long list of rich and famous tenants. The most famous is John D. MacDonald's fictional hero, Travis McGee, who lived and operated his salvage business from his houseboat docked at the Bahia Mar Marina, Slip F-18. Many of his adventures took place on waters that we have already sailed.

To the north, the Intracoastal continues as a narrow condo canyon past Pompano Beach, the Hillsboro Inlet (with reliable ocean access), Deerfield Beach and the classy and high-priced Boca Raton. The waterway widens quite a bit at Lake Boca Raton, which connects to an inlet of the same name. Translated directly from Spanish, the name mean's "mouse's mouth" or inlet. Finding this curious, I delved deeper and learned that the lake was denoted on an old chart as "Boca Ratones." This translates more aptly to "Thieves Inlet," which could be something of an historical embarrassment for this upscale city.

Farther to the north is Delray Beach, then Lake Worth, Palm Beach and its inlet. An old-style, wood-trimmed motor yacht tied up along the Palm Beach seawall and pedestrian walkway will serve as a hint that interesting things are to be found here. Palm Beach is a good place to stop and take out your collapsible bicycle for a self-guided tour of the neighborhood of the undeniably rich and famous. Or, better yet, to take out your yachting blazer and ascot and hire a Bentley for a more upscale encounter. Henry Flagler's famous Breakers Hotel is a great place to enjoy a double martini under medieval tapestry. Alternatively, a popular lunch counter on quaint, picturesque Worth Avenue provides a more egalitarian meeting ground for old money and new.

Proceeding north from Palm Beach, we come to Jupiter, then St. Lucie Inlet (ocean access), the mouth of the St. Lucie River, and the town of Stuart. This is an access point to the Okeechobee Waterway, which we discussed earlier. From the St. Lucie Inlet, continuing north up the Indian River Lagoon and up somewhat misnamed "Indian River," we come to Ft. Pierce and its inlet.

Like Ft. Lauderdale and many others, Ft. Pierce it was originally established as a military base from which to fight the Seminole Indians. It became a tourist destination with the opening of Flagler's Florida East Coast Railroad. It still has the feel of a small, old Florida town. It is also the home of the Harbor Branch Oceanographic Institution, which, among other things, searches the ocean depths in a submersible craft looking for organisms that could be used in new drugs.

Proceeding north from Ft. Pierce, we come to Vero Beach, then Melbourne. There the barrier island configuration becomes more complicated, hosting Cocoa Beach, Port Canaveral and its inlet, Merritt Island and the Kennedy Space Center. After leaving the shuttle launch pads astern, we notice that the Intracoastal becomes narrower. We pass the Ponce de León Inlet, the town of Daytona Beach and the Matanzas Inlet, named for a bloody Spanish vs. French event in Florida history mentioned in this book's chapter on weather.

North of Daytona Beach comes St. Augustine, the oldest European-founded city within the boundaries of the U.S. and Canada. St. Augustine's history probably starts with Ponce de León. It was founded to guard the Florida coast, traveled by treasure ships en route to Spain. The town was raided by Sir Francis Drake and later the Castillo de San Marcos was built to guard the harbor. A short visit to the fort and historical buildings of this town will provide a deep appreciation of its long history.

Approximately 30 miles north of St. Augustine comes the mouth of the St. Johns River, providing access to the ocean on the east. Another 30-some miles north lies Fernandina Beach on the Georgia border. Sailing or motoring there would complete our coastal navigation of Florida.

## St. Johns River

Turning west and traveling a few miles up the St. Johns River brings us to Jacksonville. Berthing that is convenient to the city's famous riverwalk is available. The river and its chain of lakes provides a path running parallel to the coast and approximately 20 miles inland. This cypress-lined path allows large boats to go southward 161 miles as far as Sanford on the shores of Lake Monroe. The total difference in height along this stretch is less than 30 feet, making for a very slow current, on which is imposed a varying tidal current.

The river offers excellent fishing for largemouth bass and shad and for sea trout, redfish, snook and tarpon near its mouth. Over its whole length it offers a wealth of animal and bird life, which includes ospreys, bald eagles and manatees, plus the usual turtles and alligators.

In the nineteenth century, the river was the major thoroughfare for the settlement of this section of the Florida interior. Steamboats transported cotton "down-river" and furnished shore communities with supplies. Later they brought winter tourists. Architectural remnants of the winter-resort age—brick buildings and large Victorian frame houses—can be found in and around Palatka, halfway "up" the river.

The St. Johns River area is replete with history, starting with St. Augustine, the struggle between the French Huguenot Jean Ribault and Spanish conquistador Don Pedro Menendez de Aviles and running through naval and amphibious skirmishes of the Civil War. The upper stretches of the St. Johns River have a colorful history, which includes an attempt by a Dr. Denys Rolle, in 1764, to establish near the village of San Mateo a plantation manned by 40 London prostitutes. The region also has an interesting Florida Cracker history replete with colorful characters who made their living fishing its waters. The fishery is commercially active to this day, and we will frequently come across places that defy classification as to time, style and purpose. Decades, architecture and function seem to blend as we round the next channelized bend in the cypress swamp and come across that long, low dock with an extended shack with tables and gas pumps. It is hard to know whether it is a marina, a fish camp, a bait store, a waterfront restaurant, or all of the above.

The total length of the St. Johns River watershed is about 270 miles. If you wish to go beyond Sanford to complete the last 110 miles, a smaller boat will be needed. But traveling inland 160 miles and coming within several dozen miles of the City of Orlando is pretty good for an ocean-capable boat.

## The Experience of Florida Boating

Let's return to my original thought that Florida gives the boating enthusiast unique opportunities to be close to the water. I have experienced this in many ways—on a canoe going down a narrow, spring-fed path across scrub prairie and into cypress swamp, crossing paths with a submerged alligator on a canoe trip on the Myakka River; in a kayak exploring gray snapper spawning grounds along mangrove coasts and getting out with mask and snorkel to see first-hand what was going on between that latticework of roots; investigating saltwater "creeks" between keys in a hard-bottomed inflatable; experiencing sunsets from the cockpit of a 34-foot sailboat at anchor; gliding over the transparent water surface on the ocean side of the Keys and watching the sea fans, brain coral heads, and grassy and bare patches glide below; throwing out the anchor, donning mask, fins and snorkel, and slipping over the side to investigate the bottom; and the thrill of sailing fast through blue water with coastal condominiums slipping by. May the Gulf Stream be with you.

Then, too, you will recall worrisome experiences—the sudden squalls, the race to take down canvas on a pitching deck with cold downdrafts blowing down your neck, or the need to keep continuous vigil during coastal navigation at night. High on this list are the uncertainties involved in entering a new inlet, which might be as described below.

Your attempt to steer a straight course is frustrated by following waves as you try to line your boat up on a narrow channel defined by two stony breakwaters that jut out from a sandy beach. An overtaking wave tries to set you sideways just before the channel mouth, but you fight it off by applying more power. As you pass the beach and dune line and come abreast of the lighthouse, you remember to get on channel 9 of the marine radio and start hailing the keeper of the bridge, which is right around the bend. The waves are a lot smaller now, but they are more chaotic from bouncing back and forth between the seawalls. After a close encounter with an oncoming, mid-size cabin cruiser whose captain doesn't realize that sailboats have to stay in the center of the channel due to their deeper draft, you notice from the behavior of the foam near the rocks that the tide is incoming and is pulling you along at five knots.

That's when you get visual verification that what lies ahead of you is, indeed, a 25-foot drawbridge and it is in the closed position. Your mast is 55 feet. Just before you start giving serious thought as to how you will turn your single-engine boat around in the narrow channel and how you will race your 9-knot engine against the 5-knot tide for an escape speed of 4 knots, a sleepy old Florida voice on the radio wishes you a good evening and the safety barriers start coming down to stop the cars and trucks. The two arms of the bridge start moving up like raised sabers to create the planned 50-foot wide gap, which is about 25 feet wide at the time your mast glides through.

You switch out of reverse and into forward gear and praise the highest being that you believe in. You thank the Army Corps of Engineers for building this bridge and the sheltering waterway behind it. Your offerings of thanks are interrupted when you are almost run down by a 30-foot Bayliner zipping along at 35 miles an hour through the manatee zone. But you do find the protected cove marked on the map of the Eastern Intracoastal Waterway. Your anchor holds well and you feel much better after your first sip of wine.

It is then that you notice the squadron of pelicans circling around a high-rise condominium, using its updraft to gain altitude. After a few minutes they have spiraled to the top. They use the height to glide to the next condo. You point this out to your mate.

Your mate says, yes, maybe they are the same pelicans we saw gliding over the dune line before we came in. Using its updraft to carry them along! Isn't that something? Clever, using the wind to get them where they want to go? Remember how they were doing that along the Sunshine Skyway Bridge to get from one side of the bay to another?

Yes, you agree, as your mate refills your glass. The sun goes down over the far side of the waterway, producing a spectacular painting in pastel blue, orange, purple and billowy white.

Such are the joys of Florida boating.

## Works Cited and Consulted

Douglas, Marjory Stoneman. *Everglades River of Grass.* 60th anniversary edition. Sarasota, Fla.: Pineapple Press, 2007.

*Florida Cruising Directory.* Ft. Lauderdale: Waterways Etc., 2004/2005.

"Florida Keys Online Guide, Dive Sites." http://www.florida-keys.fl.us/divesite.htm.

"Force-E South Florida Dive Centers." http://www.force-e.com/dive_sites/wreck_diving_sites/wreck_diving_sites.shtml.

Ohr, Jim and Pete Carmichael. *Florida's Fabulous Canoe and Kayak Trail Guide.* Hawaiian Gardens, Calif.: World Publications, 2004.

Papy, Capt. Frank. *Cruising Guide to the Florida Keys.* 3rd ed. Minnetonka, Minn.: Publication Arts, 1981.

_____. *Cruising Guide to the Florida Keys, with Florida West Coast Supplement.* 10th ed. Bluffton, S.C.: F. Papy, 1998.

Rhodes, Captain Rich. *Cruising Guide to Florida's Big Bend.* Gretna, La.: Pelican Publishing, 2003.

White, Robb. *The Lion's Paw.* New York: Doubleday, 1946.

Young, Claiborne. *Cruising Guide to Eastern Florida.* Gretna, La.: Pelican Publishing, 1987.

_____. *Cruising Guide to Western Florida.* Gretna, La.: Pelican Publishing, 2000.

# Sunsets, Sunglasses, and Celebrities on the Small Screen
*Valerie E. Kasper*

The earliest images of Florida come from the explorers, specifically the Spanish conquistadors. Juan Ponce de León, who sailed with Columbus on his second voyage, eventually discovered Florida and was so taken with its beauty he named it La Florida (LAH flow REE dah) or "place of flowers." However, Álvar Núñez Cabeza de Vaca, a conquistador who was captured by Indians in Florida and lived for years with the tribe, wrote about Florida's dark side: the heat and humidity, the insects (particularly the mosquitoes), and sunburn. Even in the sixteenth century, the paradox of Florida's beauty was interpreted by those who saw it, and passed on to those who might never see it.

Centuries later, not only those who live in Florida can appreciate this paradox, but, thanks to television, the entire world can experience Florida's vast array of images, from serene sunsets and beautiful sandy beaches to destructive hurricanes and bloodthirsty mosquitoes to senior citizens and the surreal South Beach Art Deco style of Miami. From television, popular culture selects its fashion fads, extracts its catchphrases, and obtains its viewpoints. The film industry came to Florida at the turn of the twentieth century and introduced the country to Florida through movies such as *Tarzan* and *Distant Drums*, which starred Gary Cooper and was set in the Everglades in the 1840s during the Second Seminole War. The television industry took a little longer. But by the 1950s, the television industry, too, had started to grow. And with it, images of the state and its inhabitants were produced and projected to its audience. Sometimes the images were positive; sometimes they were negative. Those who lived in Florida could be seen as uneducated Florida Crackers or well-educated astronauts working for NASA. Florida itself could be seen as a beautiful paradise or a treacherous swampland. These images were the beginning of popular culture's relationship with the Sunshine State.

And although Florida "missed out on much of the Golden Age of television," due to a federal freeze that prohibited the creation of new stations (Florida Trend), it certainly caught up and produced an abundance of television shows filmed entirely or partly in the Sunshine State. Television came to Florida in 1949 through stations in Miami and Jacksonville, and once the freeze on new station creation was lifted in 1952, many more stations appeared. By the 1970s, Florida was the third largest film producing center in the United States, and in 1973 the Florida Motion Picture and Television Association was formed, followed by the Motion Picture and TV Services Office in 1974.

Although Florida is no California or New York, she has held her own over the past 50 years. Since 1958, hundreds of television shows or series have used Florida as their filming location at least once. From the early years of ocean-centered shows such as *Flipper, Sea Hunt,* and *Surfside 6,* to the middle years of space travel in *I Dream of Jeannie,* retirement in *The Golden Girls,* and action packed crime in *Miami Vice,* culminating during recent years in a host of reality shows such as *The Real World: Key West, Miami Animal Police,* and Hulk Hogan's *Hogan Knows Best,* television has helped create Florida's image. In addition, Florida has hosted a range of educational/documentary shows and talk shows, and even Food Network has used Florida to film some of its cooking shows. South Florida has produced the most televisions shows, with Miami leading the way. Besides English-language shows, Florida is also home to a multitude of Spanish-language television shows such as *¿Qué Pasa, USA?*

This chapter explores television shows shot within Florida either in their entirety (full seasons) or partially (partial seasons or individual episodes). Sometimes, the only connection to Florida, though, is the front shot of a house, which is the case in *The Golden Girls*. The chapter also explores the misconceptions many viewers have of certain popular shows believed to be shot in Florida, but actually shot elsewhere, such as *The Golden Girls, Empty Nest,* and *Nurses,* which are all set in Florida, but shot in California. These three shows, which are spin-offs of one another, are considered by many to be Florida shows, and therefore produce an image of Florida that many people believe is reality. Any show connected to Florida affects the image that the nation, and possibly even the world, has of Florida as a state of fun, sun, and vacation. While examining shows filmed in Florida, this chapter will touch on reasons producers and/or directors choose Florida as a location for filming, such as its good weather, its romantic atmosphere, or, in the case of Jackie Gleason, its abundance of golf courses available year-round.

The image of Florida as the Sunshine State with its subtropical climate, beautiful sandy beaches, and romantic sunsets has long brought people to its shores. One of the prominent images of Florida has been that of a paradise. This is seen in many of the television shows produced the decade following the freeze of the 1950s. During the 1960s, a host of shows depicting Florida as a tropical paradise aired, such as *I Dream of Jeannie, Flipper, Surfside 6, Gentle Ben, Lassie,* and *Sea Hunt*.

The first three shows portray Florida as a coastal paradise, while the last three shows portray the paradise of Florida's interior landscape. *Surfside 6* starred Troy Donahue, Van Williams, and Lee Patterson as three hip young detectives who lived and worked on a houseboat moored across from the Fontainebleau Hotel on Miami Beach. Wealthy socialite Daphne Dutton (Diane McBain) lived on the yacht next door, and Cha Cha O'Brien (Margarita Sierra) was the

Fontainebleau's resident night club singer. The Fontainebleau Hotel was considered the most luxurious hotel on Miami Beach at the time, so the show gave viewers a taste of Florida's wealthier side. The series lasted from 1960 to 1962. Up the eastern coast, *I Dream of Jeannie* astronaut Captain Tony Nelson's (Larry Hagman) space ship malfunctioned and he crash landed on an island in the South Pacific, where he discovered a 2,000-year-old bottle that housed a genie (Barbara Eden) who was banished to her bottle for not marrying the Blue Djin. Jeannie used her powers to return Captain Nelson and herself to Cocoa Beach, where they lived platonically at 1030 Palm Drive for the next four years.

During this half-hour sitcom that ran from 1965 to 1970, several images of Florida appear. First, it shows Florida as a coastal paradise, for what man would not want to work for NASA, live in Cocoa Beach, and have a beautiful genie call him master? Second, it merges this fantasy paradise with reality by offering real places in Cocoa Beach, such as Bernard's Surf Restaurant. Though most of the sitcom was filmed in California, the show's producer, Sidney Sheldon, was quite familiar with Cocoa Beach and referenced places in the area often. In addition, rocket launches from Cape Kennedy as well as shots of Patrick Air Force Base are seen in the show. Merging the realistic images of Cocoa Beach with the fantasy of Tony and Jeannie's life authenticates the viewers' image of what Florida must be like. Third, it offers Americans an escape from reality during a decade that saw increased political tensions, increased divorce rates, and also the rise of the civil rights movement and feminism. *I Dream of Jeannie* created a fantasy life that was a complete escape from real life, something many Americans were desperately seeking. In addition, the show provided a view of small-town life. Despite the fact that Nelson worked for NASA, he lived in the small town of Cocoa Beach, not Miami Beach. This small-town atmosphere, in combination with its fantasy counterpart, gave the show a sense of innocence, despite Jeannie and Tony not being married and Jeannie wearing a revealing harem costume every day. Maybe the innocence came from the censors not allowing Jeannie to reveal her bellybutton on screen. The edict from the censors was that Jeannie's harem pants had to be waist-high. Jeannie's bellybutton didn't debut until 1985, when they filmed their reunion show.

Another view of small town life and innocence is shown through shows where the main characters aren't human. *Flipper*, which ran from 1964 to 1968; *Gentle Ben*, which ran from 1967 to 1969; and *Lassie*, which ran from 1954 to 1971, all centered on a small-town family and its pet. The Ricks (*Flipper*) lived in Coral Key, Florida; the Wedloes (*Gentle Ben*) lived near the Everglades; and Lassie's families lived in small towns. These rural settings offered the audience a nostalgic look back at America during a time when many people lived in suburbs and divorce rates were climbing. These shows again blurred the lines between reality and fiction, but in an innocent way. What kid didn't dream of having a dolphin as a pet and seeking adventure?

In addition to the local, small-town settings, these shows also offered a nostalgic view of family life. *Flipper* was a show about a game ranger named Porter

Ricks (Brian Kelly), who was the chief ranger at Coral Key Park in Florida, and his two sons, Sandy (Luke Halpin) and Bud (Tommy Norden). The show centers around their adventures with their pet dolphin, named Flipper, whom they saved after a hurricane left him injured. He adopts the family and lives in the tropical lagoon outside their house. Like *Flipper*, *Gentle Ben* centered around a family and its adventures with a creature — this time a bear. The father, Tom Wedloe (Dennis Weaver), was a game warden in the Florida Everglades. His son Mark (Clint Howard) has a special relationship with a bear named Ben. The story follows the friendship between Mark and his bear. Unlike *Flipper* and *Gentle Ben*, *Lassie* only filmed one episode in Florida. During the 1965 season, an episode entitled *Lassie the Voyager* was shot in Alexander Springs, Florida. Lassie was a collie who showed incredible maternal instincts as she protected her family time and again from harm.

Although *Flipper* and *Gentle Ben* have different settings, they both were produced by Ivan Tors Studios and were filmed in Florida. *Flipper's* 100 episodes were filmed in a lagoon at the Miami Seaquarium, where the setting of Ranger Rick's house and dock were built for the show. *Gentle Ben* was set in the Florida Everglades, but filmed at the studios in Miami. Whereas *Flipper* offered a more tropical setting with palm trees, a beach, and an ocean, Gentle Ben's setting was more wilderness and wetlands. Flipper's family might encounter sharks in the ocean; Gentle Ben's family might encounter alligators in the swamp. Lassie's one episode was filmed at Alexander Springs, which is part of the Ocala National Forest. It is a hybrid of the other two settings. The spring water is a brilliant, clear, aqua color, but it is surrounded by a subtropical forest of oak trees, pine trees, and sabal palms. All three of these settings offered different, but equally exquisite, scenery and showed the blissful beauty Florida had to offer.

That same beauty existed not only on land, but also under the water. Through shows like *Sea Hunt* (1958–1962), which also was produced by Ivan Tors Studios, viewers discovered the underwater experience. In the story, Mike Nelson (Lloyd Bridges), an ex-Navy scuba diver, becomes an underwater investigator. Throughout the seasons, Mike outmaneuvers criminals, saves people's lives, solves crimes, investigates murders, stops drug smugglers, and searches for buried treasure. And he does it all in 30 minutes with time to spare to deliver a message to the audience about ocean conservation.

But the biggest attraction of this show was simply the underwater paradise itself. In this series, Ivan Tors took coastal living from above the sea to under the sea and combined a crime series with adventure. This added a different aspect to the crime/action/adventure genre, especially during a time when scuba diving was new to most people. Thanks to the expertise of underwater cinema photographer Lamar Boren, at least half the show was filmed underwater (Phillips and Holmes 102), so each episode was filled with crystal blue water and exotic sea creatures. The series was filmed in Miami and Silver Springs, Florida. Silver Springs, which is in the middle of the state, has clear, light blue water that allows for beautiful underwater filming. It showed that the interior of Florida is just as spectacular as the coastal areas. In addition to showing viewers the interior landscape of Florida, it also introduced an entire generation to scuba diving and inspired many to learn to scuba dive.

Many directors and producers filmed in Florida because of the beauty and the climate, both of which were conducive to filming. However, in the mid-1960s, Jackie Gleason relocated *The Jackie Gleason Show* from New York to Miami Beach, Florida, where it remained until the end in 1970. It was said Gleason moved the production to Miami Beach so he could play golf year round (McNeil 423). A public relations person from Miami, Hank Meyer, had heard Gleason was restless in New York, especially in the winter when he couldn't play golf, so he suggested Gleason move south (Goss 28). CBS spent $250,000 to relocate Gleason and his crew. They even built a state-of-the-art television studio next to his favorite golf course (Nelson 69). In order to relocate his cast and crew, Gleason chartered a train and dubbed it "The Great Gleason Express."

*The Jackie Gleason Show* was a variety show with comedy skits, guest stars, and Gleason's famous catchphrase, "And away we go." But its greatest legacy was the immensely popular skit, *The Honeymooners*. Gleason introduced *The Honeymooners* as a comedy skit during his first variety show in 1951, and the popularity of this skit that revolved around two lower middle class, married couples from Brooklyn kept viewers entertained for decades. The Kramdens and the Nortons lived in the same apartment building, and Ralph Kramden (Jackie Gleason), who was a bus driver, and Ed Norton (Art Carney), who was a sewer worker, were always trying to achieve better lives for themselves and their wives through get-rich-quick schemes that usually backfired, which led to arguments with their wives and catchphrases such as "to the moon" and "one of these days." But all ended well, and each episode concluded with another catchphrase, "Baby, you're the greatest." These catchphrases became part of popular culture, and even when Gleason's show was canceled in 1970, the catchphrases remained part of popular culture.

Although Florida's tropical landscape and coastal paradise were not used, nor needed, to film the skits for *The Jackie Gleason Show*, they are most certainly one of the reasons Gleason moved his production and his home to Miami Beach, thereby bringing one more televised show to Florida. At the beginning of every show, Gleason displayed to the nation why he moved to Miami Beach: as a helicopter flew along its beautiful, sandy beaches and brilliant blue water, an announcer would exclaim that Miami Beach was "the sun and fun capital of the world." Miami couldn't have asked for better advertising, and "the press and the local economic boom which accompanied hosting a hit TV show eventually brought millions of film and TV production dollars to south Florida" (Goss 30).

All of the previously discussed shows ended their runs in the early 1970s, and it was not until the 1980s that Florida saw another drastic change in television. The '80s brought a new type of television, more sophisticated, artistic, better. This was a time of "quality television," which meant "shows with a particular set of characteristics that we normally associate with 'good,' 'artsy,' and 'classy'" (Thompson 16). One of the main reasons for this change in television was cable. The rise of cable television in the 1980s caused network television to strive harder to produce more sophisticated programming because it was now competing with a cable box that brought viewers more variety, with channels like HBO, where the movies were more visually appealing and available 24 hours a day. Two other techniques utilized in prime time during the 1980s were the serial format, in which stories continued from episode to episode, and the cliffhanger, which left the season in a suspenseful situation so viewers would return the following season. All of these qualities came together for NBC in 1984 when it took a chance on a show called *Miami Vice*, a show that not only embodied the style of the 1980s, but created many of its own, and also put Miami Beach on the map.

*Miami Vice* was a police drama that centered around two detectives on the Miami Metro-Dade Police Vice Squad. James "Sonny" Crockett (Don Johnson) and Ricardo "Rico" Tubbs (Philip Michael Thomas) battled international drug trafficking, prostitution, Miami's underworld, political corruption, and a host of other criminal mischief. Crockett was white; Tubbs was black. Crockett was from the south; Tubbs was from New York. This debonair duo was supported by a multicultural squad of detectives, and that is where the similarities with other cop shows in the genre ended. Although *Miami Vice* was only on the air (excluding syndication) for five seasons, its effects are still seen throughout the country today. Not only did *Miami Vice* change the look and sound of television, it changed popular culture by prompting many of popular culture's most remembered styles, such as designer shoes without socks, Ray Ban sunglasses, and the five o'clock shadow. It also continued the coastal paradise image of Florida, though the small-town innocence of previous decades was replaced by big-city excitement as the show focused on Miami. However, instead of downtown Miami, the show focused on Miami's South Beach area.

*Miami Vice* was a groundbreaking show in the 1980s that started on a piece of paper that read: MTV cops. Legend has it that Brandon Tartikoff, NBC programming chief, wrote these two words on a piece of paper and wanted someone to implement it, and Anthony Yerkovich, former writer and producer of *Hill Street Blues*, created *Gold Coast*, which eventually became *Miami Vice*. Tartikoff visualized an expanded MTV music video, so popular in the 1980s. He wanted fast action, complex camera angles, music synchronized with the images, and bold color, so it was not unusual in *Miami Vice* to see someone showered with bullets in slow motion as synchronized music from Phil Collins, Willie Nelson, or Iron Maiden played alongside the action.

Originally, Tartikoff wanted the show set in New York, but quickly dismissed the idea for Miami. Yerkovich was fascinated by south Florida, even when he was working on *Hill Street Blues*. He thought of Miami as a "modern day American Casablanca" (Zoglin). He liked the socioeconomic gathering in Miami, especially the Cuban refugees and the Cuban-American community that had a substantial existence in the area. He liked its reputation for drug deals and money laundering. Yerkovich said he wanted the city to serve as another co-star; he wanted it to serve as a protagonist (Schmalz).

Although rock music, flashy visuals, and hip fashion were not new ideas, Yerkovich used *Miami Vice* to bring that contemporary look to television through the show's music, location, and fashion. That look didn't come without a price, a price of $1.2 million per episode. The music alone could cost up to $50,000 per episode (Golden 127–8). The music might have been costly, but it enhanced the storylines. It was used in synchrony with the story's plot, and sometimes in place of dialogue. It showed mood and tone. The music was part of an ensemble, so music would be combined with other elements to produce a certain effect. In one episode, the streets were watered down to provide a reflection of the moon at night, and Crockett and Tubbs drove down the secluded, glittering, moonlit street at the end of the episode as the music played. The music was not just background music; it was substance. According to Thomas Carter, who directed the pilot, it was "psychological subtext" (Zoglin).

Miami was uneasy about a crime show using its city as a location, especially since it focused on the international drug trade, but as the show's popularity grew, so did Miami's reputation as a hip, multicultural epicenter. The introduction to the show, alone, provided Miami with fantastic promotional material. It portrayed Miami as a coastal paradise with pink flamingos, bikini-clad women on powder soft sand beaches, and a boat cruising through the ocean. So every Friday night *Miami Vice* invited its audience to escape from reality and dive into its coastal paradise where the men were as beautiful as the women.

All of this brought Miami Beach, particularly South Beach, into a prominent place with viewers. Miami was no longer seen as a place to retire, a place of Cuban refugees, a place of drug trafficking and crime. It was revitalized, both physically and mentally. When *Miami Vice* started filming in the South Beach area, it was a seedy section of town. However, as interest in the area increased, due in part to the show, the area transformed. The Art Deco district of South Miami Beach was placed on the National Register of Historic Places, and the Army Corps of Engineers restored the Deco buildings along Ocean Drive (Doll and Morrow 120), which *Miami Vice* used to show a modern city. When a building wasn't the correct color, because earth tones were not allowed on set (Bogle 279), it was repainted to reflect the Miami-dolphin turquoise, tropical pink, and sultry violet colors of a stylish, contemporary city. Over time, that once seedy section of town became chic and full of trendy clubs and outdoor cafes. It even acquired a new name: SoBe.

In addition to a hip location and billboard music, *Miami Vice* created two cops who never looked so good. Crockett's ensemble of the Italian sports coat over a pastel colored T-shirt with white slip-on designer shoes and no socks complemented Tubbs' double-breasted suits with silk shirts and ties. They took the five o'clock shadow from grunge to gorgeous. Men throughout the nation started imitating the *Miami Vice* look. They made designer clothes and the casual look popular. Until this show, no one would have worn a T-shirt under an expensive jacket, much less roll up the sleeves. Crockett and Tubbs set the fashion standard for the 1980s.

Through location, music, and fashion, *Miami Vice* merged fantasy with reality by changing fashion, by using popular music, and by using actual buildings in the Miami area. Many times, the artists singing the songs appeared in the show. Sheena Easton played a rock star; Crockett was her bodyguard. He was protecting her until she could testify in court in a racketeering case, but he fell in love and eventually married her. She was later killed off. In addition to real-life rock stars, many of the buildings seen throughout the show were authentic. Lincoln Road Mall, the pink Alexander All-Suite Luxury Hotel, homes from Star Island, and the Miamarina, where Crockett kept his boat, could all be seen throughout the seasons of *Miami Vice*. Ocean Drive and Biscayne Boulevard, where many of the chase scenes were filmed, are actual roads in Miami (Golden 124–6). The famous flock of flamingos in the introduction was filmed at Parrot Jungle and Gardens. Even the characters' lives were given south Florida personae. Crockett was a former University of Florida football star who was drafted to Vietnam and later became a Miami vice officer who's divorced, lives on a boat, and has a pet alligator named Elvis. Even Tubbs, a former New York detective, fit into the Miami flavor with his Caribbean looks and his Cadillac convertible.

Unfortunately, the show that had a huge impact on popular culture could not stay within its budget, and after five seasons executive producer Michael Mann decided it needed to be sold into syndication to recoup its investment (McNeil 545). But over the next two decades, other shows appeared and built upon the *Miami Vice* tradition, and still others replaced it with more sophistication. It wasn't until the twenty-first century that more sophisticated shows appeared in Florida. However the early '90s produced two shows that combined Florida actors with the Florida lifestyle, the boating lifestyle in particular.

Don Johnson's character may have been a former University of Florida football player whose career was ended by an injury, but Burt Reynolds was in reality a football star for Florida State University, Florida's longtime rival, before a knee injury ended his longtime dream of a professional football career. It was that injury that led Reynolds to become an actor who eventually made his home in Jupiter, Florida. Burt Reynolds starred in another crime genre series, *B.L. Stryker*, in 1989. Another actor who made his home in Florida was Terry Bolea, a.k.a. Hulk Hogan, who lives in Belleair Beach, Florida and also had a crime series in the 1990s called *Thunder in Paradise*. Neither series made much of a spark. During the 1989–90 season, Reynolds worked close to home because *B.L. Stryker* was filmed in Palm Beach. In it, Buddy Lee Stryker, a retired New Orleans private investigator, returned to Florida to live on his boat. Hulk Hogan's character, R.J. "Hurricane" Spencer, is an ex–Navy Seal who is now a mercenary living on Florida's gulf coast. He and partner Martin "Bru" Brubaker (Chris Lemmon) fight villains in their souped-up, high-tech boat called Thunder.

The two shows have three things in common: the main star lives in Florida, both shows only lasted one season, and both shows feature a boat. Reynolds and Hogan are homegrown boys. Both grew up in Florida, graduated high school in Florida, and attended a state university. Though they have lived other places, and they may own homes in other cities, they both remain loyal to their Florida roots. And although both of their shows lasted only one season because they brought nothing new to the crime/adventure genre, they did, however, make the idea of owning a boat very appealing, thereby promoting the coastal paradise image of Florida yet again. In *Thunder in Paradise*, the boat is a prototype Spencer's buddy, Brubaker, made for the government. It is futuristic and full of high-powered gadgets (think Kit in Knight Rider without the voice). It brought excitement and adventure to Florida's waterways as the main characters sped along the aqua green Gulf of Mexico with sea spray coming off the boat's bow. In *B.L. Stryker*, Reynolds's character, as did Johnson's character before him, offered the romance of living on a boat: no yard to mow, the vivid sunsets, the soft slapping of the waves, and the freedom to change locations on a whim. Though the plots and storylines might have needed more substance and creativity, the shows certainly offered the notion that owning a boat was pleasurable and exciting.

But it is the new century that brings three very dynamic new crime dramas and one nighttime soap opera to Florida's coast: *CSI: Miami*, *Burn Notice*, *Dexter*, and *Cane*. What *Miami Vice* lacked in substance in the 1980s, these shows make amends for in 2000. These shows combine a dynamic cast with cutting edge technology and old-fashioned know-how. Two are filmed entirely in south Florida. The other is set in Miami, but mainly filmed in southern California. However, by its fifth season, it was the world's most popular show.

According to the BBC and Reuters, that series was *CSI: Miami*, which is the tropical offspring of *CSI: Crime Scene Investigation*. Lieutenant Horatio Caine (David Caruso), a former homicide detective, heads a south Florida team of forensic investigators amid the sultry tropical surroundings and cultural crossroads of Miami. His team includes Calleigh Duquesne (Emily Proctor), a bilingual southern beauty with a specialty in ballistics; Eric Delko (Adam Rodriguez), an underwater recovery expert who knows all the twists and turns of the Florida waterways; and Ryan Wolfe (Jonathan Toggo), a former patrol officer who specializes in blood and trace evidence. In addition to the team, there are Alexx Woods (Khandi Alexander), the knowledgeable medical examiner; Natalia Boa Vista (Eva LaRue), the enigmatic DNA specialist; and Detective Frank Tripp (Rex Linn), the gruff homicide detective with an appreciation for CSI.

Even though most of *CSI: Miami* is shot in Los Angeles, it offers viewers warm, sunny views; the clean, modern lines of the city, and beautiful people — something audiences can either relate to or dream about. Unlike its sibling shows, *CSI: Crime Scene Investigation* and *CSI: New York*, it has a different, brighter, lighter look to it. Like *Miami Vice* before, the characters, both good and bad, are sexy, well-dressed, and well-spoken. The forensic team drives around Miami in Hummers. The background shows Miami's opulence with magnificent mansions; flawless, bikini-clad bodies; and harbors filled with luxurious yachts. Team members use their high-tech touch screen computers to solve crimes. And they do all this without breaking a sweat (in Miami's 90-plus degree heat), soiling their clothes, or messing up their hair. The show portrays Florida's clean, coastal living. Only about five episodes a year are shot in south Florida, which happens to be where Caruso lives. The irony of living in the city where the show is set, but commuting to California, where the show is filmed, should not escape viewers.

Caruso says they shoot several episodes a year in Miami to capture "the seduction of the city" (Garvin). However, he also concedes that their "real fans know the difference between the episodes shot in studios and those done on location" (Garvin). And interestingly enough, they do. Popular culture now has a say in television; it's called blogging. Many professional television critics have sites, as do many of the studios. From the blogging sites, America (and beyond) can voice its opinions, and voice them it does. In one blog entitled, "If this is Miami, I'm Gloria Estefan," the author lists an array of problems with *CSI: Miami*'s authenticity. From setting and cast to lighting and soundstage, he compares the show to Miami. He explains that "there are very few Latinos or Cubans in this Miami; only one African American, and so far, no gays" (Skippy). He doesn't count the characters of Khandi Alexander or Adam Rodriguez because they act like caucasians. He also points out the multitude of dialects in Miami from "Fidel Castro to Jerry Seinfeld's Uncle Leo, retiring in Boca," and the only thing the show offers is a South Carolina, southern accent from Emily Proctor's character (Skippy). His last gripe is, of course, the setting. Miami knows Miami, and California ain't it.

Blogging, and the Internet in general, has also expedited worldwide coverage of catchphrases and other anomalies from television. Whereas Jackie Gleason's catchphrases were spread by word of mouth, which might take years, nowadays the Internet cuts that time into days. Where television audiences once had to wait for David Letterman, Jay Leno, or *Saturday Night Live* to parody their favorite television persona or show, nowadays any member of society can post his own parody.

A quick Internet search can uncover numerous parodies on a television character. Something as simple as sunglasses can get the entire Internet buzzing. Ray Bans might have made Don Johnson sexy, but David Caruso's use of sunglasses has made him fodder for the masses. In every episode of *CSI: Miami*, Horatio Caine arrives to the scene of a dead victim. He slowly walks around and assesses the situation. Usually at some point, he will place his hands on his hips. He will discuss the evidence with one of his team, and at just the right moment, Caine will turn, cock his head sideways, and deliver a classic one-liner, as he slowly puts on his sunglasses. Some classic one-liners are:

"You don't spend $1,000 on clothes you're not going to wear."

"So, we have a victim that started out the weekend big man on campus and ended it dead on arrival."

This body language and deliverance of one-liners has found its place in popular culture. There are Web sites and YouTube videos dedicated to Caine's sunglass usage and catchphrases. In an interview with David Letterman, Jim Carrey called Horatio Caine a "scene buttoner," meaning he closes the scene so no one can retort. Caine just walks away after his one-liner; there is no time to reply. Caine's attitude; slow, terse dialogue; and sunglasses have placed him at the center of many heated debates. The audience, including critics, either loves him or hates him. Either way, thanks to the Internet, they can all have their own opinions.

The one thing *CSI: Miami* lacks that Florida's second new crime drama of 2000 has is humor. *Burn Notice*, which is filmed entirely in Florida, offers the same light, bright view of Miami, and in this case, it really is Miami. But it brings a refreshing sardonic humor with it. It also introduces an entirely different protagonist. Michael Westen is Horatio Caine's doppelganger. They are both intelligent men who always solve their cases. But Westen is confident, without appearing arrogant. He is clever, without appearing condescending. His one-liners are more witty than cheesy.

*Burn Notice* is a cross between *Bourne Identity* and *MacGyver*. Michael Westen (Jeffrey Donovan) receives a burn notice from the CIA after serving his country as a covert operative for the past ten years. A burn notice means he no longer exists. The CIA jeopardizes his life, freezes his bank accounts, dumps him in Miami (where he happens to have family and friends), and blacklists him. The show focuses on his struggle to discover why he was burned, while he accepts freelance jobs to pay the bills. As a civilian, he reconnects with his best friend, Sam Axe (Bruce Campbell), a former Navy Seal and military intel operative, who now lives in Miami drinking mojitos and entertaining rich women; and his ex-girlfriend, Fiona Glenanne (Gabrielle Anwar), an ex–IRA operative he dumped without explanation. The last of this ensemble is Michael's chain-smoking, hypochondriac mother, Madeline (Sharon Gless), who finds clients for him while playing cards with her neighbors.

Two of the elements *Burn Notice* executes successfully are fun and energy. Although Miami is usually seen as a coastal paradise in shows, *Burn Notice* also portrays it as a character, and this character is fun and energetic, fast-paced yet casual. The darkness of some crime dramas such as the *Law and Order* series is replaced by lightheartedness. The series achieves this through three means: humor, voice-overs, and characters, all of which are interconnected. Humor runs through the show, the voice-overs, and the characters.

Throughout the show, Westen provides voice-over narration, briefly informing the audience about certain aspects of the spy business. For instance, he misses the old days before car air bags. For a spy, an air bag is a hazard because it deploys upon impact. This isn't beneficial when chasing or evading bad guys. This particular voice-over comes as Westen is driving backwards to elude Miami's finest. In another instance, Westen reveals how fighting in bathrooms is advantageous because there are many hard surfaces to slam your opponent into, which is easier on the knuckles.

The voice-overs augment the humor, but the chemistry between characters adds energy to the show. The two women in Westen's life add more color to his world than the Miami scenery. Westen's ex-girlfriend Fiona mixes model looks with bad attitude, but she's not eye candy. She's the kind of girl who shoots first, enjoys it, and asks questions later. She and Michael have a complicated relationship, and according to Matt Nix, the show's creator, Michael and Fiona "are two people who really don't have anybody else that they can be with. Anybody else is going to be afraid of what Michael does, and it sort of turns her on, and anybody else for Michael is going to be uninteresting" (Veitch). However, despite their past, she has agreed to help him determine who burned him. In one episode that epitomizes Fiona's character, she utilizes a concealed stun gun in an attempt to subdue a villain who deals in human trafficking. While Sam watches, the criminal knocks her to the ground and grabs her leg as she clutches the stun gun, points it toward his nose, and pulls the trigger. As Sam runs toward her, Westen's voice-over informs the audience that electrocuting someone while he is holding your leg causes both of you to suffer the voltage. At which point Fiona, knowing this, pulls the trigger and both fall unconscious. When Sam approaches the two bodies, his only comment is that Fiona is one crazy chick. It is this type of humor that propagates the energy in this fast-paced show and solidifies the chemistry between the central characters.

The second woman in Westen's life is his mother, who sports a short, gelled, mussed-up, platinum blonde do, gold hoop earrings, a cigarette between her fingers, and a lot of over-the-top melodrama that drives her son crazy, but in a loving way. Despite Westen's annoyance, he always ameliorates the situation, even when it's just a broken coffee pot. However, he holds his upbringing responsible for his current career choice. He tells the audience that "people with happy families don't become spies. A bad childhood is the perfect background for covert ops" because such people don't trust anyone, they're use to getting smacked around, and they don't get homesick. The dynamics between Westen and his neurotically needy mother are humorous, and the audience can feel his frustration, yet he loves her, and their endless bantering brings endless comedy and authenticity to the storyline. Who can't relate to a relationship with mom? Madeline Westen's constant interference makes most viewers appreciate their own mothers.

Because *Burn Notice* is filmed in Miami, the show radiates sun-soaked scenery. The crew has worked in abandoned concrete plants, warehouses damaged by Hurricane Andrew, and a Miami office building. In the office building, Westen has to cut through a concrete ceiling and dive out a large window to avoid capture. Though the building was real, the ride out the window was shot on a sound stage because the actual window was an expensive hurricane window. In addition to the hurricane window, there are shots of jalousie windows, pink plastic flamingos, and night clubs. While doing surveillance work from a garage, Michael and Fiona are actually sitting atop the largest adult novelty store in South Beach. Even the scenery provides humor in the show.

This character-driven, action-packed, crime drama portrays Miami as a fun-filled vacation in the sun, with a casual environment where action is always just a stun gun spark away. The pilot actually won a 2008 Edgar Allan Poe Award, honoring the best in mystery, in the category Best Television Episode Teleplay.

The Florida scene becomes a little more serious, and in some instances darker, in *Cane* and *Dexter*. *Cane* illustrates the growing influence of Latinos in south Florida. It centers around a Cuban-American family dynasty of sugar cane growers, and it's set and filmed in Miami. It is the first network series to focus positively on the Cuban exile experience and give credence to the Latino population in south Florida. It shows a family of successful, articulate, educated Latinos. Executive producer Jonathan Prince believes it will "educate the rest of America about everything from the Pedro Pan exodus of children from Cuba to the tension between those who left the island and those who stayed" (Garvin).

In *Cane*, Alex Vega (Jimmy Smits) faces opposition from his brother-in-law (Nestor Carbonell) when he marries into the Duque family. His father-in-law (Hector Elizondo) is looking to pass down the family business, possibly to Vega, whom he thinks of as a son. Another opponent to the family business is the Samuels family, a prejudiced, white family competing for dominance in the sugar cane industry. The family saga, at its heart, is an immigrant's story of those who succeeded, continue to struggle to maintain the business and the family, and are willing to protect the business and family.

Even though the show was based on the memories of screenwriter Cynthia Cidre, who was asked by the CBS entertainment president to create "something personal" (Deggans), there was one problem: Palm Beach's Fanjul family. Cidre created the show based on her memories of "her childhood, and immigrating to Miami in the fourth grade, when her father worked as a chemist in the sugar industry" (Deggans). However, the Fanjul family is one of the nation's largest sugar manufacturers, and its members built their empire after fleeing Cuba — a severe similarity to *Cane's* back story. After some legal dealings, the Fanjuls and CBS came to an agreement. Sadly, though, the series only lasted one year.

Once *Cane* was canceled, Smits moved onto another Florida drama in its third season — *Dexter*. This dark drama explores the mind of serial killer Dexter Morgan (Michael C. Hall), who happens to work for the Miami Metro Police Department as a blood splatter analyst. As a young child with a terrible secret, Dexter was adopted by Harry Morgan, a Miami police officer. His father recognized his sociopathic personality and taught him to channel it constructively by killing those who deserved to be killed, such as murderers and rapists.

What allows viewers to like this sociopathic killer is the ethical dilemma of killing those who deserve to be killed. Is he hero or villain? In addition, *Dexter* uses techniques shared with *Burn Notice*: it has voice-overs, it's fast-paced, and it's humorous. The audience is allowed into Dexter's world though his voice-overs, and the show is humorous because of his dry wit. "Another beautiful day in Miami," he says with typically dry humor in one episode. "Mutilated corpses with a chance of afternoon showers." Dexter also has a certain self-awareness.

He realizes he is socially damaged, but his charisma allows the audience to like him, but makes them wonder about the reliability of his character. Can someone who protects his sister and plays cheerfully with his girlfriend's kids be permanently damaged? These characteristics add lightness to the darkness, and they challenge the viewer to loathe this affable serial killer.

Despite the bright, new shows in the same old genres, the twenty-first century brought something new to television: the reality show. And television would never be the same. No longer would someone have to have talent in order to be a movie star, nor would reality have to be real. According to those in the industry, there are many benefits to shooting reality shows in Florida: good weather in the winter, a diverse population that provides diverse characters for show, and talented crews at a reasonable price (Gale). However, do reality shows portray Florida in a positive light? It depends on the reality show.

Florida has seen its share of reality shows. In two shows, Florida is portrayed as Babylon, as seven strangers live in spectacular mansions in South Beach (1996's *The Real World: Miami*) and in Key West (2006's *The Real World: Key West*). In other shows, celebrities are shown, for better or worse, living their ordinary lives (*Hogan Knows Best*). And still other shows document the professional lives of tattoo artists (*Miami Ink*), police officers (*COPS*), and animal control officers (*Miami Animal Police*). Depending on the show, Florida's image could be positive or negative. Either way, reality television has certainly affected Florida's image and popular culture in a number of ways.

Although many reality shows use Florida for a season, such as *The Real World*, there are three filmed entirely in Florida: *Hogan Knows Best*, *Miami Ink*, and *Miami Animal Police*.

The county of Miami-Dade covers more than 2,000 square miles, ranging from South Beach to the Everglades, and the 20 animal control officers of *Miami Animal Police* receive almost 2,500 calls a year (Miami Animal Police). In addition to average domestic animals, officers also contend with exotic animals, such as alligators, boa constrictors, and monitor lizards, which is when they call private companies skilled in removing wild animals from urban settings. Most animal control officers handle stray dogs and cats, maybe some livestock. However *Miami Animal Police* reveals a different story: officers deal with cock fighting, dog fighting, raccoon attacks, pythons in public restrooms, alligators on freeways, and bats in palm trees. Because of these officers, viewers receive an education, and Miami is seen as more than an urban center full of pampered pooches.

The second show filmed in Florida also offers its viewers an education. About one in eight Americans have a tattoo, studies say, and the industry has more than doubled since 1990 (Matheson). While tattoos still signify rebellion and resistance for some, they've also become a mainstream form of art and expression for many in popular culture. Tattoos are not only body art; they make a statement about and by the person they adorn, which is why a reality show about a tattoo parlor, its clients, and its employees has lasted four seasons on the TLC network.

Miami Ink is about a tattoo parlor in South Beach. During each show, customers request and tattoo artists create tattoos of various shapes and sizes for various reasons. Each customer has a story of love, loss, accomplishment, or commitment to parallel the art work they request. In addition, the tattoo artists providing the exquisite artwork have their own dramas to discuss. It's not just the skill of the artists that makes the show popular; it's the interaction between the artists and their customers that adds interest and energy.

Did you know the first tattooing machine was based on the design of the door bell?

*Miami Ink's* parlor has a plethora of emotion and art. Many celebrities have inked tattoos to symbolize their commitment to a relationship. However, popular culture has seen what happens when those relationships sour. According to Ami James, one of the tattoo artists, "Tattoos last longer than romance" (Pervos). The show's artists also fulfill emotional needs. Mark Zupan, captain of the United States quadriplegic wheelchair rugby team that competed in the Paralympic games, also known for his appearance in the 2005 film *Murderball*, came into the shop. They were able to finish a tribal tattoo on his arm. In other episodes, clients have gotten tattoos to help them over a death or to memorialize a death. *Miami Ink* even worked with the Make-A-Wish foundation by allowing a child to come watch them work. Other interesting episodes have featured a circus sideshow worker who wanted a tattoo of a rubber-chicken prop, a graffiti artist who wanted a tattoo of her artwork, and recording artist Lloyd Banks, who wanted a tattoo to commemorate the release of his latest album.

Did you know that sailors who had an anchor tattoo once were believed to have sailed the Atlantic Ocean?

Now in its fourth season, *Miami Ink* is one of the network's most highly watched shows, with five and six million viewers each week, and it has created spin-offs: *LA Ink* and *London Ink*. The show tries to avoid the stereotypical image of partying drunks who stumble into tattoo shops late at night for some permanent body art they'll probably regret the next morning. Instead, it tries to focus on educating its viewers. It shows the skill and thought that go into each tattoo.

Did you know Winston Churchill's mother had a snake tattooed on her wrist?

The final reality show shot completely in Florida is *Hogan Knows Best*, which centers around Terry "Hulk Hogan" Bollea, a former pro-wrestling star, and his wife, Linda; daughter, Brooke; and son, Nick. The show began in Belleair Beach, where Hogan owned a 17,000-square-foot, million-dollar mansion, but later moved to Miami, where he bought a $12 million bayfront estate on Miami Beach's North Bay Road. Hogan has maintained that the move had nothing to do with legal battles with neighbors, who took him to court because of the menagerie of animals he kept on his property. Instead, he says, he moved to further the careers of his children. In the show, Hogan is portrayed as a stern but good-hearted father who only has the interests of his family in mind. He loves his wife, tries to advance his daughter's singing career, and encourages his son's love of cars and racing.

Unfortunately for the Hogans, reality became too real last year when Nick, who was 17 at the time, was in an automobile accident that left his best friend on life support. He eventually was charged with reckless driving and serious bodily injury, which is a felony, and sent to jail. Soon after, Linda Bollea filed for divorce after 22 years of marriage and started dating a 19 year old. All of this, of course, has become fodder for the media, and Hogan contends the reality show has hurt his family. He believes the show "exacerbated the faults in his marriage" and his celebrity status hurt Nick during his court experience (Fletcher). He said Nick's persona in *Hogan Knows Best* was not the real Nick, but the public believes his television persona is accurate. Hogan believes this persona, and his son's celebrity status, hurt his son in court. Interestingly enough, many bloggers believe Nick was shown too much leniency due to his celebrity status.

The argument, though, has some merit. Many critics contend that "reality television" is an inaccurate description for this genre because producers design a show, carefully select the participants, and place them in artificial environments designed for "maximum emotional impact" (Hirschorn). In some instances, producers have been accused of re-shooting or asking participants to perform a certain way. Ami James of *Miami Ink* says he is nothing like his character. He says reality characters are "portrayed the way the editing room wants to portray" them. "The show is only 40 minutes" out of an entire week, so editors focus on their own agenda (Pervos). If this is true, could Hogan be correct? Could reality television hurt those it catapults into celebrity status?

Although some believe reality television to be an outrage against culture, others see it as an essential part of popular culture. Reality television has become such an integral part of popular culture that in 2008 the Academy of Television Arts and Sciences announced it will give its very first primetime Emmy Award for Outstanding Host for a Reality Show or Reality Competition. Reality television will probably continue into the future for several reasons. First, it's cheaper to produce than quality television, so networks can use it as filler, thereby allowing them to spend more money on other programming. Second, reality shows fill a void. In conventional television shows, "stock groups of characters grapple with endless versions of the same dilemma" (Hirschorn). Reality television, on the other hand, offers something different—the unrestricted, unlimited ability to broach taboo cultural issues. Values and beliefs collide, which makes for fascinating television. Last is the human factor. Watching real people act in unexpected ways is more exciting than predicting the end of *CSI: Miami*, where Horatio Caine always closes his case.

An extension of reality television is true-crime television, in which the show uses an actual crime, usually a murder, and real people to tell the story. Some shows focus on a popular crime of the day, while others revisit cold cases, historic crimes, or notorious murders. Shows such as *The Investigators, Foren-*

sic *Files,* and *Body of Evidence* are true-crime shows. *Body of Evidence,* starring renowned criminal profiler and homicide investigator Dayle Hinman, guides the viewer through some of her most puzzling cases and explains how they were solved. These baffling crimes often have no eyewitnesses, little evidence, and no apparent motive.

Hinman is from Florida. She grew up in West Palm Beach and graduated from Florida State University with a degree in criminology. She began her 26-year-career in law enforcement in 1975, working as a cop on the beat at Florida State University. She spent five years as a deputy for the Leon County sheriff, including a stint in the department's underwater recovery dive team, and was eventually trained in the criminal investigative analysis division at the FBI's behavioral science unit. Hinman, who is based in Tallahassee at Florida's Department of Law Enforcement, was one of the first detectives to be trained in forensic profiling under the FBI's legendary John Douglas. She is one of a handful of women in her field, and she has successfully investigated hundreds of criminals, including infamous Florida killers like Aileen Wuornos, Danny Rolling and Ted Bundy.

In each episode, Hinman takes the viewer behind the scenes to show how her team of law enforcement experts uses its skills to investigate and solve murders. The show has focused on serial killers, disappearances, and sexual predators. In one episode, Hinman's team is stumped when a popular woman is found bludgeoned to death in her bedroom. They suspect her millionaire husband, but he has an airtight alibi. In another episode, a hurricane blows through Florida leaving several dead, but one death wasn't due to the hurricane. Hinman's team investigates a criminal's fiendish plot to use a natural disaster to conceal a murder. By the end of each episode, Hinman and her team put the pieces together to reveal the murderer, the motive, and the means.

Many viewers believe *The Golden Girls, Empty Nest,* and *Nurses* were filmed in Florida. However, they were only set in Florida; they were shot in California. These three shows, which are spinoffs of one another, are considered by many to be Florida shows, and because of that they have a substantial impact on Florida's image. Who would have thought that a sitcom about four retired women, one of whom was a stroke victim, would become so popular, not to mention cast Florida in a positive light? But *The Golden Girls* changed the perception society had of retirees and of Florida being jam-packed with a geriatric populace. It made yuppies realize their parents could be self-sufficient, and it made boomers realize retirement might be pleasurable.

All four women contributed equally to the energy and success of the show, and it often explored socially conscious themes, even controversial themes such as homophobia, domestic violence, healthcare, illegal immigration, and older women's sex lives. Sexual insinuation and some profanity were routine on the program and added to its energy. Sophia's stroke, which rendered her incapable of diplomacy, cunningly allowed the show to comment on popular culture. Sophia could get away with comments other characters were unable to pull off.

Despite the Miami setting, the only connection the show had to Florida was the address of the house the women occupied, at 6151 Richmond St. in Miami. No such street exists in Miami. Instead, the original house was based on a home in Pacific Palisades, California. After the first season, Disney built a model of the home at its studio in Orlando.

In 1987, an episode of *The Golden Girls* was used to create another series about the 55-and-older population. It was called *Empty Nest*, and it was equally as popular. Instead of women, this show focused on a widower, Dr. Harry Weston (Richard Mulligan), and his two grown daughters (Dinah Manoff and Kristy McNichol), who have returned to live with him, thereby making the title ironic. It was almost the opposite of *The Golden Girls*. Blanche is chasing men; Harry is rejecting feminine advances. Sophia is sharp-tongued and cynical; Harry is passive and compassionate.

In 1991, *Empty Nest* spawned its own offspring, *Nurses*, a sitcom about a group of nurses working in the same hospital as Harry Weston, the Community Medical Center. All three of these series were produced by the same person, Susan Harris; were set in the same city, Miami; were played on the same night, Saturday; and on the same network, NBC. This unique situation allowed the characters and shows to cross over, which allowed for intertextual themes across the three sitcoms. One example is the 1991 hurricane episode, in which Dinah Manoff (*Empty Nest*) appeared on *The Golden Girls*, Estelle Getty (*The Golden Girls*) visited *Empty Nest*, and Park Overall (*Empty Nest*) and Betty White (*The Golden Girls*) appeared on *Nurses*.

Although the shows were not filmed in Florida, they still produce an image of Florida because they are set in Miami. Just having the setting in Miami causes society to make connections because television is an influential force in popular culture today. Whether television portrays reality or fantasy, it can trigger national changes, such as fashion, music, and catchphrases. Whether it's Don Johnson's wardrobe or David Caruso's one-liners, the social impact television has on America is profound. And with the introduction of the Internet and blogging, that impact proliferates. Besides the effect of television on popular culture, individual shows have an effect on the filming location, in this case Florida. Most of the shows discussed in this chapter have placed Florida in a positive light and shown those unfamiliar with the state its coastal paradise image. Even those mistaken for Florida shows bolstered Florida's image. By doing so, they have brought people to the Sunshine State, which brings money to the state. In addition, shows filmed in Florida bring money into the economy by providing jobs. *Burn Notice* alone "puts a lot of people to work over a long period of time. And it puts Florida in front of the world, almost like a product placement" (Persall). So thanks to television, the placement of Florida in front of the entire world allows society to experience a vast array of images of the Sunshine State and allows Florida to continue to change popular culture's fashion, catchphrases, and viewpoints.

## Works Cited and Consulted

Bernhard, Brendan. "South Beach Riot." *The New York Sun*. February 6, 2007. http://www.nysun.com/arts/south-beach-riot/48049/?print=6773277121.

Bogle, Donald. *Prime Time Blues: African Americans on Network Television*. New York: Farrar, Straus and Giroux, 2001.

Deggans, Eric. "Jimmy Smits Raises 'Cane.'" *The St Petersburg Times*. September 14, 2007. http://www.sptimes.com/2007/09/14/Tv/Jimmy_Smits_raises__C.shtml.

Doll, Susan, and David Morrow. *Florida on Film*. Gainesville: University of Florida Press, 2007.

Fletcher, Alex. "Hulk Hogan's Son Requests Jail Changes." *Digital Spy*. June 3, 2008. http://www.digitalspy.co.uk/showbiz/a97326/hulk-hogans-son-requests-jail-changes.html.

"Florida in TV." *Florida Trend*. March 2008. http://floridatrend.com.

Gale, Kevin. "South Florida Receives Triple Dose of Reality TV." *South Florida Business Journal* 26 (September 2003). http://www.bizjournals.com/southflorida/stories/2003/09/29/story4.html.

Garvin, Glenn. "Behind the Scenes with CSI: Miami." *The Daily Collegian*. May 8, 2006. http://media.www.dailycollegian.com/media/storage/paper874/news/2006/05/08/Entertainment/Behind.The.Scenes.With.csi.Miami-1922226.shtml.

———. "New Fall CBS Television Show 'Cane' about Cuban Americans in Miami." *The Miami Herald*. May 18, 2007. http://havanajournal.com/cuban_americans/entry/new-fall-cbs-television-show-cane-about-cuban-americans-in-miami-9922/.

Golden, Fran Wenograd. *TVacations*. New York: Pocket Books, 1996.

Goss, James P. *Pop Culture*. Sarasota, Fla.: Pineapple Press, 2000.

Hirschorn, Michael. "The Case for Reality TV." *Atlantic Monthly*, May 2007. http://www.theatlantic.com/doc/print/200705/reality-tv.

"If this is Miami, I'm Gloria Estefan." *Blog Critics Magazine*, October 4, 2002. http://blogcritics.org/archives/2002/10/04/204958.php.

Matheson, Whitney. "A True Tale of Tattoo Envy." *USA Today*. July 30, 2003. http://www.usatoday.com/life/columnist/popcandy/2003-07-30-pop-candy_x.htm.

McNeil, Alex. *Total Television: The Comprehensive Guide to Programming from 1948 to the Present*. New York: Penguin Books, 1996.

"Miami Animal Police." Animal Planet. http://animal.discovery.com/fansites/mapd/about/about.html.

Nelson, Richard Alan. *Lights! Camera! Florida! Ninety Years of Moviemaking and Television Production in the Sunshine State*. Tampa: The Florida Endowment for the Humanities, 1987.

Persall, Steve. "Florida's Budget Shortfall Could Curb TV, Film Productions Here." *St. Petersburg Times*. July 27, 2008. http://www.tampabay.com/features/movies/article734339.ece.

Pervos, Stephani. "Miami Ink's Ami James Leaves His Mark on Chicago." *Oy! Chicago*. http://www.oychicago.com/article.aspx?id=864&terms=Miami+Ink.

Phillips, Louis, and Burnham Holmes. *The TV Almanac*. New York: Macmillan, 1994.

Schmalz, Jeffrey. "Miami Journal; Sun Sets on Show that Redefined a City." *The New York Times*. May 18, 1989. http://query.nytimes.com/gst/fullpage.html?res=950DE2DF1738F93BA25756C0A96F948260.

Thompson, Robert J. *Television's Second Golden Age*. New York: Continuum, 1996.

Veitch, Kristin. "Burn, Baby, Burn: Creator Matt Nix Puts Us on Notice." *EOnline*, July 3, 2007. http://www.eonline.com/uberblog/detail.jsp?contentId=3743

Zoglin, Richard. "Cool Cops, Hot Show." *TIME*, September 16, 1985. http://www.time.com/time/printout/0,8816,959822,00.html.

# Dangerous Game: Snakes, Gators and One-Ton Sharks

*Steve Glassman*

Owing to its subtropical climate, many sinuous waterways, and large tracts of wilderness cheek by jowl with populated areas, Florida arguably leads the densely peopled areas of first-world countries in the threats posed to humans by wildlife. Sound like hyperbole? Consider this.

In Palatka, the neighbor of Fire Marshall Joe Guidry shouted to the fireman for help. A five-foot eastern diamondback rattlesnake was slithering through his yard (*see* Fatal under WORKS CITED). Guidry grabbed his sidearm and came running. He emptied his pistol into the snake. Excited by the encounter, Guidry acted without thinking. He pulled his trophy's body from under a shed. The serpent snapped to and drove its fangs into his arm. Guidry felt his lips tingling as he stood, a sure sign of venom poisoning. He was rushed to the emergency room, where 18 vials of antivenin were administered — to no avail. Even with optimal medical treatment, he succumbed.

Sanibel is a ritzy island community just offshore from Ft. Myers in the southwest corner of the state. On September 11, 2001, a date known worldwide for terrorist attacks, Robert Steele walked his dogs, as he frequently did, near his home along a trail near the Ding Darling National Wildlife Refuge (*see* Alligator Attacks 675). A different sort of terrorist — an alligator less than eleven feet long — lay in ambush. The reptile attacked Steele and dragged him into a nearby canal. Steele's wife, hearing his anguished cries, splashed into the water and struggled to save her husband — to no avail. His lower leg had been "traumatically amputated" by the relatively small, 300-pound gator. Steele died from blood loss before help could arrive. Across the state in heavily populated Broward (Ft. Lauderdale) County, Yovy Jimenez went out for her usual evening jog (Bodies). While stopping on a bridge over a canal to enjoy the sunset, she allowed her feet to dangle over the water. An alligator leapt from the water, clamped down on her legs and dragged the young woman under the surface. Her partially eaten body was found the next morning. Her death was one of three attributed to alligator attacks that month.

Thad Kubinski was a 69-year-old retiree who had immigrated to the St.

Petersburg area for the good life (Hunter). Part of the good life was a morning dunk off his dock into Boca Ciega Bay. He started one August morning, as usual, with a dive into the warm salty waters. Lurking under the dock was a nine foot bull shark. Kubinski never reached the shore alive. The neighbors considered Boca Ciega Bay safe from shark attack because of its relative shallowness. Yet sharks have killed in even shallower Florida waters. A year later, eight-year-old Jesse Arbogast was wading in the Gulf of Mexico near Pensacola. A seven-foot bull shark slashed at him. An alert uncle grappled the boy — and the beast — to shore, the boy's arm still in the shark's mouth. The limb was retrieved from the creature's maw. Surgeons attempted to reattach it, but the massive blood loss overwhelmed the child's system, and he died from his injuries. On average, 80 to 100 documented shark attacks occur worldwide each year. At least a third of those attacks, and sometimes almost one half, happen in Florida (Facts about sharks).

Many other forms of wildlife pose occasional threats to humans or their pets in the Sunshine State, such as Burmese pythons, crocodiles, leaping sturgeon and manta rays. We'll concentrate on the major threats and give a passing nod to the minor ones in this chapter. First, let's take up the creature everyone has a fascination with (either negatively or positively) — snakes. Florida is home to six venomous types. Five are pit vipers (rattlesnakes, water moccasins and so on) and the sixth, the eastern coral snake, belongs to the cobra family. Of the three coral snake species north of the Rio Grande, the eastern, which occurs in Florida, is the most venomous (Sanchez). Nevertheless, it poses little danger to humans. Only .5 to 1 percent of the 6,000 or so snake bites in the United States each year are attributed to coral snakes. These snakes are small, rarely more than two feet long, and quite secretive (Eastern Coral). In my many years of tramping along hiking trails in the Florida woods, I can, offhand, only recall seeing one live coral snake, which I identified by the old saw, "black and yellow kill a fellow, red and black, friend of Jack."

As it happened I had lost the trail and was wandering in a patch of low hammock (very deep, swampy woods), and I was feeling pretty glum. It is entirely possible for experienced woodsmen to stay lost for days in such areas, and though I spend much time hiking in the woods, I don't consider myself an experienced woodsman. Then I spied the coral snake. It was brilliantly colored, with day-glow red bands separated from equally attractive and bright black bands by small rings of yellow. It was colorful enough to be a necklace, and it was probably no longer than a necklace, perhaps fifteen inches. The creature was hanging along the trunk of a palm tree, its tail in a hole in the trunk. On seeing me, it flailed about, trying to untangle its empennage from the hole. It dropped to the ground and attempted to flee by a strange hopping motion. It was apparent that the tiny creature was more afraid of me than I of it, and reminded me that I as a human was the master of the environment, even in deep woods. Shortly, I regained the trail, but I continued to feel a kinship to that coral snake. For a time we had been two lost and lonely souls in the woods.

All the other coral snakes I've seen have been roadkill. The most notable was discovered not far from my house on a residential street along which I jogged daily, miles from open country. I was unable to convince the adjacent homeowner to dispose of the body, and so the ever diminishing brilliance of its outstretched form was ground into the pavement by tires for several days. Given the heavy landscaping around many Florida homes and this little fellow's secretive nature, I would imagine it is more common in urban environments than most of us think.

The only coral bite I have ever heard of happened on an Ocala golf course. Someone discovered a banded snake thirty inches long (Snake Bite). Naturally, the golfers were about to do the Lord's work by killing the animal with their clubs. A golfer who had kept snakes as a youngster intervened. Figuring it was the similarly banded king snake on account of its great length, he carelessly picked up the reptile. It bit him. He endured a many-day ordeal in the emergency room, which for a time left him immobile from the neck down. As his body lay inert, the doctor tactlessly told him that permanent paralysis was one of the indications of coral snake bite. It was a distinct possibility. As it happened he recovered fully, but his example should ring in the ears of any putative Steve Irwin who sees a coral snake and thinks even vaguely about picking it up.

The venom of the eastern diamondback is not as potent as the coral snake's. In fact, several rattlesnakes have clinically more powerful venom. Nevertheless, as must be apparent from the Palatka incident above, the eastern diamondback rattlesnake, owing to its large size and ability to deliver a potent shot of venom, is one of the world's deadliest serpents (Diamondback). It is also the largest rattlesnake in the Americas and one of the world's biggest venomous serpents.

In legend, the eastern diamondback grows to as long as eight feet, and weighs ten or more pounds. The more usual adult size is four to seven feet with five and a half feet appearing to be the average. One study cited a captive snake that weighed 5.5 kilograms, or about twelve pounds, and another paper said specimens have grown to 26 pounds under laboratory conditions. Length is important because the snake can strike up to half or more of its body length; accounts vary, and some claim the diamondback shoots two thirds of its length, meaning a seven-foot snake could hit a target four or so feet away. As unlikely as such a distance seems, it may be a useful to think about when dealing with the creatures in the wild. Its fangs are the longest of any rattlesnake, and may measure up to an inch in length. Body weight is important because on average the eastern diamondback can produce 410 milligrams of venom with large individuals yielding as much as 1,000 milligrams. A lethal dose for a human is about 125 milligrams. Experts figure that the chances of death from a "severe" bite, even with medical assistance, range between 30 percent and 40 percent.

This creature inhabits all geographical regions of the state of Florida with the exception of watery locations, but its preferred habitat is dry, sandy areas such as pine-palmetto flatwoods, spruce-pine scrub and the like. But it may be well to bear in mind that the diamondback markings mimic live-oak leaf litter.

Its relative decline in numbers appears to be because of its inability—fortunately—to adapt to evolving land use patterns in the state. In other words, it does not live comfortably in suburban environments. Optimal temperatures for the eastern diamondback range from 65 to 75 degrees. During warm periods the snake seeks the natural air conditioning of gopher tortoise (and other) burrows, and occasionally during very hot periods in the summer, when the temperature seldom drops below 75, it will go into a state of aestivation. By the same token, during cold snaps in the northern part of its range, which reaches along the coastal plain to the Carolinas, the southern half of Georgia, and then along the gulf plain to the Florida parishes of Louisiana, it'll fall into a sort of brumation or near-hibernation. Spring and autumn, the snake hunts early to midmorning. During the winter it hunts around midday, and in the long Florida summer, it's basically crepuscular or nocturnal.

The eastern diamondback, like all pit vipers, has special sensory organs located in the pits between the eye and nostril. These organs read the heat signature of objects, with warm-blooded mammals giving off the best defined image. In short, pit vipers, like American GIs, come equipped with night vision. During the warm months of the year, a diamondback will curl up comfortably at night near a log, hollow stump or the base of a tree, and wait for a rice rat, woods mouse or cottontail to hop within fifteen inches, the effective range of its night goggles and an easy striking range for an adult snake. Once the snake strikes the animal, it immediately detaches and allows the prey animal to beat an apparent escape. The reason for this, it is surmised, is to prevent injury from the thrashing of an animal as large as a rabbit. Another reason is that its venom not only dispatches the prey animal, but also begins the digestive process while the bitten creature slinks off to die in private. By the use of sight, smell and taste, the snake, rapidly flicking its tongue, follows the dying rodent, the odor of the venom being the chief marker in the scent trail.

The diamondback also uses its senses to find a mate (Courtship). Pheromones released by receptive females draw males from as far as a half mile. When more than one male arrives on the scene, the suitors do the serpent version of arm wrestling. They rise up and attempt to throw each other to the ground. The winner gets the girl. All this goes on in April, and the mother, taking no chances on being stuck with a deadbeat sperm donor, will mate with more than one male. In August, a dozen or so foot-long babies are live-born in a gopher tortoise den or similar burrow. Scientists refer to the newly born as neonates, and they each have a single button on the tail and enough venom in their glands to kill a human. The mother will keep an eye on her brood for a couple of weeks before they are left to their own devices.

There are up to ten different kinds of toxin in diamondback venom. It was long believed that rattlesnake venom was only hemotoxic—or destructive of blood particles—but neurotoxins (or nerve damaging) toxins are also present. For unknown reasons, different combinations of this cocktail of venoms may be found in different specimens of the same species—and even in different fangs of the same snake. A Pacific Coast rattlesnake once was determined to have yellow venom in one fang and white venom in the other. The white was practically harmless, and the yellow quite powerful. Supposedly, snakes in northern Florida have more potent venom than those in the southern reaches; this may be a wives' tale or a considered judgment.

Venom requires a great deal of energy to produce. It is too valuable for the creature to waste on something it can't eat. Being a highly evolved species, the diamondback has the ability to withhold venom. Young snakes are more dangerous and venomous than older ones because they have not learned discipline. They tend to eject all of their venom even in defensive strikes. When a large critter such as a human blunders into its range, the diamondback — and other pit vipers — frequently lashes out with a dry or only partially envenomed strike. Many weird folk remedies for snakebite, chewing tobacco, kerosene, whiskey and on and on, appeared effective to practitioners because there was in essence nothing to cure, the bites being dry. Somewhere between 20 and 50 percent of rattlesnake bites are of this kind. Enraged and hunting snakes, on the other hand, fully envenom their bites, meaning it is not wise to annoy a snake and then get bitten. The diamondback can strike and return to coil so fast the process appears only as a blur to the human eye. The cycle occurs in one quarter second. Fortunately, every highly excited diamondback I have ever encountered has been in the open and easily maneuvered around. Their rattles sound more like a leak in a high-pressure hose than a rattle, and the speed and power of their false strikes should cow anyone with a penchant for showboating a la the cable TV nature boys. Other diamondbacks I've encountered, on the other hand, were so laid-back that a little mild pushing could not coax them to pose coiled for my camera.

I know of two non-provoked diamondback bites. One occurred to a friend of a former student. The student had written a paper about his buddies' rattlesnake hunting exploits. It ended in the death of the only snake they caught. When I saw this student some time later, I asked him in passing if he had been hunting snakes. "Naw, we don't do that anymore," he said. "One of my pals got bit and the insurance company said they wouldn't pay if another of us was hit." He then related that the three friends were walking through the woods on a snake-hunting expedition. The first passed by unharmed, but the second one was nailed by the snake, which none of them saw. I learned about the other case on the web. It happened to a Hillsborough (Tampa) County deputy (Boey). He too was struck while hiking in the woods. He was a certified snake handler and called on to rid areas of troublesome reptiles. He too was struck without warning, perhaps by a hunting snake that he stepped too close to. All this has led me to rethink my common habit of hiking alone in the woods, often outside cell phone range. I always wear low-top hiking books for the support they provide to the feet, but I may add high tops, and never again will I venture into the forest in shorts. Heavy jeans add a layer of protection against snakebite, and they have the added benefit of helping to repel the almost always present red bugs and ticks.

The population density of the eastern diamondback is not high. For instance, in a four year study of snakes observed on a three mile stretch of rural roads in prime diamondback habitat — upland pine woods— in Hernando County, only one diamondback was observed (Enge). A similar study using slightly different techniques found only two, whereas the studies found 33 and 197 Florida black racers, respectively. There is, however, no reason to be complacent, because the authors of this study believed the diamondback population had been undercounted.

The pupils of the eastern diamondback stand like vertical slits, a trait shared in Florida only by the other four species of pit viper. Of the four, two are regarded as relatively venal and two as nonfatal. Put the water moccasin and the canebrake rattler in the potent category. Old timers claim a dog struck by a cottonmouth moccasin has a fair chance of survival, but no chance if hit by a diamondback. The canebrake is the southern name for the timber rattler. In our area it inhabits swampy locales, including (obviously) canebrakes. In the north it is considered only mildly venomous but laboratory tests show its venom to be deadly. The copperhead is a northern species that just barely penetrates the upper tier of Florida counties. Its bite is very mild, as venomous serpents go. The pygmy rattler averages only 12–18 inches in length, but it makes up for its diminutive size with its adaptability and an outrageously touchy nature. These things can be found everywhere — in urban and suburban areas as well as the countryside. Nursery plants often harbor this unwelcome stowaway. This little fellow is as feisty as the diamondback is retiring. It can be counted on to strike without bothering to shake its diminutive tail, which may not be recognizable as a rattle even if heard. Aside from in garden centers, bites have been and frequently are recorded in backyards and even nursing homes. Fortunately, the venom is not considered extremely dangerous unless the victim is in a debilitated state. Probably most reading this do not need to be told to seek medical treatment, if bitten by one of these little guys. Many rattlesnake fatalities occur to those who are complacent about their bites. In a study of eight recent rattlesnake-caused deaths in Arizona, three turned out to be experienced snake handlers who did not seek treatment.

The Centers for Disease Control recommends that anyone bit by a poisonous snake should first of all keep his wits (How to). Proper attention will, in almost all instances, save the victim's life. Observe the bite area. Remove venom that may be on the skin. Remove all jewelry in case swelling makes it impossible to get off later and cause serious problems. Keep the injured area (a limb in almost all cases) below the heart. Do not engage in violent physical activity, such as trying to kill the snake for purposes of identification. Killing the snake, though useful, is not necessary because all pit viper bites are treated more or less the same — and the coral snake is very distinctive. Get to a hospital emergency room for observation and probably injection with antivenin, and treatment for anaphylactic reactions (to the antivenin) if necessary. Treatment within the first two hours is essential for best results.

Scientists in Singapore conducted a study of Asian folk cures for snake bite (Samy). The venom they chose, probably because it happened to be the easiest to obtain, was that of the eastern diamondback. Preparations were made from a number of plants reputed to be used for snake bite in folk medicine. The result was injected into lab mice and a lethal dose of venom administered. Surprisingly, several of the plants gave the mice almost complete immunity to diamondback venom. The most effective was something called false sarsaparilla, and coming in second was the gloriosa lily. Though native to Asia (and Africa), the gloriosa lily has long been grown in Florida gardens. A bit further north but covering the range of the eastern diamondback, it freezes to its roots in the winter but comes back as a perennial. It is not outside the realm of possibility that medical technicians may devise an expedient self-treatment for snakebite from this or other plants, which would be a real boon for outdoorsmen and third-world folks outside the range of convenient medical care. Only recently has rattlesnake venom been studied for its medical properties. Owing to its effects on the circulatory system, much may be learned from such studies.

Miami's Southwest 8th Street has long been known as the Tamiami Trail. On the far west fringe of the city, the trail crosses Krome Avenue running north from Homestead. Sometime in the 1990s, the Miccosukee tribe built a casino on the northwest quadrant. Hundreds of thousands of patrons are drawn to the casino and hotel complex every year, enough to provide every Miccosukee man, woman and child, about $50,000 in income. Also drawn to the spot are a variety of people not interested in gaming. One of these was 36-year-old Justo (or Jose) Padron. He was CEO of Tamiami Medical, a corporation which had billed the U.S. government more than $7 million dollars, mostly for therapy for HIV patients, and $2.3 million dollars had been paid to his company, with more than a third of a million dollars in cash showing in the company's ledgers. Padron had an unusual background for a CEO, having been arrested more than a dozen times since 1989 (Prosecution). He'd been convicted of such crimes as burglary, robbery and drug possession. He was classified as an habitual felon by the state of Florida, and the feds had seized Tamiami Medical's books. Padron was in the parking lot of the casino trying to steal a car for a quick getaway. But a vigilant security guard called police, who arrived, catching the miscreant CEO in the act. An accomplice wisely surrendered. But Padron had violated parole. If caught, he'd go to jail. He took off running. Police followed. Arriving at the lake surrounding the property, the police stopped. But Padron boldly leapt into the water. Police heard snapping sounds. Then they heard anguished cries. What was left of Padron's body was later recovered along with two alligators, neither quite ten feet long.

The American alligator is one of the world's 23 species of crocodilians (Classification). The crocodilian order hearkens back 250 million years, with the appearance of the archosaurs, ancestors of both the crocodilians and the dinosaurs. The crocodillians assumed their modern form about 100 million years ago (*Alligator mississippiensis*, American Alligator). This makes the order one of the oldest on the globe. They are frequently referred to as saurians, because they are the closest living relative of the dinosaurs. In the days before a giant asteroid plunged into the Yucatan and destroyed the dinosaurs' world order, crocodilians swam in cypress swamps beside their larger reptile brethren. The dinosaurs perished, but sixty-five million years later the crocodilians (and the cypress) are still with us, and often they are the apex predator in the ecosystems in which they are found. It may be useful for those living in (or visiting) Florida to keep in mind that the alligator is the apex predator in all watery habitats in the state including aquatic-terrestrial interface. Something else to bear in mind is that a human falls on the outside edge of the general size and shape of the preferred prey, which range from insects and small crustaceans to large mammals.

Quiz show science frequently ponders such important questions as whether alligators are crocodiles—and vice versa. The correct answer is that all alligators are crocodilians, but no crocodile is an alligator, because the order breaks into two families, the alligator and the crocodile. There are eight species on the alligator side of the family, six of which are referred to as caimans and live in the neotropics below the Rio Grande. The black caiman of South America is superficially almost identical to our American alligator in size and shape, though not the closest in terms of scientific classification. That designation falls to the Chinese alligator, which lives in the Yangtze River basin and has been almost extirpated in the wild. Though quite small as crocodillians go, growing to just over six feet in length, the Chinese alligator is responsible for one of the most familiar reptile icons on earth, the Chinese dragon. It seems likely that these little reptiles, in days gone by, accounted for many a missing Chinese peasant, if not in fact then at least in myth.

The American alligator grows much larger than its Asian counterpart. It ranks third (along with the black caiman and probably the American crocodile) in terms of size of the 23 crocodilians. Males grow to be twelve to thirteen feet in length, while females usually are less than ten feet. Occasionally a fourteen-foot gator is spotted and larger ones are reported from time to time. There have been historical claims of alligators measuring seventeen feet in Florida and nineteen feet in Louisiana. Both alligator species are much more cold-tolerant than any other crocodilian. The range of the American alligator takes in the whole southeastern coastal plain, going as far north as northern coastal North Carolina through the southern half of Georgia to the extreme corner of southeastern Oklahoma and lowland eastern Texas. Those northern areas experience very cold weather, at least occasionally, every winter, and now and then prolonged cold snaps. The alligator is equipped to deal with it. Scientists have shown that gators are capable of exposing their nostrils in freezing water (American Alligator). The rest of the body hangs down at a 30 degree angle into relatively warmer water. The more normal way gators deal with cold weather is by tunneling under banks. There they lie in a state of brumation. Even as far south as Central Florida gators are scarce in mid winter, being holed up in their relatively warm underground bunkers. Mild periods might find them out on their favorite beach, catching some rays. In far south Florida they are pretty common all winter long. Driving along the Tamiami Trail (U.S. 41 from Naples to Miami), you can sometimes count gators in the hundreds lying on the bank of the canal, warming up in the sun.

Most of the tropical crocodilians are green to grayish in color. The darker color of the gator may be useful in soaking up northern sun. For their wide distribution, alligators are most common in Louisiana and Florida. A useful index for their relative population may be nuisance gator calls. In an average year, Oklahoma has 4 to 6, Texas 460, South Carolina 750, Louisiana 3,000 to 4,000 and Florida 17,000 (Langley). The alligator can be found in every county and area of Florida including the Florida Keys. There is some evidence that the south Florida climate may not be optimal for them. Gators in Everglades National Park tend to be somewhat thinner than central Florida creatures, owing, it is believed at least in part, to heat stress, although the relative lack of nutrition in the Glades, which is not nearly as rich in food sources as the cable channel nature shows would have you believe, may also be responsible.

Alligators can be found in almost any aquatic environment, ranging from spongy marsh and shallow swamps to mangrove-fringed saltwater bays. Many true crocodiles, such as the American crocodile, which shares the gator's south Florida range, have salt extruding glands. Alligators lack these so their forays into salt and brackish water are short-lived, but I've known one gator in Everglades National park that spent its days in a cattail-lined pond and which regularly at night crawled across the campground at Flamingo to Florida Bay, making for an interesting sight for those tenting in its path. Large bull gators hang out in deep water (American Alligator). Large females stay in open water until successfully bred. Then they move to marsh or lake edges where they construct beehive shaped nests up to a yard in diameter. The nests consist of mud and decaying vegetation which, along with summer temperatures, incubate the eggs. An average nest temperature below 88 degrees in the mid trimester of the sixty-day incubation period will produce all female offspring. A range of 90 to 92 will produce all males, and a temperature above 93 will yield a higher proportion of females. On hearing the young peeping in their shells, the mother gator, which lurks about to protect the nest from raccoons or other predators, may open them. She takes the young in her mouth and carries them to water. Sometimes she helps the neonate break through the leathery shell of the egg. Gator mothers have also been known to bring food to their young, which are perfectly capable of feeding themselves by hunting small prey, insects, snails, minnows and so on. A mother gator looks after her young for at least a year. She keeps track of little ones by clicks made by her brood. Woe to anything that attempts to molest her children. Subadults large enough to fend for themselves generally remain among aquatic weeds and away from potentially cannibalistic large bull gators.

Alligators mature sexually at about six feet. But as with humans and other social animals, simply reaching sexual maturity is no guarantee of successful courtship and mating. The breeding season falls in April and May. Sexually receptive females move into deeper water seeking bull gators. The courtship, again like human courtship, tends to be long and drawn out. It involves body posturing, snout rubbing, water slapping, and bellowing. The process requires hours or days to complete, and about a third of alligator nests contain eggs with more than one sperm donor, all of which come from only the larger bull gators. A male ten feet or less has almost no chance of siring a clutch.

The American alligator, like the beaver and the bison, is one of the few non-human animals capable of significantly altering its environment (Campbell). As noted above, alligators can burrow under banks. They also engineer pools in the Everglades and perhaps elsewhere. The Everglades, proper, is a large prairie mostly of sedges and grasses that is inundated only part of the year. In the very dry period in the spring before the rains begin to fall in May or early June, the small ponds created by gators act as a significant refuge for aquatic species, as well as for the alligator. These pools, known prosaically as alligator holes, can be as small as six or seven feet across and just a foot or so deep, to many yards wide and scratched down to bedrock. They may be occupied by a lone bull male or by a female looking after her year's brood of hatchlings. Aside from the gator, the holes provide homes for wading birds, fish, amphibians and aquatic insects, and gator nests also provide habitat above the level of the rising waters later in the summer. A gator hole — usually with mother gator and brood — can be found at the end of the boardwalk into the Fakahatchee swamp adjacent to Collier-Seminole State Park east of Naples.

Crocodillians (including alligators), unlike other reptiles, have a four-chambered heart, a feature shared with birds and mammals. The crocodilian heart has a special feature. It allows oxygen to be pumped only to the vital organs. This means a large gator can submerge and remain underwater for a couple of hours. The larger the gator the longer it can remain underwater without breathing. Pressure sensors on the gators' snouts allow them to target prey underwater, and sensors in other parts of their bodies may also assist. They have keen eyesight, used to spot prey above water, and their vertical iris expands at night to give them owl-like vision. The creatures' brain, however, weighs less than one-half ounce. This could mean the alligator and other crocodilians, though advanced in some sensory elements, are incapable of learning. That has been the long-time assumption of very well-regarded scientists such as Archie Carr and Thomas Barbour. They posited that the alligator, like most creatures, had a "natural fear of man." This assumption was made by observers in the early to mid twentieth century.

The very first European to write about alligators, a putative member of the ill-fated French attempt to colonize Florida by the name of LeMoyne, reported that Indians were terrified of alligators because of frequent alligator attacks (Himes). He left pictures of beasts more reminiscent of Chinese dragons than the reptiles normally spotted in the Sunshine State. Two centuries later, William Bartram, in experiences gained just before the American Revolution, also reported monster alligators which attempted to "molest" him, as the Quaker naturalist quaintly put it. John Muir, during his cross-Florida tramp shortly after the Civil War, reported that black people and dogs exhibited great fear of alligators because they were specially targeted by the beasts. By the mid twentieth century, however, naturalists claimed that alligators had a natural fear of man and could be depended on to retreat in the presence of humans.

What had happened in the meantime? The economy of early Florida was supported by extractive industries. Most of these were on the cottage level, and chief among them was hunting and trapping. The most valuable animal, both on account of its numbers and the dollar value of its hide and meat, was the alligator. The Civil War helped populate Florida, as Confederate draft dodgers filtered throughout the state, pushing into locales that previously had been occupied by the Seminoles. These folks were well-armed and supported themselves on a catch-as-catch-can basis. For the best part of a hundred years, they waged war on alligators. Whether the alligator changed from a vicious predator upon humans to a creature that is afraid of them is a judgment beyond my capability. What is clear is that the species sensed its role had changed once the alligator became a protected species, which occurred in the mid 1960s on the state level and in the 1970s on the federal level. At that time, the alligator was believed to be on the point of extinction.

In a few short years, the creatures were being seen once again throughout the state. I even saw them in the canal alongside Red Road in the heart of Miami by the early 1980s. Scientists now estimate that about 300,000 alligators inhabited the state in the '60s. As early as 1976, biologists from the Florida Game and Freshwater Fish Commission puzzled over the disturbing new data. This data included the unthinkable, alligator attacks on humans, some of which had resulted in death. In particular, they revisited the old assumption that gators were docile beasts, citing LeMoyne and Bartram. Most of us continued in the belief that all such alligator attacks were anomalous. We believed that the attacks could be accounted for by gators going for mistaken targets or gators having been fed by humans. Whether you want to call the alligators' incredible response to a changing environment intelligent or not, it is clear that the creature has the ability to readily adapt. It is equally clear that when the alligator feels no pressure to avoid humans, it can seek them as prey.

A recent study by an Australian medical team may provide some needed perspective regarding the relative viciousness of the American alligator (Caldicott and Croser). Northern Australia is inhabited by one of the nastiest menaces in the reptilian world, the estuarine or saltwater crocodile. Members of this species, during World War II, dispatched 980 Japanese troops pinned down by British fire in a mangrove swamp off Burma. (Naturally, as with all such claims, not all accept the verdict of English naturalist Bruce Wright, who was with the British forces.) A lone saltwater croc called Whiteback—like some saurian Moby Dick—is claimed to have devoured thirteen in Sarawak, Malaysia. I personally know of two islanders who were fishing, one inland in a freshwater stream, the other spearfishing at night, killed by these extremely efficient and vicious predators.

For that, the authors of the Australian paper take American alligators very seriously. For instance, they note that a fairly typical bull gator of just under twelve feet can exert a crushing power with its jaws of about 2,000 pounds, enough force to smash "a pig's skull with ease [or] lift a small utility vehicle." Coupled with the well-known death roll, this crushing force allows the reptiles to tear off chunks of larger animals. The scientists cite the American alligator as one of three species of crocodilians worldwide known as threats to humans. Strangely enough, there have been many more documented attacks by American alligators in Florida than there have been attacks by saltwater crocodiles in Australia. For instance during the thirty-odd years of the study, only 64 people were attacked by salties in the three northern states of Australia; only 17, or about a quarter, were fatal. In Florida during the same period there were hundreds of alligator attacks, with about the same number of fatalities. In Australia, only the largest and most powerful saltwater crocodiles were involved in the attacks. In Florida, alligators as small as six feet attacked humans. In both Australia and Florida, most attacks were made on people swimming or standing in the water. However, in both places humans on land were also objects of the reptiles' attention. In Australia, one person sleeping on a beach was killed by a saltie, and in another incident, a crocodile entered a tent and killed both of the sleeping inmates. In the past I have camped on sandbars in alligator-infested waters, and I have slept on the deck of my houseboat when I could hear bull gators roaring. Neither of those things will occur in the future — at least not unless I'm convinced a gator cannot invade my space. Nor will I dangle my hands or feet off a boat or dock. Formerly, I would not allow dogs in the water near me. Now I will not allow them near the bank. I will continue canoeing through alligator-inhabited swamps, but I will not be as cocksure of myself as I was in the past. People spend tens of thousands of hours in prime gator habitat without incident. There is no reason for undue alarm, but there is no good reason to take unnecessary chances either.

One fine September day two fishermen, trolling two miles off Hollywood Beach, Florida, got a strike. The fish that strike produced was a lunker. It turned out to be a 9.5-foot-long, 370-pound tiger shark. Curious, as fishermen frequently are, about what their catch had been eating, they cut into the stomach. Tiger sharks are the original garbage mouths. One was found to have in its stomach "two empty cans, a plastic bottle, two burlap sacks, a squid, and an 8-inch fish" (tiger shark). This one had a size 10½ high-top Adidas tennis shoe, black and white in color, in its stomach (Iscan). It also had a white gym sock, and inside the sock was a human foot, complete with undigested tissue and hair and the connecting two leg bones. A femur, presumably from the other leg, was also in the shark's stomach. A shark's tooth was embedded in the foot. Forensic science was able to determine that the victim was a white male about five feet nine inches tall in his late twenties. The victim was, however, never identified.

Of the three species of shark most dangerous to man, the most notorious, the great white, rarely enters Florida waters. It is a temperate-zone creature that prefers cooler waters, although the occasional great white will nose around Florida coasts in the winter. Few people are in the water then and so its threat potential here is practically nil. The other two dangerous Elasmobranches are the tiger shark and the bull shark. Both call Florida home in a big way.

The tiger shark is a member of the subclass ominously called requiem sharks. It has a blunt nose with a heavy body forward and a gracefully tapering fuselage that ends in a distinctive sickle-shaped tail. Characteristically, its sides are striped or spotted. The tiger shark's teeth and bite pattern are distinctive. Each tooth is viciously curved with saw-like edges and a deep notch on the outer margin. The upper and lower teeth match in size and shape and decrease in size as you move backwards. Gestation requires fourteen to sixteen months, producing ten to 80 pups. This can be a very big fish. Mature females grow to fourteen feet. Males reach maturity at seven to nine feet and females at eight to ten feet, with weights ranging up to 1,400 pounds. The biggest specimens may reach seventeen feet and weigh a ton. The tiger shark inhabits a wide range of habitats and locales. Although basically a tropical species, it moves north during the summer months and returns in cooler periods. Because of its proclivity for warmer climes, it is absent from Europe and the Mediterranean, but can be found in the open Pacific and on many other coasts, including Florida's. It seems to prefer murky inlets and harbors.

The fact that the tiger shark is a large, opportunistic feeder and that it hangs around coastal waters where people swim makes it a danger to humans. More attacks are attributed to tigers than any other shark except for the great white. It is entirely possible, however, that the most dangerous shark species is neither the tiger nor the great white. That distinction probably belongs to the bull shark, another of the aptly named requiem sharks. The bull shark generally sticks to the tropics and subtropics, except in eastern North America, where it ranges into temperate waters in the summer. This shark is somewhat smaller than the tiger, the very largest growing to eleven and a half feet and weighing 500 pounds (Bull Shark). The average male weighs in at 200 pounds and is seven feet in length. Its snout is blunt, being wider than long. That, coupled with its feisty nature, gives it the common name of "bull." It has extremely small eyes with presumably weak eyesight. This probably owes to the fact that it frequently inhabits murky coastal waters and presumably does not greatly rely on its eyesight to feed. The relatively small size of this species should be no comfort to beachgoers. Its rather generic "shark-like" shape makes it difficult to identify accurately, and its habit of nosing close to shore, even appearing in freshwater, coupled with its extremely aggressive nature account for specialists' upgrading this species on the list of maneaters.

Almost certainly the bull shark is Florida's number one attack shark. Although extremely dangerous, it is a quite interesting species. Bull sharks, for instance, can live for extended periods far away from the sea. It has long been known that sharks inhabit two large lakes in Nicaragua. The resemblance of those sharks to the bull shark was noted. However, only recently has it been determined that the so-called Nicaraguan shark is indeed the bull shark. Individual specimens go to and from the Caribbean via a rapids-filled stream, leaping like salmon. Most fishes, whether marine or freshwater, keep the same balance of salt in their bloodstream as occurs in the outside environment, a process called osmoregulation. Scientist have learned that the bull shark manages to maintain its salt content in freshwater by urinating frequently (Heupel). The bull shark is sometimes called the Zambezi shark, presumably from its residence in that large river in south central Africa. The bull shark has also been seen in freshwater in North America, having been reported north of St. Louis in the Mississippi. One claim even put one in the Great Lakes. Probably the most famous example of the bull shark escaping the notoriety that should have been its due occurred in New Jersey in 1916, in a series of four shark attacks. Peter Benchley was inspired by them to pen *Jaws*. As usual, a great white was fingered for these attacks, and for good reason. A great white was caught nearby with human remains in its belly. Two of the attacks occurred up a coastal stream forty feet wide. This is bull-shark, not great-white, habitat. For this reason authorities now believe that, by an incredible coincidence, two sharks were in involved in those four human deaths, and that a bull shark was likely one of them.

In Florida, bull sharks have been reported far up the St. Johns, which for some reason harbors many other salt or brackish species such as stingrays, needlefish, blue crabs, croakers, and, on occasion, enough redfish to support a temporary fishery. The Caloosahatchee has long been known to be frequented by bull sharks and no doubt the other large (and perhaps small) rivers in Florida have a larger population of bull sharks than believed.

So what are your odds of taking a dip in a Florida stream or off a Florida beach and ending up as a subject for a Peter Benchley sequel? You probably will not be disappointed to learn the answer is very slim. Despite hype such as this found in a blurb for a Princeton University Press book called *The Shark Watcher's Handbook*— Avoid Florida. Almost 40 percent of recorded shark attacks have occurred in Florida's waters. The combination of 1,277 miles of coast, dangerous sharks, and millions of bathers leads to the inevitable"—your chances, according to the same blurb, of being struck by lightning in Florida are six times higher (Shark Watchers). In fact, most of the supposed shark "attacks" that occur in Florida are mere shark bites inflicted on surfers by small species such as blacktips or spinners (Shark Attacks). Surfers seek out turbulent waters, and the flash of their hands or feet resemble baitfish in the murky water. The fact that the shark attack file is located in Gainesville may well be the reason these minor bites, all or many of which are documented in the media, end up in the file.

Of the 357 attacks listed by the file in the three most active Florida counties, only one fatality was recorded, and that was in 1934. In fact, there have only been thirteen documented fatalities from shark bite in Florida in more than a century. Those thirteen deaths appear few compared to the 111 Florida bicycle-related fatalities in a fairly recent year. Homicide deaths in Florida average about a thousand, more or less, per year, and about three thousand vehicular deaths are recorded in the state per year. Clearly, of the three threatening creatures discussed here, sharks are the least fatal — and the easiest to avoid. Stay out of salt water and you have a 99 percent certainty that you will not become a meal for these toothy killers. By the way, those minor bites suffered by surfers and others, while rarely life threatening, should not be taken lightly. Any trauma in salt water runs a high risk of infection from a whole slew of potent bacteria, not the least of which are two related to cholera, *Aeromonas hydrophila* (brackish water only) and *Vibrio vulnificus* (Aeromonas and Vibrio). These "gram-negative" bacteria are the contaminants in the oyster population that force a closing of the Apalachicola and other shellfish beds now and then. More than half of those with a severe case of ingested bacteria die. The mortality rate for serious infections, such as can occur from a shark bite, runs about 25 percent. Emergency room physicians frequently put shark bite victims on an antibiotic regime immediately after diagnosis. In short, any shark bite, as well as any other significant salt (or fresh) water injury such as coral cuts, stingray puncture and the like should be treated with a great deal of respect.

Those with a tendency toward anxiety have better reason to dwell on alligator attacks. Fatal alligator encounters in the past fifty years, while less than two dozen, show a disturbing trend toward the more frequent. Even more unsettling to those of us who like to worry about things are the number of attacks on land. This chapter began with the story of a man walking his dog near his home who was dragged into a marsh by a gator. That man violated, no doubt without thinking, the rule of taking dogs near water. The reptile probably was after the dog but got the less-nimble owner by default when his pet danced away. Not far from the venue of that attack, a landscaper was working in a yard with a waterfront when she was assaulted by a twelve-foot monster gator and hauled into the nearby lake (Harding). Two others working nearby heard her screams and saved her from the beast. But she succumbed later to the infection that set in to her massive wounds; bacteria similar to those found in salt water occur in fresh water and alligators' notoriously germ-laden mouths.

The rule of thumb used to be to not allow dogs and children in the water together. The new rule of thumb probably should be not to allow pets or children near water unless you are absolutely sure no gators are in the vicinity. If aquatic weeds (lilies, pickerel weed and the like) are present, assume gators may be lurking about. This is not sensationalism; this is good sense. Statistics regarding snake bite were more difficult to obtain, possibly owing to the fact that unlike shark or gator attacks, each bite is not recorded religiously by the media.

The estimates of the total number of bites nationwide varies wildly. Most "authorities" agree that about a third are caused by people trying to handle snakes, and that alcohol is frequently a factor. The best recent study was conducted by an MD at a Tennessee research facility (Daley). North Carolina clocks in with the highest rate of snakebite at nineteen per 100,000 residents, possibly because of snake-handling religious practices. The national average was four per 100,000. In the two recent decades covered by the study, Texas had the most snakebite fatalities with 17, and Florida came next with 14. Each had less than one fatality per year. A study conducted in Florida in the mid 1950s showed three deaths in each of the two years in that study (Parrish). This might indicate snakebite treatment is better today than fifty years ago. It seems just as likely to me to reflect the changing economics and land uses in the state. Even as more people move into rural subdivisions, fewer people make a living by extractive industries and so are less likely to annoy an eastern diamondback in a face-to-face encounter, and probably the mentality has changed a bit too. In days gone by, people considered they had a duty to kill every diamondback they saw. Nowadays the live-and-let-live mentality holds sway, which is a boon to both serpent and man. Even recreational use of the outdoors has become more mechanized, with hunters proudly sitting in car stands and crashing through the woods astride four-wheelers. I have even noticed a decline in urban outdoorsmen, as I meet many fewer citified hikers on my forays into the woods, and areas that formerly were quite busy on weekends, especially on sunny mid-winter weekends, stay quite unpopulated year-round — while RV campgrounds and the like become increasingly more populated.

Two crocodilian species inhabit Florida. The least common, the American crocodile, at one time lived as far north as Cape Canaveral, but in the last century it was almost entirely eliminated from our fair state. A remnant population hung on in the toe of Florida. For many years members of this species were considered complete recluses (*Crocodylus*). The only way an ordinary citizen got a glimpse of one was when it collided with his automobile in that mangrove-fronted stretch of U.S. 1 that passes from Homestead to Key Largo, and this situation was feared to perhaps doom the ever-diminishing population. Now, however, the crocodile has at least temporarily made a comeback. In a recent camping trip to the Everglades, I saw one sunning himself near the marina, and others on islands in Florida Bay. Historically in Florida the gator has been regarded as the more aggressive species, but rangers in the Everglades told me the crocodiles at Flamingo drove the gators away. This is more in keeping with the crocodile's fearsome reputation worldwide. To date, there has never been a human death attributed to crocodiles in Florida, and in fact, I have not even found evidence of a crocodile attack. This may change now that the creatures are becoming more common and habituated to humans in places like Flamingo.

A serious — but funny — wildlife menace to humans in Florida is flying fish. I am not talking about those small, winged fishes of the open ocean. Rather I am talking about the kind of large fishes, of many species, Florida has been known for since time immemorial. Years ago, while attempting to launch my canoe on the Suwannee River near Manatee Springs State Park, I witnessed one of the most amazing things I've ever seen in Florida. A silver-colored, fish-like creature bolted from the water and then plunged back into the Suwannee. I estimated it was ten feet long. Using the snake principle that your estimate is at least twice as long as the real object reduced the footage to a mere five feet. I had no idea what I had seen. But I paddled just a few hundred yards and decided I'd had enough for that day. That was back in the 1980s. I had no idea that a species of sturgeon, called the gulf sturgeon, lived in that river and other rivers of the panhandle (Gulf Sturgeon). The gulf sturgeon can grow to eight feet, weigh 200 pounds, and frequently, for unknown reasons, leap up to six feet into the air. The color of this sturgeon is bronze or brownish rather than silver. The gulf sturgeon has been completely protected since 1991, and nowadays in the late spring through the fall, jumping adult sturgeon are a common sight on the lower Suwanee. Also common on that river are speeding boats (or jet skis) with the requisite skimpily clad sunworshippers in the bow. Signs warning of the danger from acrobatic, 200-pound fish are posted everywhere. Many boats do not appreciably slow, nor do the Ra-worshippers abandon their posts on the foredeck. Occasionally, one is knocked for a loop. According to a New York Times article, "Injuries have included a broken pelvis, a fractured arm and a slashed throat" (Goodnough). Boaters continue to roar down the Suwanee and other rivers, and—can you believe this?—gripe that this 200 million-year-old inhabitant of the river threatens their safety. Now and then leaping fish pose a danger elsewhere in the state, such as recently in the Keys when a large eagle ray struck and killed a woman (Goodnough).

The Burmese python is native to Burma, Malaysia, and Thailand (Burmese python). They are among the largest snake species on the planet, commonly growing to 20 feet, with a weight of about 190 pounds. Like the pit vipers, they have sense organs that home in on warm-blooded prey. They are opportunistic feeders, generally seeking warm-blooded birds and mammals. Thanks to the Internet, a widely distributed photo of a python that attempted to swallow a man-sized alligator shows they occasionally attack reptiles, and that they also are a potential threat to humans. The occasional python has long inhabited the Sunshine State, and I have personal knowledge of individual specimens, including a twenty footer, captured or killed in Central Florida going back to the 1980s. These snakes were probably released (or escaped) into the wild by pet owners who couldn't figure out what to do with a pet that had outgrown its welcome. However, in the past decade, pythons have begun to breed in the Everglades (Serpents). This fact worries park officials, who have captured 350 of the large critters to date, and figure at least 3,500 remain in the wild. Burmese pythons, to maintain themselves, must eat their weight in a year (Revkin). After devouring a large rodent or bird, they curl up in the sun. The additional warmth is needed to help digest their catch.

Burmese pythons are just one of many exotic species that have attempted to colonize the Sunshine State. Most find the local creatures too competitive and fail to establish a foothold. Others do very well at first. The alarm, sometimes hysterically, is raised. An example of this is the walking catfish. This creature was believed by usually level-headed biologists to pose a big threat to the state's ecosystem. The ease with which it appeared to crowd out native species in individual locations and then move on to the next wetland—by walking overland on its fins—supported this view. Nowadays, the walking catfish is well established in the Sunshine State, but local predators have adapted to its presence, and natural controls are in place. It is still not welcome, but it is no longer considered a dire threat. It remains to be seen whether the Burmese python will follow a similar pattern. My guess is that it probably will, after time, simply become another interesting Florida curiosity. In the meantime, I think I'll make double sure no reptile, of any kind, can gain entry to my camper while I am camping in the Florida wilds. You probably should do the same.

## WORKS CITED AND CONSULTED

Achenbach, Joel. "One Man's Pet, Another's Invasive Species." *The Washington Post*, April 18, 2008: A1.
"Alligator Attacks Fact Sheet." Florida Fish and Wildlife Conservation Commission. November 29, 2005.
"Alligator mississippiensis." http://www.flmnh.ufl.edu/cnhc/csp_amis.htm#name
"American Alligator." University of Georgia Savannah River Ecology Laboratory.
"Bioluminescent algae leads to bull shark attack." Where Light Meets Dark.com. http://www.google.com/imgres?imgurl=http://www.wherelightmeetsdark.com/images/news watch/Andrea_Lynch__bull_shark_victim_sm.jpg&imgrefurl=http://www.wherelight meetsdark.com/index.php%3Fmodule%3Dnewswatch%26NW_user_op%3Dview%2 6NW_id%3D334&h=290&w=400&sz=21&tbnid=vNgYrI8A7k0J:&tbnh=90&tbnw=12 4&prev=/images%3Fq%3Dbull%2Bshark&hl=en&sa=X&oi=image_result&resnum=1 &ct=image&cd=3
Blech, Jörg. "Serpents in Paradise: Burmese Pythons Invade Florida." *Der Spiegl*. http://www.spiegel.de/international/spiegel/0,1518,456018,00.html.
"Bodies of 2 Women Found Sunday; Third Woman's Body Found on Wednesday." Associated Press. May 14, 2006.
Boey, Valerie. "Hillsborough County Deputy Warns Others to be Careful of Snake Bites." http://www.tampabays10.com/news/local/article.aspx?storyid=53246.
"Bull Shark." http://www.flmnh.ufl.edu/fish/gallery/Descript/bullshark/bullshark.htm.
"Burmese Python." Honolulu Zoo. http://www.honoluluzoo.org/burmese_python.htm.
Butler, Joseph A., Todd W. Hull, and Richard Franz. "Neonate Aggregations and Maternal Attendance of Young in the Eastern Diamondback Rattlesnake, Crotalus adamanteus." *Copeia* 1 (1995): 196–198.
Caldicott, David G.E., et al. "Crocodile Attack in Australia: An Analysis of Its Incidence and Review of the Pathology and Management of Crocodilian Attacks." *Wilderness and Environmental Medicine* 16: 143–59.
Caldicott, David G.E., Ravi Mahajani, and Marie Kuhn. "The Anatomy of a Shark Attack: a Case Report and Review of the Literature." *Injury* 32: 445–453.
Campbell, Mark R., and Frank J. Mazzotti. "Characterization of Natural and Artificial Alligator Holes." *Southeastern Naturalist* 3: 583–594.
Centers for Disease Control and Prevention. "How to Prevent or Respond to a Snake Bite." http://www.bt.cdc.gov/disasters/snakebite.asp.
"*Crotalus adamanteus*, eastern diamondback rattlesnake." http://animaldiversity.ummz.umich.edu/site/accounts/information/Crotalus_adamanteus.html.
"*Crocodylus acutus*" http://www.flmnh.ufl.edu/cnhc/csp_cacu.htm.
"*Crocodylus niloticus*" http://www.flmnh.ufl.edu/cnhc/csp_cnil.htm.
Cruz-Martínez, A., X. Chiappa-Carrara, and V. Arenas-Fuentes. "Age and Growth of the

Bull Shark, *Carcharhinus leucas*, from Southern Gulf of Mexico." *Northwest Atlantic Fish Science* 35: 367–374.
"Current Classification." htttp://people.clemson.edu/~jwfoltz/WFB300/subjects/crocs/crocs.htm.
Daley, Brian James, and Jacob Barbee. "Snakebite." eMedicine from WebMD. http://www.emedicine.com/med/TOPIC2143.HTM.
"Death ray: Killed by a flying giant." *The Daily Telegraph* (Australia). March 22, 2008.
"Diamondback Rattlesnakes—Largest North American Venomous Reptile." http://www.tigerhomes.org/animal/diamondback-rattlesnake.com.
"Eastern Coral Snake." http://people.wcsu.edu/pinout/herpetology/mfulvius/index.htm.
Enge, Kevin M. and Kristin N. Wood. "A Pedestrian Survey of an Upland Snake Community." *Southeastern Naturalist* 1: 365–380.
"Facts About Shark Attacks." Princeton University Press. http://press.princeton.edu/releases/m7256.html.
"Fatal Alligator Attacks." http://www.southeasternoutdoors.com/wildlife/reptiles/fatal-alligator-attacks.html.
"Fatal Rattlesnake Bites." http://www.southeasternoutdoors.com/wildlife/reptiles/fatal-rattlesnake-bites.html.
Federal Drug Administration. "*Aeromonas hydrophila*." http://www.cfsan.fda.gov/~mow/chap17.html.
———. "*Vibrio vulnificus*." http://www.cfsan.fda.gov/~mow/chap10.html.
"Florida Alligators." http://www.goldiproductions.com/comingbackalive/animalalligator.html.
"Florida Law Enforcement Agency Uniform Crime Reports 1980 to 2005." http://www.disastercenter.com/crime/flcrime.htm.
Florida Museum of Natural History. "Tiger Shark." http://www.flmnh.ufl.edu/fish/Gallery/Descript/Tigershark/tigershark.htm.
Florida Wildlife Commission. "Division Of Law Enforcement Field Operations. Weekly Report. May 12–18, 2006." http://myfwc.com/law/Weekly/2006/OPERATIONSWEEKLY5-19-06.pdf.
Flynn, Hal. "Media Finally Reports Shark Attacked by Man!" http://scholar.google.com/scholar?q=alligator+attacks+in+florida&hl=en&lr=&start=20&sa=N.
Gillingham, James C., Charles C. Carpenter and James B. Murphy. "Courtship, Male Combat and Dominance in the Western Diamondback Rattlesnake, *Crotalus atrox*." *Journal of Herpetology* 17: 265–270.
Goodnough, Abby. "Summertime. Fish Jumping. That's Trouble." *The New York Times*, July 4, 2007. http://www.nytimes.com/2007/07/04/us/04sturgeon.html.
"Gulf Sturgeon Facts." http://cars.er.usgs.gov/Marine_Studies/Sturgeon_FAQs/sturgeon_faqs.html.
Harding, Brett E., M.D., and Barbara Wolff. "Alligator Attacks in Southwest Florida." *Journal of Forensic Science* 51: 674–678.
Heupel, Michelle R., and Colin A. Simpfendorfer. "Movement and Distribution of Young Bull Sharks *Carcharhinus leucas* in a Variable Estuarine Environment." *Aquatic Biology* 1: 277–289.
Himes, Tommy C., and Kent Keenlyne. "Alligator Attacks on Humans in Florida." Southeast Association of Game and Fish Commissioners, thirtieth annual conference, 1976.
Huber, Daniel R., Christina L. Weggelaar, and Philip J. Motta. "Scaling of Bite Force in the Blacktip Shark *Carcharhinus limbatus*." *Zoology* 109: 109–119.
Hunter, Rod. "Sharks on the East Coast." http://www.surfingthemag.com/news/surfingpulse/shark-071305/index.html.
Iscan, M. Yagar, and Barbara W. McCabe. "Analysis of Human Remains Recovered from a Shark." *Forensic Science International* 72: 15–23.

James, Daniel. "A Review of Nuisance Alligator Management in the Southeastern United States." *Proceedings 4th International Urban Wildlife Symposium* (2004): 182–185.

Juckett, Gregory, and John G. Hancox. "Venomous Snakebites in the United States: Management Review and Update." *American Family Physician* 65 (April 1, 2002.) http://www.aafp.org/afp/20020401/1367.html.

Langley, Ricky L. "Alligator Attacks on Humans in the United States." *Wilderness & Environmental Medicine* 16: 119–125.

Noonburg, Greer E. "Management of Extremity Trauma and Related Infections Occurring in the Aquatic Environment." *Journal of the American Academy of Orthopaedic Surgeons* 13 (July/August 2005). http://www.jaaos.org/cgi/content/abstract/13/4/243.

O'Connell, Martin T., Travis D. Shepherd, Ann M.U. O'Connell, and Ransom A. Myers. "Long-term Declines in Two Apex Predators, Bull Sharks (*Carcharhinus leucas*) and Alligator Gar (*Atractosteus spatula*), in Lake Pontchartrain, an Oligohaline Estuary in Southeastern Louisiana." *Earth and Environmental Science* 30: 567–574.

Ogrosky, Kirk. "Prosecution and Defense of Criminal Health Care Fraud Cases: U.S. Department of Justice Perspectives for the Future of Enforcement." Health Care Compliance Association's 12th annual compliance institute, April 16, 2008. Washington D.C. http://www.compliance-institute.org/pastCIs/2008/post/W6/SessionW6.pdf.

O'Neil, Mary Elizabeth, Karin A. Mack, Julie Gilchrist, and Edward J. Wozniak. "Snake bite Injuries Treated in United States Emergency Departments, 2001–2004." *Wilderness and Environmental Medicine* 18: 281–287. http://www.wemjournal.org/wmsonline/?request=get-abstract&issn=1080-6032&volume=18&issue=4&page=281.

Parrish, Henry M. "On the Incidence of Poisonous Snakebites in Florida: Analysis of 241 Cases Occurring during 1954 and 1955." *American Journal of Tropical Medicine and Hygene* 6: 761–765. http://www.ajtmh.org/cgi/content/abstract/6/4/761.

Pillans, R.D., et al. "Rectal Gland Morphology of Freshwater and Seawater Acclimated Bull Sharks *Carcharhinus leucas*." *Journal of Fish Biology* 72: 1559–1571.

"Poisonous Snake Bites Elderly Woman." http://www.news4jax.com/news/13699006/detail.html.

"Pygmy Rattlesnake Bites Man at Wal-Mart." http://www.local6.com/news/9569525/detail.html.

"Rattlesnake Bites Woman Twice at Lowe's." http://www.local6.com/news/9792489/detail.html.

Revkin, Andrew C. "A Movable Beast: Asian Pythons Thrive in Florida." *The New York Times*, July 24, 2007: F1.

Rice, Aaron N., T. Luther Roberts, and Michael E. Dorcas. "Heating and Cooling Rates of Eastern Diamondback Rattlesnakes, *Crotalus adamanteus*." *Journal of Thermal Biology* 31: 501–505.

Samy, Ramar Perumal, et al. "Ethnobotanical Survey of Folk Plants for the Treatment of Snakebites in Southern Part of Tamilnadu, India." *Journal of Ethnopharmacology* 115: 302–312.

Sanchez, Elda E., et al. "The Efficacy of Two Antivenoms against the Venom of North American Snakes." *Toxicon* 41: 357–365.

Schmid, T.H., and F.L. Murru. "Bioenergetics of the Bull Shark, *Carcharhinus leucas*, Maintained in Captivity." *Zoo Biology* 13: 177–185.

"Shark Attacks." Florida Museum of Natural History. http://www.flmnh.ufl.edu/fish/sharks/isaf/isaf.htm.

"Sharks attack two teens at Florida beaches. Is it safe to go in the water?" *People*, July 11, 2005: 62–3.

"Snake Bite! A Man Survives Being Bitten by a Poisonous Snake." *Golf Digest*, July 1999. http://findarticles.com/p/articles/mi_m0HFI/is_7_50/ai_54949017.

Suncoast Herpetological Society. "Pre-Cautions and Helpful Facts." http://www.kingsnake.com/suncoastherpsociety/SHSven.htm
Taylor, Emily N., and Dale F. DeNardo. "Reproductive Ecology of Western Diamond-Backed Rattlesnakes (*Crotalus atrox*)." *Copeia* 1 (2005): 152–158.
Tennessee Herpetological Society. "Snakebite Statistics." http://www.tennsnakes.org/snakebite_statistics.htm
"When Critters Drive Us Crazy." *Sarasota Herald Tribune.* March 4, 2008. http://proquest.umi.com/pqdweb?did=1439679301&sid=1&Fmt=3&clientId=17916&RQT=309&VName=PQD.
Woodward, Allan R. and Barry R. Cook. "Nuisance Alligator Control in Florida, USA." *Crocodiles: Proceedings of the 15th Working Meeting of the Crocodile Specialist Group.* Gland, Switzerland (2000), 446–455.
Zucco, Tom. "Gator Attack Ends Protection on Island." *St. Petersburg Times,* September 20, 2004. http://www.sptimes.com/2004/09/20/Tampabay/Gator_attack_ends_pro.shtml.

# Hollywood East
## Linda B. Moore

A debate has long raged among sociologists and philosophers regarding whether media merely reflect or actually influence society — the age-old conundrum of life imitating art or art imitating life. Perceptions gained from media are seldom universal. Those who hold just the tail of the elephant, for example, without seeing the whole animal, and those who feel only the trunk have very different visualizations of the pachyderm. The same argument exists for audiences who view films. Each person comes to the screen with a unique background of knowledge, and each leaves with a different perception of the movie's message. The Sunshine State, "once referred to as 'Hollywood East,' has been the location for countless films from the 1910's through to the modern era" ("Movies and TV in Florida"). As "major studios such as Universal, Disney, and MGM" relocated to the state, Florida — by 1995 — became "the third largest movie-making state" behind California and New York ("Movies Filmed in Sarasota"). Audiences worldwide have seen movies either with Florida settings or with references to Florida on the big screen, on DVDs, or at their television box offices. Some of these audience members have actually visited the state; others have not and never will. Yet all these viewers have internalized some perception of the state from these movies. Some viewers come away with a picture of lush, tropical marshlands; others of pristine, sandy white beaches and crystal waters occasionally churned up by hurricanes; still others with visions of drugs, gangs, and crowded cities. Some see poverty and prejudice; others see luxury and affluence. For viewers, native Floridians and tourists are a mixture of teenagers gone wild on spring break, of grey-haired seniors living in trailers or boarding homes while searching vainly for the restorative elixir of Ponce de León's Fountain of Youth, or of criminals hoping to find either a new start or their fortune in the state.

Vince Whibbs, former mayor of Pensacola, Florida, began most of his public speeches by describing the Pensacola area as "the western gate to the Sunshine State where thousands live like millions wish they could" ("Pensacola"). Though also used by other locations, this slogan's truth reveals the imagery painted by many Florida films. From the Panhandle to the east coast, west coast, and the most southern tip of the Florida Keys, the Sunshine State represents a paradise of escape for many: a place to escape for relaxation, a location to escape and rebuild a troubled life, or a final, rewarding destination for retirement. Like

John Milton's *Paradise Lost*, Florida's long film history represents a picture of paradise lost for many of its natives and visitors.

In 2008, Florida's movie and film production entered its 110th year. The Sunshine State's earliest movies were actually late nineteenth century newsreels of soldiers in the state during the Spanish-American War. Today the state's Office of Cultural and Historical Programs contains a vast collection of Florida movie memorabilia in the form of posters and other artifacts explaining that until the 1920s, Jacksonville, Florida, competed favorably with Hollywood, having some 30 studios and more than 1,000 movie actors ("Florida Movie Poster Collection"). In 1908, Kalem, the first film company in Jacksonville, produced *A Florida Feud; or, Love in the Everglades*, the first narrative film produced in Florida. This silent movie pictured stereotypical poor whites and became "a box-office and critical success because of the location work, which was noted in the trade publications of the day" (Doll 2). Several other production companies soon followed Kalem to Jacksonville, which became known as "The Winter Film Capital of the World" between 1920 and 1928. At that time Richard Norman began producing films aimed mainly at African American audiences (Florida Vacation). These films offered a very different picture from the stereotypical servile roles of African Americans at this point in history. They also offered African American audiences a place to see movies, and Norman studios remains today to celebrate this rich era of film making in Jacksonville. Florida's mild climate provided excellent settings for these early 1920s films, starring such notable actors as John Barrymore, Rudolph Valentino, Gloria Swanson, and other familiar box office names.

At first a "silent film capital," the state later hosted "talkies" and is especially remembered for its production of Tarzan films, many of which were filmed at scenic Wakulla Springs, near Tallahassee, during the 1930s and 1940s. Films continued to be produced in the state during the 1950s and 1960s. Tourism information notes that the current Greenwich Studios in South Florida, near Miami, were involved in production of the underwater shots for the 1965 James Bond movie *Thunderball* (Florida Vacation). With the 1970s came the blockbuster *Jaws* (1975); *Jaws 2* (1977), filmed in Navarre Beach on Okaloosa Island; and later *Jaws 3-D* (1983), three movies responsible for striking fear into most potential Florida swimmers. A recent press release inviting Floridians to "Shine in Movie and TV Scenes," mentions Jim Carrey's *Truman Show* (1998), filmed in Destin's Seaside and Arnold Schwarzenegger's *True Lies* (1994), filmed in the Keys, as prime examples of recent Florida movie settings. This same press release contains Florida Governor Charlie Crist's statement that "Florida has a strong film and entertainment industry that represents an important line of business for our economy" (Kayemba). Besides the billion dollars that the more than 5,000 production companies have poured into the Sunshine State, Florida films have had a vast impact on how not only Floridians but the rest of the world view the state (Marth 243).

Film buff Paula Tran is familiar with four states currently noted for movie production and imagery—New York, Texas, Florida, and California. She sums up Florida's character portrayal as the most "fair" of the four. In New York, she says the characters are superficially "snooty"; in Texas they are "rednecks"; and in California they are "ripped" heroes rescuing the "bimbo *du jour*." Florida, however, is the "Stradivarius among these fiddles." Her take on character images from these states seems right on target, as she goes on to note that the scenery in which these characters co-exist reminds us of freedom, of that seductive need we all have to escape. The most interesting thing about Florida films, she notes, however, is the image of the characters created: "frenetic Ace Ventura searching for the Miami Dolphins' mascot; bumbling, sweet-tempered Gaylord Focker trying to soothe conflicts between his in-laws" in *Meet the Fockers* (2004); the "fiercely brutal" characters in *Scarface* (1983); the incompetent lawyer played by William Hurt, and the "hot and sensual Matty Walker (Kathleen Turner) in *Body Heat*" (1981). These characters are composites of Floridians. This critic goes on to note that "a significant part of the uniqueness that is Florida derives from the blended population there—ranging from the New York retirees to the fading Faulknerian 'Southern aristocracy' to the fiery Cuban refugees." She goes on to say that whereas a homogenous culture is "vanilla ... a wild confluence of cultures [produces] brilliance" (Tran).

Florida has long been pictured as an escapist's paradise, the place to vacation or retire, and these images of beach relaxation are abundant in Florida films, as are images of retirees in both luxurious and poor accommodations. However, movies like *The New Klondike* (1926) that picture shady real estate scams suggest that paradise is sometimes hard to attain. In this movie buyers are promised "man-made islands of sand and coral," which turn out to be swampland. The Marx brothers also satirize land scams that developed during Florida's land boom in the mid 1920s in one of the first "talkies," *The Cocoanuts* (1929), in which Groucho Marx attempts to sell lots in Cocoanut Manor, "an undeveloped tract of land" next door to the Hotel de Cocoanut, which he manages (Doll 254–58). America's Great Depression in the 1930s stalled pleasure vacations to the state for a time. Alluring as they are in reality, Florida's subtropical climate and beautiful beach land are simply too good to be true for many tempted to travel to its shores, and this truth is fused indelibly into many Florida films.

Water is a consistent, often life-giving but sometimes dangerous image in Florida films—whether as crystal, blue-green waves crashing onto white sandy beaches, a soothing afternoon shower, or pelting, wind-driven drops in a Florida hurricane. Water can be cleansing, providing excitement to tourists as they splash in pools or in the warm Gulf waters. It provides an avenue for boats of all kinds—cruise ships, sailboats, or high speed motorboats. Water proves a home and sanctuary for dolphins like Flipper but can also hide Jaws and predatory alligators, producing dangerous situations. For the Cracker (initial use was for someone born in Florida) family in *The Yearling* (1946), water is both a blessing and a curse as it waters their crops, but then destroys them in six days of hard rainfall. For Elvis Presley, who plays Toby Kwimper in the 1962 musical

*Follow That Dream*, water provides the reward he searches for in coming to the state. A disabled veteran, Kwimper homesteads in Florida, eventually setting up a fishing business along the Gulf Coast. Successfully defending his business in a lawsuit, Kwimper hears the judge deliver a message many viewers perceive indirectly from other Florida films: "The spirit of the pioneer is still functioning today. It's what has made this country great" (Fernandez 88). An adventurous spirit has brought many outsiders to Florida in search of relaxation, money, physical health, or love.

Florida's water provides escape and an entertainment paradise. Images of bikini-clad females in such movies as *Where the Boys Are* (1960) firmly establish Florida as America's Spring Break capital. However, as Fernandez notes, subsequent Spring Break movies like *Springbreak* (1983) shift the emphasis from a "moral" female view to one in which the female characters display a more savvy, sexual nature. In more recent Spring Break movies such as *Revenge of the Nerds II: Nerds in Paradise* (1987), the male has become an ineffectual nerd. This movie introduces other types of characters and themes that begin to emerge in Florida films: gays, African Americans, and Cuban terrorists (Fernandez 115).

Images of gays and lesbians in Florida films have largely followed stereotypes, and these roles have been treated with both negativism and humor. In an early movie, *A Florida Enchantment* (1914), women successfully transform into men with the help of a magic seed. Men, on the other hand, find themselves being chased by police and other straight citizens after ingesting the seed and exhibiting feminine behavior. It is interesting that the movie's director, Sidney Drew, uses St. Augustine's Ponce de León hotel, a luxurious 450-room structure "to signify the luxurious lifestyle of his characters" and features "characters in white lace dresses and summer suits ... in lush gardens" (Doll 11). Rejuvenation does not successfully translate to sexual transformation, however, according to the movie. Despite the state's being called the "Gay Riviera" by some, many Floridians still seem reticent to find alternate lifestyles acceptable, though academics have recently resurrected *A Florida Enchantment* for film festivals and for discussions of sexual reversals (Doll 8). Even in more modern movies such as *Some Like It Hot* (1959), *Ace Ventura: Pet Detective* (1994), and *Birdcage* (1996), alternate lifestyles are either treated humorously or met with disgust by some of the movie characters. For example, in a hilarious scene in *Ace Ventura: Pet Detective* (1994), Jim Carrey tries to wipe a kiss from a transgendered character off his lips. Far from a laughing matter is the movie *Monster* (2003), a biography of Aileen Wuornos, prostitute and lesbian, convicted and executed for killing seven men in central and northern Florida during 1989 and 1990. According to Doll, Wuornos, played by Cherize Theron, comes across as a "sympathetic sociopath ... at once frightening and pitiable," again, hardly a "normal" or acceptable person (219). Whether humorous or horrific, alternative lifestyles are presented in many Florida films, leading viewers to ponder the variety of lifestyles in paradise.

Images of African Americans' roles in Florida movies have evolved through the decades from stereotypical roles of maids, servants, and farmhands to more positive and significant roles in current movies. Florida is a southern state, and with that title comes the burden of prejudice and bigotry in the nation's eyes. Some films have dealt with racism in an attempt to explain the issue's historical roots. For example, *Rosewood* (1997) dramatizes tragic historical events resulting in mob violence that destroyed the small Florida town of Rosewood's African American population. Some movies have offered moral lessons by examining friendships between whites and African Americans. Fernandez offers two such movies: *Bright Victory* (1951), a movie in which a blind soldier befriends an African American, and *Treasures of Matecumbe* (1976), a movie similar to Twain's *Huckleberry Finn* in which a white boy and his African American friend search for treasure in the Florida Keys. More positive roles for African Americans began to emerge with the movie *Body Heat* (1981), in which African American J.A. Preston's detective character is instrumental in solving Matty Walker's husband's death (Fernandez 179–184). Now, it is not unusual to find African Americans involved in complex, important movie roles, often as policemen or politicians. Other ethnicities, however, have not achieved the status of African Americans and Cubans in Florida films. Though some interest was developed in Greek sponge divers in the 1930s and 1940s in films such as *Down Under the Sea* (1938) and *Sixteen Fathoms Deep* (1948), for the most part immigrant Filipinos, French, Asians, Poles, Germans, and others have been largely ignored by Florida filmmakers, who have chosen instead to exploit Cuban stereotypes.

Iconic movie images have evolved of the Sunshine State that are both positive and negative—from sunshine, crystal waters, pristine beaches, palm and orange trees, pink flamingos and dolphins, shells, and the Fountain of Youth (seemingly available at luxurious high-rise hotels) to hurricanes, murky swamp waters, humidity, sharks and alligators, poverty-stricken migrant labor camps, and high-speed chases of Cuban drug lords by sometimes-corrupt Miami policemen. Early Florida movies often picture poor but moral Cracker characters such as those in *The Yearling* (1946), based on Marjorie Kinnan Rawlings' 1938 Pulitzer Prize–winning novel about pseudo wealthy gold-diggers who move into the state seeking rich husbands. Florida, especially south Florida, has long been pictured as a playground for the wealthy in movies like *Moon Over Miami* (1942), in which the characters find love. *Moon Over Miami*, a top-notch musical starring Betty Grable "in her first film with top billing," is an example from the Golden Age of films that "epitomizes the kind of romantic fantasy associated with this genre" (Doll 145). According to Kay Latimer, one of the "husband hunters" in the film, Miami is "where rich men are as plentiful as grapefruit and millionaires hang from every palm tree" (145). Other movies like *The Big Street* (1942), on the other hand, afford no reward for women like Lucille Ball, paralyzed in an accident, who futilely travels to Florida hoping for both physical healing and love from wealthy film co-stars such as William Orr, receiving neither (Fernandez 103).

Perhaps the most popular image of Florida presented through the movies is that of a paradise, a place to regenerate and to spend the last years of one's life peacefully. Henry Flagler and Henry Plant, belonging to the "dubious group of business giants known as the robber barons" in the mid-nineteenth century, are largely responsible for making Florida "America's sun porch" by draining swamps, laying railways, and building resorts in the state (Doll 286–87). This picture of Florida as a tourist destination persisted in many films that were either produced or set in the state. The movie *The Truman Show* (1998) stars Jim Carrey as a character manipulated by a television production company into believing his staged life is real. Adopted in infancy by the company and surrounded by actors, Carrey grows up in a television-created "sphere." The dramatic satire pictures the New Urbanism movement of the 1980s in which Seaside, Florida, was built. A Golden Globe award-winning movie, *The Truman Show* was nominated for three Oscars, and the town of Seaside presented the perfect location "for a story about a man whose life was too good to be true" (Doll 245). Recent films, however, continue to explore the relationship between true happiness and physical surroundings, suggesting, as Doll does, that true happiness lies within the person rather than depending on his ideal surroundings (288).

Many movies present older or physically feeble characters who have moved to Florida. However, the lifestyle of these characters, often forced to live in nursing homes, trailer parks, or boarding houses, is not always what they had planned. In *The Crew* (2000), Burt Reynolds, Richard Dreyfuss, and Seymour Cassel are retirees living in a South Beach rooming house. Shortly after their move to Florida, the men revert to their criminal past to survive, finding themselves taking a contract to kill. A quirky, but somewhat more positive image of still active retirees occurs in *Meet the Fockers* (2004), where Barbra Streisand (Roz) teaches sexual techniques to senior citizens in the Coconut Grove community. Ron Howard's science fiction sequels *Cocoon* (1985) and *Cocoon: The Return* (1988) explore the ideas of aging and regeneration when six retired citizens living in a retirement home find themselves miraculously rejuvenated after swimming in a pool containing cocoons of aliens. Making a deal with the aliens, the three couples ironically leave Florida (and the planet) for a life of immortality. In the sequel they return to Earth, with four of them deciding to stay and face normal aging and death. Only two of the six opt for immortality. Florida is not always the paradise advertised for movie characters who come to the state for healing or retirement. It is, instead, a lost paradise as exemplified by Ratso (Dustin Hoffman) in *Midnight Cowboy* (1996). Crippled and sick, Ratso has dreamed of running on Florida beaches filled with beautiful women. However, the movie ends tragically, but not unexpectedly, with Ratso dead in Jon Voight's arms on a bus traveling to Florida. Had Ratso reached Florida, he would not have been miraculously restored to strength. He would not have raced along Florida's beaches.

Many of the recent crime-ridden films reflect a *film noir* style of moviemaking popular in America during the 1940s and 1950s, but continuing today in many Florida films. Derived from French for "black film," *film noir* provides a "black slate on which the culture [can] ascribe its ills and in the process produce a catharsis to help relieve them," explains Ellen Smith (151). Florida's sometimes dark and almost always damp, humid atmosphere is perfect for *film noir*, with its "tacky theme bars on the beach, humid nights, ceiling fans, losers dazed by greed, the sense of dead bodies rotting out back in the Everglades," as Roger Ebert describes in a review noted by Fernandez and Ingalls (153). Characters in *film noir* style movies display existential characteristics; they are isolated, troubled, ambiguous, but loyal to friends. This style did not die out by the 1960s as many think. It is still evident in some recent Florida films, most of which clearly display the *Paradise Lost* theme. Especially reminiscent of *film noir* are four movies with Florida ties. In *Key Largo* (1948), Edward G. Robinson's sweaty character soaks in a bathtub and smokes a cigar. The sweltering heat of the closed hotel lobby and the darkness of an impending storm add to the murky atmosphere. Lauren Bacall is the "good girl" and Humphrey Bogart is the "disillusioned hero" who struggles against the hand he has been dealt (Smith 152). In true *film noir* fashion, Frank McCloud represents the psychologically damaged soldier who finally destroys the villains, gangsters intent on completing a counterfeit deal, to return to Nora, played by Bacall. The hurricane becomes a metaphor for the increasingly edgy situation in which the gangsters become more and more nervous. Descriptions in *Key Largo* of the movie's raging hurricane are very similar to an actual category-5 hurricane that occurred in 1935, whose 250 mile per hour winds knocked out stretches of the railway Henry Flagler had completed in 1912 (Doll 61). This movie pictures the dark and frightening reality of Florida hurricanes and the presence of disturbed, violent, and criminal characters.

*China Moon* (1994), with its murky atmosphere and continuously falling rain, is another example of *film noir*'s somber tradition. The film's "femme fatale ( Madeleine Stowe), who seduces a top-notch, but flawed, detective (Ed Harris) and then manipulates him into helping her dispose of her abusive husband" is reminiscent of *Body Heat* (1981), another prime example of *film noir* in which Kathleen Turner (Matty Walker) seduces William Hurt (Ned Racine) to kill her husband. The character of Kyle Bodine in *China Moon*, played by Ed Harris, is not a "corrupt antihero." He is, instead, taken in by the somewhat sympathetic but manipulative Rachel, played by Madeleine Stowe, who "develops genuine feelings for her patsy" (Doll 92).

Both the sweltering heat and the immoral relationship of the characters are indicative of *film noir*, a type of film that is often "misrepresented and misunderstood." *Film Noir* is "a type of crime drama ... famous for its dark visual style" (Doll 84). Doll goes on to say that the film's femme fatale tempts and manipulates the story's male characters (usually detectives or lawyers) with her "sensuality and sexuality." Endings of *film noir* movies are seldom happy, suggesting a dark side of life. Matty Walker (Kathleen Turner) in her classic line to Ned Racine (William Hurt), "You're not too bright. I like that in a man," forewarns the imperceptive and drunken Ned of his impending setup. Besides its reflection of the dark *film noir* genre, *Body Heat* also echoes land speculation deals mentioned in several earlier Florida films. Matty's husband has become wealthy through his real estate deals doing what's necessary to gain power and money (Doll 86). Once again, the perceptive viewer questions whether Florida's land boom and subsequent land bust has actually helped or hurt the state with its incidents of swindling and its overbuilding of condominiums, highway systems, and entertainment industries that often destroy much of the state's natural beauty.

Perhaps the best example of *film noir*'s "corrupt [and] morally ambiguous" characters is in the brutal 1983 movie *Scarface*, which pictured Cuban immigrants as Miami mobsters involved in crime (Smith 157). Such films often picture the Sunshine State's natural tropical beauty as flawed by overbuilding, crime, corruption, and danger. Much of the movie was shot in Hollywood because of protests at the portrayal of Cubans in the film. Based on a 1932 film, the 1983 *Scarface* has been criticized for its excessive violence. Tony Montana, played by Al Pacino, brutally claws his way from dishwasher to drug lord in the film. Scarface becomes addicted to cocaine, a drug that eventually leads to the character's downfall. A poster for the movie seems to sum up the lost paradise imagery quite well: "In the spring of 1980 ... thousands [of Cubans] came in search of the American Dream. One of them found it on the sun-washed avenues of Miami ... wealth, power and passion beyond his wildest dreams.... He loved the American Dream. With a vengeance" (Doll 150).

In his violence, Tony Montana seems to represent that evolving, dangerous image that viewers have formed of Florida from films beginning in the late nineteenth century—the idea that Florida is no longer a land of paradise waiting to afford a new beginning to the downtrodden and afflicted. The state's lush resources—crystal clear water, rich foliage, and wildlife—have taken a backseat to images of overbuilding and danger in current films. Gone are images of moral characters, friendly animals, and a mild subtropical climate. Florida's commercialism and pandering to tourist entertainment has produced unpleasant scenes of crime and drugs. Though some movies still picture the paradise, that paradise has surely been lost in many of the current movies that are either shot in or reference the state. Carl Hiassen, a Florida novelist whose many books have been adapted for films, once said: "The Florida in my novels is not as seedy as the real Florida. It's hard to stay ahead of the curve. Every time I write a scene that I think is the sickest thing I have ever dreamed up, it is surpassed by something that happens in real life" (quoted in Solomon). Florida's movie images are truly varied in nature. Whether seen as reflections of paradise or of dangerously drug-infested, overbuilt cities, the perception of the state lies with the movies' producers and ultimately with the viewers.

## WORKS CITED AND CONSULTED

Doll, Susan, and David Morrow. *Florida on Film*. Gainesville: University Press of Florida, 2007.

Fernandez, Susan J., and Robert P. Ingalls. *Sunshine in the Dark: Florida in the Movies.* Gainesville: University Press of Florida, 2006.
Florida Tourism Industry Marketing Corporation. "Movies in Florida." Visit Florida.com. http://www.visitflorida.com/movies/.
Gorin, Janice. "Florida Movie and Poster Collection." Division of Historical Resources. http://www.flheritage.com/museum/collections/posters.
Kayemba, Paul. "New Florida Guide Invites Travelers to Shine in Movie and TV Scenes." http://media.visitflorida.com/travel/news/?ID=931.
Marth, Del, and Martha J. Marth. *Florida Almanac 1999–2000.* Gretna: Pelican, 1999.
"Movies and TV in Florida." Florida Memory: State Archives of Florida. http://www.floridamemory.com/PhotographicCollection/photo_exhibits/movies.cfm
"Movies Filmed in Sarasota." http://www.simplysarasota.com/MovieLocations.html.
"Pensacola." http://www.emeraldcoastinfo.com/pensacola.htm.
Smith, Ellen. "Subtropical Film Noir." In *Crime Fiction & Film in the Sunshine State: Film Noir.* Edited by Steve Glassman and Maurice O'Sullivan. Bowling Green: Bowling Green State University Press, 1997. 151–164.
Solomon, Deborah. "The Way We Live Now: Questions for Carl Hiassen." *The New York Times Magazine*, July 25, 2004.
Tran, Paula. Personal e-mail. May 19, 2008.

# "'If you don't like this town get out and stay out'": Ernest Hemingway's Key West

### E. Stone Shiflet and James H. Meredith

In an April 21, 1928, letter, Hemingway writes to Maxwell Perkins about the conditions in his soon-to-be-new hometown, Key West, Florida:

Tonight is a big night (Saturday) although not so cheerful because another cigar factory has closed down. This is a splendid place. Population formerly 26,000 — now around ten thousand. There was a penciled inscription derogatory to our fair city in the toilet at the station and somebody had written under it — "if you don't like this town get out and stay out." Somebody else had written under that "Everybody has" [*Selected Letters* 276].

While Hemingway remains one of the most celebrated former residents of Key West, the relationship between this now fabulously successful tourist town and its fabulously successful favorite son was not always quite so harmonious, although by no means was it ever rancorous. For the most part, Hemingway found Key West an ideal place to work, play, and earn a living. For its part, Key West has always found Hemingway a source of commercial success.

Because Ernest Hemingway is that rare American individual who has reached both professional fame as a writer and intellectual and who has also simultaneously reached and maintained celebratory fame as an icon in the popular imagination, he is as much a legendary figure as he is an historical one. Most of the public at large arguably knows more about the myth than they do his actual biography, and this is especially true in Key West, where his home is privately held and seems to be used more for entertainment or commercial purposes than it is for educational ones. Not that there is necessarily anything wrong with entertainment or commercial purposes. But for the purposes of this essay, what is essential to understand first are the facts behind Hemingway's moving to Key West, including his real estate transactions; his record-breaking fishing exploits; his anger at Julius Stone and the New Deal bureaucrats' attempt at restoring the local economy in the 1930s by making Hemingway a tourist attraction (in "The Sights of Whitehead Street: A Key West Letter" he claims his house is No. 18 in a compilation of 48 things to see there); his experience with the Great Hurricane of 1935 and the death of the veterans; and, finally, his celebrity life with the

Florida locals and especially his often apocryphal exploits at Sloppy Joe's, then, and how he is commemorated now. This chapter explores the symbiotic, but nevertheless complex, and the almost secularly sacrosanct (the oxymoron is intentional) relationship between Hemingway, the iconic American writer, and the modern emergence of Key West from economic disaster to its current status as a popular tourist destination and commercial venue. While Twain and Hannibal, Missouri, and Faulkner and Oxford, Mississippi, may have complex legacies between writer and place, they have nothing to compare with what is still between Hemingway and Key West.

Ernest Hemingway and his second wife, Pauline, arrived in Key West in April 1928, about the time the letter to Perkins was written, after hearing about the town's tropical wonders from fellow writer Dos Passos. Hemingway and Pauline had been living a very comfortable life in Paris until that March, but Hemingway felt an urgent need to return to the states and this island paradise sounded just great, especially with its supposed lack of tourists, its inexpensive cost of living, and its availability of sport fishing. The initial 1928 visit to Key West also coincided with a remarkable conceptual breakthrough in the development of what would eventually become Hemingway's 1929 novel *A Farewell to Arms*. In his brilliant documentary book about the making of that novel, Michael Reynolds writes:

> In early March, 1928, Hemingway began to write a story that he had been trying to get on paper for almost ten years.... It was not the first time he had attempted the novel; he had been working over the material in various forms since the winter of 1919.
>
> When Hemingway returned to the plot of *A Farewell to Arms* three years later in 1928, his attitude toward his material had changed considerably from the period of the "Ur Farewell." ... At some point between 1925 and 1928, he came to realize that Caporetto was the key to the war in Italy and that he must take that disaster into account in his novel, he knew of the precedent set by Stephen Crane in *Red Badge of Courage* of inventing seemingly firsthand experience, and he realized the potential of the reading he had begun years before on the Italian war....
>
> All of this he must have done before March of 1928, when he actually began writing *A Farewell to Arms* [*Hemingway's First War* 281].

With Pauline pregnant with his second child, Gregory, and he now conceptually full of the novel that would make him even more famous than he was already becoming, Hemingway came to this new home in the United States ripe with life's potential. According to James McLendon in *Papa: Hemingway in Key West*, Ernest and his wife "arrived on the closing day of the first week in April, 1928" (22). By April 1938, when Hemingway would start the long process of separating from Pauline, move away from Key West, and set up his new residence at the Finca Vigia in Cuba with Martha Gellhorn, he would have published *Death in the Afternoon* (1932), *Winner Take Nothing* (1933), *Green Hills of Africa* (1935), and *To Have and Have Not* (1937), which is a remarkable string of creative accomplishments by any measure. This trip to Key West would also initiate a decade-long period of tremendous literary productivity that would only be altered again in 1937 with his work on the Spanish Civil War and the start of his tempestuous relationship with Martha Gellhorn, who would become his third wife and who would take him in a whole new literary direction.

Hemingway's initial residence in Key West was on Simonton Street, which was named for John Simonton, who had bought the island for $2,000 in 1819 along with his partner John Whitehead, from its original owner, Pablo Salas, the postmaster of St. Augustine during the last Spanish occupation of Florida (Ogle 5). The Hemingways initially moved into an apartment above the local Ford motor vehicle dealership, the Trevor-Morris Company. Pauline's Uncle Gus (Gustavus Augustus Pfeiffer), an Arkansas businessman who made his fortune in a cosmetic company, Hudnut Perfumes, had purchased for them a Model A Ford, which was supposed to have been on the loading docks awaiting their arrival in Key West. When the automobile was not there as expected, Hemingway contacted the Ford dealership, which then offered to have the inconvenienced couple stay in the apartments above the dealership until their new vehicle arrived. They resided in those apartments until the fall of that year, when they moved into a rental house at 1100 South Street (McLendon 50).

At the end of 1928, Hemingway's father committed suicide, which changed the son's life in Key West dramatically. His father had throughout his life suffered from bouts of often severe depression, and had lost a considerable amount of his savings in ill-considered Florida land deals (and he was not alone by any means) and had also been suffering through painful bouts of angina as well. He shot himself with a pistol in his Oak Park home. Hemingway was on his way back home from New York City. He was riding on a train with his oldest son, Jack, who had just returned from Europe where he had been living with his mother, Hadley, his father's first wife. Ernest left his young son in the care of a Pullman porter and made his way back to his hometown. After attending to funeral arrangements and taking care of the future financial needs of his mother, Grace, Hemingway returned home to Key West saddened by his loss, and took all of his wrenching grief with him as he finished the first draft of *A Farewell to Arms*. He never returned to Oak Park again. In Key West, Hemingway's feelings about his father's personal retreat from life were probably worked through in the revising of the manuscript, which is about Frederick Henry's disastrous retreat from Caporetto, the historical humiliation of the Italian Army, and how Henry's warm feelings about life turned cold walking back to his hotel in the cold rain. Eventually, Hemingway would more directly discuss the issue in *For Whom the Bell Tolls*, which was begun in Key West during the late 1930s and finished in Cuba in 1940.

With the subsequent success of *A Farewell to Arms* bringing him even more fame and professional security, Hemingway was able to make his family more secure in Key West as well. On 28 April 1931, almost three years from the date of their first visit to Key West, Ernest and Pauline Hemingway officially purchased their home at 907 Whitehead Street, named after the same John Whitehead, a house they had previously been renting. They paid $8,000 in cash for the property. The money had been given to them by Pauline's ever-generous Uncle Gus.[1] At the time that they purchased it, the house was basically a dilapidated relic, which had to be totally restored. Although still weak from her third son Gregory's cesarean birth (her second in two years), Pauline started the long process of remodeling the home, starting first with the two-storied carriage house that would eventually serve as her husband's writing room. In *Ernest Hemingway in Key West*, Marsha Bellavance-Johnson writes about this coral-stone house, which is just a block off of Duval Street:

> It was built in 1851 by Asa Tift, a wealthy shipping magnate. The coral was quarried at the site and the hold became the basement. It's a Spanish Colonial style with floor to ceiling windows, opening onto porches which circle the building on both levels....
>
> Eventually Pauline refurbished the home. The décor was a blend of her European antiques and fine oil-paintings with animal trophies and artifacts from their world-wide trips. Landscaping and a pool were added and a brick wall built to discourage sightseers who were attracted by Hemingway's increasing fame [43].

Hemingway soon began writing in his converted second-floor office in the small outbuilding that stood behind his residence, an old carriage house. The structure had once been home to the house servants (Bellavance-Johnson 45). While Hemingway would live in this house until he separated from Pauline, she maintained a residence there until her death on 1 October 1951. After the death of Hemingway in 1961, his surviving wife, Mary, and the estate eventually sold the house. It was eventually purchased by Bernice Dickson, who opened it as a museum in 1964. The house has remained in the Dickson family ever since. In 1968, the house was listed on the National Register of Historic Places, and it has been the locus of much Papa-grist for the popular-imagination mill.

Arguably, the most notorious Papa legend in Key West has to be the six-toed cats that now famously reside at the Hemingway house on Whitehead. These cats allegedly descend from felines Hemingway owned while he lived there. In *Hemingway's Cats: An Illustrated Biography*, Carlene Fredericka Brennan writes that perhaps these cats may not have come from Hemingway at all:

> Despite popular belief, according to son Patrick, Ernest Hemingway did not own cats when he and his second wife, Pauline, and their two sons, Patrick and Gregory, lived in Key West at 907 Whitehead Street. According to an article written by Mark Burrell in the *Miami Herald* on August 21, 1994, Patrick Hemingway stated that even though his father was fond of cats, he did not possess a single cat in Key West [13].

Yet despite these disputations, the origin of these cats has recently evolved into an international story. According to a 31 July 2006 story in the *Guardian*:

> The U.S. Department of Agriculture wants to fine the museum's owners up to $200 (£107) a day for "exhibiting" the animals without a licence, according to a

lawsuit filed in Miami, but the trustees insist that tourists pay to see the house, of which the cats are merely residents.

"They're comparing the Hemingway house to a circus or a zoo because there are cats on the premises," said Cara Higgins, the museum's lawyer. "This is not a travelling circus. These cats have been here forever" [Luscombe].

Bellavance-Johnson offers the following explanation: "Even now the famous 'Hemingway' cats still roam the grounds. One legend has it that a poor spinster neighbor, Miss Marie Chappick, took in numerous cats. Those cats adopted the 907 Whitehead Street home after 'Papa' Hemingway started feeding them" (43). No matter what the circumstances actually may be, the lineage of these cats may ultimately not be the real issue. It all depends on whether you care if facts get in the way of an opinion. These cats reinforce the Hemingway myth in the popular imagination in a paradoxical way, so their existence as Hemingway's cats trump the truth no matter what, and, therefore, they have become living, almost apostolic representatives of his Key West life. The notion that they are warmer and fuzzier representatives of the often-portrayed hyper-macho Hemingway may, in fact, give the story more legs, or toes, if you will.

The other lasting Hemingway image associated with Key West in the popular imagination is his deep-sea fishing exploits and sportsman accomplishments, which, unlike so many other aspects of his Key West mythology, have been built upon facts rather than legend. *New York Times* reporter Paul Greenberg writes, in "A Fish Tale," about the potential number of Hemingway's deep-sea catches:

> Hemingway was a frequent but inconsistent record keeper. In his archive room at the John F. Kennedy Library in Boston, the numbers are there, sort of. During one 180-day stretch in 1933–34, the *Pilar* logs reveal a catch of 10 marlin, 2 sailfish and 9 sharks. But in an article in *Esquire* describing the typically slower spring run of that same year, Hemingway said the *Pilar*'s catch was 51 marlin.... If we assume an average annual catch of 40 fish and a ratio of four marlin to every tuna, that would make for something like 800 marlin and 200 bluefin tuna.

No matter how you count them, hypothetically or not, Hemingway was unmistakably a proficient deep-sea fisherman. He was a founding member and lifetime honorary vice president of the International Game Fish Association and a member of the International Fishing Hall of Fame in Ft. Lauderdale, Florida. As a consequence of his well-documented accomplishments, a different sort of Hemingway mythology was spawned, a legend built upon countless period photographs of the smiling man standing triumphantly next to his gigantic catches, as well as one built upon his own self-fashioning.

This self-fashioned myth was a modern mass multi-media creation. While the primary facts may be true about his fishing, the mythological amplification occurs in the marketing of Hemingway as the image of modern masculinity. From 1933 to 1936, beginning with the inaugural Autumn 1933 issue, Hemingway wrote 26 articles for Arnold Gingrich's *Esquire: The Quarterly Magazine for Men* ("Hemingway and the Magazines"), which was created specifically to celebrate and market American masculinity. Just as repetition is an ancient rhetorical device, so repetition is arguably the most effective means to market a public image, and thus it was with the repeated image and description of Hemingway as the confident voice of masculine sportsmanship in a period when the concept of masculinity was being threatened by the Great Depression, unemployment and financial and emotional failures and public breakdowns, F. Scott Fitzgerald's essay, "The Crack-Up," (*Esquire*, February 1936) being the perfect example. Additionally, Hemingway's location in remote Key West, a place conducive to an exotic lifestyle, reinforced the carefully crafted image of a man not only of the world but above it all as well. With Hemingway's help, *Esquire* became a monthly magazine with the January 1934 issue, after only four or five months in business.

The magazine was an immediate success. It is illuminating that Hemingway's name was repeatedly advertised on the top of the first three covers, October 1933, January 1934, and February 1934 — four of the first five issues, continuing again with the April 1934 issue. After that he had something in almost every issue that year and into 1935. Regardless of who else was included in an issue, his name was always first either on the list of fiction or non-fiction writers. With titles like these, "Marlin off the Morro: A Cuban Letter," "Out in the Stream," "Remembering Shooting-Flying: A Key West Letter," "On the Blue Water," it is easy to see how Hemingway's "Letters" spoke to the directly to the *Esquire* readership, which was probably looking for escape from the challenges of daily life, and looking to feel good about itself as well. From the very beginning, *Esquire* succeeded by marketing clothes and products to American men. While Hemingway was never a clothes-horse by any stretch of the imagination, his tactile writing about traditionally masculine pursuits was perfectly well suited for *Esquire*'s type of marketing approach. In the inaugural edition, founding editor Arnold Gingrich asserts that

> *Esquire* aims to be among other things, a fashion guide for men, but it never intends to become, by any possible stretch of the imagination, a primer for fops. We have been studying men, and men's clothes, for many years, and we have come to the conclusion that the average American male has too much inherent horse sense to be bothered very much by a lot of dress rules that nobody but a gigolo could possibly find either time or inclination to observe. On the other hand, we feel that men have long since ceased to believe that there is anything effeminate or essentially unbusinesslike about devoting a little care and thought to the selection of clothes [94].

In his very first "Letter" to *Esquire*, "Marlin off the Morro: A Cuban Letter," Hemingway writes:

> Getting up to close the shutter you look across the harbor to the flag on the fortress and see it is straightened out toward you. You look out the north window past the Morro and see that the smooth morning sheen is rippling over and you know the trade wind is coming up early. You take a shower, pull on an old pair of khaki pants and a shirt, take the pair of moccasins that are dry, put the

other pair in the window so they will be dry the next night, walk across the corner to the café and have breakfast [137].

The Morro, of course, is the most famous of Havana landmarks and was even more well-known in 1930 because many Americans traveled to and through Cuba than they do now. Despite many fashion trends since then, approximately 75 years hence, khaki pants (Ralph Lauren trademarks them as chinos) and hand-stitched moccasin (L.L. Bean markets a bullet proof pair) remain timeless American clothes classics and perpetual bestsellers and the companies that make them are continual buyers of expensive magazine advertisement space. If you were a 1930s northeastern businessman and reading this passage for the first time, on a weekend, a vacation, or on the train to work, these ubiquitous casual clothes just became the stuff of romantic adventure. Moreover, even a cursory look at men's clothing advertisements today reveals a very similar setting in which to sell clothes. It typically involves a setting of obvious, but unstated, romantic potential: an unmade bed, wet towels, a well-known landmark, and clothes. No matter what is there, there is a story to be told. Yet while there maybe some stylistic similarities between this writing and that found in his serious fiction, there are fundamental differences between the two. The "archetypical" Hemingway masculine style is more apocryphal than actual. Yes, you heard it here: there is no monolithic, masculine Hemingway style; instead, there are many styles. Hemingway did not change his basic style of writing to sell fashion; instead, the idea that men's clothes were fashion and that it was appropriate to think about them that way became commonplace in America at the same time as Hemingway became famous, and that change has made a big difference in American culture ever since. F. Scott Fitzgerald's work at first greatly profited from this very phenomenon; his characters seem to be dressed right out of the Brooks Brothers catalog. Hemingway (and Fitzgerald as well) was writing modern, unadorned, specific, and descriptive prose that is anchored strongly in a concrete sense of place several years before the businessman, with pockets full of discretionary cash, became a major focus of American marketing in the later 1920s. For his part, Hemingway ended his regular contributions to *Esquire* in 1937, after his worldview and focus completely changed with the civil war in his beloved Spain and the threat of worldwide fascism beginning to dominate his attention.

However, even before he went to the Spanish Civil War in spring of 1937, another serious event occurred that reminded Hemingway that the world was a dangerous place no matter where you lived. On 5 September 1935, Ernest Hemingway piloted his cabin cruiser, the *Pilar*, into Lower Matecumbe Key, some seventy-five miles north of Key West. Instead of trolling for sport fish, he was searching for survivors of one of the most powerful hurricanes to ever land on the U.S. coast. He found carnage he had not seen since he was an eighteen-year-old ambulance driver on the Italian front.[2] The category-5 Labor Day hurricane was "the type that people dread most: deceptive, slow moving, impossible to predict, and immensely powerful. As late as the evening of September 1, weather forecasters remained unsure of precisely where or how hard the storm would hit" (Ogle 177). The hurricane eventually roared across the Keys and hit the western side of the Florida peninsula, leaving behind death, destruction, and carnage of historic levels for a hurricane: "Buildings collapsed into piles of rubble, which the wind transformed into weapons of destruction and death" (Ogle 179). As part of a volunteer group organized by Monroe County Sheriff Karl Thompson, Hemingway was one of the first to view what remained in the aftermath. As he wrote Maxwell Perkins on 7 September, "Nothing could give an idea of the destruction. Between 700 and 1,000 dead. Many, today, still unburied. The foliage absolutely stripped as though by fire for forty miles and the land looking like the abandoned bed of a river. Not a building of any sort standing.... Saw more dead than I'd seen in one place since the lower Piave in June of 1918" (*Letters* 421).

The World War I analogy was not inappropriate. Among the storm's victims were 259 veterans who had been working on the island helping build a bridge linking Lower Matecumbe Key with Jewfish Key, part of an ambitious Florida initiative to span the thirty-five mile gap in the Overseas Highway that hampered the flow of tourism into Key West. These former soldiers had been living among three camps stretched between Lower and Upper Matecumbe since late 1934 in order to avoid a reprise of the 1932 Bonus March on Washington, D.C. At its height, the collective camp population numbered 684, the residents representing a surprisingly diverse cross-section of America: among them were draftsmen, lawyers, high-school principals, actors, and at least one professional boxer (Drye 48). Others were, apropos of Depression-era stereotypes, itinerants. Hemingway took the veterans' deaths personally, and not merely because of his close identification with those who had witnessed combat; he had encountered at least some of these men before, during their frequent furloughs in Key West, where they could prove a rowdy force when their frustrations boiled over into drunken brawls (Ogle 176). According to Carlos Baker, Hemingway himself barely missed becoming the victim of one vet who liked to summon patrons at Sloppy Joe's to his side, knock in the head with his crutch, and then rifle their pockets to fund his bar tab (*Writer as Artist* 207).[3]

Immediately after returning from relief efforts at Matecumbe, Hemingway wrote "Who Murdered the Vets?," a searing indictment of bureaucratic callousness that — as its title suggests — accused Franklin D. Roosevelt's administration not of reckless indifference or even manslaughter but of homicide for abandoning the veterans to the dangerous South Florida tropics:

> Whom did [the veterans] annoy and to whom was their possible presence a political danger?
> Who sent them down to the Florida Keys and left them there in hurricane months?
> Who is responsible for their deaths?
> The writer of this article lives a long way from Washington and would not know the answers to these questions. But he does know that wealthy people,

yachtsmen, fishermen such as President Hoover and President Roosevelt, do not come to the Florida Keys in hurricane months [Trogdon 168].

Published in *New Masses*—a leftist journal Hemingway had long disparaged— "Who Murdered the Vets?" is usually seen as inaugurating Hemingway's short-lived stint as a proletarian writer. Two years after the hurricane, that stint would culminate with the publication of the long-gestating *To Have and Have Not*, a novel whose paradigmatic distinction between the moral veniality of the rich and the noble struggles of the working poor would prove one of the decade's more complex repudiations of New Deal politics. It is no secret that Hemingway chafed at the bureaucratic machinations of Key West's primary New Dealer, Julius Stone, who with good intentions wanted to turn the city into a tourist haven, largely at the expense of the writer's privacy. Especially in scenes that reference the Roosevelt administration, *To Have and Have Not* contains several passages whose feral tone could fit seamlessly within "Who Murdered the Vets?"

Besides its important glimpse into the troubles of these Bonus March veterans who met their ignominious fate on the Keys, *To Have and Have Not* also depicts the overall struggles of the conchs during the Great Depression as well. Boat captain Henry Morgan, like just about everyone else on the island, is in a life and death struggle for economic survival. Morgan, a proud individualist, learns too late that "no matter how no man alone ain't got no bloody fucking chance" (Hemingway *To Have* 225). Hemingway almost learned that lesson too late himself, adding those words on the last draft before publication, right after he returned from his first and most important visit to the front lines of the Spanish Civil War in spring 1937. The movie version of *To Have and Have Not*, starring Humphrey Bogart and the teenaged, but nonetheless alluring Lauren Bacall, turned out to be far more popular than the original novel. The movie script was of course revised by William Faulkner, and turned out to be his best Hollywood effort ever. The movie version has none of the Great Depression travails in it at all. In the 1940s, when the movie was released, the economic threat of depressed capitalistic markets had been over shadowed by the rise and near total domination of worldwide fascism, led primarily by Germany's Adolf Hitler and his Nazi party. Instead of being set in Key West, the movie is set on the French island of Martinique, after the collapse of France during the German invasions in which the Vichy government was established as a Nazi puppet regime. The American Morgan, whose native U.S. was still neutral at the time, gets caught in international intrigue as he is hired to help an important Free-French leader and his wife to freedom. The only tie to America's most southern point of land is that Morgan's boat is noticeably registered in Key West. To make sure that the audience gets this point, the camera momentarily focuses in on the name of the city, stenciled on the boat's side wall. Although the movie has very, very little to do with the original novel and, regrettably, with Key West, it is the most popular and critically successful movie adaptation of one of Hemingway's novels.[4]

There is one more aspect of Hemingway's life in Key West that has a life of its own: Sloppy Joe's and the annual Papa Look-Alike Contest that occurs in July every year. The bar has its origins in an establishment called The Blind Pig, a location that Joe Russell began renting for $3 a week right after the repeal of Prohibition allowed him to operate his speak-easy in the open. The Blind Pig quickly was renamed Sloppy Joe's, which was located on the south side of the 400th block of Greene Street and was "fully three times as large" as the tiny original, illegal one located at the corner of Front and Duval Streets (McIver 51, 48). "On May 5, 1937, Sloppy Joe's moved again, this time just a half block to the southeast of Greene and Duval Streets," or, more precisely, 201 Duval Street, where it still operates today (McIver 51). Hemingway supposedly took an old urinal from Sloppy Joe's when Russell moved to this last location. Allegedly, Hemingway used it as a drinking trough for the feral cats he probably never owned, but this has been questioned, especially since the ever-thrifty Russell moved everything he could from the older location into the new one and would need every available urinal. Russell bought the building, formerly known as the Old Victoria Restaurant, for $2,500.

"For the past sixty [or so] years [Sloppy Joe's] has remained essentially the same" (Bellavance-Johnson 33), and it has been living off the Hemingway legacy ever since. "Now, [however,] the music is electronically amplified and there's a counter which does a brisk business in Hemingway memorabilia. The bar also sponsors events during the annual July Hemingway birthday celebrations" (Bellavance-Johnson 33). The bar hosted its 28th Papa Look-Alike Contest in 2008 as well as the 11th Annual Running of the [Key West] Bulls. It remains a heavily contested event. In 2007, for example, 125 men competed for the look-alike honors, with all the contestants resembling Hemingway during the last two years of his life in Cuba, instead of the more vigorous Hemingway of the 1930s. Historical accuracy, especially when it has to do with a commercial enterprise, has become subordinated to the myth in the popular imagination.

Gail Sinclair and Kirk Curnutt, in their introduction to *Key West Hemingway: A Reassessment*, address this issue directly. They write about the conflicted legacy of Hemingway as a serious literary figure and as the valuable commercial commodity that he so poignantly represents today in Key West:

> For many observers, the belief that Key West was more of a venue for celebrity showmanship than artistic accomplishment has been reinforced by the city's posthumous treatment of its most famous resident. Throughout Paris, Pamplona, Ronda, and Venice, one can gaze reverently upon plaques and busts that unobtrusively commemorate Hemingway's connection to these sites. Key West, meanwhile, is home to vendors hocking an obnoxious array of Papa paraphernalia, including T-shirts, beer coozies, Zippo lighters, and, for a time at least, nostalgia cruises on yachts called the *Pilar* that looked nothing like the thirty-eight-foot cabin cruiser that Hemingway docked at the island's abandoned Navy Yard [Manuscript 15–16].

As a consequence of Hemingway having once famously lived in Key West, a walk today down Duval Street is a commercial enterprise in itself, yet one that nonetheless has a unique edge to it. This is nothing like the decidedly homogenous, family-oriented marketing famously found in Orlando, a city which primarily owes its existence to Disney. Key West, on the other hand, would exist whether or not Hemingway had ever lived there at all, but it indeed would have been a very different place now. In real estate, as well as in the development of noteworthy places, it is always location, location, and location. The unusual location of Key West, with its island setting and isolated position as the most southerly American spot of land, makes it an ideal place for people to feel more liberated to be themselves, whether it is in their imagination or even in their sexual identity. In the end, therefore, Hemingway's legacy in Key West may exist today more in the popular imagination than it does in historical fact, but that may have been inevitable from the very beginning of the relationship between this complex man and the equally complex island community.

## NOTES

1. Despite the commercial success of *A Farewell to Arms*, Hemingway and Pauline were never able to live off of his earnings. In fact, Hemingway used a lot of the novel's advance money from Scribner's to make his mother more financially secure after the suicide of his father, which left her in rather difficult circumstances. He also used the money to buy his boat *Pilar*.
2. More information about Hemingway and the 1935 Labor Day hurricane will be found in *Key West Hemingway: A Reassessment*, Gail Sinclair and Kirk Curnutt, eds., (Gainesville: UP of Florida, forthcoming in 2009).
3. Hemingway tells this story himself in his *Esquire* essay, "He Who Gets Slap Happy," published in August 1935, just one month before the Labor Day hurricane.
4. Probably, the best adaptation of a Hemingway short story was *The Killers*, starring Burt Lancaster and Ava Gabor. Legend has it that it was supposedly Hemingway's favorite adaptation — he always enjoyed looking at Ava Gabor.

## WORKS CITED

Baker, Carlos. *Hemingway: The Writer as Artist*. Princeton: Princeton UP, 1963.
Bellavance-Johnson, Marsha. *Ernest Hemingway in Key West*. Ketchum, Idaho: The Computer Lab, 2000.
Brennen, Carlene Fredericka. *Hemingway's Cats: An Illustrated Biography*. Sarasota, FL: Pineapple P, 2006.
Drye, Willie. *Storm of the Century: The Labor Day Hurricane of 1935*. Washington, DC: National Geographic, 2002.
The Ernest Hemingway Home and Museum Web Site. http://www.hemingwayhome.com/HTML/main_menu.html.
"Hemingway and the Magazines." The U of South Carolina Libraries. www.sc.edu/library/spcoll/amlit/hemmagazines/hem.html
Hemingway, Ernest. *Selected Letters, 1917–1961*. Edited by Carlos Baker. New York: Scribners, 1981.
_____. "Marlin off the Morro: A Cuban Letter." *Esquire* (Autumn, 1933). *By-Line: Ernest Hemingway*. Edited by William White. New York: Scribners, 1967. 137–143.
_____. "The Sights of Whitehead Street: A Key West Letter." *By-Line: Ernest Hemingway: Selected Articles and Dispatches of Four Decades*. Edited by William White. New York: Scribners, 1967. 192–197.

_____. *To Have and Have Not*. New York: Scribners, [1937] 1996.
Gingrich, Arnold. Quoted in *Esquire* (September 2008): 94.
Greenberg, Paul. "A Fish Tale." *The New York Times* http://www.nytimes.com/2007/08/12/books/review/Greenberg-t.html?_r=1&oref=slogin. 12 August 2007.
Luscombe, Richard. "Claws Out over Hemingway's Six-Toed Cats." *Guardian* 31 July 2006. (http://www.guardian.co.uk/world/2006/jul/31/books.usa)
McIver, Stuart B. *Hemingway's Key West*, 2nd edition. Sarasota, FL: Pineapple Press, [1993] 2002.
McLendon, James. *Papa: Hemingway in Key West*. Key West: Langley P, 1990.
Ogle, Maureen. *Key West: History of an Island of Dreams*. Gainesville: UP of Florida, 2003.
Reynolds, Michael S. *Hemingway's First War: The Making of "A Farewell to Arms."* Princeton: Princeton UP, 1976.
Sinclair, Gail and Kirk Curnutt, eds. Introduction. *Key West Hemingway: A Reassessment*. Gainesville: UP of Florida, forthcoming in 2009.
"Hemingway's Look-Alikes." Sloppy Joe's Bar. http://sloppyjoes.com/lookalikes.htm
Trogdon, Robert W, ed. *Ernest Hemingway: A Literary Reference*. New York: Carroll & Graf, 1999.
_____. *The Lousy Racket: Hemingway, Scribners, and the Business of Literature*. Kent, OH: Kent State UP, 2007.

# The Space Coast: Where Dreams Meet Possibilities

*Tammy Powley*

> I dwell in Possibility —
> A fairer House than Prose —
> More numerous of Windows —
> Superior — for Doors —
>
> Of Chambers as the Cedars —
> Impregnable of Eye —
> And for an Everlasting Roof
> The Gambrels of the Sky —
>
> Of Visitors — the fairest —
> For Occupation — This —
> The spreading wide my narrow Hands
> To gather Paradise —
>
> — Emily Dickinson

American poet Emily Dickinson describes the vision of possibilities which originally helped found the United States, a nation built by dreamers. Everyday realities like gas prices and political issues may attempt to ground us in the here and now, but they do not keep us from envisioning a future of possibilities as we look up into the night sky, beyond this world. Some of these dreams seem merely to be fantasies fueled by talented science fiction storytellers like Gene Roddenberry, famous for his creation of *Star Trek*, now a popular science fiction franchise, and Philip K. Dick, whose stories became embedded in blockbuster American movies such as the now classic *Blade Runner* and later-produced movies *Screamers*, *Total Recall*, and *Minority Report* ("Films"). However, science fiction has become reality to many Florida residents in a state some still consider a paradise, and those who live and work on the Space Coast of Florida, the home of Kennedy Space Center (KSC), have first-hand knowledge of this. The rest of the nation, though not physically located as closely, has also shared this experience, especially when it comes to the relationship of pop culture and space exploration. Hollywood, California — not Hollywood, Florida — has been responsible for shaping much of what we think when it comes to exploring the heavens, and now the two are fused, as science fiction often crosses over into scientific facts.

One of the most significant scientific resources today in Florida is the KSC, home to the National Aeronautical and Space Administration (NASA) and numerous aerospace contractors. Unequivocally, the KSC has been responsible for some of the nation's most astounding scientific accomplishments, while its development also resulted in creating Florida's historically recognized Space Coast, once a vast area of undeveloped swamp land that now coexists with rocket boosters, launch pads, and aeronautical engineers. Florida's cultural identity is tied to the space center, and in this chapter I examine the notion that Florida's Kennedy Space Center has been responsible for more than just great scientific discoveries. It has helped build a nation of dreamers.

I frame this essay in history, purposefully selecting major historical milestones rather than attempting to include the entire history of the KSC, a topic already covered very well and in some detail by many other authors. Historic events related to the KSC are naturally responsible for shaping much of the nation's related popular culture as well as space culture; however, eyewitness narratives from local citizens add to the insights of more famous participants who have lived these dreams and, in some cases, nightmares which have encompassed the Space Center. Without their stories, the text simply becomes a group of facts with no discernable connection to the dreams and possibilities that have helped to develop an iconic relationship that most of us recognize, whether or not we are Florida natives, when we think of Florida's Kennedy Space Center. I focus on the following questions: How did the KSC initially develop from a possibility into a reality and affect the cultural environment of local residents? What was the vision of the original, newly transplanted space center residents? How did the KSC impact the national consciousness and become integrated into our nation's psyche, as well as affect our popular culture? Does this iconic relationship and connection to popular culture still continue in the twenty-first century, and if so, how does it inform the nation's dreams of future possibilities?

## The Right Stuff at Cape Canaveral

The Space Coast of Florida refers to Brevard County, one of the largest counties in Florida. Like much of the state, the original inhabitants included Native Americans and later, Spanish explorers. Its large coastal area and access to rivers such as the Indian River and Banana River provided plenty of natural resources for living off the land, and even today, a surprising amount of wildlife still manages to negotiate a life between housing subdivisions and golf courses. By the mid–1800s, pioneers prompted by land grants started to settle in the area as well, especially after the Civil War, when "defeated Southern soldiers and northern veterans as well moved their families to the unoccupied frontier to seek new lives and opportunity" ("Brevard County History").

Originally part of an even larger area, by 1905 Brevard broke off and established its current boundaries, located now between Indian River County to the south and Volusia County to the north. The famous Flagler railroad continued to bring more residents to the area who made their living off citrus farming, commercial fishing, and tourism until World War II. Currently, Brevard has a population of over 500,000, with 16 cities and towns, and includes a huge stretch (72 miles) of Atlantic Ocean beach ("Brevard County History").

Like much of present-day Florida, Brevard County is still a tourist destination. Within close driving distance to Disney World, Epcot, and other theme park attractions, it is also home to one of the most famous beaches in the country, Cocoa Beach; however, its economic and cultural foundation changed considerably after World War II when the United States government took proactive measures to become a leader in what was then considered true rocket science. In an unprecedented and controversial step, the government established the Army Ballistic Missile Agency in Huntsville, Alabama, using a team of German scientists, "men who a year before had been using their genius to try to stop the Allied efforts for victory in Europe" (Faherty 4). Headed by Dr. Wernher von Braun, the group was assembled in order to start developing, building, and testing missiles for the United States Army. Eventually, this team moved to what was originally a testing ground called Cape Canaveral, a more remote area of Brevard surrounded by water, and ideal for running and monitoring missile testing. By the 1950s, both the U.S. Army and U.S. Air Force were conducting numerous tests at Cape Canaveral. These initial steps into a scientific space frontier were the beginnings of what evolved into a national aerospace industry that would plant much of itself at Cape Canaveral, and thus the county was aptly nicknamed the Space Coast of Florida. This time marked the early stages of a monumental manned space program, some of which was later romanticized in Tom Wolfe's *The Right Stuff*. First published in 1979, the book's popularity with a public hungry for heroes propelled it to the big screen in 1983. It may have been about thirty years after the fact, but eventually, Hollywood did catch up and realize this true story was worth telling. In an un–Hollywood-like approach, the tale is told with surprising accuracy. It begins with the test pilots who were attempting to break the sound barrier, then goes into the selection of the first pilots to be trained as astronauts, following this with the Communists' slap in the face with the launch of Sputnik, and finally culminates with the success of three space missions manned by Alan Shepard (played by Scott Glenn), Gus Grissom (Fred Ward), and John Glenn (Ed Harris). Cape Canaveral plays a significant part in this narrative account, as the story wraps up with astronaut Gordon Cooper (played by Dennis Quaid) flying Mercury-Atlas 9 from Cape Canaveral's Launch Complex 14 (*The Internet Movie Database*).

## KSC Emerges from the Muck

Before anything else — before man walked on the moon and before the shuttle flew teams of astronauts into space — the space center complex had to be imagined and built. Of course, "built" may not be the correct word to use considering the initial development of the center, where those involved made do with what they had available at the time. Maybe "assembled" might be more appropriate, considering that the Cape Canaveral Missile Test Annex included a slab of cement (which was poured directly over sand), plywood scaffoldings, and trailers. This was the site of the first successful launch from the Cape in July of 1950 called Bumper 8, a two-stage missile, and this was where many other launches soon followed (Faherty 7–8).

One of the witnesses to Bumper 8 was Elizabeth Bain, who was responsible for monitoring radar equipment during testing and who has the distinction of being the first female to work on a launch pad. In September 2000, Bain and other retired KSC workers participated in an ongoing oral history project. She was interviewed about her experiences working at the Cape and moving to Cocoa Beach, which at the time had little in the way of housing or other amenities. A single mother of two, she was offered a position as a chief clerk and moved from New Jersey to Florida. She eventually went to work for the Air Force because of a lack of male personnel due to the Korean War. In an interview, she explains how she came to work at the Cape:

> Well, they were so short of men to take care of radars and things, that they asked me if I knew anything about radar because I had worked, you know, with people that had been into this thing. I was exposed to what they were talking about and knew what a radar set was and everything. So they said, "OK, you're going to go to the Cape." There were two other ladies that went up with me, but they were able to work in an air-conditioned van that was not on the pad. Where with me, I worked with Dick Jones's group, and it was in a rinky-dinky little truck-type thing, that had all the equipment and things in it printed "interference control." So the GIs that were there, about five or six, kind of felt sorry for me, so they said instead of you sitting in this truck why don't you let us work it out so that you can sit outside the truck and do the radar out there. That was the way we ended up [11].

All of these people — Elizabeth Bain, the GIs, and other members of the small team who began at the beginning, imagining, making do, working around whatever obstacles presented themselves — had some understanding of the significance of the work they were doing. However, as Bain explains, their picture of the future was not completely clear: "Although we were aware that they would take certain steps to go further and further, we had no idea what it would eventually come to. All of us were very proud of the fact that we were actually able to do something" (19).

KSC, at this point, was still evolving and remained an unclear vision in the minds of those closely involved in the process. This process went into overdrive soon after the Russians launched Sputnik and the space race began. It took the president of the United States, John F. Kennedy, to focus the lens and clearly outline what was expected of the nation's space industry:

> I believe that this nation should commit itself to achieving the goal, before this decade is out, of landing a man on the Moon and returning him safely to the Earth. No single space project in this period will be more impressive to mankind, or more important for the long-range exploration of space; and none will be so difficult or expensive to accomplish [quoted in Pyle 13].

This challenge literally launched the Mercury, Gemini, and finally Apollo programs. We did make it to the moon. President Kennedy, however, would not live to see this happen many years later with the landing of Apollo 11 on July 20, 1969 (Pyle 43), and after the president was assassinated, his name was used to unite the Cape Canaveral Testing Annex and the Launch Operations Center (operated by NASA) to officially create the John F. Kennedy Space Center (Day), today most often referred to simply by the acronym KSC.

## From Tropicana OJ to "We Have Lift-Off"

From 1950 to 1969, a considerable alteration occurred for Brevard County affecting both residents and the surrounding environment. The launch pad where Elizabeth Bain worked was not the only spot that lacked infrastructure. When she naively agreed to live temporarily in the house owned by the man who interviewed her, Bain had no way of knowing what a tremendous favor he was doing for her and her children, because at the time there was no rental property available. They would have had no place else to stay on Cocoa Beach. The condos, surf shops, and mini-marts that now crowd the island were nonexistent; the little "row houses" were the only housing, and most of them were occupied by native residents (Bain 10). Norris Grey, who also participated in the September 2000 oral history project, was a serviceman stationed on the base at the time. He lived out on the launch area, literally sleeping on the pad and eating C-rations for two weeks as he and other servicemen prepared for the Bumper launches. Because there weren't enough barracks for the men to sleep in, they set up World War II mosquito bars right on top of the launch pad, and that's where many of the security and infantry men slept (Gray 16).

William Barnaby Faherty discusses the changes that occurred in the area in his book *Florida's Space Coast: The Impact of NASA on the Sunshine State*. "During the years 1950 to 1960, when the Cape changed from an area of citrus groves, sand bars, and swamps to a major launch site, Brevard became the fastest growing county in the country.... Brevard [saw a population] increase of 371 percent [and] the median income had risen to $6,123, the highest in the state" (15).

Not all of this income came from residents employed directly by the Air Force or NASA; independent contractors became very much involved in the transition from citrus farming to space exploration as they took on countless support roles needed at the time. Today, many of these contractors such as Lockheed, Grumman, Boeing, and Harris play an even bigger role in the operation of the KSC, especially the shuttle, the area's most recent manned space vehicle project. Technically related services were not the only services needed. With such a large facility to operate, the KSC needed food vendors, security, and transportation. All of these smaller industries spun off the initial aerospace industry and infused the area with jobs, which in turn, enticed more people to move to the Space Coast.

One area of the Space Coast that realized enormous change was Port Canaveral. At one time, it was a small port used mainly by shrimp boats, and later by Tropicana to ship orange juice north. Today some of the largest cruise ships in the world dock and load tourists who will be traveling on ships owned by Disney, Carnival, and Royal Caribbean. Minnie Mouse, appropriately sporting a sailor suit dress and heels, greets travelers as they arrive and climb aboard. Access to rivers like the Mississippi made the small port a perfect match for the needs of the space program, which would use it to transport large pieces of equipment. Years of dredging helped expand the port so that it could accommodate larger ships, opening it up to more opportunities and eventually converting it into "one of the busiest cruise and commercial ports in the Western Hemisphere" (Faherty 161–2).

The general population was, for the most part, open to these changes, understandably interested in earning wages that far exceeded those of citrus pickers and packers. But, as in many rural areas, some community members were reluctant to welcome the "missile people" with open arms (Faherty 15). Not everyone was happy to see these changes happen, but there was really no way to stop them as Cape Canaveral, Cocoa Beach, and the surrounding areas exploded with growth.

## Locals Get Lost in Space

The dream of living and working in Florida came true for those who took a chance on a new life and moved to the area. This unique cultural environment attracted northern transplants to the Sunshine State lured by the promise of high-wage jobs and a semi-tropical way of life. "Men of science and industry, academics and engineers, politicians and dreamers, in short, people from all walks of life, united in an unlikely alliance to reach to the Moon. It was a time like no other" (Pyle 13).

Even with the catastrophic Apollo 1 accident that killed astronauts Gus Grissom, Ed White, and Roger Chaffee during a simple spacecraft check in 1967 (Pyle 18), the influx of newcomers continued. Most were there because of the Apollo program. These included engineers like Charles Lynch, who had spent time at Eglin Air Force Base in 1955, and, after finishing his enlistment, went on to earn his engineering degree from Northrop Aeronautical Institute in California with the intention of becoming part of the space program. A few years working for various aerospace contractors, first in Texas and then in Alabama, taught him the value of a government position that might pay a little less but provide more security for his family. He managed to land a coveted position as a NASA engineer, and in August 1967 moved from Huntsville, Alabama, to the bedroom community of Rockledge, Florida, along with his wife and three young daughters, ages 4 months, 4 years, and 8 years old. Looking back now, even though he had lived in Florida before, he admits they "didn't know what to expect" and discovered "Huntsville was already civilized [compared to the] poor housing in the area. A few people were still living in campers and trailers.... The Humphrey Bridge was still made of wood.... It was the end of old Florida."

The Lynch family was typical of the countless numbers who came due to the Apollo missions, which had become the primary focus of the KSC and NASA, starting with Apollo 7, which launched in October 1968 (Pyle 18). The race to the moon had officially started, and more Apollo missions would follow as these once-new residents transformed into Space Coast locals. Each launch brought with it a kind of energy that spread throughout the community. I was one of those locals, and though very young, I still remember the huge number of people who lined up across from the pad and along the waterway to watch each launch. We'd load up in VW vans and pickup trucks ready for a day of festivities, bringing picnic lunches and lawn chairs as we prepared to wait it out. It was a massive party complete with moms who would bring cakes decorated like missiles, offering free slices to anyone who happened by. Once we witnessed the launch, we all fell silent and thoughtful, proud and amazed at what we had shared, and we still thought of this moment days later after the lawn chairs were put away and our sunburns had subsided. Lynch described it as "a strange feeling" similar to a carnival atmosphere: "You had all this excitement, and then everyone would be quiet, for two or three weeks, before it all started over again [for the next launch]."

This Moon craze was not just a hot topic in Brevard County or the State of Florida. The early to late sixties was packed full of movies that related to space adventure. The Moon, especially, was the focus of numerous B movies: *Moon Pilot* (1962), *First Men on the Moon* (1964), *Hercules Against the Moon Men* (1964), and *Rocket to the Moon* (1967) ("Movie Listings by Genre"). All of these had some sort of scenario placing men on the moon, much like the real-life goal of NASA. On the smaller screen, space travel was given a more domestic flair with the television show, *Lost in Space*, where a family of astronauts is thrown off course and continues to travel to alien worlds as its members try to find their way home. This show ran from 1965 to 1968 and was basically the equivalent of *The Brady Bunch* in space (Phillips). All of this media attention continued to idealize the notion of man in outer space.

Of course, with every boom there comes a bust, and while Apollo 11 brought us to the Moon, the brass ring that everyone was after, what followed was an unexpected change in the political atmosphere and ultimately the last mission to the moon with Apollo 17 in December 1972. Plans were in the works for Apollo 18, 19, and 20, and all the launch hardware was in place to follow through with these missions, but the U.S. Congress of the early '70s did not have the vision of its predecessors (Guillemette). The space race by this time was long over and the political climate no longer looked favorably on space exploration, so the Apollo program ended, and "Brevardians moved from space to earth, namely to keep their jobs as layoffs soared toward the ten thousand mark" (Faherty 112). Though Faherty goes on to point out that the layoffs did little to affect the growing population of Brevard County, this is primarily because of a change in demographics than because most workers found local jobs after losing their positions at the Cape.

In 1972, I was nine years old and many of my friends' parents had lost their jobs. I may not have had a full understanding of the crisis going on, but as I rode my bike around my neighborhood, the row upon row of "for sale" signs was unnerving. One friend of mine confided that they might have to move back to New York because her dad's company was going back there. To keep his family in Florida, he sacrificed his career as an aerospace technician to become the manager of a local drug store, a far cry from the launch pad but enough of a living to allow him to support his family. But many families were not that lucky, and little by little, KSC employees moved away and were replaced by retirees. Charles Lynch explains how this happened: "Many houses were empty. People just walked away from their homes. That's when the retirees came down here. It was like grocery shopping. They could pick almost any house they wanted and just take over the payments. We really didn't have that many retirees around here until then." The bust eventually turned around, though the glory days of the early Apollo years would never be matched. Apollo was not the end of the KSC or NASA or the Space Coast. Skylab followed and "became the bridge to sustaining manned space flight while the nation opened up new avenues to Space exploration" (Faherty 118). One of these avenues eventually led to the Space Shuttle Program that, like Apollo, had its share of successes and disasters. The Space Coast population now consisted of more than just "missile people," and the nation continued to look at this area of Florida to inspire.

## Genies and Guinea Pigs

Cocoa Beach, in particular, found favor with a national audience. If someone asked you where you were from and you mentioned any city on the Space Coast other than Cocoa Beach, most Yankees would not comprehend. Even if you didn't live in Cocoa Beach, it became easier to say so just to give at least a vague understanding of your location. To most non-natives, Cocoa Beach *was* the Space Coast because, more than any other area in Brevard County, it saw a concentrated dose of development during the early Apollo days. This included hotels, office buildings, nightclubs, and restaurants, and the "nation came to identify the space program with Cocoa Beach rather than with other communities in the vicinity" (Faherty 16). This fascination with Cocoa Beach, NASA, and Florida's part in space exploration spilled over into pop culture with the television show *I Dream of Jeannie*, the creation of Sidney Sheldon. Airing for the first time in 1964 and running for five consecutive seasons, its main characters include a 2,000-year-old genie and an astronaut (Lundquist). They share the roles of protagonist and antagonist, creating comedic scenarios that intertwine slapstick with space missions. U.S. audiences now had a little of the Space Coast in their living rooms, via a television show, once a week. This show still airs through reruns and DVD collections. The city even renamed a street after the show: "I Dream of Jeannie Lane" (Duggins x). Much like the space center, the television show has become an icon of the era.

Space was becoming a romanticized frontier both in real life and in the fantasy world created by Hollywood. Following *I Dream of Jeannie* and *Star Trek* on the small screen came space adventures for the big screen with such motion picture epics as *2001: A Space Odyssey* (1968), directed and co-authored by Stanley Kubrick; the *Star Wars* series (which began in 1977) from writer and director George Lucas; and of course, *Star Trek*, which crossed over to the cinema in 1979 with its first of a series of movies starting with *Star Trek: The Motion Picture* (The Internet Movie Database). Movies about cowboys and cops were being replaced by stories that took place in other worlds, in a future that movie-goers could only imagine. Astronauts were the new Lone Rangers who could virtually take audiences on new adventures to new worlds.

Major Nelson and Captain Kirk were fictional characters, but real astronauts like Alan Shepard and John Glenn were just as popular, becoming celebrities at the space center, and their presence at Cape Canaveral during the '60s "electrified the place ... transform[ing] lazy little Cocoa Beach into a high-tech boom town and a rocking, rollicking hot spot. The young engineers and their families built homes, schools, churches" (Thompson 204). The Space Coast was no longer a sleepy county of citrus farmers and fishermen and had evolved into a national leader in technology, a home to heroic astronauts as well as unimaginable scientific discoveries. In his biography of Alan Shepard, *Light This Candle: The Life and Times of Alan Shepard America's First Spaceman*, Neal Thompson talks about the instant hero status conferred on the original 110 test pilots just for being nominated by NASA, as well as about Shepard's thoughts on the strict selection process that followed:

> The selection committee was looking for men "who were not only in top physical condition but had demonstrated that they had the capability to stay alive under tough and dangerous assignments." Skeptics ... would snicker that what NASA really wanted were guinea pigs. But Shepard didn't see it that way. He saw aviation at "a crossroads, and space was the new turning point ... something new and important" [161].

Each Apollo launch brought Americans together emotionally and spiritually as they listened on radios or watched their televisions to hear if the astronauts were successful, and if not, as in the Apollo 13 mission, if they would make it safely home to Earth. This powerful, real-life story was moving enough to prompt a movie version in 1995: *Apollo 13*, directed by Ron Howard and starring Tom Hanks, Kevin Bacon, and Bill Paxton. Characters in the movie illustrated a fictionalized version of the story that was in many ways accurate, particularly when it came to showing how the entire country was watching and waiting for the safe return of its heroes, in reality astronauts Jim Lovell, Jack Swigert, and Fred Haise. These were nationally shared experiences, not just the property of locals or NASA employees, and even critics of the space program had to agree that America had surpassed the Soviets in the space race. We had won.

The Space Shuttle program made another big connection to mainstream America. It no longer limited astronauts to male pilots from one of the branches of the U.S. armed services. Dr. Sally Ride was the first woman in space as part of the 1983 *Columbia* mission. Astronauts from other countries such as Holland, West Germany, and Canada also participated, as well as the ill-fated school teacher and civilian Christa McAuliffe, who died during the *Challenger* accident in 1986. Other reasons the shuttle caught the attention of average Americans included the large number of flights and the airplane-like structure of the spacecraft which "added a new thrill" to this program (Faherty 132–134). Even the program's first spacecraft was named after a fictional spaceship everyone knew very well: *Enterprise*, from the popular syndicated television show *Star Trek*. In the beginning, it seemed possible that space flight would one day become just as common as flying in an airplane.

The horrible accidents of *Challenger* and later of *Columbia* in 2003 were sobering reminders for the nation that space flight was anything but common, at least not yet, and that space exploration was still dangerous. In 1986, it seemed unbelievable that the first accident even happened. Much like the Kennedy assassination, most of us who were old enough to remember the incident also remember where we were and what we were doing when it happened. It's a day we will never forget. My own experience was particularly eerie. I was listening to the radio, wearing my circa 1980s Walkman, while conducting research at the University of Central Florida's library, when I heard a brief news flash from the radio station. I stopped with a stack of books held in my arms and looked around at all the other students and staff who were quietly going about their business, obviously unaware of what had just happened. I realized no one in there could tell me if what I had just heard was correct (as this was well before Internet access in school libraries), so I rushed outside and looked up into the sky. The tail smoke was normally visible even as far as Orlando, but that day I couldn't find it. I saw a friend of mine walking by the library entrance and immediately told him what I had heard. Of course, he told me I had to be wrong. That just wasn't possible. The events in each of our stories may differ, but the experience was still the same: shock, disbelief, and grief. Unlike the rest of us, McAuliffe, the first lay person to attempt space travel, seemed to realize the risk she was taking, and as her well-known quote indicates, she also was aware of the importance of this attempt. "I touch the future. I teach" (iCelebZ.com).

## Looking in the Rearview Mirror

With so many other issues crowding America's psyche in the early twenty-first century, it may seem difficult to believe there is still room for us to dream about space. Confessions of Space Shuttle astronauts such as Mike Mullane, who talks in his autobiography about his experience in 1987 as one of the 29 men and 6 women to be selected for the program, may even seem naive today: "I dreamed of feeling the crush of a rocket's G-forces on my body and of seeing the great globe of Earth behind my ship. I dreamed of the day I would fly a rocket as part of the 'Conquest of Space'" (22). This kind of overwhelming excitement harks back to the early years of the shuttle program, which may not have been as electrifying as the Apollo program, but is unmatched today. It is uncertain whether the U.S. will find a successful program that will bring back the glory days of space exploration and thus generate the same kind of excitement, especially in the public mind.

Politically, the atmosphere is still not as encouraging as during the Kennedy era, and with a real war going on, though removed from our soil, it is hard for the ordinary citizen to focus on the possibilities of space. The majority of space missions now are unmanned robots or satellite launches. In fact, the Space Shuttle will be in mothballs soon, and dreamers like Mike Mullane will only be found in autobiographies on quiet library shelves rather than in the spotlight during a launch. So what is next for the KSC and NASA? How can they continue to inform the nation's dreams of future possibilities, and is popular culture even paying attention any more?

Apollo fever is certainly only a memory now, but according to Pat Duggins, a longtime journalist for National Public Radio whose voice is associated instantly with the topic of space exploration, the narrative is not necessarily over with the retirement of the shuttle. "It's a story of lost dreams, facing change, and new dreams to come" (xi). These new dreams he talks about are, in fact, grounded in the old technology that made Apollo so successful. Theorist Marshall McLuhan's notion of the past affecting the future describes the philosophy that NASA seems to have adopted with some of the programs it has planned for the future: "We look at the present through a rear-view mirror. We march backwards into the future" (75). In many ways, NASA and the team at the KSC are looking into their rearview mirrors and modeling aspects of the Apollo program that seemed to work so well back then.

The Moon is back in view for the Space Coast, and Mars has been added as well. Both are planned destinations for the latest space program called Constellation, which will use the KSC to maintain ground operations including launch, recovery, and landing. The Ares and Orion spacecraft will be launched from well-known Launch Pad 39-B, previously used for both Apollo and the Space Shuttle. Their missions also sound very familiar: "Ares I is an in-line, two-stage rocket that will transport the Orion crew exploration vehicle to low Earth orbit. Orion, which will eventually carry humans back to the lunar surface, will accommodate as many as six astronauts" (*Kennedy Space Center*). Another similarity is the physical design of Orion, which looks very much like the old Apollo rockets. The cone shape is restored, replacing the airplane-like design used during the shuttle years. NASA, at least, is trying to build momentum again by using its Web site at www.nasa.gov to present a modern marketing concept through content and videos aimed at contemporary, web-savvy audiences, with the mantra, "at NASA, exploration powers inspiration, innovation, and discovery." The International Space Station has had a human presence since 2000 and the Constellation program has goals which mirror those of Apollo—traveling to the space station in 2014, returning to the moon by 2020, and building an outpost on the moon. This seems encouraging for the United States to be inspired again by the "Conquest of Space" (Mullane 22).

It has taken over 35 years for another Moon mission, and according to Rod Pyle, those who worked closely within the original Apollo program believe that they all "had a dream that the powers in Washington and the nation at large may no longer share" (180). However, Pyle makes a good argument as to why the nation should continue to dream about space exploration and act on that dream. We had a successful Moon program before, so we should continue. It will push and expand our technological capabilities. Mars is the next closest planet which "feeds the human soul." And finally, if the U.S does not continue, we will lose our competitive edge to another country or countries which continue progressing their space technology (180). If we stand still and do not attempt to move forward, even if it is just a few steps, it is the same as taking many steps backwards.

As a product of the Space Coast's rocket fever, growing up in Brevard County and later working at the KSC writing operation and maintenance manuals as my first real job out of college, I choose to be optimistic. The general public currently may be unconcerned about the future of space exploration; however, future space programs look promising. As Constellation has the opportunity to prove itself and make history like its model, Apollo, the gaze may one day return to the KSC and to the people on the Space Coast who continue to support the space program. Even so, there will always be dreamers like Alan Shepard, Elizabeth Bain, Christa McAuliffe, Mike Mullane, and Charles Lynch who are able to "dwell in Possibility" (Dickinson).

## Works Cited and Consulted

Bain, Elizabeth M. "Interview." Kennedy Space Center Oral History Project. September 25, 2000. http://www.ksc.nasa.gov/kscoralhistory/.

"Brevard County History: A Brief Introduction." Brevard County. http://www.brevard county.us/history/history-summary.cfm.
Day, Dwayne. "Cape Canaveral." U.S. Centennial of Flight Commission. http://www.cen tennialofflight.gov/essay/SPACEFLIGHT/KSC/SP46.htm.
Dickinson, Emily. "I dwell in Possibility." *American Poems*. http://www.americanpoems. com/poets/emilydickinson/10609.
Duggins, Pat. *Final Countdown: NASA and the End of the Space Shuttle Program*. Gainesville: University Press of Florida, 2007.
Faherty, William Barnaby. *Florida's Space Coast: The Impact of NASA on the Sunshine State*. Gainesville: University Press of Florida, 2002.
"Films." Philip K. Dick.com. Philip K. Dick Trust and Electric Shepherd Productions. http://www.philipkdick.com.
Gray, Norris. "Interview." Kennedy Space Center Oral History Project. September 25, 2000. http://www.ksc.nasa.gov/kscoralhistory/.
Guillemette, Roger. "Project Apollo." U.S. Centennial of Flight Commission. http://www. centennialofflight.gov/essay/SPACEFLIGHT/apollo/SP19.htm.
"The Internet Movie Database." Amazon.com. http://www.imdb.com.
"Kennedy Space Center." National Aeronautical and Space Administration. http://www. nasa.gov/centers/kennedy/home/index.html.
Lundquist, Patterson. "Concept." I Dream of Jeannie. http://www.idreamofjeannie.com/.
Lynch, Charles. Personal interview. May 27, 2008.
McAuliffe, Christa. "Christa McAuliffe Quotes/Quotations." iCelebZ.com. http://www. icelebz.com/quotes/christa_mcauliffe/.
McLuhan, Marshall and Quentin Fiore. *The Medium is the Massage: An Inventory of Effects*. Madera: Gingko Press, 2001.
"Movie Listings by Genre." Films and TV. http://www.filmsandtv.com.
Mullane, Mike. "Sputnik." In *Riding Rockets: The Outrageous Tales of a Space Shuttle Astronaut*. New York: Scribner, 2006. 18–23.
Phillips, Mark. "The History of TV's Lost in Space." *Lost in Space* the Classic Series. http://www.lostinspacetv.com.
Pyle, Rod. *Destination Moon: The Apollo Mission in the Astronauts' Own Words*. New York: Collins, 2007.
Thompson, Neal. *Light This Candle: The Life and Times of Alan Shepard America's First Spaceman*. New York: Crown Publishers, 2004.

# Cuban Miami: Manufacturing Casablanca
*Rafael Miguel Montes*

At the tail end of a relatively nondescript strip mall in Hialeah, Florida, a place now known more for its congestion and factories than for the pink flamingoes of its defunct race track, stands what some may consider a spectacular display of hubris. Located across the street from a twenty-four-hour Walgreen's and next to Angelita's Dolar [sic] store, The Morro Castle cafeteria has been feeding people for the last two decades. Known as one of the few places in South Florida where one can purchase a full breakfast for fewer than three dollars, the cafeteria prides itself as one of those restaurants transported directly from the island prior to the revolution. Its name was slightly different in the Havana of the 1950s, but *El Castillito*, baronial but diminutive and somewhat anonymous then, gained notoriety upon its owners' move to the city of Hialeah. Now rechristened and sharing its name with the colonial fortress at the mouth of Havana Bay, the restaurant deems itself an enduring symbol of Cuban exile culture.

Behind its plate-glass entrance, located directly next to the sliding window counter where waitresses in black polyester uniforms pour espressos and offer buttered Cuban toast to the walk-up crowd, you enter a world of exile nostalgia. Photographs of the original restaurant façade in Havana, small postcards from the forties from Cubana Airlines offering round trip flights from Miami to Havana and back for thirty dollars, and snapshots of famous performers and politicians who dined at *El Castillito* act as potent reminders of the past. The nostalgic collage vies for the patron's attention to such an extent that one may miss the framed first dollar earned in America by the owner of Morro Castle, or the two-year-old restaurant review from a local newspaper, or even the well-preserved snapshot of the head waitress, Amelia, an employee since the early fifties, at her American citizenship swearing-in ceremony. The entrance wall is not so much a requiem for the past, but a coherent synthesis of a cafeteria's history lived in two places. The wall implies the notion that many "Cuban exiles realized that their identity was dependent upon a continuity between past and present, and between Cuba and the United States" (García 93). This continuity hinged upon not only the preservation of Cuban culture and traditions in exile but also the acknowledgement that the dreams of an eventual return diminished with each passing year in Miami. In other words, a Cuban past and an American future, though not necessarily mutually exclusive, sets in motion a present that might be viewed by some as a case of cultural paralysis or dogged anti-assimilation (Croucher 77).

It would be very simple to view the cafeteria as just another example of Miami's Cuban population failing to understand its location in the United States and not some mythical North Havana. The dining room wall is dominated by a mural painted by one of the sons of the owner of the original fortress which gives the restaurant its name. Beneath a sky-blue backdrop, from one of the castle's walkways, four young men in white linen shirts and tan gabardines look upon the diners enjoying breakfast in Hialeah. Frozen in time and in space, the two owners and the original line cooks from the original restaurant in Havana are smiling at your decision to eat in their establishment. Though in real time, the real world of twenty-first century South Florida, three of the four are deceased and the youngest is approaching eighty, the mural is a nod to a heritage and a history that invokes where this place you are now eating breakfast all began. Over the top or not, it would seem rather closed-minded to demand or even suggest that these memories of immigration, of lives lived elsewhere, are apt symbols of regret or ingratitude. Exile should not entail an absolute severing of the root, a denial of one's past in order to ensure immersion in the present of the new nation. One may see the mural and the mural only and not see the paper placemats emblazoned with the highway map of Florida, or the cheeseburgers and chicken fingers on the menu. One may see the mural and the mural only and deem this place excessively ethnic, exotic, foreign, without bothering to read the signs of hybridity, synthesis, and biculturalism all around. One may see the mural and the mural only and see only what one already decided to see.

According to noted Florida International University sociologist Lisándro Pérez, "The Cuban presence in Miami is evident in a myriad of ways. The 'Cubanness' of the area is manifested not only in demonstrable terms, such as economic activities and cultural events, but also in a more tangible manner, such as ambience" (83). Citing David Rieff's 1987 travel narrative *Going to Miami: Exiles, Tourists, and Refugees in the New America*, Pérez reaffirms the writer's belief that multiple waves of Cuban migration have altered and "largely taken control of the atmosphere of the city" (83). Despite the sociologist's brief nod to the economic and cultural impact brought about by the Cuban population in Miami, the ambiguous nature of the rest of the assertion proves somewhat more problematic. Dealing in auras, senses, feelings, and vibes, Pérez caters to the same forms of subjective perceptions of the city that has often seen Miami transformed, in the popular imagination, into a hypertropical oasis of supermodels, linen suits, clacking dominoes and unrepentant hard-line Republicans dreaming of a free Cuba. Neither the New Casablanca nor Paradise Lost, Miami is "the multicultural crest of the wave of the American future" (Grenier and Stepick 1).

Packaging Miami as either a foreign landscape of unusual rituals and practices or a momentary destination for taste-makers, supermodels, lifestyle addicts, and the glamourati has been one of the most significant tactics used to establish the city's sense of otherness. Arguably, it is this re-definition of the city, usually from the perspective of those who only momentarily call it home, that is the image of the city that dominates the global conversation. Whether it's a Travel Channel episode entitled "The World's Sexiest Beaches" showing South Beach or it's a pan of the magic city intercut with bikini-clad models walking the beaches during an airing of The Latin Grammys, the viewer captures the message that Miami is the mythical land of the beautiful, the tanned, the toned. Given the inattention to all other potential images available here—the elderly waiting at bus stops in triple-digit temperature or blocks-long lines of people outside the Immigration and Naturalization building praying for an appointment to even get in the building—it seems only natural for the authentic Miami to disappear behind and beneath the gloss of the manufactured one.

Controlling images and creating illusions is the potentially dangerous byproduct of the media industries who well understand the allure of pop culture and our unending obsession with that culture. Unwilling or unable to deal with the complexity—the messiness—of people or places or events, producers of popular culture deal with metaphors, icons, texts easily read and equally easily understood. The power of the popular is in its imaginary cohesiveness and its ability to have *all* speaking the same language of experience and *all* recognizing the same objects regardless of the strength of our experience or the power of our recognition. Visual shorthand and experiential shorthand offer so much mass veracity to the image or to the text that it begins to seem true and to feel true. This new truth, much more enticing for its imagined completeness than the old subjective collection of half-truths and near-truths gives popular culture its most significant power. In the realm of pop culture, Miami is not the piecing together of the tales of the immigrant, the refugee, the model, the millionaire, the migrant worker, and the playboy. It is one thing and only one thing. It is not your hometown.

It is in the realm of travel literature that one most readily sees this attempt to create a singular definition of a visited location. Authors of travel narratives tend towards narrating their own Anglo shock instead of exploring a multicultural city built upon the inclusion of, and conversations among, multiple countries and diverse populations. The aim of this chapter is to explore the mechanics of this genre of literature and how much of the meaning in this type of writing depends on a number of preconceived notions of the writer. From popular representations of the Cuban exodus and the allure of South Beach nightlife to Rieff's work, Joan Didion's *Miami* and Alexander Stuart's *Life on Mars*, all offer a compelling portrait of a city dissected by those only expecting to be tantalized by tropical passion and castigated for their monolingualism. Their Miami is quite different from the comfortable home I've inhabited for almost four decades and can only exist as they have imagined. The city can only truly be as foreign as they expect it to be.

## Travels into the Heart of Cubanness

For Joan Didion, arriving at Miami International Airport results in a type of submergence that makes her feel as if she has landed underwater. Her "experiencing certain weightlessness" evolves into a "heightened wariness of having left the developed world for a more fluid atmosphere" (23). Thus begins her narrative of the city of Miami — an aqueous, permeable waterscape that, due to its status as less-developed, allows Didion to develop it to her own specifications. The author's reconstruction of the city engages two of the most common tropes of Miami-based travel narratives: tropicalia and Havananess. Written during the pastel proliferation of *Miami Vice* and in the aftermath of nationally telecast images of tent cities erected under superhighways, one could excuse Didion's exuberant depiction of Miami's heat with its "hot colors, hot vice, shady dealings under the palm trees ... similar to that of pre–Revolutionary Havana" (52). Yet in the midst of all that sizzle, there are portions left uncooked.

Even a cursory glance at these lines from Didion's work offers this reader, located in Miami and born in Cuba, evidence of the author's derogatory attempts at local portraiture. The common stereotype of Hispanics as temperamental, passionate, and given to moments of uncontrolled spiciness relegates the population to an area outside of reason, intellect, and logic. The hot temperature of the city affects the internal Hispanic heat that ties Hispanics to the landscape to such an extent that they cannot even hope to raise themselves to the level of traveler that Didion certainly has achieved. For Didion, vice and other surreptitious activities also become central to the Cuban character because exiles are trapped in the politically-charged nexus of counterrevolutionary activity, political assassination aspirations, and narcotics trafficking. In other words, the city is submerged and the economy is subterranean. Yet another blind spot for the author is the tacit assumption that Havana is the supreme signifier of the island itself. Havana, short-hand for the many provinces of Cuba as well as each of these areas' local customs and dialects, funnels the entire island into a confining package.

Narrowing the island perspective by privileging the capital, the seat of Castro's government, although culturally naïve, is narrative genius. The reason for Didion's reductive maneuver is due, in part, to the intent of the text itself. By tropicalizing Miami, and thus aligning the city with Havana, Didion allows herself to explore the interconnectedness between the two areas. Although this is not a unique perspective, since much critical work on Miami relies on this paradigm, this particular text's evocation of the Miami-Cuba contact zone sets up a historically-frozen community that has found itself incapable of overcoming the Cuban Revolution or the failed Bay of Pigs invasion. Didion's documentation of political minutiae, ranging from the infiltrations of covert operatives, to the presence of the CIA, FBI and other national policing agencies, to paramilitary organizations performing maneuvers in the Everglades, creates for the reader a Bond-inspired city of intrigue.

Plots thicken and pages turn; however, the Cubans bear the brunt of the narrative by being cast as exiles whose longing for home has become so acute that they've taken up arms to liberate the lost homeland. According to Didion, "Miami Cubans ... take their stand on a higher ground, *la lucha* as a sacred abstraction, and any talk about 'interests,' or for that matter 'agreements,' remains alien to the local temperament, which is absolutist, and sacrificial, on the Spanish model" (110).

The suggestion of absolutism, in light of the writer's agenda, stands as one of *Miami*'s ultimate ironies. By explicitly constructing a monolithic community too caught up in the struggle to engage with the American culture of self-interest (Didion 110), the multi-faceted political stances of Miami Cubans, changing through the advent of acculturation and further instances of exodus, are undermined by day-to-day exigencies of fighting the good fight — the abstract *lucha*.

Although all Miami Cubans seem to be conservative ideologues bent on dethroning Castro, the characters in Didion's book are mainly terrorists, anti–Castro community leaders, and besieged (fire-bombed) anti-embargo victims of the first two segments of the population. Didion's evaluation of Miami as a floating diaspora (121), exchanges cultural interrogation for lurid details of political betrayal. This maneuver permits her narrations of intrigue and espionage to undermine any semblance of cultural exploration. Eschewing examination for the sake of entertainment, a common stumbling block of travel narratives, makes *Miami* a potentially dangerous document. Conceived as a spirited, rhythmic, passionate portrait of the city (Didion 126), it is, ultimately, composed of silences, volatile (sub)plots, and temporal paralysis. Didion's Miami of 1987 is Matanzas's *Bahía de Cochinos* of 1961, is Dallas's Deely Plaza of 1963, is Kennedy's visit to the Orange Bowl of 1962, is Reagan's speech at Dade County Auditorium of 1983 — an intricate network of military, governmental, and revolutionary moments.

From this swirl of temporal and geographic dislocations, Didion rarely strays in her narrative of political intrigue and Miami subterfuge. On the rare occasions when she attempts to discuss the ceremonies and customs of Cuban exile culture, her voyeurism bears a strong resemblance to outsider superiority rather than cultural reportage. What you sense throughout the descriptions of the people who populate the city is an incessant need, on Didion's part, to reinforce the tropical fusions she perceives to be the essential component of the Cuban character. Her narrative lens captures images of Miami Cubans running around and attempting to blow each other up; when they stop running and stand still, Didion perceives them through a hazy, Caribbean filter which wholly marks them as other, as different, as, ultimately, lesser.

For Didion, the female guests at a *Liga Contra el Cancer* charity function render an "effect [that] remained lush, tropical, like a room full of perfectly groomed mangoes" (53) Furthermore, the male Cuban community in this Miami sees itself in the throes of a constant battle against communism: "In the Cuban view, the world turned" upon the axis of "conspiracy and allegiance" (Didion

78) willing to die for "*la patria*" or perish in "*la lucha*" (Didion 77–8). In other words, the men of Cuban Miami long for homeland and are willing to destroy themselves in the name of democracy and liberation. The women, on the other hand, are passive fruit in "Bruno Magli pumps and silk and linen dresses" (Didion 53), doing their part to keep up a less important good fight, namely, self-sacrificing acts of charity.

In her role as detached onlooker, however, there seems a tacit denial that power can be wielded without some degree of responsibility. Miami-based terrorism and tropical imagery, to a bilingual native of Cuban descent, fails to either appeal or appall because the text seems almost fictional, despite its extensive bibliography. Personally, I have never seen this Miami. I have seen small strip mall offices where ex–political prisoners gather one night of the week to talk politics and military history. I have seen brief hunger strikes over detainee neglect at the Krome detention center that have ended soon after the news camera vans drove away. However, I have also seen a Cuban-American population whose desire to return to Cuba permanently, post–Castro, diminishes radically, as well as an American-born second generation, born to Cuban exiles, with only a marginal understanding of Spanish. Not offering this type of all-inclusive portrait of Cuban Miami, and convincing readers that her vision of the city is a factual document, Didion chooses to narrate a decidedly foreign and conspicuously unassimilated population more for effect than for veracity. A somewhat assimilated enclave whose old guard is dying and whose new guard maintains some traditions as it operates in a global economy makes for a much less dramatic read.

Didion herself scoffs at ethnic opportunists who come to the city for a couple of days to create a culturally troubling portrait for glossy travel magazines. She is enraged by the "condescension" of those "inclined to reduce the particular liveliness and sophistication of local Cuban life to a matter of shrines on the lawn and love potions in the *botánicas*, the primitive exotica of the tourist's Caribbean" (61). However, even though she sees herself as temporary native and not a freelancing tourist, Didion is not above succumbing to her own sense of cultural myopia:

> Almost any day it was possible to drive past the limestone arches and fountains which marked the boundaries of Coral Gables and see little girls being photographed in the tiaras and ruffled hoop skirts and maribou-trimmed illusion capes they would wear at their *quinces*.... The favored facial expression was a classic smolder. The favored backdrop was one suggesting Castilian grandeur, which was how the Coral Gables arches happened to figure [54].

Despite the class fantasy inherent in the community's celebration of the *quinces*, Didion's descriptive technique ridicules the spectacle by focusing attention on a sequence of stereotypes that some inexperienced observers may perceive as actual components of Cuban-American culture and the families that uphold this culture. The mock smolder of the decorated girl is witnessed by the "machismo" of a brother or boyfriend and the doting mother "in dark glasses

... protect[ing] the symbolic virgin.... Point[ing] out the better angle, the more aristocratic location" (Didion 54). Macho men and overbearing mothers and hopeless debutantes act out their aristocratic delusions in Didion's eyewitness account and the author chooses to report the events without commentary. By choosing not to explain how the *quinces* ceremony acts as an important rite of passage and a vital moment of cultural preservation, nor how the aspirations to aristocracy attempt to allay the grief of having lost everything and being forced to begin again in exile, Didion reduces the proceedings to the level of outlandish absurdity. By actively engaging in analytical silence, Didion does more than watch. She dismisses.

In sharp contrast to Didion's dismissive "monarch of all I survey" (Pratt 201) persona is the sensory-driven narrator of ethnic fusions created by Alexander Stuart in *Life on Mars*. This particular Miami travelogue emphasizes the city as an amorphous space station, an alien world of aliens, where the inhabitants arrive at a moment's notice and transform themselves. Constantly shuffling identities, people passing through Miami recreate themselves "under the sensualizing and democratizing influence of extreme heat" (43). According to Stuart, "Nothing is fixed in a town where for many people their main project in life is themselves—reinventing their history, their sexuality, or, in the case of so many models and work-out junkies, their bodies" (43).

Stuart's perspective on local culture, fueled by the ingestion of a variety of mind-altering pharmaceuticals, is quite protean in nature. Gone are the (counter)espionage hysterics of a community of terrorized exiles. In its stead, Stuart reintroduces the many communities that manage to inhabit the city of Miami. Criss-crossing the Deco district of South Beach, the Mediterranean revival setting of Coconut Grove, and the "heart ... of Miami's Cuban population" (87) that beats on *Calle Ocho*, the traveler seeks to incorporate the many cultures that, like himself, also criss-cross the cityscape.

Despite this democratic paradigm shaping the entire project, the transplanted British novelist finds it nearly impossible not to succumb to the same estranging tendencies so prevalent in Didion's text. Despite casting America as a "virus, invading my soul, destroying my Britishness, my faith in humanity, my quiet calm and natural reserve" (7), the distancing mechanisms inherent in the travel narrative preserve the outsider persona even within the metamorphic atmosphere of outer space. Stuart's land of changeable identities is a disorienting space somewhere between the First World and the Third World: "Miami does not feel like America or Cuba.... It's stranger than that—like Frank Sinatra crossed with Luis Buñuel, or Flipper trapped in a labyrinthine fiction by Borges" (14). The fact that this genre relies on the author's consistent reinforcement of his/her subject matter's inaccessibility is vital to underscore at this juncture. A major aspect of the travelogue's contrived nature is its unspoken claim that the narratives presented are accidental or even spontaneous. This strategy permits the author to place him/herself in an equally ambiguous position. In this case, Stuart purports neither to shape the text nor select the subjects in order to advance the notion that he is narrating first-hand experience, as it comes racing by, and also attempting to include these experiences, at a moment's notice, into his ever-expanding intercultural vocabulary. In other words, Stuart is the antenna, receiving passively all the Miami satellites' transmissions.

The main predicament of this confused spectator perspective is ultimately its willingness to devalue the subject matter for the sake of maintaining the disorientation intact. Various cultural practices of the Cuban community in Miami suffer, at different points in the text, in Stuart's desire to cast himself as the perennial outsider. The most virulent portrait of the exile community is painted within the *Botánica el Indio Amazónico* section. Stuart's attempt at narrating the proceedings within the *Santería* market is weighed down by demeaning stereotypes and condescending gestures of othering. The promise of cultural exchange within the site's network of Cuban, Miamian, and African roots is utterly nullified by Stuart's fixation with the aforementioned textual mechanisms that formulate the traveler as an alienated, confused eyewitness: "I duck inside a smaller, more promising establishment, the *Botánica el Indio Amazónico*, its window filled with kitsch religious statuary, ceramic Native American figurines, heavily decorated with painted feather head-dresses and beads, and a whole range of other weird shit demanding immediate investigation" (88).

One wonders what type of investigation Stuart plans to pursue after reducing the accoutrements of a "four-thousand-year-old Nigerian religion" (89) into a diorama of kitsch and shit. Furthermore, it is imperative to note that the investigation that does ensue fails to promote a further understanding of the surroundings or of the religion. Unable to overcome the language barrier while conversing with the "tiny old Cuban woman behind the counter" (89) and unwilling to have his future divined by "a large, somewhat retarded-looking man in a feather head-dress and Native-American garb" (91), Stuart exits the shop with the results of the perfunctory investigation in tow. "This place is weird: voodoo, doll worship, hexes, and curses, are in the air" (92).

The almost imperceptible movement from weird shit to weird place accentuates the author's unwillingness to engage, participate, or even learn from the exchange. He enters and exits the store with the same set of beliefs. The difference, however, is the experience permits him to view the two members of the Cuban community as distorted images lessened by their obedience to otherworldly, in the narrator's eyes, cultural practices. Somewhere between "tiny old" and "large somewhat retarded" stands the untouched and untouchable Stuart. In fact, the author is so oblivious to the element he is in that he continually miswrites *botánica* as *botánico*. That one mistyped vowel functions as a visible trace for the dismissal of the cultural importance of the entire experience.

These squandered chances, perhaps due to the travel narrative's requirement of authorial bewilderment, are quite numerous throughout *Life on Mars*. Despite Stuart's nearly incessant references to Miami's reputation as a site of identity transformation, it seems almost ironic to gauge how very little his own identity transforms when he experiences the "foreignness" (231) of the territory.

Individual transformation may be part of the activity of the members of the city; however, the outsider/insider, white/non-white categories seem absolutely fixed. The author's "excellent social biopsy of the city" (Hiaasen) at times turns malignant in the racially/ethnically-charged contact narratives he chooses to relate.

A dinner party at Mitchell Wolfson's private supper club ends with a tour of the city chauffeured by the "millionaire philanthropist" (234). Wolfson, according to Stuart, "whisks us outside to the striking luxury of his white 1962 Cadillac Fleetwood, complete with whitewall tyres, leather upholstery, streamlined dashboard and a stylish radio which sadly doesn't work but seems to promise a twilight zone of broadcasts from the early 1960s" (236). The busted radio may not transmit the sounds and voices of the early sixties, but the racialized landscapes that Stuart and the other passengers encounter from within the safety and comfort of the Cadillac's "white" luxury, evokes the political atmosphere of the time.

Traveling through South Beach, the white signifier of class and privilege meets the natives: "Drunken couples—Hispanic, white, black, gay, straight—spill across the street in a confusion of colours, sounds, and smells: music, snatches of conversation in Spanish and English; sweat, perfume, liquor. Bodies thump against the almost stationary car; faces gaze in, eyes popping, mouths broadening in mostly generous smiles" (237).

Part Conrad, part Gunga Din, Stuart's narration of the incident sets up a series of class and color boundaries which immediately bring to mind Florida's ugly history of racial segregation, Jim Crow laws, and ethnic friction. The inebriated throng, a carnival of races, colors, and sexualities, is sharply contrasted to the straight, white men and affluent Europeans trapped in the "stationary" vehicle. The immobile whiteness, namely the car and its occupants, seems protected from the sensuality and the confusion exhibited by the teeming South Beach masses. The contact zone here, marked by "thumping bodies," is further racialized by the "broad" mouths and "popping" eyes of the seemingly predatory crowd. Physically stereotyped and capitulating to the sensual (sexual), the threatening, uncontainable, spilt crowd is further contrasted to the author's intellectual pursuit of putting it into words from his vantage point of class and culture.

When movement ensues, Wolfson wonders if the passengers "dare" to go on a "risky Adventure" to the "night-time netherworld of Overtown and Little Haiti" in the "this most conspicuous of vehicles" (237). This night journey into the metaphoric heart of darkness concludes the evening. However, in Stuart's depiction of the ethnicities and races and sexualities of Miami, what the reader essentially concludes is that the author is unable to speak from a place other than one bound by whiteness and privilege. The Cadillac voyage, in Stuart's hands, becomes a moment of automobilistic apartheid where all those who are not like him are reduced and othered for the sake of preserving his position as First World narrator. Going to Little Havana, Little Haiti, or Liberty City, for members of those respective communities, is not an "Adventure"; it is a chance to go home and relax after commutes, supervisors, and eight-ten-twelve-hour work days. From the manufactured beauty of South Beach, where Stuart resides and constructs his text, Miami may be the place where people "test-drive a transformation" (43); however, in the daily grind of traffic and labor, Miamians are, regardless of color, origin, or orientation, despite Stuart's narrative, locked on planet Earth.

Trapped by what Pérez-Firmat deems the "protocol of the travel journal, as if visits to Miami were expeditions into a foreign country" (*Hyphen* 19), David Rieff, the last author I have chosen to explore in this chapter, chooses to explain Miami as a much less expansive territory than either Didion or Stuart. Neither underwater nor outer space, Rieff's Miami is a network of enclosed spaces where ethnic and non-ethnic groups collide and conflict. Within these claustrophobic contact zones, exiles, tourists, and refugees in the New America, as his subtitle suggests, attempt to exchange culture and identity information. However, in proclaiming that "it is precisely the degree to which Cubans feel at home in Miami that makes the Anglos disenfranchised, homeless" (141), the promise of reciprocity collapses. Barter and interchange fails in the decidedly foreign battleground of ideologies the author chooses to impose upon the city during his gathering of impressions.

Given the book's genre, it seems obvious to choose the airplane as the apt metaphor for discussing the concept of multicultural enclosure. Momentarily confined in a pressurized cabin, journeying through an equally confining, metaphoric boundary labeled national airspace, Rieff observes the colors and languages he suddenly finds himself surrounded by in perhaps too close quarters. Amidst the "solid clumps of Spanish" and the "faces of the travelers [which] were unfamiliar" (19), the writer recalls the tired, racist trope of exotic unfamiliarity: "It was just what the Anglos said: Going to Miami was like going to a foreign country and see[ing] broad, stoical, Indian faces; dark-skinned women with heavily piled, dyed blonde hair; a general increase in corpulence and diminution in height" (19).

You wonder if Rieff is the only Anglo on the flight. These descriptions of difference, filtered through the first-person narration of the travel writer, set up a variety of troubling distinctions. It is not so much how broad, corpulent, or diminutive the passengers seem to be, but how, by placing himself as lone observer, Rieff sees himself as the paradigm of height, or weight, or an entire series of other physical characteristics. The textually reinforced passivity of the subjects under scrutiny, I would argue, makes it nearly impossible to read these variations as either genetically, culturally, or linguistically induced differences. In the hands of travel writers, not just Rieff, they enter the realm of imperfections. Despite supporting a narrative apparatus that purports to uphold the two essential components of the travel journal, exploration and comprehension, the third element commonly employed, disorientation, negates the hope of fulfilling the other two. In essence, the stranger will, by his/her very nature, perceive the land as strange.

Even more sinister, perhaps, is the distinct possibility that the writer, for the sake of the text, will do more than make the surroundings unfamiliar. Sometimes, as Rieff does in his experiences at the Versailles restaurant on *Calle Ocho*, he dismisses reality altogether. Taking a respite from the "smell [of] tropical air" and "the shock of feeling that distinctive Caribbean breeze against the skin" (42), Rieff enters the confines of the aforementioned eatery at midnight: "Sipping coffee in the new Versailles (a restaurant in its Miami incarnation), as I listened to the speeded-up Spanish, the clink of dominoes, and reveled in the overwhelming smell of rice and beans, I could have been along Havana's *Malecón*, staring out toward Florida" (42).

The conflation of Cuba-identified images serves Rieff's purpose of geographical conflation. By Havanizing Miami, he is able to insinuate a seamless connection between two cities central to the experience. The rapid-fire Spanish and "overwhelming" smells mark his outsider status. What seems peculiar about the experience is the sound of "clinking dominoes" within the establishment. Versailles is a restaurant. Patrons of the "quaint, kitschy, noisy" (Pérez Firmat, *Hyphen* 134) diner are primarily there to sate their hunger for home-cooked Cuban food. Why Rieff chooses to interrupt this activity with the misplaced noise of an impromptu domino tournament seems, on the surface, a mystery. However, given the compression of images in the passage, and the impressionistic nature of the genre, whether dominoes are now part of the Versailles experience for everyone is irrelevant. They are part of the exile experience and the Cuban experience, and, for Rieff and his primary readership, that is sufficient enough to introduce the game into the proceedings, regardless of whether or not its inclusion makes logical sense.

Hemmed in by the text's explicit assumption that going to Miami is not remarkably different than going to Havana, Rieff's collapsed globe avoids the political and cultural tension between the two territories. The evocation of the restaurant is quite different in the hands of a Cuban-American author and scholar who understands and underscores the emotional power of a place like this. Pérez-Firmat's Versailles, a powerfully iconic image of Cuban Miami history discussed in his seminal *Life on the Hyphen: The Cuban-American Way*, is the "glistening mausoleum" where the "history of Little Havana — tragic, comic, tragicomic — is written" (*Hyphen* 135). His reading of Versailles radically diverges from Rieff's composite by pointing out how divided the two cities, Miami and Havana, actually are from each other.

Pérez-Firmat's appraisal of the multiple mirrors and glass surfaces at the Versailles restaurant, oddly omitted by Rieff, creating a "Cuban panopticon" (134), eloquently reveals the exile's forced acknowledgement that one is eating Cuban food in Miami and not in Cuba. It is more than the entrees and the bodies that are multiplied. The awareness of "displacement — the pain of exile" (Pérez-Firmat 179) is also multiplied in these reflective surfaces. For this writer, "the hall of mirrors is also a house of spirits.... My idea of immortality is to become a mirror image at the Versailles" (Pérez-Firmat 135). It is within this vocabulary of displacement that Pérez-Firmat negotiates what he had earlier identified as the Cuban condition — the realization that no amount of fabricated attempts at verisimilitude will bridge innumerable geographic and historic divides.

Rieff's ultimate pronouncement of Miami as "that great, tempting orifice, sucking the immigrants north" (210) and a city where "even the refugee can be tourists as well" (211) accentuates the supreme conceit of the entire project. A journey that begins in the multiethnic confines of a Boeing 747 leaving LaGuardia Airport ends at the check-in counters of Miami International Airport. Apparently, the experiences in Miami, book-ended by scenes of arrival, departure, and constant motion, have taught Rieff little about Cuban Miami's ambiguous sense of home and place. Unaware, or consciously forgetting, the travel restrictions, the embargo, the politically-driven unwillingness to return, for some, and the economic inability to return, for others, Rieff makes everyone around him a traveler as well: "Now, the simple accessibility of the entire world via air travel makes ... forgetfulness all but unattainable.... Thus in Miami every alien and immigrant cannot but know that the journey home requires nothing more than some cash and a ride to Miami International" (210–1). Rieff's belief in the power of movement, regardless of historical and political truths, makes us all equal. It also makes us more like him.

## Myami: Lessons Learned Standing Still

During a recent trip to my local Cuban bakery, a place which I, much to the consternation of my immediate family, visit altogether too frequently, the owner called me back to her private office. Behind a cluttered desk overflowing with receipts, post-it notes, and faxes, a tower of dangerously leaning cardboard boxes dominated the back wall. One of the boxes had been razored open and placed on what would have been her office chair. The owner was very excited to show me the new catering brochures she had just had printed for her bakery. The glossy pages were quite impressive. Beneath the gothic-inspired logo of the bakery, professional photographs of meat pastries and fruit-filled tartlets dominated the page. Close-up shots of fondant cakes, intricately decorated, dominated the foreground. She had obviously spared no expense in making these hand-produced works of art the calling card for her six-franchise bakery empire.

On the reverse of the colorful page, a list of her specialties and catering packages appeared in flawless black print. Items, prices, descriptions all arranged in neat columns. Although the owner, a single mother of two, had left Cuba in the Mariel boatlift of 1980 and catered to a predominantly Hispanic clientele, she took special pride in having printed bilingual brochures. Every Cuban item had its American translation directly next to it. *Croquetas* were now labeled *croquetas*—croquettes. *Pan Cubano* read *Pan Cubano*—Cuban bread. Realizing the tower of boxes before me represented thousands upon thousands of these printed catalogs as well as several thousand dollars of self-promotion, the English professor inside me hesitated upon seeing a rather major mistranslation.

Under the wedding cake section, the traditional *Pastel de Tres Pisos* had been translated not as three-tier cake but as three-tear cake. The customer in me who had been raised on her food and had never recalled a word spoken in English at the bakery paid the error little mind. The academic in me could not fathom how someone who has spent nearly three decades in Miami feeding so many and possessing the entrepreneurial wherewithal to own half a dozen businesses, cannot spell tier. How exactly could she, her American-born sons, and her Cuban-American printer have caught this mistake? Uncertain of which role to play, I complimented the photography and the design but also mentioned that there was a spelling error in one of the entries. I explained to her that "tear" means *lagrimas*, as in *llorando* (shedding tears), and "tier," with an "ie," means *pisos*. Taking the brochure from my hand, she scanned the page, found the error, grinned, and said, "¡Ay, m'ijo! Let 'em learn now that most marriages end in tears!"

The lesson her reaction imparted is both significant and true. As a successful businesswoman who has acquired more wealth than I'll probably ever see through her hard work, determination, and a truly unmatched product, she inhabits a Miami that is not one of linguistic precision or vocabulary perfection. She operates not within the exigencies of the native tongue but works towards pleasing other parts of the mouth — the sweet tooth, the sugared lips. Good food and good service needs no language and certainly none of my highly specialized skills. The palate neither knows nor needs grammar. The line of customers beginning at the counter and snaking out past the door not only represents her achievement on her own terms and in her own language, but also a city whose multiple populations, always seemingly from elsewhere, have always recognized that real power is not in communication but in understanding.

## WORKS CITED AND CONSULTED

Croucher, Sheila L. *Imagining Miami: Ethnic Politics in a Postmodern World*. Charlottesville: University Press of Virginia, 1997.
Didion, Joan. *Miami*. New York: Simon and Schuster, 1987.
García, María Cristina. *Havana USA: Cuban Exiles and Cuban Americans in South Florida 1959–1994*. Berkeley: University of California Press, 1996.
Grenier, Guillermo J., and Alex Stepick III, eds. *Miami Now! Immigration, Ethnicity, and Social Change*. Gainesville: Florida University Press, 1992.
Pérez, Lisandro. "Cuban Miami." *Miami Now! Immigration, Ethnicity, and Social Change*. Gainesville: Florida University Press, 1992. 83–108.
Pérez-Firmat, Gustavo. *Life on the Hyphen: The Cuban-American Way*. Austin: University of Texas, 1994.
Rieff, David. *Going to Miami: Exiles, Tourists, and Refugees in the New America*. Boston: Little, 1987.
Stuart, Alexander. *Life on Mars*. London: Black Swan, 1997.

# The Highwaymen and Other Black Icons
*Edmondson Asgill*

Not surprisingly, Florida's image in the national consciousness was shaped to a great extent by a number of African Americans from various fields. The primary focus of this paper will be on the recently rediscovered black "highwaymen painters," whose paintings are sought after with a vengeance today. But there are others that have contributed to the image of Florida, including such figures as Howard Thurman and Mary McLeod Bethune and two outstanding literary authors, Zora Neale Hurston and James Weldon Johnson. These will be discussed, albeit briefly, at the end of this essay.

In the '50s a group of black painters emerged in Ft. Pierce, from a section known as Blacktown, in Indian River County. They were mostly unskilled workers who by a stroke of good fortune discovered they could escape the only option then available to them, a very difficult life working in citrus groves picking and crating oranges and grapefruits. They discovered a talent for painting and a consumer market in need of art at basement prices. By the '80s that consumer taste had run its course, and the group had virtually disbanded. In the '90s, however, there occurred a resurrected interest in their work, and those of the original crew who were still alive suddenly found fame and even greater fortune. And this reenergized interest in highwaymen painting is not about to let up.

The origin of the highwaymen painters is not entirely shrouded in mystery, but in recent years, as they have become popular and their paintings increased in value, many fans, attempting to claim proprietorship to some sensational revelations about these painters, have speculated hugely and drawn self-gratifying conclusions. As Ken Hall noted, "anecdotal history" has become the genre for this. A case in point: there would have been none of these painters if there had been no A. E. Bacchus! A. E. "Bean" Bacchus is generally considered the grand patron of these artists. Also, Jim Fitch is claimed to have coined the label "highwaymen," a word that creates an aura sufficiently sensational and intriguing. The image of these painters has been raised to legendary status to the extent that the claims above have to be questionable.

Bacchus was a veteran landscape artist who retired to Florida to live out an epicurean and freethinking lifestyle. Attracted to his home in Ft. Pierce were a variety of artists including writers such as Ian Fleming of James Bond fame and

Zora Neale Hurston, the celebrated black female writer from Eatonville. All this liberal social gathering was at a time when tension between the races was high: the civil rights movement was picking up momentum in defiance of the increasing atrocities of the Klan. A house in Mims, Florida, belonging to Harry T. Moore, then leader of the NCAAP, was fire-bombed; Jim Crow was having a jolt of resurgence given the impunity racists enjoyed; and blacks had few opportunities but harassment from the police once they were outside their socially and politically assigned station in life as farmhands, domestic workers, or unschooled apprentices (Monroe).

So it was rather audacious and unquestionably deserving of praise for Bacchus to open his house to all and sundry, including black workers who were aspiring artists. These were self-taught artists who had a natural love and talent for painting even though many were not highly educated. Bacchus met Harold Newton, the first of the highwaymen painters, whom he encouraged to capture the idyllic Florida landscape of his imagination (Monroe 5). Thus, Bacchus became the father of the Indian River School of painters who were later renamed the "highwaymen painters." But Bacchus's relationship to Newton was more advisory than mentoring. Newton was already painting religious images before he met Bacchus—and continued to do so. Many of his paintings have the characteristic three birds representing the Trinity. Compared to what they could make in a month picking oranges, the black painters discovered they could make the same amount of money in a day painting! Bacchus encouraged these black painters to pursue the Florida landscape motif, which was his major impact on them. Beyond the camaraderie and his encouragement to work on landscape painting which would make them financially independent, he hardly influenced the quality of any of the work of the highwaymen. His role in the "discovery" or mentorship of the highwaymen painters is obviously overplayed and exaggerated. Bacchus, himself a product of the Hudson School of landscape painters, was a formally trained artist who had a technical regard for scale and spatial perspective. The highwaymen painters had no such regard for form.

Newton and the later crop of highwaymen painted, invariably from memory, an idyllic, but not necessarily romanticized, landscape of the Florida they knew intimately. They did not need, nor did they take advantage of, a subject in their immediate view when they painted. Their paintings were exaggerated and impressionistic, demonstrating, albeit unwittingly, reminiscently intuitive and residual traces of a deeply rich African cultural tradition of art: a complete disregard for form, proportion, and reality. Art is not a faithful reproduction of life but a surrealistic impression that allows much for the imagination. They painted purposefully for the utilitarian potential of the work, in their case, the immediate profit motif.

One is reminded of Alice Walker's classic short story "Everyday Use," where she contrasts African and Western aesthetics of art in Dee's attitude towards the quilt which was deliberately left to her sister, Maggie, to remind Maggie of her grandmother, and the kitchen utensils which Maggie and her mother simply recognized for their utilitarian, functional "everyday use." Dee, on the other hand (ironically calling herself Wangero Leewanika Kemanjo, a clearly misguided attempt to recall her African heritage), is only capable of seeing these objects from her Western-trained educational lens as art to be displayed on a wall for her similarly Western-educated friends to observe and admire from a distance, not to use. The black painters created evocative and suggestive statements of the imagination with an eye clearly targeted at a buyer. As one highwayman aptly put it, even if crudely, "A painting was not done until it was sold" (Monroe 9). Hezekiah Baker, another highwayman, remarked, "We didn't paint for perfection. We painted for color" (PBS interview).

The Florida which these black artists painted was one they instinctively knew too well. That Florida, fortuitously, was already appealing to the popular imagination of unspoiled, verdant (even savage) flora, moss-laden trees and a brisk kaleidoscope of bright colorful bushes and plants, marshes, raging ocean waves, animals indifferent to human presence, typical cumulus clouds (precursors to Florida's brisk but violent afternoon summer storms and hurricanes), and radiant golden orange-colored setting suns. Elements of the creeping modern world were seldom included. Their paintings were almost always devoid of human beings and the trappings of the modern world—cars, houses, public buildings, etc. They were not consciously painting some illusion the buyers wanted, nor were they deliberately avoiding replication of the real world that buyers might wish to escape from. The buyers they targeted wanted to reward the painters for their effort and wanted to decorate their offices as cheaply as they could get away with. These buyers were neither skilled in art appreciation nor were they in search of escapist art, as many pundits of highwaymen painting would have us believe.

It is obvious that Bacchus did not attempt to teach Newton and the other painters or to discourage their technique or style: their flaring colors, inexact proportions, or disregard for finesse and perfection. He may have been fascinated by what many have come to describe as primitive or vernacular art. America was just about to recover from a patronizingly drunken obsession with a popular but misguided view of African American artists of the Harlem Renaissance, an obsession sarcastically labeled "The Cult of the Primitive" when the "Negro was in vogue"(Glicksberg). Of course, while some Harlem Renaissance artists may have suffered this cult syndrome to gratify their white audiences, many Renaissance writers and critics resented this unflattering fascination with the exotic and the savage. This cultic appreciation was not a distinguishing or deserving mark of authenticity for the African American writer.

Two writers in particular, Imamu Amiri Baraka and Langston Hughes, responded to this misguided fascination with exotic and patronizing gestures towards African American literature, Baraka in his play, "Dutchman," and Hughes in "Slave on the Block." Harlem Renaissance writers may have been wrongfully hailed for indulging the African American dialect in their writings or for evoking the savage, untutored character in their heroes as we find in

Chesnutt's "The Goophered Grapevine" and Fisher's "The City of Refuge." But they were not necessarily writing for a white audience. In fact, Harlem Renaissance writers were no longer interested in writing for a white readership but were more interested in producing a body of literature that appealed to readers from their own heritage.

It seems possible, therefore, that Bacchus may have been more patronizing than helpful to Newton and the rest of the highwaymen. It was the initial highwaymen painters, Harold Newton, Alfred Hair, R.L. Lewis and Al Black, who taught the others. The three other painters who formed the original core of the highwaymen were James Gibson, Roy McLendon, and Livingston Roberts. These were students, not of Bacchus, but of Newton and Hair. The majority of these initial highwaymen never met Bacchus. Undoubtedly, he was first to recognize the talents of the initial few, to assist with materials and cash, and to freely open his house to them at a time when it was daring to socialize with poor blacks. It is reported that he often appealed to the highwaymen painters to slow down when they became more conscious of the quick fortune to be made than of the quality of the paintings (Monroe 7), but his influence on their art was negligible.

If Bacchus could claim to have any decided influence on any of the highwaymen, then it had to be on Alfred Hair. He was introduced by his high school art teacher, Zanobia Jefferson from Lincoln Park Academy, so he could receive formal tutoring (Monroe 5). She first recognized Hair's talent and love of painting. But even then, Hair quickly departed from Bacchus's tutelage and rehearsed high art and resorted to a formulaic, assembly-line style to mass produce paintings without much detail; his only motivation was to make quick money, not to produce lasting art. His paintings were strictly suggestive and full of color. Newton, on the other hand, was a more careful artist; he injected details into his paintings and is generally regarded as the most accomplished of all the highwaymen painters. Bacchus, it seems, preferred their untutored and informal paintings — raw, unpolished, irreverent, unabashed and indifferent to a critical world.

Another dubious element in the mythology of these black painters relates to the sobriquet, "highwaymen," first coined by Jim Fitch in 1994, almost fifty years after Harold Newton, the first of the black painters, had sold his first painting. Jim Fitch, a promoter of Florida art tradition, was inevitably bound to run into the works of the black painters. He was bewitched and quickly became one of the earliest avid collectors of their work. The label "highwaymen" has stuck ever since, even though at least one of the original painters, Sam Newton, Harold Newton's brother, has denounced the label and refuses to be associated with it (Beatty 58). The word may carry negative connotations of daredevil, criminal activity, but this was not Fitch's intention. The name is more a testament to the artists' persistence to break away in a daring way from the limited life of drudgery which the racist climate in American made available to them at the time.

Of course, the painters did not have occupational licenses and did not wish nor dared to buy them; they had to avoid attracting attention to themselves. They needed to avoid the tax collector and the police for breaking solicitation ordinances. They sold their paintings from the trunks of their cars. They essentially trekked along U.S. 1, which ran north/south along the Florida Atlantic coast. From Ft. Pierce in the south, they went as far north as Jacksonville and inland and west to Orlando, Tampa and sometimes as far northwest on the panhandle as Tallahassee and Panama City. They went in search of sympathetic patrons. Their journeys invariably took them away from their socio-economic stations and neighborhoods to lawyers' offices, doctors' clinics, banks, offices of insurance agents and real estate brokers, and, their mainstay, cheap motels along the Florida Atlantic beach strips. So it is not difficult to imagine, given the political and social temperament of the times, that they could be easy targets of police interceptions and harassments. They had to move discreetly and hurriedly and gather their wares quickly in order to dodge the ever vigilant, over-zealous police.

But this is not the whole picture. We know some of them actually set their paintings up on roadsides, where some cops, becoming patrons, were tickled by the notion of a black painter. In another case, a councilman is supposed to have insisted a painter purchase an occupational license before he would buy a painting. In any case, to avoid the vagaries of trying to sell their paintings on the highways or in neighborhoods where they were generally not allowed, the painters came up with a new strategy, a brainchild of Alfred Hair. The painters did not all have to try individually to sell their works. They kept painting and chose a point man who was sent out to do most of the selling.

Even though the term "highwaymen" might have negative connotation, the catchy label has certainly done the painters a world of good; it has imbued them with bravado, calculated cunning and legendary fame far beyond their wildest dreams. They had no illusions of being prodigies in the field. They painted fast, sold the paintings faster than they could dry, lived fast, and dodged the law as best they could. Now, by an ironic twist of good fortune, thanks to the nickname given them by Fitch, they are sought by art aficionados. Legislators have inducted them into the Florida Hall of Fame. A slew of imitators, wheelers and dealers cannot afford to miss out on this bonanza, and surviving highwaymen painters, not to be outdone, are today on the lecture circuit, are guests at galleries and art shows throughout the country and on radio and TV documentaries, and are even holding forth through their own Web sites. Even art teachers have included the highwaymen in their curricula in high school.

A third conundrum created by pundits is tantamount to a mischaracterization of the quality of the highwaymen's paintings. Their works have been given a number of names, many of which are patronizing and not quite complimentary: "vernacular art," "motel art," "folk art," "primitive art," "artless art," etc. They have even been described as "artists by default" (Monroe 2), presumably given the conditions by which they came to discover their calling. Jim Fitch claimed they learned "by osmosis," which is a rather cryptic denial of the highwaymen's own abilities. Indeed, the paintings were marked by all kinds of imperfections and infelicities: inaccurate or deliberately imprecise depictions, gross disregard for verisimilitude, exaggerated sketches that begin to suggest caricatures, and sometimes blatant infelicities, such as a limb from a tree suspended in space or a fingerprint smudge intruding in a blue sky that would make an aspiring or committed artist cringe.

Many paintings suffer from cracking, which happens when a primer, dry to the touch but not properly cured, is overlaid with paint. They also suffered from poor handling and consequent smudges when the final product, still wet, was loaded up for the market. Another infelicity was the inattention to obvious details: the absence of a signature, or a ball point pen used instead of a brush for the signature, untitled works that were not dated, or paintings signed by someone hired to sell the painting, so that authenticity of a particular work becomes speculative. But these annoyances should not diminish the value of the raw talent of these painters, even though they were not polished in art schools.

Given the impact they have had and continue to have on the contemporary art world, they obviously had talent, which often came through, despite the speed with which they painted to make quick money, and the consequent lapses in proficiency. They were not concerned with leaving an imprint of their worldview or making a political statement in their art. The primary motivation of the original highwaymen was to escape poverty. They were not conscious of marketing a sylvan, idyllic image of Florida sought after by their northern neighbors and visiting tourists from abroad. Even to allege that they inadvertently reshaped reality and thus contributed to a "mass conspiracy" of illusion (Monroe) is a quite a stretch for a body of unselfconscious painters who knew they could paint well enough to escape the painfully limited option that life in the South offered them. Willie Daniels, a highwayman painter himself, claimed that "Harold Newton's paintings looked so realistic that a rabbit being chased by a dog would be fooled and run directly into the painting" (Beatty 23).

This is how the highwaymen went about their work. They bought cheap Upson boards used by construction workers for their paintings. These boards have been discontinued since the '80s when the Upson Company went out of business, so it is not difficult to tell an original highwayman painting. The 4 × 8 boards were often cut up, usually into 2 × 3 pieces. For framing, they used cheap, white, crown moldings. To give the final product an antique look, the white moldings were brushed with gold or silver paint. The painters often competed to see who could paint the fastest. Many of them could produce 20 or more paintings in a day. James Gibson once painted a hundred pictures in a twenty-four-hour marathon (Monroe, Phenomenon). Robert Butler produced one of his memorable paintings in twenty minutes while the camera was rolling, and Al Black could paint an entire mural in less than thirty minutes. The paintings were loaded up in cars to be sold before they were completely dry or cured. The crown moldings helped somewhat but did not always prevent smudges. Depending on how desperate the painter was for cash or the predisposition of the buyer, the paintings went for anywhere from a mere $10 to $40.

To increase sales as business boomed, the painters had to mass-produce paintings efficiently and sell them quickly before law enforcers could obstruct their business. They began to congregate to distribute their workload. They soon created something like a production line. They employed apprentices to set up, as it were, a template. These apprentices cut the boards and added the moldings while others primed the boards or painted the initial background shades. Alfred Hair, for example, employed novices during the day to prime and paint the background of his boards. These he would finish the same night, overlaying the background with standard mental pictures he already had in view, making only slight variations. In a carnival atmosphere of beer and barbeque, a team worked into the night, apprentices cutting the Upson boards, adding crown molding or priming, while the experts painted. The next day, still wet with paint, another team of salesmen moved out to sell the paintings.

Many of these apprentices soon discovered their own talent (that is if they had not already known they had it) or learned very quickly. There was just too much money to be made and too much fun in the process to go back to toiling as farmhands. Al Black was a notorious slick talker who initially did most of the selling for the other painters. Then he learned to restore wet paints that were smudged. Before long he was painting and later mentoring many of the later highwaymen. Brothers soon joined brothers: Harold's brothers, Sam and Lemuel; Ellis and George Buckner; and Johnny and Willie Daniels all became painters. In all, there were twenty-six "original" highwaymen painters.

Al Black is perhaps the most colorful of all the highwaymen painters (after Alfred Hair who died too early and tragically in a barroom brawl). He started as an apprentice for Al Hair and graduated to become a hustling salesman and a restorer of damaged paintings. Before long he had mastered the craft and was painting himself, making $5,000 a week and living very extravagantly and dangerously too. Too slick for his own good perhaps, he was eventually jailed for cocaine possession and has been in and out of prison ever since. He has the singular notoriety of painting murals in prison which have brought peace and pleasure to inmates and prison staff. As one guard put it, he has turned the "prison into a museum." One health worker commented that his prison murals "allow the imagination to go places and to think differently than what the environment dictates," and another said his prison murals have created a safe space for employees and inmates alike to meditate, "a tranquil beauty and wonder to the prison environment" (Minton).

Not all the highwaymen painters were poorly educated. A few of the later highwaymen painters were quite educated. R.L. Lewis took art classes when he was recovering from a football knee injury. He attended Edward Waters College, graduated from Florida Agricultural and Mechanical University with a B.A. in art education, and taught high school for years. He started painting when he was very young, receiving his first payment of $2 for his rendition of the Last Supper. Fred Strickland, from far-afield Gainesville, was a jet engine specialist who served in the Marines and worked in the aerospace program at Kennedy Space Center for forty years.

By the 1980s many of the highwaymen's paintings had been discarded or relegated to garage sales. The artists had produced somewhere between 50,000 and 100,000 paintings (Monroe, "Phenomenon"). Many never ended up rich or singularly famous. Money came too easily and went too fast. They celebrated life flamboyantly, drove flashy cars, and lived riotously and dangerously. Many have died. At twenty-nine, Alfred Hair was murdered in a barroom fight. Robert Butler, one of the few who have made it big, unfortunately lost many of his paintings when the house in Lakeland where he kept many of his originals burned down.

The highwaymen were inducted into the Florida Artists Hall of Fame in 2004. Their paintings today adorn the Governor's Mansion and the Tallahassee House of Assembly, mayors' offices, libraries, galleries, museums, Epcot, hospitals and schools. The highwaymen and their paintings appear at benefits. Al Black's prison murals were catalogued by the state of Florida in 2001. Jim Minton described Al Black's work as "inspirational symbolism ... embedded with the attributes of divinity" and reported in the newsletter he and his wife issue a proclamation by then–Secretary of State Glenda Hood: "Their artistic visions have greatly contributed to our state's cultural heritage"(Minton).

A resurgence of interest in the highwaymen landscape painters and their paintings began in the '90s. Some speculate that this is a reaction to the deleterious consequences of modern incursions which are destroying the sylvan landscape—construction of highways and buildings, and traffic and the concomitant estranged human relationships which seem to be inescapable routines of life in the twenty-first century. Whatever the case, the surviving highwaymen have seized on the new interest in their work and have resumed painting. Now there are a host of other painters, some of them well-meaning copyists who are cashing in on the fervent interest in highwaymen-style landscapes. However many of them are trained and their paintings are generally more technically correct. Even some of the surviving highwaymen have "improved" their paintings by imitating the style of tutored artists. All the same, the pre–1993 paintings are the most desirable today, especially those with the rare incidence of people and buildings. With this sudden notoriety has come a host of charlatans marketing paintings as authentic highwaymen products, and hustlers who have attempted to exploit some of the not-so-savvy highwaymen landscape painters. One was offered $300 a week salary for rights to all his future works (Klinkenberg).

Realistically today, the paintings go for anywhere from $500 to $5,000. Harold Newton sold a painting for $34,950. The current record price for a highwayman painting is $42,000. Other successful painters are James Gibson, R.L. Lewis and Robert Butler. Gibson's 5' × 4' painting depicting sunset over Boca Ciega Bay near St. Petersburg, where Governor Charles Crist grew up, is now housed in the Governor's Mansion. That painting alone without the frame and mounting brought $18,000. Gibson was the featured artist for Black History Month in February 2008 (www.floridablackhistory.com).

Many of the surviving highwaymen today have their own Web sites (Gibson, Lemuel Newton, Issac Knight, Roy McLendon, Willie Reagan, and Willie

Daniels, for example), and they are in demand for appearances at schools, libraries, museums, galleries and benefits. Collectors are combing garage sales in hopes of finding an original highwaymen painting. Many documentaries have been produced on the highwaymen painters. "The Highwaymen: Florida Outsider Artists" is narrated by Spencer Christian and is available on VHS, DVD and CD (Everglades Production). Another, "The Highwaymen, Legends of the Road," features interviews with Robert Butler and Ann Carroll, the only woman in the original group of highwaymen (Arts Connection). In fact, Robert Butler has been advertised on QVC. Avid collectors Mr. and Mrs. Geoff Cook now issue a monthly online Highwaymen Newsletter of news and tidbits, and host an annual Highwaymen Festival the second Saturday in June (wwwfloridahighwaymen.com).

There are, of course, many other interesting African Americans from Florida who have made their mark on the national landscape — except these individuals are not nationally recognized for their Florida origins; having been born in Florida has not been a defining aspect of their success. On the other hand, Zora Neale Hurston and Weldon Johnson, or Thurman and McLeod Bethune, though they are no longer alive, are constantly in view and their work and reputations continue to resonate in academic studies and in cultural celebrations nationally.

Howard Thurman (1899–1981), whose house in Daytona Beach is today a national monument, has been listed as one of greatest preachers of the twentieth century in *Life* magazine. He was the first dean of a white university in this country and the first pastor of an interracial and intercultural church in the U.S. He published over twenty books, in addition to giving many public lectures. His sermons and meditations were a constant source of inspiration to America's greatest civil rights leader, Martin Luther King Jr. Mary McLeod Bethune established a school in 1904 today known as Bethune-Cookman University, which over the years has attracted national and international students. She was a founding member and first president of the National Association of Negro Women and a member of President Roosevelt's advisory team on black affairs. First Lady Eleanor Roosevelt was a personal friend of Mary McLeod and as first lady made personal visits and stayed at her house, also now a national monument, on the campus of Bethune-Cookman University (Long). The influence of these two outstanding individuals may be somewhat muted today and they no longer attract huge fans nationally, yet their names when mentioned in certain astute circles still do raise eyebrows in admiration and awe.

Annual events reflecting Florida's black history are the Juneteenth festival and the re-enactments of Civil War battles, such as the Battle of Olustee in Lake City. The Emancipation Proclamation went into effect on January 1, 1863, but many in Confederate states only came to know about it on June 19. Juneteenth is recognized today by blacks in many states, including Florida, as a time for celebration. The Olustee re-enactment, started in 1976, is held in the middle of February and usually runs Friday through Sunday. These two festivals are family and community celebrations marked by very similar activities—memorial services, parades, speeches, lectures, entertainment, food fairs, advertisements, arts and crafts, competitions, announcements, fundraising activities for special projects in the communities, and of course, the re-enactments and musical and theatrical performances (Fears). These festivals have become very popular for blacks in Florida, particularly for their historical significance: they provide educational opportunities to fill the gaps not popularly acknowledged in school curricula and oral discourse. For example, they address the roles of slaves and freed black soldiers in the confederacy and the Union in a variety of combat and non-combat positions, they describe the inventions of slaves, and they offer stories and depictions of what daily life was like for blacks during slavery and the Civil War.

James Weldon Johnson from Jacksonville and Zora Neale Hurston from Eatonville are long dead, Hurston in 1960 and Johnson in 1938, but they continue to exert some influence on the popular imagination. Weldon Johnson wrote "Lift Ev'ry Voice and Sing" (Wintz 50) for a school celebration of Lincoln's birthday, and his brother, Rosamond Johnson, set it to music. Today this composition has been rightfully appropriated as the "Negro national anthem." It's an uplifting song rendered lustily with fervor and pride as a standard feature on many formal occasions and celebrations in the black community. The song is a testament to the abiding faith and surviving strength of African Americans in spite of the terrible hardships they have been through, even from the very dark days of Jim Crow:

> Bitter the chast'ning rod,
> Felt in the days when hope unborn had died;
> Yet with a steady beat...
> We have come over a way that with tears have been watered
> We have come, treading our path through the blood of the slaughtered....
> God of our weary years
> Keep forever in the path, we pray.
> Lest our feet stray...
> May we forever stand,
> True to our God,
> True to our native land.

Another part of Weldon Johnson's work that continues to appeal to the popular imagination is his sermon poems. Not particularly instructive from a strictly doctrinal perspective, *God's Trombones* is a collection of seven stylized lyrical dramatizations of biblical events and stories, an enduring vernacular tradition today of preaching in the black church throughout America. Paul Lawrence Dunbar was the first to render the sermon as a verse poem in "Ante Bellum Sermon" (Dunbar). Many of the popular televangelist preachers, Rodney Parsley for example, are reputed to have attracted large congregations to their churches because they now preach like black Baptist pastors.

"The Creation," one of the sermons in *God's Trombones*, is a favorite recitation piece for children in the African American community and a standard choice in dramatic contests in schools and colleges today. This same stylized poetic sermon plays a pivotal role in a modern short story similarly titled, "The Creation," by Maxine Clair (164). In this short story, the main character, Wanda, has selected Johnson's "The Creation" for major local and state drama competitions. Her friend, Folami Quander, belongs to a sect of African Americans who live apart from mainstream American culture and are jealously guarding their African beliefs and traditions. To Folami and her family, the creation is not the biblical one of the Christian God. They believe Obatala formed the earth and created the orishas, who have personalities not unlike human characters. With Folami's assistance, Wanda is able to lend to Johnson's poem a vigorous dramatic orientation that is informed by the characters of the gods in the panoply of Yoruba theogony. Needless to say, she won the local tournament — although she was later denied a spot at the state championship because of her color.

These two poems demonstrate the cultural role Weldon Johnson has had in the national contemporary imagination. But there is even another work by Weldon Johnson that occupies a special place in our popular culture.

American law once defined non-white as anyone with one percent of black blood. Many who cannot be identified as black from their very fair complexion have safely made the choice to pass as white. "Passing" improves their social and economic standing in the society and this issue has been one of the themes unique to American literature. *Passing* (1929) is the title of one of Nella Larson's novels. It has tragic consequences for its heroine. Langston Hughes presents an ironic twist to this same theme in a short story, "Who's Passing for Who," when a white couple, not to be denied the opportunity to enjoy a culturally rich and memorable night of entertainment in Harlem, passes as black. But Weldon Johnson from Florida was the second of the many writers to have explored this emotionally painful subject boldly in his seminal novel, *The Autobiography of an Ex-Colored Man* (1912). Charles Chesnutt's *The House Behind the Cedars* (1900) was the first of this sub-genre.

In Johnson's book, the true love between the narrator's white father and his mulatto mother is squelched by their different racial circumstances. The narrator at first assumes he is white until reality enlightens him otherwise. When he leaves school, he decides to attend college in Atlanta to learn more about his heritage. But this does not happen: his money is stolen in a boarding-house, and he has to abandon his dream of a quality education. He drifts through a number of prodigal experiences, surviving mostly by his musical talent. He discovers "ragtime," which together with Negro spirituals he recognizes as a product of the genius of the black race. He finally decides to make something out of himself as a result. He returns from Europe to the Deep South to learn more about the rich musical heritage of black people and to record that history. But unfortunately, before he can achieve his goal, he witnesses the horror of a lynching, when a young black male is publicly burned alive, a crime which the law is totally incapable of preventing. Completely drained emotionally, humiliated and ashamed that a race of people could be treated so horrendously with impunity, he opts for the easy way out, choosing to forsake his race and to pass for a white man. As he puts it at the end of the novel, he sold his "birthright for a mess of pottage."

The landscape of race relations in America and the peculiar predicament of the mulatto have left deep psychological scars (Bullock and Davis). The mulatto is often portrayed as a tragic figure in literature, and "passing," as an inconvenient option for the faint-hearted, is a dilemma with which African American writers and thinkers have had to wrestle. The poems and the novel of Weldon Johnson occupy a cherished and lasting niche in the popular imagination of America.

Though Zora Neale Hurston died poor and in virtual obscurity in 1960, many biographies have since been written about her. Much attention was given to her after Alice Walker made efforts to locate her gravesite and to reissue her books. Hurston grew up in Eatonville, where an annual Zora Neale Hurston cultural festival is celebrated proudly today. This festival was initially intended as a scholarly investigation by scholars and fans of her life and work, but the festival has become a week-long major cultural event for vendors of African American artifacts, paintings, books, music, food, and clothing fashions; for cultural groups (choral, dance, theater, music performers); and for extra-curricular school field trips.

Hurston's historical importance cannot be gainsaid. She is regarded today as one of the earliest African American feminist writers. In her novels she has tried to recreate the beautiful, evocative language of blacks from the wealth of their vernacular folklore. *Of Mules and Men* is a fictionalized, anthropological attempt to capture the imaginative folkloric genius and evocative imagery of black dialect. As a researcher in anthropology, she studied religious beliefs and practices in the Caribbean, which she recorded in *Tell My Horse*. Almost fifty years after her death, Zora Neale Hurston remains indisputably the most popular black writer from Florida, widely read by the public and studied in schools. Two of her popular novels, *Their Eyes Were Watching God* and *Jonah's Gourd Vine*, were, indeed, set in Florida.

*Their Eyes Were Watching God* is probably the most widely read and studied of all Hurston's writings. With the momentum of the feminist discourse of the last forty or so years, it was logical that scholars and essayists recognize her for her pioneering role in the movement. But she never avowed feminism; her feminist orientation is not strident. Hurston is, deep down, a hopeless romantic rebel who writes to celebrate life and love in spite of the seemingly insurmountable obstacles, cruelties, and tragic consequences of the actions of her characters.

*Their Eyes Were Watching God* is a woman's search for a genuine love not tainted by extraneous concerns—not the social security in an atrophied marriage with Logan Killicks, nor the wealth and societal preeminence Joe Clarke offers but which entraps her in a Blakean kind of prison. (See William Blake's "Song"). Janie rebuffs all these inconvenient social comforts and scorns the judgment of a society which would readily frown on an older woman in love with a younger and penniless Tea Cake. Tea Cake offers, not marriage, but adventure and unconditional love. Janie recognizes the worth of his offer and runs away with Tea Cake in order to liberate herself from a patriarchal domination which stifled her first excursions into marriage. Unfortunately, her liberation is short-lived. Tea Cake dies. She returns unrepentant and scornful of those eager to condemn her for running away soon after her husband's death for a life of adventure with a man whose very name, Tea Cake, is a characternym suggesting reckless living. This romantic triumph of the woman who defies the prescribed societal role has endeared many readers to Hurston's work even today. The very lyrical opening paragraph of the novel presages this romantic triumph for Janie: "Ships at a distance have every man's wish on board. For some they come in with the tide. For others they sail forever on the horizon, never out of sight, never landing until the Watcher turns his eyes away in resignation, his dreams mocked to death by Time. That is the life of men" (1).

For Janie, certainly, her wish did come in with the tide. This romantic streak recurs in *Jonah's God Vine*. The main characters are absolute working-class blacks with very little education. But despite John's incurable philandering propensities, the reader recognizes John and Lucy as celebrants in an enviable idyllic romance. John writes to Lucy: "When you pass a mule tied to a tree/Ring his tail and think of me," to which Lucy responds: "Long as the vine grow 'round the stump/You are my dolling sugar lump" (52–53). John is rudderless once Lucy dies; she was the one who had been "spreading carpets for his feet and breaking off the points of thorns." But their love is eternal, almost reminiscent of Heathcliff and Cathy's in *Wuthering Heights*, by Emily Bronte. At his lowest, when John has lost his church and the esteem of his parishioners, his eternal love, Lucy, appears in a dream vision and directs him away from Sanford, where life had become unlivable, to Plant City, where he finds temporary respite in the arms of Sally Lovelace. She will eventually play the role of the surrogate mother to John's neglected children. Sally is a catalyst for John to redeem himself, for Lucy had only wished for John to lead a life of example. When he meets Sally, who offers him all the creature comforts that should make him forever grateful, his only thought is to make his peace with Lucy. "Let Lucy see it too, Lawd, so she kin rest. And be so pleased as to cast certain memories in de sea of fuhgitfulness where dey will never rise tuh condemn me in de judgment" (191). When he falters this time in that inexplicably mindless submission to the temptation of a simpleton in Oviedo and breaks his pledge to Lucy, it is time for him to return in death to her, where he belongs.

Zora Neale Hurston has also contributed to the popular culture in Florida through her fascinating ability to reinvent into memorable rhetorical masterpieces black folk imagery from the African American vernacular legacy with all its rhythmic syncopations, its emotionally painful imprecatory burdens, its humor, its proverbial characterizations of humans and animals, and its folk wisdom. "Jump at de sun," a spectacular encouragement to live one's dreams to the fullest, is today found in diverse places such as engravings on paperweights and, in fact, is part of the title of one of Hurston's biographies (Porter). Lucy brags of her petite frame when John tries to belittle it: "Ahm uh li'l piece uh leather, but well put together" (35). John, not often equal to the verbal contests with Lucy, moans: "Jes' 'cause women folks ain't got no big muscled arm and fistes lak jugs, folks claims they's weak vessels, but dass uh lie. Dat piece of uh red flannel [her tongue] she got hung 'tween her jaws is equal tuh all de fistes God ever made and man ever seen" (96). On gossipers, "Some of 'em so expert on mindin' folks' business dat dey kin look at de smoke comin' out yo' chimney and tell yuh whut yuh cookin'"(119).

When John summons the courage to run from his oppressive stepfather, he stands before the burnt-off trunk of a tree to excise the man's memory by "throwing the character of Ned Crittenden [his stepfather] upon it." In an ironic double entendre with very suggestive sexual innuendo which foreshadows his tragic flaw, he asserts his manhood which his stepfather had vainly tried to crush: "Ahm jus' lak uh old sho—soft when yuh rain on me and cool me off, and hard when yuh shine on me and git me hot" (47). His inability to control his libido ultimately destroys him.

Not happy at the prospect of her daughter marrying John Pearson, Lucy's mother Emmeline is itching for a fight with her daughter. "Ah means to beat her 'til she rope lak okra, and den agin Ah'll stomp her 'til she slack lak lime" (67). Her hostility raises consternation in her husband, Richard Potts. "Whut make you got tuh plow so deep, Emmeline?" (68). Later she says of her soon-to-be son-in-law, "Maybe he got cloths, but he ain't got a chamber pot tuh his name nor bed to push it under" (77).

Howard Thurman and Mary McLeod Bethune are now household names beyond the borders of Florida. Festivals such as Juneteenth and the Olustee Battle Re-enactment in Florida are noteworthy events acknowledging the significant contributions of blacks in America and attract ever-increasing audiences today. The literary legacies of Zora Neale Hurston and Weldon Johnson have reflected well on African Americans in Florida. But of even more interest today is enthusiasm for the paintings of highwaymen.

The highwaymen painters do not even remotely approach the intellectual accomplishments of Thurman and McLeod or of Hurston and Weldon Johnson. But they are the current focus of public excitement. These landscape artists were, I am sure, surprised that they could sell a painting for $40 in the fifties, and suddenly have money to spend on things they could only have dreamed of, when their friends and neighbors took a month to make the same amount. They may have even been amused that people would pay such money for work which they themselves did not see as a sacred mission, the way most artists generally do.

Jim Fitch might have been searching for a sensational name for these black painters, and though it is exaggerated and somewhat inaccurate, "highwaymen" has unleashed a tidal wave of curiosity and created a growing body of fans who cannot get enough of these painters and their paintings. Short on schooling, the painters still had talent. The public knows good art when it beholds it. Whatever the artistic value the public may place on each of these figures, they all have had influence. These talented African Americans have influenced not only the development of popular culture in Florida, but in the nation as a whole. Reason enough to "Lift Every Voice and Sing."

## WORKS CITED AND CONSULTED

Baraka, Imamu Amiri. "Dutchman." In *Norton Anthology of African-American Literature*. Edited by Henry Louis Gates and Nellie Y. McKay. 2nd ed. Norton, 2004. 1946–60.
Beatty, Bob. *Florida's Highwaymen: Legendary Landscape*. Orlando, Fla.: Historical Society of Central Florida, 2005.
Blake, William. "Song." In *Norton Anthology of English Literature: The Major Authors*. Edited by M.H. Abrams et el. 5th ed. Norton, 1987. 1317.
Bullock, Penelope. "The Mulatto in American Fiction." *Phylon* 6 (1945): 78–82.
Chesnutt, Charles. "The Goophered Grapevine." In *Norton Anthology of African-American Literature*. Edited by Henry Louis Gates and Nellie Y. McKay. 2nd ed. Norton, 2004. 604–13.
_____. *The House behind the Cedars*. Boston: Houghton Mifflin, 1900.
Clair, Maxine. "The Creation." In *Literature Without Borders*. Edited by George R. Bozzoni and Cynthia A. Leenerts. Upper Saddle River, N.J.: Prentice Hall, 2001. 164–180.
Cook, Geoff. Floridahighwaymen.com. www.floridahighwaymen.com.
Davis, Arthur P. "The Tragic Mulatto Theme of Langston Hughes." *Phylon* 16 (1955): 195–208.
Dunbar, Paul Lawrence. "An Antebellum Sermon." In *Norton Anthology of African-American Literature*. Edited by Henry Louis Gates and Nellie Y. McKay. 2nd ed. Norton, 2004. 910–12.
Fears, Mary L. Interview, April, 2008.
Fisher, Rudolf. "The City of Refuge." In *Norton Anthology of African-American Literature*. Edited by Henry Louis Gates and Nellie Y. McKay. 2nd ed. Norton, 2004. 1225–36.
Fitch, Jim. "The Highwaymen" *Antiques & Art Around Florida*, Winter/Spring, 1995. www.aaaf.com/fews9501.ktm.
Glicksberg, Charles. "The Negro Cult of the Primitive." *Antioch Review* 4.1 (1944): 47–55.
Hall, Ken. "The Highwaymen." www.go-star.com/framer/highwaymen.htm.
"The Highwaymen: Florida's Outsider Artists." VHS/DVD/CD. Public Broadcasting Service, 2002.
"The Highwaymen, Legends of the Road." VHS/DVD/CD. Directed by Jack Hambrick and Howard Brassner. Public Broadcasting Service, 2008.
Hughes, Langston. "Slave on the Block." In *The Short Stories of Langston Hughes*. Edited by Donna Akiba Sullivan Harper. New York: Hill & Wang, 1997. 32.
_____. "Who's Passing for Who." In *The Short Stories of Langston Hughes*. Edited by Donna Akiba Sullivan Harper. New York: Hill & Wang, 1997. 190.
Hurston, Zora Neale. *Jonah's Gourd Vine*. 1934. New York: Harper, 1990.
_____. *Mules and Men*. 1935. New York: Harper, 1990.
_____. *Tell My Horse*. 1938. New York: Harper, 1990.
_____. *Their Eyes Were Watching God*. 1937. New York: Harper, 1990.
Johnson, James Weldon. *The Autobiography of an Ex–Colored Man*. New York: Dover, 1995.
_____. *God's Trombones: Seven Negro Sermons in Verse*. New York: Penguin, 1976.

Klinkenberg, Jeff. "The Highwaymen." *St. Petersburg Times*, August 6, 1995. www.sptimes.com/news/091700/news_pdf/florida/the_highwaymen.shtm/.

Larsen, Nella. *Passing*. Edited by Carla Kaplan. New York: Norton, 2007.

Long, Nancy Ann Zrinyi. *The Life and Legacy of Mary McLeod Bethune*. Cocoa, Fla.: Florida Historic Society, 2004.

"Looking for Zora." http://members.tripod.com/chrisdanielle/alicebio_4.html.

Minton, Jim and Carol. Newsletter. www.highwaymenartist.com/events.html.

Monroe, Gary. *The Highwaymen: Florida's African-American Landscape Painters*. Gainesville: University Press of Florida, 2001.

———. "The Highwaymen Phenomenon." www.aarf.com/fehwyphen01.htm.

Porter, A.P. *"Jump at De Sun": The Story of Zora Neale Hurston*. Minneapolis, Minn.: First Avenue Editions, 2003.

Walker, Alice. "Everyday Use." In *Norton Anthology of African-American Literature*. Edited by Henry Louis Gates and Nellie Y. McKay. 2nd ed. New York: Norton, 2004. 2437–43.

Wintz, Cary D., ed. *The Harlem Renaissance: A History & an Anthology*. Maplecrest, N.Y.: Brandywine, 2003.

# The Dazzling Lure of Treasure Hunting
### Kathleen Robinson

Tales of treasure litter Florida's cultural and geographical landscape. In fact, one of Florida's earliest visitors, Spanish explorer Ponce de León, was lured there by Native American myths that spoke of the ultimate treasure, immortality. Unlimited youth and life motivated the Spanish explorer to travel to the shores of Florida. However, Ponce de León's search was fruitless, and his tenure in Florida was cut short (Thompson). Yet as the story of Ponce de León continued to be told, Florida became culturally synonymous with treasure. The lure of treasure enticed others to the Florida peninsula through popular myths, stories, books, films, novels, and songs. The representation of treasure in connection with Florida has continued to draw visitors who seek rewards to be uncovered in the Sunshine State. A historical exploration of various Florida myths of treasure and treasure hunters showcases why and how treasure and the hunt for treasure is inextricably linked to representations of Florida in popular culture.

Florida had many colonizers beginning with the Spanish, French, and British, and ultimately ending with people from the United States in 1821 ("Timeline of Florida"). All the colonizers reported the Florida landscape as a beautiful, yet dangerous, tropical environment. Most had a sense of untold wealth and treasure within easy grasp. A belief in easy treasure led to a stereotypical view of Florida as a treasure trove. The sense of untold and unfound wealth lured many to the state during Florida's early history. But this chapter focuses on the popular culture representations of treasure in the late nineteenth, twentieth and twenty-first centuries and how these representations relate to other cultural representations of the Sunshine State.

## Tales of the Early Treasure Seekers

In the late 1800s, Americans began to settle Florida, and these early settlers discovered a landscape of both beauty and muck. When the United States officially acquired Florida in 1819, the waters were littered with shipwrecks—Spanish, French, British, and American (Fox 2). Knowledge of these wrecks helped to paint Florida as a place where treasure was literally strewn below the surface of the water. Many settlers salvaged and scavenged shipwrecks, an occupation commonly known as "wrecking," as a means of subsistence, albeit sporadic. These early Florida treasure-hunters were the forerunners of the modern-day treasure hunter. As the early treasure-hunters or wreckers sought to establish their livelihoods, they were motivated to locate ships and to secure the goods on the ships not by civic duty but by personal greed. Noted Florida historian John Viele, in *The Florida Keys: A History of the Pioneers*, observes that for these early Floridians "wrecking was the mainstay of the economy. Nearly every citizen derived his living in some way or another from the business" (22). But not all of the wrecking was on the up and up. Some early Floridians took to the water as pirates or privateers. However in the 1820s, piracy was brought under control by Admiral David Porter and his campaign to eradicate pirates in Florida. Interestingly, the occupation of wrecking in Florida's early history foreshadows the treasure hunting in Florida waters through the following decades. In fact, the traditions established by the wreckers helped contribute to the mythology of Florida as a treasure-heavy place, through information, maps, and stories.

The volatile waters of the Florida straits created a fertile ground for wrecked ships and for the individuals who salvaged in these waters. Many of the settlers during the 1800s took to scanning the watery horizon looking for ships and storms. Making a livelihood through the retrieval of goods and money from downed and wrecked ships was considered respectable. Images of wreckers, early treasure hunters, appeared in texts and guides about Florida circulated in American parlors and salons. Most early textual representations of Florida are attempts to entice Americans to visit the state. Sydney Lanier, Georgia poet and scholar, explains in his 1876 travel narrative for consumptives, *Florida: Its Scenery, Climate and History*, that Key West "is headquarters also for the Florida wreckers, into whose hands the reefs throw many a prize" (156). Lanier, one of the earliest writers to link shipwrecks and treasure hunters for a popular audience, traveled and spent time in Florida. The image of the Florida treasure hunter also appears in Lanier's poem "A Florida Sunday," written in Tampa in 1877. The opening lines read:

> From cold Norse caves or buccaneer Southern seas
> Oft come repenting tempests here to die;
> Bewailing old-time wrecks and robberies [lines 1–3, 142].

In "A Florida Sunday," Lanier's romanticized view of wrecks and robberies creates a linkage, treasure brought forth through the sinking of ships.

The themes of Lanier's work were popular, and more than likely, these romanticized views of treasure and the Florida seas contributed to treasure seekers' desire for adventure and easy money. John Viele, in *The Florida Keys: The Wreckers*, observes:

The combination of heavy shipping and a powerful current ... following close to dangerous reefs made the Florida Keys the site of a great many wrecks, especially during the nineteenth century. Ships were wrecking on the Florida Reef at the rate of almost once a week in the middle of the nineteenth century (the collector of customs in Key West reported a rate of 48 wrecks a year in 1848). For a period of almost 100 years, wrecking captains and wrecking vessels in the Keys had to hold a license issued by the Federal court. In 1858 there were 47 boats and ships licensed as wreckers [54–5, 166].

The wrecking industry continued to contribute heavily to the Florida economy and to establishing a connection between Florida and the treasure hunter. Due to the overwhelming amount of revenue brought in by the wrecking industry, on March 3, 1825, Congress passed the Federal Wrecking Act, which decreed: "All property, of any description whatsoever, which shall be taken from any wreck, from the sea, or from any of the keys and shoals, within the jurisdiction of the United States, on the coast of Florida, shall be brought to some port of entry within the jurisdiction of the United States" ("Chapter 19").

The Federal Wrecking Act of 1825 has created a legal course for all salvagers and treasure hunters in Florida since. Florida wreckers operated as businessmen, but their image was of maverick treasure hunters, salty seamen, and romantics seeking fame and glory. These images of the treasure hunter continued to be refined.

Wreckers created an immense amount of fodder for tales and stories about the period. In 1940, Key Wester Thelma Strabel wrote a three-part serial novel in the *Saturday Evening Post* titled *Reap the Wild Wind*. Strabel's plot focuses on the Key West wrecking industry during the 1840s. In 1942, Cecil B. DeMille adapted the story for the big screen. DeMille's *Reap the Wild Wind* strays from Strabel's story, yet still has wrecking as its focus. Staring John Wayne and Paulette Goddard, *Reap the Wild Wind* tells the story of Loxi Claiborne, who is running the family salvage business due to her father's death. The film follows Loxi and Jack through trials and tribulations and contains a lengthy section complete with a legal trial which investigates the rights of the salvager. DeMille's work won two Oscars. Both Strabel's and DeMille's work glorify the wrecking industry and idealize the men and women who pursue the work. Much as Lanier's poetry and non-fiction spoke of the money to be made, Strabel's and DeMille's fictionalization presented the idea that wrecking was a way to get rich in the late 1800s and the early 1900s. Salvaging declined as shipwrecks grew less common and the early vessels were all plundered. The next phase of Florida treasure hunting and cultural representations of the hunters begins.

## Seeking Treasure in the Ground

As the wrecking industry declined, many visitors and residents of Florida shifted from looking to the sea for treasure and transitioned to examining the soil for treasure left by the early colonizers. During the late 1800s and early 1900s, crude methods of recovery focused mainly on access to the treasure or wreck. Ideas circulated in many popular news publications and journals about the richness of life in Florida. Mirroring the sentiments of Lanier's poetry and travel narratives, reports of the time spoke of the hunt for unclaimed treasure just beneath the land. On May 28, 1897, *The New York Times* reported the discovery of treasure on Amelia Island in Florida. The $45,000 treasure was discovered by two parties, first by one group posing as scientists and second by Chris Pinckney, who stole the charts of the alleged scientists. The 1897 article explains that Pinckney involved local Floridian George Gause in discovering Spanish doubloons valued between $32,000 and $39,000 in a buried box. Pinckney departed under the ploy of converting the coins to cash, and Gause realized that he had been duped.

Gause solicited legal counsel with W.A. Hall, who garnered governmental permission to hunt for the treasure at a percentage of one-half. The article continues with the suggestion that Gause found Pinckney in New York, and that the team then double-crossed Hall. In addition, the article further explains the treasure fever which infected the community on the island. "The town is greatly excited over the matter, and amateur treasure seekers are at work daily digging around old trees on the island. Over four acres in one place have been dug over in this way." The 1897 report of treasure hunting heralded a new dawn of wrecking and treasure hunting on the Florida landscape, presented to the American public. Inherent in *The New York Times* piece is the linking of treasure hunters with espionage and intrigue.

Many individuals were lured to the tropical landscape by tales of endless sunshine, abundant money and hidden treasure. In October 1908, *The New York Times* reported five Harvard students chartering the America's Cup defender *Mayflower* to search for a sunken Spanish galleon and treasure. Due to poor weather and damage to the vessel off the coast of Florida, the sailors were found in need of rescue. The article reports that one of the rescued sailors was "reluctant to tell anything about his part, and none would say whether or not they got near the scene of the supposed sunken treasure." Once again, America was exposed to the idea that Florida was the place to go treasure hunting and the geographical location of untold wealth. Episodes like this became subject matter for popular fiction, especially juvenile fiction. Of course, *Treasure Island* always incited adventure and treasure hunting, and many authors used factual stories of Florida treasure hunters to create stories of American treasure hunting and adventure for American youth. One such author, Fisher Ames Jr., created a story in 1909 that spoke of treasure hunting in Florida. Ames's *By Reef and Trail: Bob Leach's Adventures in Florida* told the story of boys fishing and hunting for treasure off the coast of Florida. The main characters, Bob Leach, Jim Murray, and Rufus, recover the treasure after a series of escapades. Building on a literary tradition that began with Robert Louis Stevenson's *Treasure Island* and on the factual history of Florida, the American public linked inextricably the idea of treasure and the rewards of treasure hunting in the Florida landscape.

Treasure-hunting continued to grow in popularity as the twentieth century unfolded. Chicago-native E.C. Cole discovered treasure off Miami in 1913 as he searched for a location for his summer home. In the August 13, 1913, *Chicago Tribune*, E.C. Cole is described as having located a "hammered iron boarding pike" with strange markings. He "deciphered" the markings and located a cache of melted gold and silver which was hammered into "squares." Cole's unearthing of treasure and the *Chicago Tribune's* presentation of the story fed the treasure hunting fervor of the early 1900s and continued to link Florida with the hope of easy wealth. Most of the early treasure hunters in Florida resorted to digging for treasure on the beaches and islands. As the first European settler, Ponce de León, had been lured to Florida by dreams of immortality, and the wreckers had been lured to the shores by sunken vessels, others were lured in the late 1800s by the thought of easy money and treasure, the new elixir of youth and freedom.

Visitors such as Henry Plant, Henry M. Flagler, and D.P. Davis decided to develop the natural treasure of the land. Early developers sought to make the land habitable; ultimately, they decided to achieve habitability by dredging and creating canals. At this time, Florida was opened to visitors seeking sunshine and good weather. In fact, many doctors prescribed time in Florida's climate to ailing individuals, and thus Florida began its long history of a transient population. However, the early developers of Florida were not interested in convalescence; they were lured by the cold hard cash that developments could draw. At the turn of the century, the American economy was bursting, fueled by oil and banking. Henry M. Flagler set about providing access to the parts of Florida not previously accessible. His railroad development enticed many Americans to what he declared the "American Riveria." The deluge of new Floridians and visitors continued throughout the early part of the century. The availability of personal automobiles helped give birth to the idea of the Florida vacation. In fact, Henry Ford kept a house in Fort Meyers, and he also participated in land speculation, a modern form of treasure hunting.

As the land was made habitable and transportation was made more convenient, many Americans began to consider the rewards of living in Florida. Charles Donald Fox in his 1925 guidebook to living in Florida, aptly titled *The Truth about Florida*, observes, "It is surprising how many men and women come to Florida without money enough to last them for a week. They seem to believe the streets are paved with gold and all they will have to do is to pick it up" (120). In American popular culture, Florida was a tropical landscape littered with buried gold and opportunities which awaited discovery. Often, settlers arrived in Florida fueled by stories about treasure. Many pictorial representations of Florida on postcards and posters showed men and women wandering the beaches, discovering coins and treasure. Hunting for treasure shifted from an industry to a Florida pastime during the 1920s.

## The Treasure Hunters Take to the Water

As diving technology continued to improve during the early 1900s, many individuals in Florida began to take to the water in pursuit of treasure. Diving technology improved greatly in 1917 when the U.S. Bureau of Construction and Repair introduced the Mark V diving helmet, which allowed for a safer diving opportunity for all ("History of Scuba Diving"). As the technology improved, so did the opportunity to locate treasure in Florida waters. The wreck of the *Urca de Lima*, a Spanish flat-bottomed store-ship, was discovered by self-proclaimed adventurer William J. Beach in 1928, using hard-hat diving gear and a metal detector (Turner). Beach's use of diving equipment opened the door to a new form of treasure hunting, and Beach was one of the first treasure-divers to obtain state permission to hunt for treasure. In 1932, Florida issued its first salvage permit to Beach, allowing him to search for and to recover materials from Spanish wreck sites. Beach did recover a number of artifacts but there is no record of Beach declaring his discoveries. However, regulations did not require him to declare or share his discoveries.

Navy diver Art McKee in 1937 began his discovery and recovery of treasure off Plantation Key. Art McKee is often considered the father of modern treasure hunting. A commercial fisherman showed McKee a pile of ballast stones and cannons off the Key, and McKee began to find silver Spanish coins, and one gold *escudo* coin dated 1721. Curious about his find, he wrote to the Archive of the Indies in Spain and received a packet of documents relating the fate of the Spanish treasure fleet which wrecked in the Florida Keys during a hurricane in 1715 (Burgess). From translations of the documents, McKee learned that the wreck off Plantation Key was the *Capitana*, or *El Rubi Segundo*, flagship of the fleet. During the next ten years, McKee and his partners searched up and down the Keys, exploring more than seventy-five shipwrecks.

In 1949, with a warehouse full of artifacts and treasure from several different wrecks, McKee opened the first museum in the world devoted to showing sunken treasures. The museum at Treasure Harbor captivated visitors with its presentation of treasure and adventure. McKee and his crew took visitors to the *Capitana* in his glass-bottom boat, and he took many of them on underwater tours in his diving helmet ("Art McKee"). McKee's treasure experience fed into the representation of the Florida treasure hunter. However, McKee did not just capture and sell the image of the treasure hunter; he also continued his search for Spanish treasure. McKee obtained a lease from the state to explore older shipwrecks, and located several other ships from the 1715 fleet. In addition to the *Capitana*, McKee and his associates found and excavated nine of the twenty-two ships lost in the 1715 hurricane. However in 1960, McKee's claim to the wrecks was challenged by rival treasure hunters, the River Rats, Tim Watkins, Olin Frick, and other divers operating aboard a ship named *The Buccaneer* (Beare). McKee went to the state to enforce his rights, as he had leased the area from the state. He learned that the wrecks were 3.5 miles offshore, and the state only had legal authority within three miles, so McKee could do nothing legally to keep rival treasure hunters from the wrecks. The fight between McKee and the River Rats perfectly reflects the greed and double-crossing inherent in treasure hunting. The element of greed would become part of popular culture as the Florida treasure hunter became an archetype.

Diving as a sport was beginning to be part of American and Floridian culture. Dive shops and tourist operations which took people into the great blue depths expanded in great numbers. The treasure hunting attempts of Beach and others began to draw attention from local newspapers and other press organizations. With television becoming part of the American cultural landscape, treasure hunting became a perfect subject. In fact, WTVJ of Miami, Florida's first television station, conducted the first underwater remote broadcast on January 20, 1957. The WTVJ mobile unit was the largest in the world at the time, and the unit filmed at a location three miles at sea off Plantation Key. The broadcast titled "Odyssey" used underwater cameras to televise live the exploration of a sunken Spanish galleon. The broadcast emphasized the discovery of treasure, and contributed to the public enthusiasm for treasure and treasure hunting. The show portrayed the ease with which treasure could be found off the Florida coast. Early and prolific treasure hunter Kip Wagner's Real Eight Company contributed greatly to the treasure myths during this broadcast. The American public enjoyed watching the divers and seeing the new "underwater" world. Feeding on this new fervor and contributing to the burgeoning sport of diving was an early television series titled *Sea Hunt*. *Sea Hunt* was an action-adventure television series which was partially filmed in Florida waters off Miami and at Silver Springs. It was the first series to focus on underwater adventures. *Sea Hunt* focused on the diving adventures of a character played by Lloyd Bridges, and aired between 1958 and 1962. Some of the more popular episodes featured underwater shots of the recovery of treasure from sunken ships of the coast of Florida. In fact, during the first season, two of the episodes featured treasure as the plotline for the show. *Sea Hunt* was the most successful first-run syndicated show at the time. Many credit the show with introducing diving to a large audience. The show is also credited with introducing the American population to the sport of treasure-diving.

## Treasure Hunting Gains Legitimacy

During the 1950s, much research was conducted about the various Spanish, Cuban, and Dutch wrecks off the coast of Florida. Most of the research relied heavily on the communication between the treasure hunters and the various governments that had the shipping records. Treasure hunters Art McKee and William Beach communicated with the Spanish government to gain access to records concerning the ships and their cargos. As the hunt for treasure intensified, so did the rivalries among the salvagers. Additionally, debates began to heat up among the various treasure hunters and the governments of Florida and the United States. Treasure hunters Tim Watkins, Olin Frick, and the various crew members known as the *River Rats* challenged McKee's rights and began to explore and to salvage artifacts (Burgess). One rivalry stands out—between two of the most well-known treasure hunters, Kip Wagner and Mel Fisher.

In the 1950s, Kip Wagner moved to Wabasso, Florida, to build a hotel. He was a novice treasure hunter. Wagner had been exposed to "stories of treasure lost and treasure found from old-timers in the Wabasso-Sebastian area" (Burgess and Claussen 82). During his early exploration, Wagner found a piece of eight on a beach near Sebastian Inlet. Wagner caught treasure fever, and he pursued many leads and used many resources such as aerial surveillance to locate more treasure. Wagner created a treasure hunting group called the Real Eight Company, after the Spanish term *ocho reales* or piece of eight. The Real Eight Company went from a loosely-formed group to a company that obtained salvage rights from the state of Florida (Burgess). At this time the governor of Florida and his cabinet owned all submerged lands under the state's navigable waters, and they could lease these areas for search and salvage (Burgess and Clausen 89). The leases could not include more than fifty square miles until a specific find was made, and then the lease could be made exclusive, so that no other individual could explore the area included in the lease. The cost of an annual lease was $100, payable in advance. The agreement also required a $500 bond and quarterly reports to the Florida Internal Improvement Fund detailing operations and listing all finds. For granting this search and salvage privilege, the state retained 25 percent of whatever was recovered, subject to state selection (Burgess and Clausen 89). At first, the Real Eight Company maintained a close relationship with the state. In fact, "to oversee the state's quarter share in all finds made, the Internal Improvement Fund selected two eminent archaeologists to work with the salvagers—Dr. William H. Sears and Dr. John M. Goggin" (Burgess and Clausen 101–102). Wagner's Real Eight Company was working with the state, but this amicable relationship would not last long.

During these early hunts, Wagner's group located *cobs*, or rudimentary coins. Most of these were gold and silver and were minted between 1711 and 1715 in Mexico City. In addition, the group discovered the Golden Dragon in the waters off Sebastian Inlet. The Golden Dragon was a gold pendant which "was the single most valuable item to come from the wrecks. It is a combination whistle, toothpick and ear spoon which hung on a complicated floral-pattern gold chain" (Burgess and Clausen 85). The Golden Dragon represents an interesting case because the piece was found in the water. In the United States, common law says that if something of value, defined as treasure, is found on land, it is finders-keepers; however if that treasure is found offshore on a state's submerged land, then, as noted earlier, it officially belongs to the state. This point was never argued, and the Real Eight Company got to keep the $50,000 the Golden Dragon drew at auction. The state received no profits from the sale (Burgess and Clausen 104).

Wagner's discoveries were detailed in a *National Geographic* story and in his own book *Pieces of Eight*. Wagner's "Drowned Galleons Yield Spanish Gold: Adventurous Divers in Florida Bring Up the 20th Century's Richest Find of Sunken Treasure" appearing in the January 1965 *National Geographic* reached an American population hungering for tales of adventure. The story captured the elements of suspense and secrecy found in treasure hunting. The treasure hunter began to be redefined from a renegade prompted by greed to a scientist lured both by the desire for wealth and the desire for discovery. The *National Geographic* story provided the treasure hunters with legitimacy, but a legitimacy that would be tested in the future by other treasure-seekers.

## Treasure-Hunters vs. the State of Florida

In 1963, Kip Wagner and his Real Eight Company attempted to salvage wrecks from the 1715 Spanish fleet lost off Florida's east coast. Ill-equipped, with his crew unable to devote its full time to the project, Wagner invited a young diver who was very interested in diving for treasure, Mel Fisher, to join him on a split percentage basis. Fisher and his crew, while working with Wagner and his company, located a cache of silver and gold coins. They collected the biggest haul ever made by a twentieth century salvager in Florida: 1,033 gold coins (Burgess and Clausen 114). Fisher and the others feared attracting swarms of treasure-hunters, so they were very secretive about the discovery. In fact, their secretiveness caused the first trouble between the salvagers and the state of Florida (Burgess and Clausen 114).

The state sent investigators to discuss the large find with the hunters. The investigators, Ed Reddick and Paul Baldwin, confronted Mel Fisher and his crew. During the three-week investigation, local and national press followed the treasure hunters and their discovery. The press depicted the salvagers as modern-day pirates reaping out-of-bounds sea treasure with the intention of beating the state out of a fortune (Burgess and Clausen 117). The Internal Improvement Fund hired a more knowledgeable source to look after Florida's archeological interests, Carl Clausen. Clausen, who has continued to contribute to the lore of the treasure hunter in his books and activities, accompanied the salvagers on their dives and discoveries, but Clausen discovered that the relationship among the state, the study of archeology, and treasure hunters was not in harmony.

A televised governor's report highlighted the state's policy on treasure and treasure hunting (*Governor's Report on Treasure*). Gov. Farris Bryant is seen on the black-and-white production describing Florida's policies on sunken treasure in Florida waters. The piece includes a small vignette in which state Treasurer J. Edwin Larson views treasure found near Ft. Pierce. Additionally, President Lyndon Johnson makes a cameo in this October 1, 1964, production. The state and the nation had caught treasure fever. Just as in the 1920s, when

Donald Fox had remarked on the myth that the Florida landscape was filled with gold, so too did this short (3:55) production contribute to the myth.

In 1964, Mel Fisher and his crews headed to the Keys, and they began diving and exploring the various wrecks in the area, much to the chagrin of the established local dive and tour boats. The contentious atmosphere between Mel Fisher and the Keys' diving population came to a head when Hugh Brown, president of the Florida Keys Underwater Guides Association, informed Governor Bryant of Mel Fisher's explorations and their effects on the wrecks, reefs, and diving activities. Suspicion in the state government grew, as some citizens and politicians believed that "tourists were being allowed to take souvenirs from the wrecks, that in fact this was perhaps one of the lures guides held out to the adventuresome tourist — a chance to go on a 'treasure hunt.' Moreover, there were even rumors that the guides may have salted the wrecks a little, dropping a few trinkets here and there" (Burgess and Clausen 127). Governor Bryant decided to let the private companies handle the salvage, as they had a better motive for managing the resources, profit. However, the relapse in governmental scrutiny only lasted until a change in governors. Governor Haydon Burns in 1965 decided to place a moratorium on all treasure-salvage leases until he could appraise the situation and determine how the state's position could be improved (Burgess and Claussen 130). During this time, only three salvage firms had legal instruments to operate: Real Eight Company, including Fisher's Treasure Salvors; the Martin County Historical Society; and the Perdido Corporation (Burgess and Clausen 130).

Real Eight Company's *Derelict* worked the waters off Sebastian Inlet and Ft. Pierce. During this effort, the divers located "a spectacle of gold coins carpeting the broad white sand" (Burgess and Clausen 131). In the days that followed this discovery, many more coins were discovered, and the Ft. Pierce treasure strike hit the headlines across the nation. Burgess and Clausen observe,

> Gold seekers came by bus, plane, car, and foot. They came in droves — amateur and professional treasure hunters, cranks, con men, crooks and the curious — all converging at the scene of the strike along Florida's southern coasts. They swarmed over the beaches between Sebastian and Wabasso, searching for coins. They shook the sleepy little towns out of their lethargy by buying every piece of scuba and skin-diving equipment local merchants had to offer. They swam or boated out to the wrecks ... in such numbers that Treasure Salvors and Real Eight had to shoo them away each time they went to work [131–132].

Florida's landscape and seascape were dotted with tourists and natives caught up in treasure fever. Kip Wagner's story in *National Geographic* fanned the flames, taking treasure hunting into the average American home. The effects of treasure fever were felt throughout Florida. The state was inundated with requests for salvage rights. The myth of a sea floor carpeted with gold coins took root in many Americans' minds, and Florida became the epicenter of American treasure hunters.

## The Ultimate Treasure Hunter, Mel Fisher

The true zenith of treasure hunting in popular culture occurred with the creation of Treasure Salvors and Mel Fisher's connection to Key West. During the late 1960s, Mel Fisher separated from Real Eight Company, and he began his own company, Treasure Salvors Inc. It was appropriate that Key West would once again become the focus for these modern-day salvagers and wreckers. Key West's long connection with the salvage of wrecks contributed greatly to the development of the treasure hunter. Similarly, Mel Fisher fit the mold of the modern renegade treasure hunter. As he established his base of operations at Key West, his family helped him in his pursuit of millions. The unique sense of adventure represented by Mel Fisher and other treasure hunters spoke to the American culture, and as the sport of diving began to grow in popularity for the American tourist, the media — the modern arbiter of culture — took notice.

As the 1970s began, Mel Fisher started exploring the waters of Key West in search of the *Atocha*, one of the ships from the doomed 1715 Spanish fleet. With a staff of diving and research experts on his tenuous payroll, Mel Fisher's Treasure Salvors Inc. slaved in the pursuit of treasure. From 1970 to 1975, Fisher's group would discover many clues and bits of treasure, but the ultimate prize, the $400-million-dollar *Atocha*, continued to elude them. In the summer of July 1975, Dirk Fisher, Mel Fisher's son, discovered five cannons attributed to the *Atocha*. However, this early success was tainted by tragedy — the sinking of one of the treasure-hunting ships, the *Northwind*, and the loss of Dirk Fisher, Angel Fisher (Dirk's wife and fellow diver), and diver Rick Gage (Smith 39). Treasure hunting was indeed a dangerous business, but it was still a very alluring proposition to the participants.

The discovery of the cannons garnered the attention of the state and federal governments. The governments, like the American public, became very interested in Mel Fisher and his discovery. They dispatched investigators to Key West. Eugene Lyon, one of Mel Fisher's hunters, recalls one of the run-ins with the government in his book *The Search for the Atocha*.

> One afternoon, federal marshals appeared on the deck of the galleon museum and approached the wooden boxes that held, in seawater, the first two bronze cannons brought up. There, addressing the guns, the officers read aloud a notice of Case #75-1416 in the Southern Federal District Court in Miami: the case of Treasure Salvors Inc., against the wrecked and abandoned sailing vessel *Atocha*. They then arrested the cannon, the best physical remnant of the ship available, and left them, as the supposed property of the salvors [Lyon 189].

The state of Florida, after studying the legal position of the parties, decided not to enter the lawsuit; they did, however, join with federal authorities to ask the Coast Guard to expel Treasure Salvors from the wreck site (Lyon 189). Federal spokesmen stated the government's position: "The entire wreck site and all the materials from it, 100 percent of them, belonged to Uncle Sam" (Lyon 190). There were many meetings and debates concerning the *Atocha*, and "Judge

Mehrtens awarded Treasure Salvors the *Atocha* without reservations" (Lyon 198). However, the federal government appealed the decision to a federals appeals court in New Orleans. According to Lyon, "On March 14, the federal appeals judge had ruled for Treasure Salvors and against the federal government. Then the Interior and Justice departments had decided that they had had enough; they had declined to appeal the case further. Suddenly the salvors realized that after seven years they had won their fight for their treasure" (Lyon 230). Finally, Mel Fisher and crew had solid legal footing on which to build their hopes. They got some help from media outlets, which highlighted and explored Mel Fisher and treasure hunting in Florida.

In June 1976, *National Geographic* did a feature on the *Atocha*. The publication detailed and displayed Mel Fisher and his crew's discoveries to a mass audience with the story "*Atocha*: Tragic Treasure Galleon of the Florida Keys." At the same time, *National Geographic* produced a documentary about the treasure hunters. Both of these publications were in preparation for a 1976 treasure exhibit in Washington. King Juan Carlos and Queen Sophia of Spain would be in attendance (Lyon 200). Mel and his wife, Deo, attended the function, and Mel presented Queen Sophia with a gold piece recovered from the wreck (Lyon 211). Additionally in 1976, Disney Films produced and released *Treasure of Matecumbe* (McEveety). The film focused on the Huck Finn-like adventures of a pair of Florida boys who were in search of treasure off Key West. Building on the treasure hunter in popular culture, the film was highly popular, and it created a desire in many youngsters to go off in pursuit of treasure. The film captured some of the danger and allure of hidden treasure, a danger and allure represented by Mel Fisher and his Treasure Salvors. *Treasure of Matecumbe* focused on the idea that treasure lay waiting in Florida waters; all you had to do was to find it, and then you would be set for the rest of your life. Yet the pursuit of treasure in the film is also linked with danger and mystery. These themes contributed to the desire of many to enter Florida waters in pursuit of the ultimate find. That allowed treasure hunters like Mel Fisher to gain more funding for his dream of locating the *Atocha*.

Following the *National Geographic* exhibit, articles were published about Mel Fisher and his treasure hunting in *Newsweek, Saga*, and *People*. Mel and Deo were even featured on *Good Morning America*. At this time, Mel Fisher launched his treasure club, allowing individuals to contribute to financing the research and in turn receive a piece of the treasure. The desire to be part of the treasure hunt was fueled by all the publicity. "On December 7, 1976, the *National Geographic* special "Treasure" aired on PBS. Thanks to the audience following the *Geographic* documentaries and the publicity buildup given the *Atocha* show, viewer interest was intense. The special outdrew any other previous public television performance and lured many viewers from prime-time network shows" (Lyon 217). But while the press was favorable, Mel Fisher's Treasure Salvors Inc. faced many economic hardships during this time. The Internal Revenue Service (IRS) impounded bank accounts, the power company shut off power for non-payment, and a rash of creditors filed suits (Lyon 225). Undeterred, Fisher kept up the hope and the hunt for the *Atocha*. Creating and maintaining a museum in Key West, Fisher continued to dive, search, and share his story with the public throughout the late 1970s and the early 1980s.

By 1985, two *National Geographic* specials had aired on TV about the search, and numerous articles and press pieces had focused the American public on Fisher's treasure hunt. Treasure diver and archeological director of the search for the *Nuestra Señora de Atocha* R. Duncan Matthewson III said, "Millions of people all over the country will see for themselves some of the wondrous things Mel and his divers discovered" (117). As millions continued to tune into the saga, the divers continued to dig and discover artifacts from the wreck. Mel Fisher's famous maxim, "Today Is the Day," was immortalized in T-shirts, museum souvenirs, and paraphernalia distributed by Treasure Salvors. In fact, in one truly unique and ingenious plan, Fisher sold shares at $1,000 a year to any investors willing to back his work. In exchange for the contribution, the individual could dive on the wrecks, have access to a percentage of the treasure found, and be part of the dream. In another stroke of genius, Treasure Salvors did not pay cash for artifacts; instead, the lucky individual got a piece of gold, or something else from the booty. A much-cited rumor has it that Mel wandered Key West with a gold finger bar, and when he spoke with investors, he would stir his rum and coke with it. He hoped to lure people with treasure and untold fortune. Another method he used was to let his divers keep their first gold piece, as he believed that this tangible evidence would cause a gold fever that only finding more treasure would cure.

When the "Today Is the Day" maxim finally came true, Fisher was on land, and rumors abound about where he was. On July 20, 1985, Fisher's son, diver Kane Fisher, radioed to Treasure Salvors' headquarters, "Put away the charts. We've found the main pile" (Smith 132). The long search for the *Atocha* was over. Kane subsequently told his father, "Silver bars are stacked like cordwood. Coins everywhere" ("Mel's Story"). Jedwin Smith, reporter and treasure-diver, recalls: "The excitement back at Treasure Salvors headquarters was almost as feverish as that at the recovery site. Beth McHaley had been on the telephone since 1:00 P.M., first calling *National Geographic* headquarters, then contacting every major newspaper from coast to coast" (137–138). With major reporters from television and newspapers arriving at Key West, Mel Fisher and his crew celebrated the discovery. It seemed that the whole world descended on the site including Jimmy Buffet, who sat on a pile of silver bars and played for the crew. In fact, Jedwin Smith references the famous photograph of Jimmy Buffet and Mel Fisher sitting atop the pile of silver bars as Jimmy Buffet sings from "A Pirate Looks at Forty."

The crush of the media created a unique opportunity for Mel Fisher as he was now able to finance and to publicize his discoveries. In addition, Mel Fisher's discovery of the mother lode and the media's subsequent affection for the treasure hunter re-launched the archetype of the Florida treasure hunter into the

American psyche. In fact, Buffet's anthematic "A Pirate Looks at Forty" captured the archetype in its success and it flaws. The treasure hunter of the late 1900s in Florida culture was driven but often a failure, a respecter of traditions, but a maverick in his pursuits—a romanticized figure with realistic attributes, in short, a combination of Key Westers Mel Fisher and Jimmy Buffet.

Following the discovery of the mother lode, Mel Fisher and his company Treasure Salvors Inc. continued to search the areas around Key West for treasure. Their searches were documented by many reporters and of course, *National Geographic*, which sent a "film crew to shoot a television special on the motherlode" (Matthewson 114). The figure of the treasure hunter continued to inspire interest and adoration, even from celebrities. "Mel had appeared on the *Tonight* show just after the motherlode was found, and had invited Johnny Carson, an enthusiastic diver, out for a look.... The press had a field day photographing Carson in his dive gear before and after the dive" (Matthewson 114). Matthewson observes, "These celebrities gave the media people something to talk about (114). In 1986, a television movie titled *Dreams of Gold: The Mel Fisher Story* starred Cliff Robertson and Loretta Swift. The story focused on Fisher's hunt for the *Atocha* treasure and contributed to Fisher's legendary status. The movie first aired November 15, 1986, not long after a drawn-out court battle between Fisher and the U.S. government over ownership of the treasure had come to a conclusion. With *Atocha* coins, jewelry, and various paraphernalia scattered around the world, and images and stories of Mel Fisher's exploits covering the globe, Florida and treasure become synonymous in the late 1980s and early 1990s. Mel Fisher died on December 19, 1998, but he continues to be part of Florida's treasure culture as his museum in Key West flourishes, and his Treasure Salvors Inc. continues to participate in the recovery of treasure and sunken artifacts.

## Continuing the Hunt for Treasure

In the 1990s and early twenty-first century, Florida and her residents still look for treasure. Treasure hunting in Florida became an industry, not the pursuit engaged of maverick treasure hunters. The modern treasure-hunters of Florida have expanded their operations to encompass more than just the coastal waters of Florida. In fact, Tampa-based Odyssey Marine Explorations discovered an estimated $500 million trove of coins and artifacts off the coast of Portugal in early 2006. The company transported the treasure to Tampa and now is facing legal action from the government of Spain. Once again, a court may be the ultimate arbiter of ownership of the loot.

Treasure and the hunt for treasure still figure tremendously in the portrayal of Florida in film and media. The 2007 film *Fool's Gold* presents the same images as earlier treasure-related films. The film uses the wrecks of the 1715 Spanish fleet as a subtext to the movie's action. With a rogue treasure hunter, the character Finn, the movie has parallels with the historical treasure hunters of Florida.

The character of Moe Fitch, an older, established treasure hunter, seems to reflect Mel Fisher. A motley group is brought together to search for the treasure, supported by a wealthy individual who desires not the treasure but the experience. This most current representation of the treasure hunter still relies on the early cultural representations of the treasure hunter which are linked to the actual treasure hunters of the past.

Treasure hunting is now driven not just by greed but also by a desire for historical discovery. Connecting to the past appears to motivate a number of treasure seekers in the modern Florida landscape. While the beaches and waters are no longer full of individuals scanning the sands and bottoms for coins or hoping to discover a priceless jewel, Florida's landscape is now filled with individuals seeking a connection to the past. Treasure remains integral to the Florida experience. From the wreckers of the late 1800s, the landowners who discovered buried treasure in the early 1900s, the beachgoers who discovered treasure as they wandered the shores of Florida in the 1920s, and the first divers in the 1940s, to the current-day treasure hunters who take to the sea with high-tech equipment and a scientific perspective, treasure maintains its primacy in Florida's image.

## WORKS CITED AND CONSULTED

Ames, Fisher. *By Reef and Trail: Bob Leach's Adventures in Florida*. New York: Brown and Page, 1909.
"Art McKee." The Treasure Wreck Chronicles: Treasure Wrecks and their Discoverers. http://thethunderchild.com/GhostGunsVirginia/TreasureWrecks/ArtMcKee.htm.
Beare, Nikki. *Pirates Pineapples and People — Tales and Legends of the Upper Florida Keys*. Miami Beach, Fla.: Atlantic Publishing Company, 1961.
Beater, Jack. *Pirates and Buried Treasure on Florida Islands, Including the Gasparilla Story*. St. Petersburg, Fla.: Great Outdoors, 1959.
Buffet, Jimmy. "A Pirate Looks at Forty." *A-1-A*. New York: Duchess Music Corporation, 1974.
Burgess, Robert F. *Sunken Treasure: Six Who Found Fortunes*. New York: Dodd, Mead, 1988.
Burgess, Robert F. and Clausen, Carl J. *Florida's Golden Galleons: The Search for the 1715 Spanish Treasure Fleet*. Port Salerno, Fla.: Florida Classics Library, 1976.
"Buried Gold in Florida." *The New York Times*, May 27, 1897. http://www.proquest.com/en-US/.
Burnett, Gene. *Florida's Past: People and Events that Shaped the State*. Sarasota, Fla.: Pineapple Press, 1996.
"Chapter 19: Wrecks and Salvages." *US Code: Title 46 Appendix Shipping*. Washington, D.C. Retrieved from www.access.gpo.gov.
"Chicagoan Finds Treasure." *Chicago Tribune*, April 14, 1913. http://www.proquest.com/en-US/.
DeMille, Cecil. *Reap the Wild Wind*. Los Angeles: Paramount Pictures, 1942.
Florea, Johnny. *Sea Hunt*. Los Angeles: MGM/Sony, 1958–1961.
Fox, Charles Donald. *The Truth About Florida*. New York: Charles Renard, 1925.
Gilpin, Vincent. "Bradish W. Johnson, Master Wrecker." *Tequesta*, 1 (1941): 3–41.
Goldstone, James. *Dreams of Gold: The Mel Fisher Story*. Simitar Entertainment, Feb. 10, 1998.
Goss, James P. *Pop Culture Florida*. Sarasota, Fla.: Pineapple Press, 2000.

*Governor's Report on Florida Treasure.* Tallahassee: State Treasury Department, October 1, 1964.

"History of Scuba Diving." Hawaii Scuba-Diving. www.hawaiiscubadiving.com.

Hudson, L. Frank, and Gordon R. Prescott. *Lost Treasures of Florida's Gulf Coast.* St. Petersburg, Fla.: Great Outdoors, 1973.

Lanier, Sydney. *Florida: Its Scenery, Climate, and History.* Philadelphia: J. B. Lippincott & Co., 1876. Retrieved from www.googlebooks.com .

_____. *Poems of Sydney Lanier.* Philadelphia: J.B. Lippincott & Co., 1892. Retrieved from www.googlebooks.com.

Lyon, Eugene. "Atocha: Tragic Treasure Galleon of the Florida Keys." *National Geographic* 149(6), 787–809 (June 1976).

_____. *The Search for the Atocha.* Port Salerno, Fla.: Florida Classics Library, 1985.

McCarthy, Kevin M. *The Book Lover's Guide to Florida: Authors, Books, & Literary Sites.* Sarasota, Fla.: Pineapple Press, 1992.

_____, William L. Trotter and Steve Roguski. *Thirty Florida Shipwrecks.* Sarasota, Fla.: Pineapple Press, 1992.

Malone, Vernon. Personal interview. July 7, 2008.

Mathewson, R. Duncan III. *Treasure of the Atocha.* New York: Dutton, 1986.

McEveety, Vincent. *Treasure of Matecumbe.* Orlando, Fla.: Walt Disney Films, 1976.

"Mel's Story." The Mel Fisher Maritime Museum. Key West, Fla.: Mel Fisher Maritime Heritage Society. Retrieved from http://www.melfisher.org/.

"Odyssey Cast to Dive Today for Treasure." *Chicago Tribune,* Jan. 20, 1957. http://www.proquest.com/en-US/.

Philcox, Phil and Beverly Boe. *Sunshine State Almanac & Book of Florida-Related Stuff.* Sarasota, Fla.: Pineapple Press, 1999.

Ray, Russell. "Odyssey Claims its Share of Loot." *The Tampa Tribune,* May 10, 2008.

Smiley, Nixon. *Florida, Land of Images.* Miami: E.A. Seemann, 1972.

Smith, Jedwin. *Fatal Treasure: Greed and Death, Emeralds and Gold, and the Obsessive Search for the Legendary Ghost Galleon Atocha.* Hoboken, N.J.: John Wiley and Sons, 2003.

Strabel, Thelma. *Reap the Wild Wind.* London: Collins, 1941.

Tennant, Andy. *Fool's Gold.* Los Angeles: Warner Bros., 2008.

Thompson, Tommy. *America's Lost Treasure.* New York: Atlantic Monthly Press, 1998.

Thompson, William, and Dorcas Thompson. *The Spanish Exploration of Florida : The Adventures of the Spanish Conquistadors, Including Juan Ponce de León, Pánfilo De Narváez, Álvar Núñez Cabeza de Vaca, Hernando de Soto, and Pedro Menéndez de Avilés, in the American South.* Philadelphia: Mason Crest, 2003.

"Timeline." Florida Memory: State Archives of Florida. www.floridamemory.com/timeline/.

"Treasure Seekers Wrecked and Saved." *The New York Times,* October 19, 1908. http://www.proquest.com/en-US/.

Turner, Buffy. "Urca de Lima: A Treasure Coast Treasure." Maritime and Yachting Museum of Florida, Stuart, Fla. Retrieved from www.mymflorida.com.

Viele. John. *The Florida Keys: A History of the Pioneers.* Sarasota, Fla.: Pineapple Press, 1996.

_____. *The Florida Keys: The Wreckers.* Sarasota, Fla.: Pineapple Press, 2001.

Wagner, Kip. "Drowned Galleons Yield Spanish Gold: Adventurous Divers in Florida Bring Up the 20th Century's Richest Find of Sunken Treasure," *National Geographic* (January 1965), 1–37.

_____, and Taylor, L.B. *Pieces of Eight.* New York: E.P. Dutton and Company, 1966.

Wilkinson, Jerry. "History of Wrecking." Keys Historeum, Historical Preservation Society of the Upper Keys. http://www.keyshistory.org/wrecking.html.

# Snowbirds Seek Solar Solace
*Steven Knapp* and *Sarah M. Mallonee*

For Dante Alighieri, the most intense part of hell is cold, not hot. Dante's ninth and lowest circle in *The Inferno* is a frozen, ice-covered land where even the tears of the damned freeze on their faces, shuttering their eyes with ice. Lucifer himself resides in this frostbitten wilderness, eternally suffering a fit punishment for his sin. Contrary to the popular image of a blazing hot Hades and red devils in flames, Dante believes that logic dictates a frozen hell. After all, hell is the point furthest removed from God; God is light, and light means warmth. Love, too, is warm and pleasant, while its absence is cold and sterile. Snowbirds, Northerners who frequent the Sunbelt during the winter months, provide evidence supporting Dante. Hell is cold and heaven is warm. The first blasts of winter launch them south by various means of transportation, as if fleeing the bat-like, flapping wings of Dante's devil, which initiate the freezing gusts of that God-forsaken place. Dante's description of hell's third circle reads like weather reports from northern regions: incessant freezing rain, sleet, hail, and heavy snow. Every year millions of migratory human beings flock south, fleeing the frozen regions of the Northeast, Midwest, Northwest, Canada, and Alaska. Florida, one of the most desirable of the warm destinations, along with Arizona, Texas, and Southern California, offers—during the months of November, December, January, February, and March—an alternative to the cold realities of snow, ice, and those ubiquitous gray skies of the northern winter.

Winterless Florida—in popular myth—is paradise. A peninsula isolated from troublesome neighbors, Florida provides more beach frontage than its rival snowbird destinations. Besides, none of the other destinations has two coasts like Florida. On the Atlantic side are miles of public beaches and even more miles of beaches with hotels, condominiums, rental houses, and the fabulous homes of the wealthy. Barrier islands stretch along the east coast from the Kennedy Space Center to Jupiter, near West Palm Beach, giving island dwellers both breathtaking sunrises and sunsets over the bordering waters. Island residents are tempted to watch the beautiful bright orange sunsets over the Indian River— the lagoon between the island and the mainland, and then set the alarm for sunrise to catch the next day's glorious reds and purples of morning. Picking a Florida coast is like picking a home site in heaven. How can you choose between two perfect places? The west coast has warm shallow water, placid Gulf seas, and some of the nicest beach sand in the world: the big, bright, crystalline sand, which is both beautiful to the eye and soft to the touch, creating a special experience, making other beaches seem somehow dirty by comparison. And, of course, Florida is the Keys: 1,700 islands, among the best places on earth. Florida is sleek cigarette boats bounding through the foamy water at sixty-five miles per hour. Florida is boating, sailing, diving, snorkeling, water skiing, parasailing, deep-sea fishing, island hopping, colorful drinks with little umbrellas sticking out over the rim, relaxation, and just plain fun in the sun. Florida is beautiful bodies in itty-bitty bikinis. For snowbirds and tourists, there is hardly anything better than getting a deep Florida tan in January, when jealous Northerners are back home wondering when they might next catch sight of that elusive yellow disk. Yes, Florida's legislators put the motto "The Sunshine State" on license plates for good reason.

Curiously for Floridians, many snowbirds leave our year-round sunshine to return to Dante's third circle as soon as reports of a thaw circulate. Most snowbirds forsake the Sunbelt long before 30-degree weather gives way to 70-degree weather in Fort Wayne, and 70-degree weather gives way to 90-degree weather in Ft. Myers. These seasonal residents, like their feathered friends, merely desire some pleasant time in a place where there is plenty of food, fun, and sun. It is certainly no secret that Floridians harbor mixed feelings about snowbirds, especially those who could stay but leave voluntarily. In fact, Floridians have a kind of love-hate relationship with these part-time neighbors, paralleled by the snowbirds' love-hate relationship with Florida. They come to us in their vibrantly colored, tropical attire — in the middle of the coldest Florida weather — complaining about New York, Boston, Detroit, Chicago, Toronto, and other infernal regions. Temperatures will be in the high sixties, or perhaps barely seventy degrees, and these curious creatures sweat profusely and dive into winter waters, which Floridians know are cold as hell. In such ways, snowbirds still show the signs of being members of that damned race of the un-elect. Why else will they not convert permanently — becoming Floridians? Why do they become one with us for a few weeks or months and then backslide, returning to the northern abyss? For Floridians, snowbirds are anomalous. Snowbirds betray a mysterious attachment to the netherworld from which they escape. Floridians, the elect of God, cannot fathom the northern allure. On the other hand, visitors to Florida sometimes find the locals unfathomable, too.

Perhaps one of this chapter's authors can add a personal note to this story that explains how Florida looked to one outsider. Steve Knapp is no longer an outsider; he is a confirmed Floridian, having lived here for over two decades. Nevertheless, his memory of his first visit to Florida in the mid 1970s is still vivid. He recalls, "Florida seemed like paradise: sunny days, warm ocean waters, and pleasant breezy nights, with wonderful places to visit and things to see." Knapp came to Florida on his honeymoon, so going out of doors would have been unwelcome in any place except paradise. What preconceptions did he have? Well, he had reports about Florida from snowbird friends, and he had mental pictures from watching television. Like other Northerners of the era, he had watched *Flipper, The Jackie Gleason Show, I Dream of Jeannie, Surfside 6,* and *Gentle Ben,* making him a veritable expert on Florida and things Floridian. Nevertheless, driving inland off U.S. 1, down miles-long, uninhabited streets surrounded by palmettos and other scrub palms, he was dumbfounded as he encountered clumps of civilization, which levitated above the swamp or scrub. He wondered: "What do these people do for a living? Where do they get the money? How can people reside in a place where the only commerce is a gas station, a bait shop, and a tiny grocery store?" Of course, at nineteen, Knapp had not yet been introduced to that burgeoning twentieth century phenomenon: retirement.

Retirement accounted for Florida's steep growth rate, which started to blossom in the 1950s. Retirees can live in places that young families, especially families planning for children, would never dream of living. To Knapp, paradise seemed like a dream — unreal — as unreal as retirement seems to any nineteen-year-old. Moreover, most of the places these transplanted Northerners lived seemed like anything *but* paradise. As Knapp drove through Florida's Treasure Coast and into South Florida, he was sure he would never live there; he would only visit the more attractive spots when vacation funds were available. Going back North was mandatory, not optional, so he left Florida with mixed feelings. Florida was different than he had imagined. There were certainly some places that had the familiar look of television, but there were also places—an incredible mix of places—nothing like he presumed they would look. Our American culture gets wrapped in layers of media images, advertisements, travel brochures, and literary images, and reality always seems a bit strange because of the disconnect. Anyone who has gone on vacation after reading one of those travel guides knows this feeling, the feeling Steve Knapp experienced on his first trip to Florida.

Before getting further into this chapter, we should attempt to define the terms *snowbird* and *Floridian.* What is a snowbird? Stated negatively, a snowbird is *not* a tourist. Why not? For starters, tourists are traveling *to* places: seeing sights, visiting exotic locations, sampling local cuisine, and experiencing the adventures of travel. Tourists go *to* Paris, France, for example. They ascend the Eiffel Tower, visit Avenue des Champs-Elysées in the evening to photograph the lights, order unpronounceable French cuisine, and sample fine wine as they tour the countryside. Tourists are on a tour, *to* someplace. Snowbirds, on the other hand, are fleeing *from* something. Snowbirds are fleeing *from* the snow, so they have different agendas. Snowbirds mix with tourists in the Sunshine State, and it can be hard to tell them apart because both groups have a superficial sameness on the outside, having donned the familiar uniform of T-shirts, shorts, flip-flops, and sunglasses. Take a closer look, however. Tourists have tickets to Disney World. Tourists are holding maps. While snowbirds have maps, they avoid consulting them in public because it is embarrassing to need a map near one's home — even one's second home. Tourists are asking store clerks for directions or for advice about local restaurants. Tourists are on a schedule. Snowbirds, on the other hand, are going nowhere, and snowbirds have all the time in the world to get there. Like the migratory fowl from which they get their name, snowbirds can settle wherever they find themselves when the weather turns mild.

At the University of Florida, researchers studying the snowbird phenomenon have settled on an ingenious definition: snowbirds visit Sunbelt locations, such as Florida, and they stay for at least thirty days. The following list is a pretty good set of criteria.

- Snowbirds frequently return to spots and places they have already been.
- Wal-Mart is their first planned stop upon arrival at their Florida destination.
- Snowbirds have a house, condo, mobile home, or other regular residence here.
- They plan to vote in Florida, but they have also requested an absentee ballot up North.
- Snowbirds want to get away, but they would prefer Florida to be very similar to where they came from up North.

This last point is a key to recognizing the snowbird. A tourist relishes the new and unusual: *viva la difference*. After all, tourists come to see new things. For snowbirds, differences are annoying and can provoke extended lectures on how things are done up North. Consciously and unconsciously, they try to duplicate their Northern living conditions—minus the snow and ice. Snowbirds want the sun, but they have grown so accustomed to Dante's hell that they would surely stay there if it were not *so* damned cold.

In the list of indicators to identify snowbirds, we include double voting: "They plan to vote in Florida, but they have also requested an absentee ballot up North." How much double voting do snowbirds engage in? Probably very little, because nobody travels clear to Florida from the infernal regions just to cast an extra ballot, but the fact is, nobody knows how much double voting occurs. The reason is simple: there is no national voter-registration database and states keep their voter lists to themselves. Snowbirds registered in Michigan or New York, for example, can simply register again in Florida and nobody knows. Why would anyone want to register in both places? There are two reasons; one reason is pretty benign, the other—double voting—is a felony in Florida. Snowbirds who come to Florida before the November election, or before a special election, can find themselves unable to vote unless they requested an absentee ballot up North, long before the election. Finding oneself ineligible to vote in Florida and unable to obtain an absentee ballot from back home can be frustrating. The easy solution is to register to vote in Florida, too.

While registering twice—North and South—is technically illegal, the snowbird voter gets flexibility. If he or she decides to come to Florida early, before the election, a ballot can be cast in Florida. The downside is that state and local offices and ballot initiatives from the infernal regions will not appear on Florida ballots. It might be of some consolation, however, to find that Florida's congressional candidates are of interest to snowbird visitors. Moreover, some of Florida's ballot initiatives directly impact snowbirds: tax law changes, and regulatory revisions, for example. Even so, snowbirds—living part time in Florida—are denied a voice in Florida's democratic process. Should people be allowed to vote wherever they happen to reside at the time of an election? Some people think so. Before taking sides on this question, consider what taxation without representation leads to.

Snowbirds have watched their share of Florida's tax burden skyrocket over the last decade because they have no legal vote in Florida. *The Wall Street Journal* reports: "Florida allows municipalities to set the taxable value of properties at different levels for permanent and seasonal residents. There have been cases of snowbirds paying property taxes 10 times as high as those of permanent residents living nearby" (Gerena-Morales). Floridians have begged elected officials for tax relief, especially property tax relief. Officials have given it to them, but it has come through initiatives such as the Homestead Exemption and Save Our Homes. The Homestead Exemption exempts the first $25,000 of property value from taxes, provided the home is the person's primary residence, not a second home, not rental property, and not investment property. Save Our Homes capped the rise in taxes to three percent or less, which was a godsend during the price escalation of the recent housing bubble, but the cap only applied to homes qualifying for Homestead Exemption. Snowbirds are getting hit so hard a Canadian snowbird association had the temerity to appear on snowbirds' behalf at a meeting of the Florida Property Tax Reform Committee in Tampa.

Votes might make a difference, and U.S. resident snowbirds are certainly tempted to express themselves at ballot boxes in Florida. To do so, they just show up at a driver's license office, or a local supervisor of elections office, and register. How many register in multiple places? Again, nobody knows, but numbers can get pretty high, as history suggests. Take Michigan's conversion to a single computerized system, which began in 1987. That state discovered "more than 600,000 duplicate registrations on the voter rolls" (NCSL). That simply means that over a half-million Michigan voters could have voted twice had they wanted to. The fact is, few voters would even *think* about voting multiple times. It can be difficult enough to get to the polls once, and it would take a level of electoral zealotry most voters lack to vote multiple times. Still, with early voting and absentee ballots through the mail, people can vote in multiple places if they have a strong enough desire to do so.

Do snowbirds vote both up North and in Florida? To find out, you would have to run a data match between Florida's voter files and voter files from Northern states. Then the voting history of any duplicates would show if, and when, they had voted twice. Even so, we would never know if the offending voters were guilty of actually doubling their votes. Theoretically, they could abstain from voting for national candidates twice while voting for ballot initiatives and state and local candidates on the respective ballots. Closing the loophole of possible double voting would likely create more inconvenience for snowbirds. Furthermore, it would probably never change an election one way or another; the numbers are too low. If every U.S. snowbird in Florida votes twice, totally unthinkable, that adds less than a million votes. Don't presidents always win by more than a million-vote difference? Besides, a single state's electoral votes, Florida's for example, can't decide the election, can they?

Snowbirds commingle with full-time Florida residents, but the snowbirds' commitment to Florida is weak. In general, these part-timers need not support the mission of their temporary residence because its mission is not really their concern. For this reason, many part-timers are never tempted to vote in Florida elections. Snowbirds are, fundamentally, from somewhere else, and while this does not visibly mark them, it differentiates them from Floridians. Saved souls and damned souls commingle in the biblical parable of the wheat and tares, too. Nevertheless, it is possible to put souls to the test and to look for telltale features that distinguish them. Along with our earlier list of indicators, one telltale feature in the interpersonal communications of snowbirds is the ubiquitous question, "Where are you from?" Just hearing this question can send some locals into fits of apoplexy. *Mars* seems like an appropriate response for these Floridians who want to scream back at their interlocutors. Nevertheless, this question is usually answered with familiar responses, such as "Oh, upstate," meaning New York State, "The Shore," meaning New Jersey, "near Boston," meaning anywhere in Massachusetts, Rhode Island, or Connecticut, and yes, even generic responses such as Ohio, Michigan, or Quebec for those who feel their inquisitors may not be sensitive to the geographic particulars. Even people who have lived in Florida for several years will reply to snowbird inquiries with these old-home locations, instead of saying Orlando, Tampa, or Miami, as the case may be. In fact, true Floridians, people who have lived in Florida most of their lives, confess to some confusion when they are asked, "Where are you from?" If they answer, "Miami," they merely prompt the follow-up question, "But where are you from *originally*?" It is difficult for snowbirds to conceive of Florida as home, and without a doubt, snowbirds see themselves as something other than Floridians.

*Floridians* are people whose home is in Florida. Is that a good working definition? Not really! After all, many snowbirds have Florida homes, too. What other qualifications might we consider? It is easy to fall back on the idea that a person's birthplace joins him to a specific locale; if so, a Floridian is—quite simply—someone born in Florida. This old lodestone cannot stand serious scrutiny, however. In fact, most permanent residents—most Floridians, if you will—came from elsewhere. Moreover, it makes no sense to treat the mere accident of birth as the only relevant fact. For example, if a Georgia-born student at Florida State University in Tallahassee gives birth here but takes the baby back to Georgia afterward, is the baby a Floridian? What if the baby was conceived outside Florida? What if neither the father nor the mother is Floridian? What if the baby spends less than a day of his life in Florida? Come to think of it, does a baby born on a flight passing over Florida become a Floridian? Does a refugee born in U.S. territorial waters off Florida's coast become a Floridian? Laws try to define such things, and many countries deny citizenship to the children of foreigners. Can some people born in a place be exempt from citizenship? Most certainly! In many countries, one or both parents must be native before a child gets automatic citizenship. Moreover, countries routinely exempt the children of diplomats from the entanglements of citizenship in the host country. And countries allow for some means of naturalization for those born outside. This makes sense. Can we deduce some definition from actual cases, however?

Consider the case of a U.S. diplomat, or member of the military, living abroad. If a diplomat has a child, her baby gets U.S. citizenship, even though the child may first come to U.S. soil months, or years, later. Should all people born outside the U.S. forfeit U.S. citizenship? Hardly! Would we grant U.S. citizenship to children born of illegal aliens and deny it to children born of legal U.S. citizens abroad? No! Nor does a person born in some locale necessarily belong in that locale. For such reasons, it takes more than the accident of birth to make someone a Floridian. Similarly, someone born outside of Florida can become Floridian. How and when do such transformations occur? Conversion is a logical necessity; those born in the city of destruction may escape to the celestial city. Some people seem too near one side to belong to the other side. While it is difficult to explain the transformations people undergo, we know that transformations occur. That is why purgatory seems so necessary in the afterlife; some neutral ground between heaven and hell seems appropriate. Snowbirds seem to inhabit this sort of space. They are transitioning into Floridians.

Uncle Fred (Steve Knapp's uncle) illustrates how conditions, both meteorological and personal, put the snowbirds to flight, and how snowbirds gradually turn into Floridians. At this point, Fred might arguably be a Floridian, but if so, he became one gradually. While living and working in Plymouth, Michigan, just outside of Detroit, Uncle Fred went through a difficult divorce some years ago. The metropolitan Detroit area is just about smack dab in the center of Dante's inferno—third circle. Anybody who has lived there during a cold, snowy winter would swear to it, if not about it. After Fred's divorce, Detroit winters seemed colder than ever. "I don't mind getting snowed in once in a while, but getting snowed in, home alone, is worse than I imagined," he confessed. While he worked at Ford Motor Company and needed to put in a few more years to collect enough pension money for a comfortable retirement, he genuinely liked Plymouth, too. "It's beautiful, six months out of the year," he said affectionately about the Detroit area. Infernal regions have their allure for many would-be snowbirds, and many committed snowbirds cannot break their ties with their old homes, either. Nevertheless, perhaps out of sheer desperation, Uncle Fred decided to save his accumulated vacation for an extended Florida stay in the winter of 1985. After four weeks he returned to metro Detroit, glad to be home. Ties to souls in the infernal region were part of the explanation. "I have friends in Detroit, and family, so I'm glad to be home," he admitted upon his return. The allure of paradise had its effect, however, and the following year Fred was vacationing in Florida again. Some observers call such repeat visitors *snowflakes*, melting too soon to earn legitimate snowbird status. How did he deal with the absence of friends in Florida? He began by importing them from Michigan.

Fred convinced his brother in Michigan to join him for some vacation time in paradise. They would even drive down together, and it was only a few years before both of them bought travel trailers in Florida. As an aside, Northerners should be aware that many travel trailers in Florida never travel — anywhere. These trailers are on permanent lots, purchased in parks that cater to snowbirds who still fancy themselves as vacationing visitors. The only traveling these trailers ever do is traveling from the RV dealership to their permanent lots. Having purchased these aluminum condos, Uncle Fred and his brother were now committed snowbirds. Naples, Florida, and Plymouth, Michigan, vied for Fred's divided affections. Fred began making ties in paradise, too. He soon acquired female friends in Naples, and they always seemed to be young, attractive, and vivacious. His Florida photographs sparked as many conversations about his hot Florida women as they did about hot Florida weather or the beautiful Florida scenery. These photos, circulated around the water cooler at Ford Motor Company, probably brought scores of other snowbirds into the annual migration, usually to Florida's west coast, following preestablished migratory patterns. Some snowbird observers link some of these settlement patterns to locations for baseball's spring training.

If baseball is America's favorite pastime, then attending the spring training games is the snowbird's favorite Florida pastime. For one glorious month, the boys of summer — or winter — ignite spring fever as they take to the field at these small — some say intimate — stadiums in towns dotted all across the Sunshine State. From St. Petersburg, Bradenton, and Sarasota on the west, to Vero Beach, Port St. Lucie, and Jupiter on the east, not to mention Winter Haven and Lakeland in the middle, this warm-up season draws plenty of team faithfuls desperate to snag autographs of their favorite players and hear the crack of the bat or the thud of a perfectly thrown ball as it hits the catcher's mitt. For snowbirds, spring training carries with it all the nostalgia of home — up North, that is. The Grapefruit League, with its storied history, has helped to link teams' fans to specific Florida landing zones by attracting flocks of winter residents, birds of a feather, who settle in close proximity to their team, their team's fellow fans, and their Northern friends. On the downside, as Uncle Fred knows, making the trip from Naples to Lakeland to see his beloved Tigers play means long lines, cramped facilities, and often a bit too much sun on these still *mild* March days. With almost no big-name players willing to mingle or meet-and-greet fans, and with split squads and frequent substitutions of first-team players for players whose names are so fresh even the die-hards have never heard them, Uncle Fred wonders when it all started to change. The whole event for Uncle Fred seems to have lost its original luster, some of its sunshine, but the myth endures, and the institution continues to draw crowds to root for the home team in this mutual home away from home.

In the beginning, when Uncle Fred first came to Florida's west coast, there is no denying that Fred was merely a migratory bird, flying an established route. He came to Florida, and he returned to Michigan a few weeks later. This dual citizenship is untenable in the long run, however. As the gospel says, "No one can serve two masters, because either he will hate one and love the other, or be loyal to one and despise the other." Snowbirds, especially the newbies, are pulled in a cosmic battle between paradise and the infernal regions. At times the infernal regions seem more like home, and at other times Florida's allure becomes so overwhelming that, like Peter in the gospels, they want to build shelters and stay. In Luke's gospel, after climbing a mountain on a getaway with Jesus and two other disciples, Peter remarks, "Lord, it's good that we're here! If you want, I will set up three shelters." In our story, each snowbird requires two shelters, one North, one South, but the divide between Florida and the North is like the divide between the celestial city and the city of destruction. Eventually, one must win and the other must lose. Newbies have no idea at first, so they exhibit nearly schizophrenic attitudes about their dual citizenship. One minute they spit venom about the snow and cold of the inferno, but minutes later, they criticize paradise. Why? It is as if Gabriel and the Devil are pulling them nearly in two. Much of the time while in Florida, snowbirds find themselves fondly reminiscing about life in hell.

Consequently, snowbirds can become critical of their southern home with little provocation. While they would never think of being the stereotypical ugly American when traveling abroad, they easily become the ugly New Yorker, ugly Wolverine, or ugly Hoosier when visiting Florida. Florida is thought of as a kind of paradise on one hand, but on the other hand it is backward, poorly educated, and filled with Southern hicks. Crackers they are sometimes called. Snowbirds can become evangelists of the North, spreading the gospel of Northern enlightenment in the still backward South. Take roads for example. Ask any Northerner about Florida's roads and you will get a lecture about roads back in [*insert state or city name*], and you are likely to be told that Florida's roads are too crowded (locals see the irony here), illogically arranged and marked, and badly maintained. While locals are aware of such problems, they hate to hear it from outsiders, and they blame many of the problems on the very snowbirds who come preaching the good news of "how we do it up North." For locals the level of frustration sometimes gets high. Locals have even proposed a solution to Florida's problems with roads, water, housing, and urban sprawl: close the Florida border. No, it is not just in California, Texas, Arizona, and New Mexico where the idea of a fence is popular.

Are we Floridians better off because of the snowbirds? A subterranean debate rages over this question. Researchers at the University of Florida estimate that about 900,000 snowbirds—staying at least 30 days—are in Florida in January of each year (Smith and House). Can this be beneficial? This estimate can easily become just a number. Consider, however, that Delaware, South Dakota, Alaska, North Dakota, Vermont, the District of Columbia, and Wyoming have fewer people than this. This influx brings a richness of culture and diversity of perspectives—a life-giving transfusion of interstate vitality. It also brings a mania associated with the season, an artificially inflated economy of restaurant patrons, grocery store shoppers, and drivers. Combined with millions of tourists, visitors choke Florida's infrastructure. When the number of visitors falls off during the summer, a magical hush falls over the towns, the businesses, and the roads. Season tickets to any one of our local fine arts theaters run, not coincidentally, from about November until May. Our local museums bring fantastic exhibitions and throw festive parties in January, February, and March, when the numbers of potential patrons are highest. It can seem as though Florida exists for the snowbirds. But having 900,000 additional residents converge on a single state, whatever the benefits, is bound to have negative repercussions. Even snowbirds are starting to acknowledge this. Uncle Fred, staying longer and longer in Florida, complains incessantly about the growth explosion and terrible traffic in Naples. He will acknowledge that most of the growth is coming from snowbirds, very much like him, and a few are even his relatives and acquaintances from up North. Snowbirds are starting to see that they themselves are largely responsible for their biggest Florida problem — other snowbirds. Yes, they have been telling tales of Florida up North. There, the story is Florida, and as the Florida story is told, it becomes the story of paradise: Florida is more like the Garden of Eden than any place on earth. No wonder more snowbirds are coming.

The reality is different from the popular perception, however. With Port St. Lucie, for example, General Development Corporation (GDC) created a town in the middle of scrub palmetto fields. GDC created this Florida town — several towns throughout the state, actually — out of nothing. The land and homes were marketed to Northerners, as a rule. Why? GDC saw a huge disparity in prices between the northeastern U.S. and south-central Florida back in the 1960s. Shrewd marketing types realized that Northerners would compare prices, not to nearby Florida locations but, instead, to their housing market up North. So while northern snowbirds flocked to Port St. Lucie to buy the bargain lots and homes, the locals wondered why anyone would pay two to three times what the local market would bear. Did Northerners get swindled? Courts would later say yes, primarily because the marketing seemed a bit too shrewd. People testified that they were taken exclusively to the company's sites and kept too busy to shop around ("Charges"). Locals had mixed feelings. If these Northerners who always claim superior ways are getting taken by Florida developers, doesn't that just show that they are even bigger rubes than the ignorant Floridians they often criticize? Should Northerners have gotten suspicious about the company's claims when they realized that Port St. Lucie had no port, and it was, in fact, miles from the ocean and even further from the closest port? Perhaps it was partly the allure of Florida that entrapped them. After all, Florida is paradise, and land and homes in paradise must be worth at least as much as similar properties are worth back in Dante's third circle, right?

Snowbirds and settlers looking for the cheapest prices often end up in the damnedest places, at the furthest outskirts of paradise. Fundamentally, they want sunshine, food, and shelter, and to remain undisturbed while they contemplate the suffering of fellow Northerners who remain behind in Dante's third circle. For example, snowbirds flock to places like Lake Placid, Florida, which bills itself "the Caladium Capital of the World." Steve's Uncle Fred went there to visit his sister, who had begun to snowbird just outside the town limits. Fred was incredulous: "There has never been a snowbird who ever heard of caladium before settling down in Lake Placid. Don't get me wrong. Lake Placid is a wonderful place, so locals from that beautiful little community should take this charitably. It's a sleepy little town with hardly anything to offer visitors. Anybody from a big city would be bored insane trying to live there." Even Lake Placid Chamber of Commerce boosters subtly acknowledge that the town is not a major tourist attraction. Sure, the chamber's Web site boasts of the town's award winning murals, and it suggests that visitors "ride through original Florida ranchlands," and "walk in primitive forests" ("Lake Placid"). Still, near the top of the Web site, the chamber gets down to serious information: "100 miles south of Orlando (on U.S. 27), 100 miles southeast of Tampa, 100 miles northwest of West Palm Beach." Okay, the town is 100 miles from anywhere. There are fewer than 2,000 residents. Honestly, tourists might pass through the town on their way elsewhere, but nobody is planning a trip to Lake Placid as tourists plan a visit to Paris, France. Why then do snowbirds flock to Lake Placid? It is peaceful to be sure, but more importantly, it is cheap. A cheap winter escape is a happy winter escape.

Lake Placid feels like escape. Face it. The "original ranchlands" have nothing to do with the allure of Lake Placid. You have to pass hundreds or thousands of "original Florida ranchlands" just to get near Lake Placid, so something else is motivating the people who come there. Sarah Mallonee's cousin who lives in Lake Placid wonders about the particular flock of snowbirds who frequent the town: "I think we only get the ones who are deaf, dumb, and blind. They come to Lake Placid because they wouldn't be able to drive in a real town. They are so old that most of them die before they return for the next season." Seriously, the Lake Placid area has some nice lakes with beautiful lakefront homes. Anybody who goes there can see the beauty of the place. The gentle hills add character to the landscape, and the trees and lakefront homes look like they could actually be in Sister Lakes, Michigan. Bits and pieces of that area are gorgeous. Realistically, however, most snowbirds get nowhere near these gorgeous properties. They are living in RV parks, mobile home parks, and cracker-box houses, sometimes miles away from the nearest water. Fred remarked about his sister's trailer: "It's on a hill, next to the railroad tracks, overlooking the highway." After a short stay, Fred concluded: "The park is populated by migrant farm workers, elderly people on meager fixed incomes, and snowbirds. Who else could tolerate their paradise shaking and rattling with the rumble of every passing train?"

Trains, developers, alligators, sharks, snakes, mosquitoes, and hurricanes cannot exist in paradise, can they? Is it possible that snowbirds are repeating Spanish explorer Ponce de León's old error—seeking the transcendent on humble earthly soil? Are snowbirds all being taken for a ride, like a huge mass of some Florida developer's clients? Has Florida been oversold in the popular culture? There is some reason to suspect so. Sir Thomas More gives us the best and most lasting name, other than the Bible's Paradise or Eden, for an ideal place:

*Utopia.* The word itself means *no-place.* Heaven on earth is literally *utopia*—nowhere. Moreover, in spite of today's Florida boosters, like Uncle Fred, Florida never was paradise. Florida was not paradise when Fred discovered it in 1985 anymore than when Ponce de León was wandering through the swamps, some say in search of the fountain of youth. Florida has always inspired outsiders with dreams that reality could never deliver. The first European explorers discovered an earthly reality that later immigrants would discover for themselves, too. Most of Florida's land is virtually uninhabitable. Its vast swamplands are teaming with alligators, poisonous snakes, inedible plants, and hordes of bloodsucking mosquitoes. In April of 1528, Cabeza de Vaca, a member of Spain's next attempt at colonization after de Leon's failure, came to Florida among a group of 300 men and 40 horses. They searched for Florida gold, but by September 22, de Vaca tells us, "we had eaten all but one of the horses." De Vaca tells of indigenous Indian tribes in America "burning the fields and woods around them to drive off the mosquitoes and to drive out from under the ground lizards and other things they eat." Only four men survived this ill-fated Spanish expedition by eventually escaping to New Spain, today's Mexico. One need not retreat to sixteenth century depictions of Florida's inhospitable natural state to see Florida's dark side, however. Just watch the Oscar-winning 1948 film *Key Largo,* starring Humphrey Bogart. It is hot in Florida, and people simply endured it before air conditioning came along. Also, hurricanes are a fact of life here. Modern Floridians get a taste of those old times when hurricanes knock out power, putting air conditioning out of service, leaving residents baking in insufferable heat. No, Florida never was, and never will be, paradise. Sir Thomas More is right to name the earthly paradise *Utopia,* nowhere. Florida may have been mistaken for paradise, but that was by outsiders listening to the hucksters, land marketers, travel agents, and, yes, even Florida's Chamber of Commerce.

Thinking about Dante's *Divine Comedy* more fittingly, Florida is neither heaven nor limbo, places the deserving go to experience God's reward for their good lives of saintliness and morality. Instead, Florida is akin to Dante's purgatory. Yes, Florida is purgatory. Here people come to suffer for their sins of omission and commission. Here the profligate lose their retirement nest egg. Here the incautious lose their retirement savings. Here the unwary lose their windfall profits from home sales in the North. Here we lose our dreams about the golden years of retirement. Here we come to terms with ourselves and the harsh realities of life. Still, we better relish our days in Florida — God's waiting room. If we purge ourselves of the baser human instincts, if we cultivate the better angels of our nature, perhaps we might, one day, see heaven.

## Afterword

Snowbirds make headlines, editorials, letters to the editor, novels, and movies all a bit livelier. While they are in God's waiting room, these snowbirds are obviously far from idle. If the more than 2,800 articles appearing last year referencing snowbirds tell us anything, it is this: snowbirds are ever-present in our minds and clearly help shape the image of Florida. Snowbirds' letters to the editor frequently reveal the needling that makes Floridians cringe: "South Florida a paradise except for..." (Ross). Alan Ross of Boynton Beach sums it all up pretty succinctly with his own personal statement when he says, "I love Florida weather and numerous other things about the lifestyle here, but I'd like to mention a few things I'd love to see changed." While this snowbird hugs his middle ground of pleasant rebuke, the pendulum swings far and wide from there. Ed Brown in Port St. Lucie feels more strongly: "The year-round residents are unbelievably rude and nasty to those of us who can still afford to head back north to escape the summer heat." He feels the wrath of the now-locals but also dishes out plenty of his own rudeness when he concludes, "We don't even encourage family to come visit any more. My one true regret is not selling and moving on a couple of years ago."

Snowbird bashing appears to be a part-time job for some locals, and newspapers frequently fill their columns with this incendiary material. The complaints are familiar and reiterate the same concerns: slow drivers, long and slow lines at stores, excessive wait times at restaurants, and a general clogging up of the well-oiled machine that is public life in Florida. In contrast to this, many more moderate locals write back to say, "Stop the pathetic snowbird bashing," and such writers remind us all to, "quit your whining" (Cormier). One kindhearted southwest Florida resident proclaims at the end of his missive, "Welcome home, snowbirds. Stay as long as you like. Our economy needs you" (Cormier).

In fact, thanking snowbirds is proper. Thanks to our snowbirds, Florida now boasts little New York style pizza joints and Mom-n-Pop places next to every Publix grocery store in the state. Thanks to our snowbirds, boccie ball, shuffleboard, pickleball courts, and golf courses pop up all over our communities. And, yes, thanks to our snowbirds, roads become more crowded and slightly unpredictable, and the wait for a table at the cheapest breakfast place in town just got two times longer. But with more green markets, art festivals, concerts, shows, and cultural events now in our state, thanks again, snowbirds, for joining us for all these activities. Everybody loves to think about, talk about, and write about snowbirds—natives and transplants alike. Snowbirds provide endless fodder for editorialists and make headlines more times than the weather. Snowbirds also provide a neat little inspiration to the creative minds who are searching for their immortality in a novel. As Joe Hensley shows us in *Snowbird's Blood*, leaving home and heading for the Sunshine State should carry an "Enter at Your Own Risk" warning. Our obsession with snowbirds remains—quite possibly—completely out of proportion to their short stay here, but their enormous impact on all things Florida makes them a conundrum worth considering.

## Works Cited and Consulted

Brown, Ed. "Unchecked Growth Caused Too Much Traffic, Crime." *Palm Beach Post*, March 9, 2008: 6E.

Cabeza de Vaca. *La Relación*. 1555. Collection of Alkek Library, Texas State University. http://alkek.library.txstate.edu/swwc/cdv/la_relacion/index.html.

"Charges Seen for Developer." *The New York Times*. February 1, 1990.

Cormier, Dan. "Stop the Pathetic Snowbird Bashing." *Charlotte Sun* [Port Charlotte], March 25, 2008.

Gerena-Morales, Rafael. "Florida Snowbirds Question Fairness of Property Tax." *The Wall Street Journal*. May 23, 2006.

Hensley, Joe L. *Snowbird's Blood*. New York: St. Martin's Minotaur, 2008.

"Lake Placid — Florida." Greater Lake Placid Florida Chamber of Commerce. http://www.lpfla.com/.

NCSL Elections Reform Task Force. "Meeting Notes." National Conference of State Legislatures, May 9, 2001. http://www.ncsl.org/programs/legismgt/elect/taskfc/notes-may9.htm.

Ross, Alan. "South Florida a Paradise, Except for..." *South Florida Sun-Sentinel* (Ft. Lauderdale), May 25, 2008: 4F.

Smith, Stanley K., and Mark House. "Snowbirds and Other Temporary Residents: Florida, 2004." Bureau of Economic and Business Research, University of Florida. http://www.bebr.ufl.edu/system/files/Temp_Residents_2004.pdf.

# Spring Break
## Jeff Morgan and Salena Coller

It all started in Hamilton, New York. Yes, that's right. The genesis of Florida as a spring break haven began in Hamilton, New York. The swim coach at Colgate University, concerned that his swimmers might get out of shape before the start of their competitive season, learned from a Colgate student who hailed from Ft. Lauderdale that the city just built "Casino Pool, which was the first Olympic-sized pool in Florida" (Reynolds). The year is 1936, and for the next half century Florida, particularly Ft. Lauderdale, became immersed in the popular imagination of Americans as *the* site for spring break.

Of course, it's not that now. City leaders in Ft. Lauderdale had seen enough by the mid-eighties and chose to stop marketing their fair city as a spring break destination for college students, who were destructive and generally spent little money except on alcohol. In fact, "commissioners once voted to purchase a riot tank with a water cannon to quell feared student rampages" (Marsh). Ultimately, traffic patterns "were reconfigured to discourage cruising, laws on public drinking were enforced, and icons of spring break bacchanalia were replaced with high-end hotels and restaurants" (Marsh). Seeing more money for the city coffers by marketing Ft. Lauderdale as a more family-oriented spring break destination, the city elders let the sun set on Ft. Lauderdale as a spring break haven for rowdy college students. Other cities, though, were apparently happy to take up the slack. Daytona Beach first stepped up to welcome these young revelers; however, for reasons Ft. Lauderdale already was well aware of, the welcome mat did not stay out long. Panama City is now the last bastion of spring break fever in Florida, the seasonal pilgrimage branching out to other locales such as South Padre Island, Texas, and Cancun, Mexico, where the legal drinking age is eighteen. In fact, Cancun is rated the number one spring break spot, followed, in rank, by Acapulco, Panama City, and Rosarito Beach in Baja. South Padre Island is ranked ninth, just ahead of Negril in Jamaica and Puerto Vallarta in Mexico. Lumped together in the middle of the pack are various North American ski resorts and European destinations, and tied for tenth are New York and Puerto Rico, the latter a U.S. territory not bound by the 1985 National Drinking Age Act, raising the legal drinking age to 21 (Crislip).

For those prepared to claim that today's youth are going to hell in a hand basket, the history of spring break would suggest otherwise. The ritual began before the birth of Christ. In ancient Greece and Rome, for example, most everyone, but youth particularly, celebrated the rites of spring by partaking in wine, dance, and love—not all that different from sex, drugs, and rock 'n' roll. The advent of Christianity somewhat slowed the inner drive to break out after a harsh winter with some spring partying. However, even in the Middle Ages spring break had its place. The spirit of Dionysus or Bacchus lived on through the centuries, but its form in the American popular imagination begins taking shape in the early twentieth century.

Two factors in the development of spring break as we have all come to know and love it are coeducation and cars. American universities were all male until the 1830s. Oberlin College in Ohio was the first university to admit women, and Mount Holyoke was the first American women's college in 1836. The American Civil War saw the rise of many Northern colleges, including female-only Vassar in 1861, and after the war many colleges started to become coeducational. When the automobile came on the scene, so did the college road trip to female-only colleges, an activity that took place in the spring once the roads became passable and everyone's hormones were high after a long, cold, lonely winter.

It didn't take long for young men and women to decide to all pile in the car together and go on a really long road trip—to Florida, an idea they could've caught from Major League Baseball. As early as 1888, baseball began the ritual of spring training. In 1888 the Washington Senators came to Jacksonville. A catcher on that team was one Connie Mack, whose Philadelphia A's came to Jacksonville in 1903 and whose grandson became a prominent Florida politician in the 1980s and '90s. In 1914, the trend kicked in with the St. Louis Cardinals coming to St. Augustine. Mack's A's were in Jacksonville, the Chicago Cubs were in Tampa, the St. Louis Browns were in St. Petersburg, and the Grapefruit League was established. Spring training brought an economic boost to these communities and added local color through the ballplayers' hijinks. Rube Waddell, the Hall of Fame pitcher, for instance, scorned in love, jumped into the St. John's River and, in another instance of temporary insanity, wrestled an alligator (McCarthy 141–43). Instances like these are the beginnings of the crazy stunts that have become a part of spring break in the popular imagination. McCarthy tells of the grapefruit dropped from a plane in 1915. Brooklyn Dodger manager Wilbert Robinson thought he was going to be catching a baseball, but it was a grapefruit that ultimately exploded in his mitt, knocking him flat, and convincing him that he was near death. And then there's Babe Ruth. In his wonderful book, *Baseball in Florida*, Kevin McCarthy covers Ruth's appetite in St. Petersburg, drinking in festive Miami, run-ins with palm trees in Palm Beach, and, of course, alligators in the outfield (148–53).

Yes, the world of sports played a key role in the development of spring break in the popular imagination. We already know of the Colgate swim team. The year after Colgate came to town, Ft. Lauderdale hosted the College Coaches Swim Forum at the Casino Pool. Two years later the Elbo Room, where you can still grab a cold one, opened on the beach. Military personnel from nearby bases joined the collegians, and spring break in Florida really began to take shape

(Marsh). Coming to Florida in the spring became a tourist event. The dollars associated with spring training are enormous. Baseball fans from the north make the annual pilgrimage to Florida to cheer on their favorite teams.

Spring training motivates many college students to take spring break in Florida, but as history tells us, they do have a few other things in mind. Clearly, sex is at the top of the list. Sex has always been associated with the spring, and by the 1960s, Hollywood was portraying Florida as an erogenous zone. The premiere of *Where the Boys Are* in 1960, which took place at Ft. Lauderdale's Gateway Theater, wasn't only about George Hamilton's tan. The movies played a huge role in characterizing Florida in the popular imagination, and the keyword was sex. At the start of *Where the Boys Are*, one of the protagonists, Merrit Andrews (Dolores Hart), debates with her "Marriage and Family" professor about whether or not a woman and man should be "playing house before marriage." Andrews even dares to mention Dr. Alfred Kinsey's new and controversial research on human sexuality. The debate between teacher and student illustrates the on-going debate about gender roles and sexuality in the United States that was forever changed by the women's rights movement, Dr. Kinsey's scientific research, and the "free love" movement in the late 1960s. In the film, all four of the girls, Merrit, Tuggle (Paula Prentiss), Angie (Connie Francis), and Melanie (Yvette Mimieux) are pressured to have premarital sex with the guys they are dating during their spring break vacation. Tuggle's love interest, Franklin (Rory Harrity), almost dumps her when she says no to sex, and later in the movie when he is drunk, Franklin is tempted to have sex with an older woman dressed as a mermaid. Three of the main characters keep their virtue while the fourth one, Melanie, is raped by an Ivy League student and suffers a nervous breakdown. The film starts out with the character Merrit talking about rebelling against the 1960s taboo of premarital sex, but by the end of the movie Merrit keeps her virtue and finds true love while her unfortunate friend Melanie behaves promiscuously and ends up being raped. In the end, the film upholds the status quo of the generation in which premarital sex is taboo.

Hollywood continued to associate Florida with spring break and sex in the popular imagination with the film *Girl Happy* in 1962. Here, Rusty Wells (Elvis Presley) tells his boss Mr. Frank (Harold J. Stone) that there are "30,000 sex-starved boys" in Ft. Lauderdale. This convinces Mr. Frank to pay for Rusty's band to take a trip to Ft. Lauderdale so that the band can protect his daughter Valerie (Shelley Faberes) from horny men who threaten her virginity. The film's songs, like "Puppet on a String," "Cross My Heart and Hope to Die," and "Do the Clam," performed by Rusty and the band, are catchy, fun, and reflect the film's theme of young love and lust. At the start of the film, Valerie rebels against her father's authority by using guilt to convince her father to let her go to Ft. Lauderdale with her friends. Throughout the film are themes of youth rebelling against parental authority and struggling with the responsibilities of independence (Doll and Morrow 294). The Italian exchange student Romano asks Valerie out and tries to seduce her on his private boat, but Rusty doesn't want to experience the wrath of Mr. Frank, so he attaches Romano's boat to a car and drives around town with the surprised couple trapped inside. Rusty ends up delivering the boat to their hotel pool and giving Valerie the phone so that she can talk with her dad. In order to keep Valerie away from Romano, Rusty dumps his current love interest and starts dating Valerie, only to fall in love with her. When Valerie finds out that her father paid Rusty to babysit while she is away on spring break, she is extremely angry with both men for not trusting her judgment as a responsible adult. There is an underlying theme of sexism in this film where the man must protect the woman from harm since she lacks the judgment and experience to protect herself. Fitting into the status quo of the era, the sexist themes reach a crescendo at the end. Here, Valerie maintains her virtue and with her father's encouragement she is reunited with Rusty. As in *Where the Boys Are*, *Girl Happy* confronts sexual reality and addresses sex with a certain morality.

These two films, though fairly risqué for their day, appear tame contrasted with the film versions of spring break that begin appearing in the 1980s. Indeed the reality of spring break also became more lewd and lascivious. Consider two articles from *Time* magazine. First, an anonymous 1965 article on spring break titled "Surf, Snow, Sex and Protest" presents a playful voice, continually using festive alliteration to describe Ft. Lauderdale in terms of "beach, broads and booze." Daytona Beach is described similarly but more sibilantly with "sex, sand, suds and sun." Interviewed Ivy Leaguers express their disdain with the low, baseness of Florida spring break. Twenty years later, John S. DeMott describes spring break revelers as survivors, referring to seven spring break deaths, most victims falling from hotel balconies. Unlike the experience of Rube Waddell, who was saved by friends, the 1985 college student visiting Florida for spring break ends with, "Either stay on the first floor or get a parachute." Things have certainly changed. In 1985, rain forced spring breakers to remain in their hotels, where at a local Days Inn "they did $50,000 worth of damage in an hour."

Details like these help explain why the vision of spring break in the popular imagination is more closely linked with those halcyon days of the early 1960s, the days of Camelot, before political, social, and cultural revolutions rocked the United States out of its comfortably numb state and into postmodern fragmentation and the denial of order. So, we keep a postcard in our mind's eye of the beach at Ft. Lauderdale in 1960, where, maybe, Annette Funicello is being chased, innocently mind you, by Frankie Avalon even though all those beach films were filmed and set in California. These images, innocent as they are (though rife with sexual undercurrent) seem preferable to the drunken college student falling to his death from a Ft. Lauderdale hotel balcony or Daytona Beach's "two month crush of 250,000 divided between Spring Break and Black College Reunion" (Hiller 104). Hiller adds that the sex and violence associated with cities like Ft. Lauderdale and Dayton Beach has led other Florida cities, like Vero Beach, to be politically committed to maintaining a small town feel (148), the feel that exists in the popular imagination when it envisions spring break in Ft. Lauderdale in the early 1960s, a time when Ft. Lauderdale "had a mid–American reputation as the most white-bread of all Florida's resorts" (232). To be sure, the vision of a Ft. Lauderdale spring break in the popular imagination is a white one, and just like the white flight that is statistically occurring throughout South Florida as the region becomes less white-bread, the search for the white-bread spring break continues north. While residents may move from Ft. Lauderdale to Vero Beach, spring breakers have moved to Daytona Beach and now on to Panama City in the panhandle. Nonetheless, what remains in the mind's eye of so many Americans is that 1960 postcard that portrayed a youthful spirit frolicking on the beach, an image attractive to most anyone who dreams idealistically of what could be, based on what once was.

## WORKS CITED AND CONSULTED

Crislip, Kathleen. "Top 10 Spring Break Hot Spots for 2008." *About.com.* 10 July 2008. http://studenttravel.about.com.
De Mott, John S. "Wreaking Havoc on Spring Break." *Time,* April 7, 1985.
Doll, Susan, and David Morrow. *Florida on Film: The Essential Guide to Sunshine State Cinema & Locations.* Tallahassee: University Press of Florida, 2007.
Hiller, Herbert L. *Highway A1A: Florida at the Edge.* Gainesville: University Press of Florida, 2005.
Levin, Henry. *Where the Boys Are.* Metro-Goldwin-Mayer, 1960.
Marsh, Bill. "The Innocent Birth of the Spring Bacchanal." *The New York Times,* March 19, 2006.
McCarthy, Kevin M. *Baseball in Florida.* Sarasota: Pineapple, 1996.
Reynolds, Christopher. "Spring Break 101: A Humble History of a Holiday Gone Wild." *The Los Angeles Times,* March 10, 2008.
Sagal, Boris. *Girl Happy.* United Artists, 1962.
"Surf, Snow, Sex & Protest." *Time,* April 2, 1965.

# Motorsports Rev Up the Economy
*Alan Pratt*

For more than a century, Florida has entertained millions of visitors, lured most often by the miles of gorgeous beaches, ideal weather, and the unusual creatures that are unique to the state. Florida in the popular mind has come to mean sunshine, palm trees, pink flamingos, lush tropical greenery, pastel-tinted bungalows, and graceful sailboats tacking off the coast. These are the experiences you see reflected in the vibrant watercolors of Winslow Homer, for example, of schooners moored in the Keys, bass fishing on Homosassa Springs, or stands of palmettos near Lake Monroe. But even with all this emphasis on the natural, Florida has another reputation — global in scope — for motorsports.

## Motorsports in Florida

Now, motorsports may not be the first thing that comes to mind when you contemplate Florida. But for a number of reasons, Florida is unusual, and famous, when it comes to motorsports. Consider this: Swamp buggy racing was invented in Florida. Swamp buggies are those tall, weird-looking things with huge balloon tires. They were invented in Naples, Florida, in the 1930s as a way to travel in the vast Everglades swamp, and they have raced there ever since. Sebring Raceway, eighty miles south of Orlando, is the oldest permanent road-racing track in the United States. Its annual "Twelve Hours of Sebring" is internationally famous. There is new race track in South Florida, the Homestead-Miami Raceway. It was built in 1993 to help the area rebound from the cataclysmic devastation of Hurricane Andrew. Even Disney World has its own speedway complete with a Mickey Mouse-shaped lake. Throughout Florida, dozens of small, mom-and-pop race tracks are open Saturday nights, places like the New Smyrna Speedway and the Volusia Speedway Park. And Florida has more motorcycles registered per capita than any other state, more than 582,000 in 2006 ("State").

Of course, the most famous motorsports events in Florida, which dwarf everything else, are the world-famous Daytona 500 and Bike Week, which occur annually in a small town of 65,000 on the east coast of Florida — Daytona Beach.

## Daytona Beach, or Rather "Daytona!"

Everyone has heard of Daytona Beach, or more likely "Daytona." As the city itself claims, Daytona is "The World's Most Famous Beach." I recall a road trip I took from California to the East Coast in the 1970s. Driving through Florida for the first time, I just *had* to go to Daytona for reasons which were unclear to me then. Maybe it was because of spring break? It's true that in the late 1980s, Daytona was the world headquarters for spring break, with hundreds of thousands of college students converging on the area, drinking, trashing hotels, and falling from balconies. However, while spring break certainly generated plenty of bad publicity for the area, Daytona's reputation — the good, the bad, and the ugly — rests squarely on motorsports.

The Daytona area has all the natural elements that make Florida so popular. The sub-topical climate gives the place long, warm, humid summers, and extremely mild winters as a result of warm ocean breezes. Paralleling the coast are long barrier islands that enclose narrow, brackish lagoons which are part of the Intracoastal Waterway. Inland are lowlands, filled with massive live oak forests, rolling pine woodlands, lakes, and marshy areas filled with mosquitoes, wild hogs, snakes, and turkey buzzards.

The beach is the thing, though. Stretching 23 miles from Ormond Beach in the north to Ponce Inlet in the south, it's bordered to the west by small dunes covered with palmettos, scrub oak, and sea oats. But this beach is not just unusual because of its length. It's wide, too — in places, five hundred feet at low tide — nearly level, and *hard-packed*. In the late nineteenth century, bicyclists discovered that it was so hard that it was perfect for riding and racing bicycles. Some hotels on the shore even offered bicycles with sails attached that allowed riders to drift down the beach from Ormond to Ponce, often without pedaling. About the turn of the century, someone realized that if the beach could support a skinny bicycle tire, it would also be a perfect surface for testing the limits of the new "hell carts," those newfangled, horseless carriages (Strickland 113). The first automobile to venture onto the beach in 1900 belonged to winter tourist C.W. Seamans (Punnett 5). This seemingly insignificant event would not only dramatically change the tiny tourist hamlets along the beach but also would forever alter the perception of Florida. In the February 1903 issue of *Motor Age* magazine, J.F. Hathaway waxed prophetic when he wrote, "The sand is nearly as hard as asphalt and very smooth. There are no stones. There is an automobile here that weighs 5,000 pounds, and it makes no impression.... It is an ideal race course and a place where world records will be made in the future" (Punnett 7).

Among the 139 drivable beaches in the world, Daytona Beach is like no other. What makes the beach unique, geologists explain, is that the sand is 97 percent quartz, washed here over eons from the mountains of Georgia and South Carolina (Punnett 14). And twice every 24 hours, Atlantic breakers pack it down until it is as smooth and hard as concrete.

It is this unusual beach that led to Daytona hosting two of the most famous motorsports events in the world. The Daytona 500 is now considered *the* premier race event for the United States, while Bike Week is arguably the largest motorsports event on the planet. Not surprisingly, Ed Hinton, author of *Daytona: From the Birth of Speed to the Death of the Man in Black*, describes Daytona as "the carotid artery through which nearly every essential element of motorsports has passed at one time or another" (xiv). He's right. No other city in the country—nay, in the world—has such a long history with motorsports, having hosted races and related events for nearly 110 years. Daytona is, in fact, the oldest and longest-running motorsports headquarters in the world, and no other city in the world has such an obvious concentration of motorsports history and motorsports activities. Evidence of this is that Daytona has least eight motorcycles and two car models named after it—far more than any other location in the world. They are:

- Manx Norton Daytona Racer (1949)
- Kawasaki 500 H1R Daytona (1971)
- Suzuki TR 500 Daytona (1972)
- Yamaha RF 400 Daytona Special (1979)
- Harley-Davidson Daytona FXDB (1992)
- Moto Guzzi Daytona (1992)
- Triumph Daytona 955i (2005)
- Suzuki Volusia 800 (2001)
- Dodge Daytona (1984–1993)
- Dodge Charger Daytona (1969, 2005- current)

Motorsports in Daytona is big—*very big*. What Hollywood is to movies, what Las Vegas is to gambling, Daytona is to motorsports. Every year, over a million motorsports fans descend on the city, most notably for Speedweeks in February when over 200,000 NASCAR fans attend the Daytona 500; the Fourth of July Coke Zero 400 with 180,000 fans; Biketoberfest in October, which brings about a 150,000 bikers; and—the big one—Bike Week in March, when over 500,000 motorcycle riders converge on the area.

## "The Birthplace of Speed": A Unique Florida Beach Creates History

It was because of the wealthy guests who stayed at the luxurious Ormond Hotel in Ormond Beach that Daytona acquired a global reputation for speed, because only the wealthy could afford such expensive toys as motorcycles and automobiles. And it was only the wealthy who could afford to amuse themselves by pushing these machines to their limits.

In fact, the first recorded automobile race on the beach involved two wealthy industrialists, Ranson E. Olds, creator of the Oldsmobile, and Alexander Winton, owner of the Winton Bicycle Company, one of the first companies to sell automobiles. The 57 mph duel between Olds is "Pirate" and Winton's "Bullet #1" took place in April of 1903 ("Daytona Beach"). It was in 1903, too, that the Ormond Hotel organized the first "Winter Speed Carnival." During this event, Oscar Hedstrom set a world record motorcycle run on his 3½ horsepower machine that he called the "Indian." He later went on to design engines for what became an American icon, the Indian Motocycle Manufacturing Company (sic). Altogether, nine American records and two world records were set at the first Speed Carnival, with a top speed for the week a blistering 68 mph (8 Punnett).

As it turned out, Daytona Beach was like nothing else in the world — the perfect testing ground for speed. Beginning in 1903 — and nearly every year for the next thirty years — the fastest motorcycles and automobiles in the world set records on this unusual stretch of Florida's east coast. In fact, "Daytona" became synonymous internationally with "speed," and it is still home to the most record-breaking race course in history. In 1904, eleven world records were broken on the beach (Hinton 44). In 1905, the death of the first of what would be many racers killed in Daytona occurred when amateur Frank Croker, the son of a wealthy New Yorker, died along with his mechanic when he swerved his 75 hp Simplex to avoid a motorcycle that suddenly turned into him to avoid an incoming wave (Punnett 28). This first death on the beach caused by the unpredictability of nature would not be the last. And it is fickle nature that would eventually play a significant role in ending beach racing.

Daytona's reputation as "The World Center of Racing," was already well-established by 1906, as this postcard excerpt suggests: "The beach makes a superb driveway and speedway for bicycle riders, carriage drives, and automobile. International Automobile Races are now held along the Daytona Beach. A glance at the views shown herein gives one only a faint impression of the beauties of this fashionable southern resort" (Ashton). In 1909, what may well have been the very first stock car race ever was held on Daytona Beach. The race had to be shortened, however, from 200 miles to 100 miles because of encroaching high tides, giving the win to Lewis Strang in his 30-horsepower Buick (Punnett 85). In 1909 the Indianapolis Speedway was completed. Compared to beach racing, this closed track offered significant improvements. Spectators could see the entire race, crowd control was easier, and charging admission was easier.

The closed-circuit auto track innovation proved to be the beginning of the end for this earliest period of Daytona's association with motorsports: "Anyone could sit on a dune and watch the races free of charge," racing historian Dick Punnett notes. "Thus, more than anything else, the lack of revenue might have doomed the beach tournaments" (96). Nearly fifty years later, this and other problems with the beach track would plague race promoter Bill France.

In the 1920s not much racing occurred on Daytona Beach, other than a few locally organized stock car races (Strickland 120). Still, in its first thirty years as the world Mecca for speed, all of the legends of racing competed on the beach. Speedsters like Barney Oldfield, Eddie Rickenbacker, Glenn Curtiss, and Sir Malcolm Campbell raced their monster cars and motorcycles on the hard-packed sand. In 1935, Campbell would claim the ultimate beach world record when his V-12, supercharged Rolls-Royce-powered Bluebird rocketed down the beach at 276.82 mph.

## Racing in the Sand Continues: The Daytona Beach Road Course

In the early 1930s, racing resumed on the beach, except that these races were run on a closed-circuit track in what is now South Daytona. The course ran up the beach and then cut through the sand dunes to reach the asphalt of the narrow beachfront Highway A1A. This was the original Daytona Beach Road Course. Years later, the course would move all the way to the south end of the beach, when William "Big Bill" France Sr. got involved. France, a race fan since he was a young boy, decided to move his family from Washington D.C., to Miami during the Great Depression to find work as an automobile mechanic. On the way south, not surprisingly, he took a side-trip to the "The Birthplace of Speed." From the Ormond Beach approach, he drove the five miles down to the Daytona pier, where the family went for a swim (Hinton 53). One can only imagine what France was thinking as he glided down that wide, flat, world-famous beach for the first time, but he decided to stay in Daytona, where he eventually purchased a gas station on Main Street and started promoting races on the beach.

In 1936, the precursor to today's Daytona 500 was born when France organized a beach stock car race. In January of 1937, he promoted a motorcycle race on the beach that actually proved to be more popular than the automobile races. About 15,000 spectators watched 98 riders from 28 states race for the $300 prize. Ed "Ironman" Kretz took the checkered flag on his Indian Scout. This was first race of what would become the Daytona 200 Motorcycle Classic, now the second-oldest continuously held motorsports event in America, just behind the Indianapolis 500 (Tucker, Tom 26).

There was something special about this motorcycle race on Daytona Beach that Big Bill couldn't have anticipated, because even during World War II when beach racing was suspended (1942 to 1946), the celebrations associated with the bike race continued on Main Street. By the time the Daytona 200 was transferred to France's new speedway in 1961, "Bike Week," as it came to called, had acquired a life of its own, growing larger and larger, eventually eclipsing the race all together. It is now the largest motorsports event in the world, and it's made Daytona's motorsports reputation truly global.

## NASCAR's Birth on the Beach

After World War II, from 1948 to 1958, France again promoted races on the beach, but he had to move further south to avoid growing development. His newly-created 4.1 mile beach/ highway loop was, in fact, at the very southern tip of the 23-mile stretch of beach. This is where the first National Association of Stock Car Auto Racing (NASCAR) events occurred (Tucker 28).

NASCAR was something that Big Bill more or less invented in December 1947 at a get-together of race promoters at the Ebony lounge atop the stylish, Art Deco Streamline Hotel on Atlantic Avenue in Daytona Beach. Of course, today everyone has heard of NASCAR, an organization which has birthed a motorsports empire involving more than 2,200 races a year in twelve different divisions. It is now the second largest spectator sport in the United States, thanks to television.

As mentioned above, stock car races were held as early as 1909 and in the 1920s. However, it was Big Bill who focused on racing the cars that people drove and were interested in, a car that they could buy, a *stock car* fresh off the dealer's floor. A radio broadcaster and long-time friend of Bill France, Ken Squier, put the implications of this idea into perspective in 2008. France "took the romance of the American with the motorcar and added the sense of loyalty to the brand and applied it to the sport. In those days if your dad owned a Ford or Chevrolet, you're going to root for the Ford or Chevrolet to win.... It was more than just a means of transportation, and he capitalized on that.... He really got it" (Wright 15). Ed Hinton ups the ante as he says that history will remember Bill France as "the only American who ever invented, nurtured, and envisioned the fruition of a whole sport, all by himself" (2).

As Daytona Beach continued to expand to the south, it became apparent that the days of beach racing were coming to a close. The vagaries of the weather, stray dogs, soft sand, and unpredictable surf had always proven to be headaches for beach racers and promoters. Additionally, racing footage shot near the stands of the notorious North Turn where most of the crowd gathered for these early races shows spectators being routinely sandblasted by cars power skidding through the sand to reach the asphalt side of the racetrack. At times, the churned sand in the north and south turns would become virtually impassable, and cars would skate off the top of them, rolling and crashing into one another. So while it was Daytona's sand that originally inspired racing on the beach, it was, paradoxically, the sand that effectively ended racing on the beach.

In 1959, Daytona's relationship with motorsports took a grand series of left turns with the opening of Bill France's International Speedway. The wild and risky scheme of carving a racetrack out of worthless swampland took years of planning and scrambling for investors. When it was completed, nearly 1 million cubic yards of earth had been moved to create the famous 2.5 mile, D-shaped "tri-oval" track with its sweeping, 31° banked turns. When France was asked why the turns were banked at precisely 31°, he said he was looking to build the fastest raceway in the world. "They couldn't lay the asphalt any steeper" (Menzer 117).

No one had ever seen anything like this speedway. In fact, it was revolutionary, allowed racing so fast that it frightened drivers. Not surprisingly, at the 1960 Daytona 500 there was a massive pile-up involving thirty-seven cars. It remains the largest car wreck in NASCAR history. In 1959, stock car driver Jimmie Thompson made this comment about "The Big D": "There have been other tracks that separated the men from the boys. This is the track that will separate the brave from the weak after the boys are gone" ("1959 Grand Nationals"). Daytona International Speedway still holds the record for the fastest race ever run, the 1987 50-Mile Busch Clash, clocked at 198 mph (Tucker, Tom 34).

First televised in 1979, the Daytona 500 serendipitously had a captive audience of millions up and down the east coast because of a huge snowstorm. And that snowstorm is perhaps responsible for the meteoric growth of NASCAR that began in the 1980s. For the fiftieth running of the Daytona 500 in 2008, as many as 35 million fans around the world watched (Willis 29).

Ironically, the Daytona International Speedway proved to be too fast. As race technology improved over the years, it became necessary to invent "plate racing" to slow the cars down. Restrictor plates limit the amount of fuel the engine can burn, thus limiting acceleration and top speed. They became required equipment on all cars at Daytona in 1988 (Tucker, Steve). Throughout its history, NASCAR has had to constantly refine its rules in order for racing to actually occur between vastly dissimilar automobiles. Now, with the exception of the body shell, which only loosely resembles a "stock car," the race cars at Daytona are essentially the same. NASCAR racing is changing, then, and long-time fans say the changes are not good.

The most dramatic and most memorable event to ever occur at the Daytona International Speedway was undoubtedly Dale Earnhardt's fatal crash in 2001. Called "The Intimidator" because of his aggressive driving style, Earnhardt was an eighth-grade dropout made good, a good ol' boy who loved hunting, fishing, and the rural life. With this and his reputation for brash, in-your-face rhetoric and rebelliousness, he exemplified what old-school, "country-boy-can-survive" stock car racing was all about. The Earnhardt persona reminded fans of the origins of stock car racing, the days of outlaws like Junior Johnson running 'shine in his souped-up sedan. Cleverly, Earnhardt embraced the bad-boy image, became the common man's hero and NASCAR's biggest money winner, and made a fortune marketing "Intimidator" collectables.

In contrast to "The Intimidator," Jeff Gordon is the new breed of driver, "the good guy," the mainstream persona that NASCAR likes to cultivate, to expand the sport's appeal. Gordon is *not* a Southerner. He's from California, and he is photogenic, soft-spoken, polished, modest, and an extraordinarily successful driver. What do these kinds of changes mean to NASCAR culture? Ken Squier, who started broadcasting the Daytona 500 in 1965, recently made this observation about stock car racing's changing image:

> It's gone corporate.... Those drivers from the start were real characters, they loved the sport but they were characters. A lot of them were real mavericks. They

were in it to win races, but they didn't care what anybody thought of them.... They did things that wouldn't be allowed today.... They weren't accountable to any sponsors like they are today. I think it's gotten more homogenized. You don't have the great characters. That wouldn't be allowed; it's big business now. People like Jeff Gordon. They're more media savvy [Wright 15].

In spite of the changes to stock car racing and NASCAR, the Daytona 500 is still "The Great American Race," and some argue the most popular racing event in the world. Due to such claims, Daytona is now home to *two* families of *billionaires*, those of Bill France's sons, Bill Jr. and Jim. Third-generation Frances, Lesa and Brian are now in firm control of the family's racing empire.

## And Motorcycles

Though Big Bill France probably didn't realize it at the time, the 1937 motorcycle race he organized would have the most profound impact on the area. Certainly the International Speedway changed the perception of Daytona forever, but it's the motorcycle, not racing, that has most profoundly changed the character of Daytona Beach.

As mentioned above, Florida has more motorcycles per capita than any other state, and the densest concentration of them in Florida is in — you guessed it — Daytona Beach. In fact, Volusia County, home of the city, has more motorcycles per capita than any other Florida county and twice as many antique motorcycles. Only Broward and Miami-Dade counties have more motorcycles than Volusia — but they have populations over four and five times larger ("Revenue"). To put this perspective, Volusia County has one motorcycle registered for every twenty residents! You won't find a concentration even close to this anywhere in Florida, or anywhere else in the country, for that matter.

So while Bike Week now has little to do with racing, it was Bill France's motorcycle races on the beach that spawned it. And *it* is now huge.

While motorcycle rallies are held all over the world, the largest are in the United States. Laconia, in New Hampshire, has the oldest; it's a nine-day event that attracts about 330,000. The Black Hills Motor Classic — "Sturgis" — which began in South Dakota in 1938, draws 400,000–500,000. Florida, though, has the distinction of hosting seven of the largest biker rallies in the nation, more than any other state (*Motorcycle* 25). For example, there is the huge motorcycle festival in Panama City, the Thunder Beach Spring Rally. The Key West Poker Run draws tens of thousands, as do Miami's Hogs on the High Seas rally, Ft. Lauderdale's Bike Show, and Tampa's Bike Fest. All of these events are growing. Look what has happened to Leesburg's Bike Fest.

A small, sleepy town of 18,000 just north of Orlando, Leesburg launched its Bike Fest in 1996, when downtown streets were closed for motorcycles, and businesses held a few sidewalk sales. About two hundred riders showed. In 2005 — just nine years later — anyone who could park within blocks of the downtown area was fortunate. Dozens of itinerant vendors set up on every bit of open space, and everywhere long lines for food and beer snaked around on sidewalks too crowded to walk on. The Leesburg *Daily Commercial* reported that 125,000 to 150,000 attended the event (O'Brien). For 2008, event organizers put the number at more than 200,000.

Of course, the largest motorcycle rally of them all is Bike Week. Every March, motorcycle enthusiasts fill every hotel, spare bedroom, and fish camp within fifty miles of Daytona—a staggering 500,000 true believers. All of the major manufacturers of motorcycles and motorcycle parts, and all of motorcycling's celebrities—from Indian Larry to Sonny Barger to Evil Knievel—everyone and everything related to motorcycles have made the pilgrimage to Daytona—making Bike Week the largest gathering of its kind on earth and the world's largest motorsports event. And it's the event that has, more than anything else, shaped the perception of Daytona, as a place without standards and without limits.

On the cover of Florida writer Steve Glassman's *The Near Death Experiment* is a biker babe in black leather, and Glassman uses the Bike Week milieu in various scenes in the novel. His description of bikers at the Boot Hill is revealing:

> In a lean-to, off to the side of the bar a clot of bruisers in leather caps and studded belts stood around a pool table holding an extension cord with two naked wires. A guy plugged the cord into his mouth. His eyes jerked, his body convulsed and he collapsed onto the floor. He flopped and wiggled. There came the smell of singed hair and charred flesh. A second guy in black leather retrieved the wire and stuck it into his mouth. His large frame buckled. He staggered, then regained his full stature. He shook his head and said, "Wow, man. What a high!" He collapsed and writhed on the floor [30].

While plenty of outrageous things occur during Bike Week, it would be rare to see anything quite this extreme. Glassman says that he met a man in Belize, of all places, who'd been to Bike Week and witnessed what is described in the novel. (More likely, one might witness something like this: While a police officer on Main Street was explaining that there really wasn't much trouble during Bike Week, he bolted in mid-sentence to run down a bikini-clad woman on a sport bike who had just pulled off her top.)

Far-fetched or not, Glassman's account is the kind of thing outsiders and the uninitiated around the world imagine about Daytona during Bike Week: a town overrun with drunken outlaws in black leather. And such descriptions, in both fiction and nonfiction, have not only added to the legendary character of Bike Week as the biggest and baddest motorcycle rally in the world but have also contributed to Daytona's global motorcycle reputation. "Go to any newsstand and look in the motorcycle section. In German, in French, in Spanish, you'll see the word 'Daytona,'" notes Mike Mathews, co-owner of Daytona Blackgold Cycles. "Daytona *is* the Bike Mecca of the world" (Griggs).

## So How Have Motorsports Shaped Daytona?

Those who drive into Daytona Beach from the west using International Speedway Boulevard will be amazed by the "superspeedway" on the right. The gigantic, gray grandstands are ten stories high in places. Twenty-five-foot black-and-white faces of various drivers, a two-dimensional NASCAR Mount Rushmore, mark the different seating areas, with the most exclusive being the Dale Earnhardt and Richard Petty towers, named after two superstars of the sport. Passing the speedway, visitors drive under a bridge announcing, "Welcome to Daytona Beach." This bridge is used almost exclusively by the more than 500,000 race fans who show up for the various annual racing events. Other than the speedway complex, visitors won't see much in Daytona to remind them of NASCAR or racing. Sure, there is a café here and there with a checkered flag motif, but that's about it.

No matter which route visitors take into the area, however, from any approach into the county—north, west, or south—they will notice something peculiar right away. The highways are peppered with billboards advertising, not NASCAR, racing, or the International Speedway, but biker bars, tattoo parlors, motorcycle dealerships, and law firms touting their expertise in motorcycle law.

The peculiar relationship between Daytona and motorcycles becomes even more apparent on weekends, when you see an unusually large number of the machines on the roads. That's so because every weekend there are numerous activities in the area *especially* for bikers. A typical event would be OB's Pan and Shovelhead party. (The Panhead engine was built by Harley-Davidson from 1948 to 1965, the Shovelhead from 1966 to 1983.) About forty of these old Harley-Davidsons rode in last year for the judging—in itself telling, as it is very, very unusual to see so many of these rare, old Harleys in one place. Hosted by a nondescript tavern outside of Deland, the free party, complete with a live band, wet T-shirt contest, and free barbeque, attracts hundreds, in spite of the withering heat and the inevitable afternoon showers of mid–August in Florida.

While the OB bash is unusual for the number of old bikes that show, biker parties around Daytona are not. Minimally, there's a *free*, bar-sponsored barbeque/party for motorcyclists *every weekend of every month*. Besides these weekly biker parties, there are poker runs for a variety of causes. All together, these biker charity events around Daytona account for close to $1 million annually and provide motorcycle fans hundreds of opportunities to congregate.

Talk to enough of these Daytona bikers, and you quickly discover one or more who moved here because he or she loves motorcycles. There's not another town in the world that attracts perhaps thousands of residents because they *love* motorcycles. The fact is, the Daytona area has the most extensive and unparalleled year-round motorcycle subculture anywhere, and motorcycle fans from all over the country—from all over the world, really—have migrated here because of it.

To support the extensive interest in motorcycles, there have to be organizations to join, places to go, and things to buy. So there are. For example, at least seventeen motorcycle clubs are active in the county, including the oldest in the state, the Daytona 200 Motorcycle Club, founded in 1943. No doubt the most convincing evidence of the Daytona area's unusual concentration of motorcycles and motorcycle culture is the amazing level of motorcycle-related commerce. Just look in the phone book. The yellow pages list more than one hundred motorcycle-related businesses.

Dozens of biker bars in the Daytona Beach area, for example, cater to and attract those who *love* motorcycles—and those who *live* motorcycles. Some of these places, like Iron Horse, Boot Hill, and the Cabbage Patch, have reputations that reach around the world. Supposedly, Boot Hill stickers have been found on the Eiffel Tower and the Great Wall of China. Sopotnik's Cabbage Patch is known the world over for its coleslaw wrestling, where nearly naked women go at it in a huge slimy pit of shredded cabbage and oil. At least a dozen other less well known joints in the area cater to bikers, places like Dirty Harry's, the Last Resort, Froggies, and Main Street Station, Wise Guys, the White Eagle, Fire Side Inn, No Name Saloon, Thunder Gulch, and Smiley's Tap. Noticeable, too, is that around Daytona, biker hangouts frequently appear and disappear: The Dog Pound and Kick Start Saloon are new; Will's, Whiskey Pete's, Panheads, and the Black Hills have vanished. In all of these honky-tonks, free for the taking, are a variety of locally published motorcycle magazines—*Renegade Biker, Florida Biker's Digest, Dixie Biker, East Coast Rider,* and *Thunder Roads*—filled with advertisements for happy hours, leathers, lawyers, parts, bikes, tattoos, and other biker specials.

Besides the numerous biker bars, Daytona is also the home of the Wyotech Motorcycle Institute, the largest school of its kind in the world; its new, state-of-the-art campus can graduate 700 technicians a year. In fact, there are all kinds of unusual businesses that focus on motorcycles. Sandi Blackmer, for instance, is "The Riding Realtor," "Specializing in finding new homes for bikers and their scoots." In her advertisements, she straddles a tricked-out Harley Softtail. *Half* of her real estate sales are to bikers (Parente). Motorcycling is so much a part of the local culture that even the local Wal-marts carry helmets, leather vests, coats, chaps, and other motorcycle-related accessories.

## Daytona, NASCAR World and Motorcycling Mecca: The Downside

It's clear that motorsports have dramatically changed the culture and the flavor of the Daytona area. And while he was not single-handedly responsible, it's pretty clear that Bill France, more than anyone else, had a thoroughgoing and far reaching impact on what Daytona is today. But what price fame?

For one thing, the events just keep getting larger. What was once "Speedweek," which France invented in 1959, is now "Speedweeks," running from late

January to February, almost four weeks. Seven major races occur at the Speedway, beginning with the Rolex 24, a 24-hour endurance race, and culminating with the Super Bowl of Racing, the Daytona 500. Bike Week, too, has grown, from a weekend event, to a week, and now officially to ten days, while it actually runs for more than fifteen.

For motorcycles, particularly, the congested roads of Bike Week are dangerous. An unnerving statistic for the Daytona area is that it has more traffic fatalities per resident than any other place in Florida—because of motorcycles. "The streets that lead to Daytona Beach are lined with spots where motorcycle enthusiasts have lost their lives," a front page article in the Daytona *News-Journal* reported (Stapleton). According to the report, the accident rate for motorcycles in Volusia County is more than twice the statewide level and more than three times the national level. And in the last five years motorcycle-related deaths have more than doubled in the county. The bottom line: More people are killed on motorcycles in Volusia County per capita than anywhere else in the nation.

To cope with the problem, the county hospital several years ago decided that all personal leave would be prohibited during motorcycle events. The problem has become so severe, however, that recently the hospital took the drastic step of suspending all elective surgeries for fifteen days to accommodate the increased carnage generated by motorcycles during Bike Week (Geggis).

And the beach where it all started? While driving on "The World's Most Famous Beach," is still permitted, racing isn't. But with the increases in the population, beach driving itself has become problematic, with traffic jams, exhaust fumes, blaring car stereos, and regularly, too, run-over sunbathers. During special events the problems everywhere are exacerbated. When the area is inundated with motorsports fans during the Daytona 500 and Bike Week, locals have to adjust their schedules—and their mindset—to accommodate the intense congestion and, at times, unruly crowds. Complaints about the noise associated with both events are common. The roar of race cars can be heard anywhere within five miles of the Speedway. Bike Week is worse. In addition to the constant rumble of motorcycles 24 hours a day for ten days, there's the dozens of outdoor rock 'n' roll bands blasting until two and three in the morning. But it's not just the noise.

The traffic during these enormous affairs becomes unbearable at times. With the races, major arteries are clogged for miles before and after. For some locals this translates into commutes that can last for hours. Near the Speedway, Embry-Riddle Aeronautical University warns its 5,000 students of the dates and times when they probably won't be able to make it to campus because of the changed traffic patterns. Bike Week traffic can be bad, too, but the event is more troublesome than just the traffic. Local standards of modesty, sobriety, and safety are further relaxed for this world-famous motorcycle get-together, while law enforcement, emergency services, and locals are required to brace themselves for what one outraged local referred to as "the March infestation."

The biggest beef for locals, however, is the conviction that motorsports activities play a major role in promoting and perpetuating the Daytona Beach area's reputation as a sleazy, honky-tonk, party-till-you-puke kind of town. That's the image of Daytona known to most — a reputation that goes back at least seventy years. Discussing the area in 1935, about the same time as Daytona Beach Road Course racing got started, Florida travel writer A. Hyatt Verrill even then was grateful that other Florida beach cities hadn't ended up like Daytona Beach:

> But, thank heaven, Palm Beach and Lake Worth had never degenerated into the type of winter playground that one finds in Daytona, Miami, and elsewhere. Although during the winter the place [Palm Beach] is filled to overflowing with visitors from the north, they are of a class far different from and better than those who transform Miami, Daytona, and other resorts into noisy, hilarious, flamboyant infernos of riotous orgies, nudity, and Bacchanalian parties" [79].

With the stereotypical motorsports fans who've frequented Daytona all these years — NASCAR's beer-swilling rednecks and Bike Week's beer-swilling, black-leather outlaws — one can understand the public-relations problem. Case in point is the recent academy-award winning film *Monster* (2003). Set in Daytona Beach, it's the story of one of Daytona's own, serial killer Irene Wuornos. What's interesting, though, is that the film confirms nearly every conceivable negative stereotype about the area. In the film, Daytona consists of ugly industrial blight or sordid slums, with derelicts behind every dumpster, corrupt cops, bankrupt social services, sleazy lawyers, and menacing bikers. One scene, for instance, is shot in the Last Resort saloon, which teems with greasy, dangerous-looking bikers. The Last Resort is still in business on Highway 1, by the way, and its ambiance is exactly as depicted.

No wonder, then, that the relationship between Daytona and the gigantic events it hosts has come to be one of love/hate. It wasn't until Bike Week of 1988, for instance — fifty years after it began — that motorcyclists were actually welcomed to the area. That's the year that "Daytona Beach Welcomes Bikers" banners were first hung across Main Street (Page 88). For years prior, the city had tried unsuccessfully to shut the event down using police intimidation and crackdowns on bikers. But beginning with Bike Week sixty-seven years ago, Daytona has more or less accommodated these gigantic affairs and even added more. Why? Because the stakes are just too high.

The economic impact of motorsports for Daytona is staggering. Bike Week, for example, generated over $350 million last year. Unable to resist the economic boon that motorcycling provides, fifteen years ago Daytona created another three-day affair for the fall called "Biketoberfest." While it doesn't yet compare to Bike Week, Biketoberfest continues to expand, having now morphed into a ten-day gig that attracts more than 150,000 motorcycle fans and pumps another $60 million into the area economy. Additionally, the International Speedway Corporation (ISC) estimates that the economic impact of racing in Daytona is equivalent to $4,000 for *each* resident of Volusia County and that it supports nearly 32,000 jobs in Florida, for a total economic impact of $2 billion (Brown).

## Motorsports and Daytona: Future Expansion

Ten miles north of Daytona Beach on Interstate 95 is Bruce Rossmeyer's $40 million "Destination Daytona," where he's just completed the world's largest Harley-Davidson dealership, a gargantuan 110,000-square-foot complex. The 150-acre site now includes several motels, condominium complexes, restaurants, nightclubs, an amphitheater, a truck stop, twenty acres of parking, a museum, and another 50,000 feet of retail space for motorcycle-related businesses. For two miles in either direction, motorcycle-related businesses are setting up shop or buying real estate for later development to stake a claim in what will be the largest collection of motorcycle-related businesses in the world. When it is complete, Destination Daytona and the surrounding area will constitute the epicenter, the Kaaba of motorcycle enthusiasts the world over.

Ultimately, the motorcycling resources in Daytona will be extensive enough to occupy even the most fanatical motorcycle fan from cradle to grave — literally. Already several Daytona funeral homes offer motorcycle-drawn hearses. The Wings and Wheels National Biker Memorial in Palm Coast is a new cemetery especially consecrated for bikers' ashes (Haug). Rev. Tom Bingol, a project organizer, is confident that motorcycle enthusiasts from around the world will pay to have a final resting place in Daytona, the Mecca of Motorcyclists.

Racing is not going to be left out, either. ISC has big plans for expanding racing activities in Daytona, too. In July of 1996 it opened Daytona USA, now the Daytona 500 Experience, which is the "Official Attraction of NASCAR." It is a motorsports theme park featuring interactive rides, exhibits and 3-D, large-screen films. And recently, ISC announced the construction of a $250 million project called "Daytona Live," a sort of NASCAR World, across the street from the Speedway. The enormous complex will include storefronts for NASCAR souvenir vendors, restaurants, and movie theaters, as well as an office tower for NASCAR and ISC.

## Prediction: More of the Same

If visitors go to the Daytona "motorsports entertainment facility," as ISC publicists now like to call its speedways, for the Daytona 500, they can experience the clamorous, colorful, carnival-like atmosphere that makes NASCAR-style entertainment increasingly popular. They will also still experience plenty of Confederate battle flags, rednecks, and Southern drawls. And even though post–Sept. 11 fans have been restricted to ice chests which hold *only* ten beers, this ostensibly for security reasons, they are still allowed to bring in as much booze as they can carry — as long as it's in a clear plastic bag. Not all of this beer is consumed during a race, though. At the 2008 Coke Zero 400, for example, disappointed fans lobbed full cans of beer at the race winner, Kyle Busch. Comedian Jeff Foxworthy's observation about stock-racing reinforces the stereotype that NASCAR—and Daytona—has been trying to shake: "You might be a redneck if you think the last four words of the national anthem are 'Gentlemen, start your engines!'" Changing stereotypes is difficult.

When the ISC lobbied for a new speedway in Washington, State Representative Larry Seaquist was quoted as saying, "These people are not the kind of people you would want living next door to you. They'd be the ones with the junky cars in the front yard and would try to slip around the law" ("Seaquist"). The message: The notion of the typical NASCAR fan as a crude, beer-swilling, Southern white male endures. ISC, by the way, has since abandoned the Washington project.

The Bike Week crowd's reputation has mellowed some because of aging baby boomers who now more often trailer their Harleys to town to act on their mid-life crises and just don't have the stamina for all-day-and-night partying. However, Bike Week and Biketoberfest, more than anything, represent an opportunity for a temporary kind of regression for those who participate in them. The "biker" image, after all, has been consciously derived from negative stereotypes. And consider this: Boot Hill Saloon during any ten-day period might sell two hundred cases of beer. During the ten days of Bike Week 1999, the saloon sold 8,300 cases (Truett 2). Thus Bike Week still conjures up images of the Daytona that Steve Glassman describes in his novel: a town run amok with heavily tattooed and bearded outlaws in black leather—wasted.

In the last decade, developers with the blessing of city leaders have spent millions of dollars in an effort to clean up, once and for all, Daytona's sleazy, honky-tonk atmosphere. This "redevelopment" has come to mean exercising eminent domain to tear down older beach neighborhoods, souvenir shops, T-shirt shops, pinball arcades, amusement rides, and saloons to make way for expensive, high-rise hotels and condominiums, exclusive restaurants, and high-end shops. If the plan is ever successful, the Daytona of the popular imagination would become a postcard memory, and Daytona Beach would take its place among the many other uninspired, overpriced, concrete condo canyons on Florida's coasts—but with an unusually hard beach, a speedway, and lots of motorcycles.

Whatever the future holds, it's likely that any intentions Daytona Beach has to appeal to high-brow society by altering its "Daytona" reputation are doomed. Seventy years of bikers, stock car racing devotees, and partying beachgoers have cast the area's celebrity in hard-packed sand. So while Florida of the popular imagination will continue to conjure images of natural beauty and relaxation, Daytona, the motorsports capital of the world, will, no doubt, likely continue to conjure images of "noisy, hilarious, flamboyant infernos of riotous orgies, nudity, and Bacchanalian parties."

I suspect that Big Bill would be quite surprised to see how his interest in motorsports changed the Daytona area. His old gas station on Main Street is still in business. It's now the "Main Street Station"—a dedicated bikers' bar.

## WORKS CITED AND CONSULTED

Ashton, Chas. "Florida: The Famous Winter Resort of America." *Exploring Florida.* Excerpt from the postcard folder. Niagara Falls, New York, 1906. http://fcit.usf.edu/FLORIDA/docs/v/vacat.htm.
Brown, Thomas. "Racing Valued at $2 Billion." *The News-Journal,* December 18, 2007, A6.
"The Daytona Beach Area's Proud Racing Heritage." Daytona Beach Chamber of Commerce. http://www.daytonabeachcvb.org/media.cfm/mode/details/id/4922
Geggis, Anne. "Halifax to Limit Surgeries during Bike Event." *The News-Journal,* October 10, 2006, A1.
Glassman, Steve. *The Near Death Experiment.* Miami, Fla.: Tropical Press, 2001.
Griggs, Melissa. "Welcome to the New Motorcity," *The News-Journal,* October 22, 2006, E1.
Haug, Jim. "R.I.P.C. (Resting in Palm Coast)." *The News-Journal,* October 21, 2006, E7.
Hinton, Ed. *Daytona: The Birth of Speed to the Death of the Man in Black.* New York: Warner Books, 2002.
Menzer, Joe. *The Wildest Ride.* New York: Simon & Schuster, 2001.
*Motorcycle Events.* St. Petersburg Beach, Florida: Motorcycle Events Association. Summer/Fall 2005.
"The 1959 NASCAR Grand National Recap." *HowStuffWorks.* http://entertainment.howstuffworks.com/1959-nascar.htm
O'Brien, Jodie Munro. "Main Street Becomes Thunder Road, Literally." *The Daily Commercial,* April 25, 2005, http://www.leesburgbikefest.com/news.htm#F3.
Page, Roby. *Bike Week at Daytona Beach.* Jackson, Miss.: University Press of Mississippi, 2005.
Parente, Audrey. "Home Away From Home." *The News-Journal,* February 26, 2006, A1.
Punnett, Dick. *Racing on the Rim.* Ormond Beach, Fla.: Tomoka Press, 1997.
"Revenue Report FY 2006." Florida Department of Highway Safety and Motor Vehicles. 1 July 2007. http://www.flhsmv.gov/html/revpub/revpub_july07_feb08.pdf.
"Seaquist Opposes ISC Track Deal, not NASCAR." NASCAR.com. 5 March 2007. http://www.nascar.com/2007/news/headlines/ cup/03/05/washington.state.track/
Stapleton, Jay. "Deaths Mar Bike Events." *The News-Journal,* October 22, 2006, A1.
"State Motor-Vehicle Registrations 2006." Federal Highway Administration, Department of Transportation. 15 Dec. 2007. http://www.fhwa.dot.gov/policy/ohim/hs06/motor_vehicles.htm.
Strictland, Alice. *Ormond-on-the-Halifax.* Holly Hill, Fla.: Southeast Printing and Publishing, 1980.
Truett, Richard. "Bike Week's New Faces." *Orlando Sentinel,* February 26, 1998, B 2.
Tucker, Steve. "All About Restrictor Plate Racing in NASCAR." *Associated Content,* March 22, 2007. http://www.associatedcontent.com/article/180120/all_about_restrictor_plate_racing_in.html?cat=24.
Tucker, Tom, and Jim Tiller. *Daytona: The Quest for Speed.* Daytona Beach, Fla.: The News-Journal, 1994.
Verrill, A. Hyatt. *Romantic and Historic Florida.* New York: Dodd and Mead, 1935.
Willis, Ken. "The 500: Great, Greater, Greatest." *Daytona 500, The News-Journal* supplement, February 10, 2008. 28–29.
Wright, Susan. "Q and A with Ken Squier." *Daytona 500, The News-Journal* supplement, February 10, 2008. 14–15.
Zaffiro, Eileen. "Bikes Fuel Annual Death Tally." *The News-Journal,* August 21, 2005, A6.

# Peculiar Presidential Politics Among the Palm Trees
*Steve Glassman*

Remember the night in 2000 when the entire nation stayed up waiting for the returns from Florida to come in and decide the presidential election? Five weeks and a Supreme Court decision were required before an end was put to that election evening. Psychologists report many of their patients were obsessed about that cliffhanger election. For some of them that night became one of those you-will-never-forget-where-you-were moments, such as when Kennedy was assassinated, or when the Challenger exploded.

Personally, I remember that night vividly. I dropped by Volusia County's Democratic headquarters just as poll workers were gathering. Shortly, it was announced that NBC called Florida for Gore. All the other channels including FOX followed suit. We were elated. The returns were in from Ormond where a friend was running for city council. She had won. I headed for that suburb and the victory party. When I got to the friend's subdivision, I had trouble finding her house. The streets were dark and there were no cars—odd party. I found her in her darkened garage. She told me the absentee ballots, the great bugbear of Democratic politicians in our county, nosed her opponent ahead. She had lost. I returned to Democratic headquarters. NBC had changed its call. Florida was back in the uncertain category, and Republican officials were assuring the media that eventually the state would end up in the Bush column. I drove the twenty miles to my house. There, late in the morning, I learned that NBC, following FOX's lead, now gave Florida to Bush. Gore conceded, but before I went to bed about three, NBC uncalled the state. At that point, the returns were too close to make a projection. The tallies ranged from 500 to 1,900 votes between the two candidates. When I woke four hours later, bracing for bad news, I learned that Gore had retracted his concession and it was still uncertain how Florida's electoral votes would be cast.

There followed five of the strangest weeks in modern political history. When they were over, the country had a new president, and the image of Florida as a chaotic banana republic, already one of the stronger alternate views of the state, had become firmly established in the national consciousness. The best part of a decade later, that evening remains firmly rooted in the national consciousness, recently inspiring an HBO movie starring Oscar-winner Kevin Spacey. So who did Floridians really vote for in 2000? The answer to that question is incontrovertibly known today, even though those votes were not recounted in 2000 thanks to the Supreme Court decision. How do I know that, you ask? Florida has a sunshine law. It allowed the Miami Herald to inspect every controversial ballot in every county in the state. The results, though widely reported in the media, were quickly forgotten and did little to settle the waters of political controversy the election whipped up. Even today, almost a decade after the election, a pall of uncertainty and discord hangs over that election. I asked several scholars and one well-known journalist to write this chapter. All declined, presumably because of the difficulty of finding the heart in the artichoke.

A book about Florida in the popular imagination could hardly go to press without a chapter about politics. So I take pen in hand myself. The fact that I was vice chairman of the Democratic party in one of the four counties in which Gore asked for a recount, though obviously biasing my viewpoint somewhat, also may allow me to provide a bit of insight. Twenty-one books on the election burden the shelves of Volusia County libraries. I gathered as many of them as were available plus a number of others, as well as some critical essays written by scholars. In order to keep what is viewed as a complicated story simple, I chose to describe three positions. One is the Bush side, the other the Gore side, and the last is a more or less objective position. One hundred twenty-four years earlier another presidential election was decided outside the ballot box, with Florida taking a leading (and controversial) role. In order to make sense of the 2000 election, I think it will be useful to revisit that election of 1876, when the Republican candidate, though a quarter of a millions votes shy of Samuel Tilden nationally, won the electoral college and was sworn in as president. Finally, I will reveal the true winner of the election, as discovered by the *Miami Herald*.

But first, let's get a barebones chronology of the events of that chaotic post election period. The day after the election an automatic machine recount, as specified by state law in the case of a close election, began. By the Friday after the election, the machine recount was completed. The Associated Press tally had Bush ahead by 327 votes, but the official total, at that point, showed Bush's lead at 960 votes with one county not reporting. The Gore campaign requested hand recounts of four counties, the three heavily populated counties on the lower east coast, Palm Beach, Broward, and Miami-Dade, and the moderately sized Volusia in central Florida. The highly urban counties used punch-card ballots which were notoriously subject to miscounting due to fouling of the punched-out "chad." Volusia, at one point, had recorded Gore's total as a minus sixteen thousand votes. Palm Beach and Volusia agreed to the request. Broward and Miami-Dade couldn't figure out what to do.

Then the fun began. Volusia began its hand recount of all 184,019 ballots, and Broward and Palm Beach recounted sample precincts of their half million each, more or less, ballots. Secretary of State Katherine Harris announced that she would not extend the November 18 deadline, five days hence, for the submitting of official election returns, and Bush lawyers attempted to halt the hand recounts. Volusia and Palm Beach, joined by Gore and the Florida Democratic Party asked a circuit court judge in Leon (Tallahassee) County to extend the deadline. The judge ruled that the deadline must stand, but that Harris couldn't arbitrarily rule out a revised tally based on the recounts, while another judge denied the Bush request to stop the hand recount. Harris, in the meantime, certified the returns from all 67 counties showing Bush with a 300-plus vote lead and proclaimed that she would officially certify the vote as soon as the overseas ballots, which by law may arrive as late as ten days after the election, were counted. Volusia completed its hand recount, garnering an additional 98 votes for Gore. The sample canvas of precincts in Southeast Florida showed small but possibly significant gains by Gore. Broward and Palm Beach then began a full hand count of all ballots. Bush lawyers sought an injunction to stop them. Gore offered — on national TV — Bush a deal. If Bush accepted the hand recounts in the four counties, Gore said he would drop all legal challenges. Bush refused. The Florida Supreme Court then ruled the manual counts could continue, and the U.S. Circuit Court denied Bush's request to stop the recounts. At that point, Miami-Dade County began to recount. It was ten days after the election.

Gore's lawyers adopted an aggressive stance against accepting questionable overseas ballots. Most of them were from servicemen and, by law or custom, did not require a postmark showing they were cast before the election ended because shipboard (and presumably other military) post offices frequently do not date-cancel envelopes. When all overseas votes were counted, most from servicemen, Bush's lead increased to 930. On Tuesday, November 21, the Florida Supreme Court unanimously agreed that the recounts should be tallied and gave the counties five days to complete the job. In response, Bush went to Florida's Supreme Court arguing that the Florida courts were trying to usurp the authority of the state's election officials. Bush also asked for recounts of overseas ballots in thirteen counties. Under pressure from demonstrators outside a nineteenth-floor office, which included pounding on the door and so on, Miami-Dade canvassers suspend recounting. Broward County completed its tally; Gore netted 567 votes. Palm Beach missed the deadline for finalizing its revote. Harris certified Bush the winner of Florida's electoral votes. Gore asked the Florida Supreme Court to order a count of contested ballots in the Palm Beach and Miami-Dade counties, about 14,000 in toto. All ballots from both counties in the meantime had been transported to Tallahassee under armed guard. Bush and Gore lawyers argued their case before Judge Sauls, who earlier ruled in Bush's favor. He agreed with Bush this time also saying there was no reason to believe a recount would change the results. The Florida Supreme Court, by a 4–3 ruling, reversed his decision. Bush's lead shrunk to 154. Counting began statewide of up to 60,000 disputed ballots in which, during the machine count, no presidential selection appeared to have been made, known as an "undervote." It was possible that many of these undervotes would indicate to an observer the intent of the voter, which Florida law specified as all that was required to tally the vote for the indicated candidate. The U.S. Supreme Court granted Bush a stay by a

5–4 vote. The counting stopped, and ultimately, the U.S. Supreme Court sided, by the same 5–4 margin, with Judge Sauls and against the Florida Supreme Court. The basis for its decision was that Bush's right of equal protection was violated because of the lack of uniform standard in the various recounts. On December 13, one month, one week and a day after the election, Al Gore conceded. This time for good.

Bill Sammon, a reporter for the conservative *Washington Times*, makes no bones about his antipathy for Al Gore. The title of his book, *At Any Cost: How Al Gore Tried to Steal an Election*, makes that plain. He argues that Gore was out of line dredging up legalistic arguments to add to his tally of votes and disputing the judgments of Katherine Harris, the Florida secretary of state charged with certifying the election. Sammon's subtext is that, for the good of the country, Gore should have accepted the 300- to 900-vote margin Bush was credited with in the approximately six million votes cast in Florida.

This book drips with partisanship. For instance, Sammon mentions that Bob Butterworth, the state attorney general and Gore campaign chair, possibly mixed his roles in the aftermath in an attempt to aid Gore. On the other hand, he consistently characterizes Katherine Harris as a public official merely trying to do her job. He neglects to mention until late in the book that Harris was Bush's campaign co-chair, not exactly the sort of thing to make for a disinterested election worker. For all this, Sammon does a good job of laying out the Republican point of view, and his account is by no means grossly unfair. If this were to be the only account of the 2000 election extant a millennium hence, a latter-day scholar would have a pretty fair understanding of the issues involved. It's unlikely Sammon's bias, which he lets be known from the outset, would unduly skew the opinion of a thoughtful reader.

Sammon begins by an examination of the snafu that caused NBC and the other networks to call Florida for Gore. In an attempt to save a few bucks, the networks all used the same exit polling data furnished by a company called Voter News Service (VNS). The pollsters were temporary workers, and their methodology was about what could be expected from temp workers, a bit erratic. The pollsters were simply instructed to accost every third or fourth voter leaving selected polls. Many questions were quite personal, having to do with salary and so on. In earlier elections, Sammons claims, it had been shown that Republican voters in these circumstances were more restrained and less likely to answer fully. The same data was reported by VNS to all networks. NBC's analysts, for whatever reason, saw the makings of a Gore victory. Although the networks claim not to pay any attention to each other, within five minutes all made the call for Gore. The result, according to Sammons, was that 180,000 heavily conservative voters in Florida's panhandle — in the Central Time Zone and one hour behind the peninsula — were disenfranchised. Many in line to vote gave up. According to a Republican pollster, this early call cost Bush about 12,000 votes.

This claim of thousands of uncast ballots for Bush is meant to counter the claim of tens of thousands of "overvotes" or misvotes in Palm Beach and other counties. In Palm Beach, because of a strange ballot called a butterfly ballot, many reliably Democratic, elderly Jewish residents, the Gore folks claimed, became confused. They cast their lot for Patrick Buchanan, suspected by many in the Jewish community of anti-Semitic sentiments—or they voted for both Gore and Buchanan. Hardly anyone, not even Pat Buchanan, believed these thousands meant to vote for him. In short, their votes were rendered meaningless so far as the presidential contest was concerned. These lost votes became the moral heart of Gore's legalistic claims. Without them, Gore's technical shenanigans could be portrayed as mere nitpicking in hopes of reversing an election. Sammon clearly regards Gore as a charlatan, and his trying to pull the carpet from under the candidate by the claim of thousands of lost panhandle votes no doubt is compelling for partisans. For the rest of us, it is food for thought.

The warm-up act for the long-running election circus began in Volusia County, whose flagship community is Daytona Beach, on election evening. There it was discovered, early in the counting of ballots, that Gore's total, in this reliable Democratic stronghold, was minus 16,000. Some fiddling with the electronic tabulator corrected that report, but the damage was done. All Volusia returns became suspect—and for a good reason. Democrats had a disturbing history, in this county, of losing close races only after the counting of absentee ballots. The Supervisor of Elections Office had become embroiled in a bitter election two years earlier. The controversial incumbent sheriff, Bob Vogel, was challenged by Gus Beckstrom, a senior police officer from an Orlando suburb who lived in a bedroom community in Volusia. Both were Republicans, and the race was officially nonpartisan. But Vogel was widely disliked by liberals. As a state trooper he had pioneered the technique of stopping motorists and commandeering any large quantity of cash. The money, always heading south, was presumably from drug sales. Critics argued that the public would be better served if Vogel confiscated the drugs heading north. Under his regime, deputies continued confiscating any large parcel of cash, once even helping themselves to $10,000 found under a bed when called to quell a domestic disturbance. The sheriff kept these and all other confiscated funds, and used the money to supplement the department's budget without any governmental oversight. Charges of racial profiling flew about, and a few of Vogel's deputies were accused of acting in a high-handed manner, including voter intimidation. Beckstrom, clearly the Republican outcast, came to be adopted by the Democrats in wrangling that mirrored the post-2000 election. Beckstrom, in what was a familiar pattern, had been ahead after the regular ballots were tallied, but lost after the absentee votes were counted.

Beckstrom's legal team asked that all absentee ballots be thrown out because it was learned that many had been re-marked by a team of election officials. Those officials were assisted by deputy sheriffs working for and presumably loyal to the incumbent sheriff. Election Supervisor Deanie Lowe explained the whole situation. The new balloting machines required marking by a felt-tip pen or a number two pencil. Without those kinds of writing devices, the machine couldn't read the ballots. In voting booths, the proper utensils were provided. Absentee voters frequently used the wrong sort of apparatus. So in order to allow the machines to read the ballots, she had her workers, including the deputies who were detailed to her office as guards, remark the ballots. To make the appearance of things even worse, according to Beckstrom, the absentee ballots had been secured by a dummie lock, and the deputies guarding the safe had access to the absentee ballots during nights when the election staff wasn't present.

All this ended, after weeks of bickering in and out of court, as one could predict. The person with the most votes, the incumbent sheriff, was declared the winner. To make amends (and not incidentally prepare for her own upcoming reelection), Deanie Lowe, a Republican in an officially nonpartisan office, circulated around the county giving presentations. One of those was staged at the DEC (Democratic Executive Committee.) I was there. Like every other DEC member, I was skeptical, even hostile, when Ms. Lowe arrived. As noted earlier, many an election of Democrats appeared to have been won when the votes were counted in the precincts, only to be lost when the absentee ballots were tallied.

The most valuable commodity someone running for office can have is name recognition. Deanie Lowe had it in our county because as a youngster she was the weather girl on the local TV station. She was a charmer then, and in that meeting, she proved still to be a charmer. She and her staff went on for an hour and fifteen minutes or perhaps longer. Charts were presented showing the changes that were going to be put into effect and other charts posted for this and that. We were bombarded with an endless flow of information and an ominous lack of organization. When the presentation was finally over, I — and I'd bet just about everyone else in that room — was sure of just two things. The first was endless relief that that gleeful tedium was finally finished and, second was that Deanie Lowe had no hand in any kind of skullduggery. I'd venture to say probably half of those fairly hard-nosed Democratics may even have voted for her in the next election.

But here we were election evening 2000, and it was just like old times. Gore had mysteriously gone 16,000 votes in the hole. The glitch that had disappeared those votes had evidently been fixed, but later sacks of ballots were unaccounted for. A sheaf here and there that had not been counted turned up in the following days. None of this was as serious as a flawed ballot design. Volusia logged 22,000 overvotes (two markings for president), proportionately more than the well-publicized overvotes in Palm Beach County that brought the butterfly lady, Theresa Lepore, national attention. Had those 22,000 voted at the same rate as the others in the county, more than a thousand additional votes would have been added to Gore's total, enough to turn the election.

All this was made more poignant by the next supervisor-of-elections race. Not surprisingly, Deanie Lowe chose to retire from the office. Running for her old job were two longtime friends and rivals. Both had started out as Democrats and county councilmen from neighboring districts in the suburban southwestern part of the county. They term limited out at the same time and decided to run against each other for the at-large council post. Either then or shortly afterward, one became Republican, and the Republican lost the race. The Democratic winner some years later ran afoul of term limits and decided to go for the supervisor of elections office. Her old rival also ran. This seemed a no-brainer. A popular incumbent county office holder running against a person she'd vanquished before. Her opponent was not only tarnished by losing her only countywide race, she had been out of the public eye for several years. But no-brainer it wasn't. The Republican won the office. We local Democrats were absolutely astonished. It is clear that it was not entirely an accident that many key elections office holders were Republicans. I am not accusing these people, or Katherine Harris, of doing anything underhanded. I'm just noting that they appear to have made an effort to get the election machinery in their hands where they were able to make key decisions about voter registration — and purging and the like.

In his book, Sammon, while soft pedaling the goings on in Volusia, looses his scorn on the Democratic counties of the Palm Beach-Miami corridor. All three counties used old-fashioned punch-card ballots. The punch card had been phased out in Volusia and most other counties of middling size and replaced with optical scan ballots that were tabulated before the voter left the area. A spoiled optically scanned ballot will, theoretically, be recognized by the machine it is fed into by the voter as the last phase of the process. That ballot is supposed to be kicked out of the machine and destroyed. The voter would then be presented with a new ballot and shown back into the polling booth. (As noted above, this mechanism didn't work in the case of the 22,000 overvotes in Volusia.) No such fail-safe mechanism had been devised for the punch-card apparatus. The problem stemmed from the so-called chad, the product punched out of the ballot. These very small paper rectangles tend to build up, and occasionally the buildup will prevent the stylus from completely liberating the chad. A quick glance, in most instances, would show a vacant hole, but when the ballot was processed through the tabulator, the hanging chad would be shunted over the hole resulting in no vote for a candidate, a so-called undervote.

Gore asked for a hand recount in the Palm Beach-Miami corridor because of the inordinately high number of "undervote" ballots. Sammon and the Republicans cried foul. There was no universal preset standard for counting the ballots. To them, such a standard clearly trumped counting what common sense would argue was the intended votes of the citizens, as evidenced by the detached but still dependent chad. Vincent Bugliosi most vehemently did not agree with the Republican position. In his book, *The Betrayal of America*, Bugliosi, one of the country's better known prosecuting attorneys thanks to his role in putting Charles Manson away, claims no partisan bias. Indeed, by his own insistence ("I consider myself a moderate"), he'd possibly be annoyed that I chose him to represent the Democratic point of view (17). He directs his outrage at the court for stepping in and stopping the process before all the votes could be counted. He minces no words: "The Court committed the unpardonable sin of being a knowing surrogate for the Republican Party instead of being an impartial arbiter of the law" (41). He goes on to say that the court's claim that Bush's right to equal protection under the law was violated "elevates audacity to symphonic and operatic levels."

The equal-protection language was added to the Constitution with the Fourteenth Amendment. It was coined with an eye to providing former slaves full rights as citizens. During the era of aggressive civil rights prosecution in the 1960s and '70s, the amendment was cited frequently to enlarge the vastly shrunken legal rights of minorities. In the case of the Florida election, the Bush legal team, headed by former Secretary of State James Baker, argued that counting "undervotes" was a violation of the equal-protection provision because the standards varied from county to county, and in fact varied from day to day in the same county.

Bugliosi notes that various methods of voting and counting the votes have been used in different jurisdictions throughout the two-plus centuries of the republic. Never before has the Supreme Court weighed in to a vote-counting fray. He quotes Georgetown University law professor David Cole, who said the court "created a new right out of whole cloth and made sure it ultimately protected only one person—George Bush." Bugliosi notes that the justices cited four cases in their ruling. He claims none of them was vaguely applicable to the 2000 election. He says that if a first-year law student cited those cases, his professors would encourage him not to waste two more years of his life in law school. According to Bugliosi, one of the cases referred to the payment of poll tax, another dealt with apportionment, and two others were legal attempts by smaller counties to give themselves more standing vis-à-vis more highly populated areas.

Bugliosi was aware of the *Miami Herald*'s recount of the undervote ballots. He thought the result of that survey was completely irrelevant. His interest was with the court. It had, for an instant, become a political body and, and as a citizen and a lawyer, he was outraged that it would forfeit its impartiality.

David A. Kaplan exhibits almost as much spleen of *Accidental President.* "Some years back ," he says in the second paragraph of his prologue, "the state adopted a new tourism slogan—"Florida, the Rules Are Different Here!" To which he responds, "Well, yes." Kaplan proceeds to poke fun at the strange (and his strangely abbreviated) demographics of the Sunshine State—"the Haitian refugees, the Jewish retirees, the native-born whites and blacks." He reviles our natural environment, "hurricanes, wildfires, and man-eating alligators," and also our peculiar institutions, notably "'Old Sparky,' the only malfunctioning electric chair in the nation." Major league bile is spent on Katherine Harris, the "Secretary of State with Those Eyelashes" and the high-grade street theater that swirled around the fate of the refugee orphan, Elian Gonzalez, in Miami earlier in the election year.

Then moving on to the national picture he says, "What we got from the system in 2000, when we peered through the looking glass, was not inspiring." After giving moderate hell to the national institutions ("the presidency, the Supreme Court and the stand-on-the-sidelines Congress hardly earned any bonus points,") he takes one final jab, calling it "an election gone bad, made worse by an almost inconceivable convergence of accidents, akin to a once in a century perfect political storm." After all this he concedes that the heart of the problem was "a vote that was basically a tie, both in the Electoral College and the actual number of votes cast for each side," by which, presumably, he is referring to the votes cast in Florida. Gore toted up a half-million vote plurality nationwide.

James Ceaser and Andrew Busch teach at universities in Virginia and Denver. They endorse the idea that the 2000 election, not only in Florida but nationally, mirrored *The Perfect Storm* of Hollywood film (and north Atlantic meteorological) fame. They make their case without the pyrotechnics displayed by Kaplan. They note that the upshot of the election produced a U.S. Senate with each party claiming 50 seats. In the House of Representatives, the parties had only been closer to parity three times in the history of the republic, and the presidential election — in terms of electoral votes — was the second closest in history. Being professors of social science, they express all this mathematically, saying that the election ranked 99.1 percent, if dead even was 100 percent. They call the election (and their book) *The Perfect Tie*. They note that the perfect tie created a storm of its own, one that destroyed many of the safeguards the republic had put in place to protect it from the sort of election chaos frequently seen elsewhere in the world. Finally, a "highly controversial" split ruling by the U.S. Supreme Court reversed a "highly controversial" split ruling by the Florida Supreme Court and settled the matter.

Almost everyone reading this chapter no doubt recalls the national ridicule to which the Florida election process was subject. Floridians, it was joked, could neither design a decent ballot, nor, as it turned out, count them. Or at least, so it seemed at the time. Ceaser and Busch address the mechanics of the Florida election. "The difference in vote totals between the two main candidates was smaller than the margin of error that the electoral mechanisms could handle." The professors may be poking fun at the antiquated voting technologies some Florida counties used. But in an election as close as the 2000 one, I doubt, if all counties hand-counted, the method deemed most accurate on a naïve level, the imbroglio could have been avoided. For some years I was the nominating chair of the faculty senate at a college. We had only 200 or so ballots. All the counters were college professors. Yet we sometimes had comical difficulty reconciling the results—and this was for elective offices that most candidates would have preferred to lose. Human nature being what it is, a result that would go unchallenged, in an election as close as Florida in 2000 would be, I think, a virtual impossibility.

One thing not much noted by those writing about the election were the Florida demographics that produced the tie. It may come as a surprise to many, but Florida is something of a demographic reflection of the country as a whole. Almost everyone is aware of the large Hispanic population of Florida. It is slightly more than 20 percent, really not all that much larger than the 15 percent of the national populace that is Hispanic. Jewish retirees and others from New York and the Northeast have long been identified with Florida, and they are rightly considered to be resident along the Atlantic Coast. But equally well represented in Florida is a large contingent of more conservative retirees from the Midwestern heartland. These folks settle predominantly on the Gulf Coast. (The saying is Easterners come down I-95 and turn left; Midwesterners go down I-75 and turn right.) The African American population of Florida is similar to the national average, and the panhandle and rural areas of the peninsula supports a Southern culture as vibrant as anyplace in Dixie. More than one central Florida municipality has a Confederate soldier on a plinth in the town square. This view of Florida as a mirror image of the nation may surprise those who think of the Sunshine State as an exotic vacation destination which is a lot of fun, but where you have to be careful about drinking the water. Given all this, it is hardly surprising that of the six million votes, more or less, cast in the 2000 general election in Florida, the tally for president was split almost dead even.

One-hundred and twenty-four years before 2000, Florida was a key player in another contested presidential election. In that year, the Democratic candidate, Samuel Tilden of New York, garnered a quarter million more popular votes than the Republican, Rutherford Hayes, out of a total of 8.5 million cast in the entire nation. The Republican party had been in power for sixteen years, long enough for the country to yearn for change. This natural yearning was helped along by a succession of scandals in Grant's administration. Though the administration's published foibles were relatively benign by modern standards, the reported corruption was probably just the tip of the iceberg. The country was fed up. Tilden was widely expected to sweep the election. The Republicans, being desperate, fought hard. The most bare-knuckle tactic consisted of "waving the bloody shirt" with slogans such as "Are you for Rebellion or are you for the Union?" and "Every Democrat may not be a rebel, but every Rebel was a Democrat," but when the totals were figured up, Tilden had a commanding 2 percent lead in the popular vote. Late in the night of election day, as the returns were reported by telegraph, almost everyone on the Republican side, including candidate Hayes himself, had given up hope of winning the presidency. A man could mount a horse in El Paso, Texas, and ride east through the border states, including Indiana, all the way to the Hudson River without leaving territory that had gone for Tilden. Nevertheless, he was one electoral vote shy of the White House.

According to Roy Morris Jr., in his *Fraud of the Century*, a sharp-eyed Republican activist at *The New York Times*, then a Republican-leaning organ, spotted an interesting trend late in the morning after the election. Three Southern states, Louisiana, Florida and South Carolina, were still occupied by federal troops and had Reconstruction governors. Of the three, South Carolina appeared to have tilted for Hayes, but Florida and Louisiana had been carried only narrowly by Tilden, by less than a hundred votes in Florida and several thousand in Louisiana. If those Southern states could be held (or turned), and a wavering Oregon elector kept in line, Hayes could still be declared winner. A telegram in the name of the New York Republican chair was sent to the governors of the southern states asking them to hang on for Hayes at any cost.

The candidates, Hayes and Tilden, conducted themselves during the post-election phase of the campaign as they did during the run-up to election day. They sat at home. In those days, it was considered indecorous to campaign on your own behalf, and it's entirely possible neither candidate voted for himself—this despite the high jinks that were a regular feature of elections of the time. The apparent lassitude of the Republican candidate did not mirror the vigor with which the Republican machine swung into action. Operatives were dispatched to the three disputed Southern states to bolster the local canvassing boards, all of which luckily were controlled by their partisans. The Republican forces in Florida included a former Ohio governor (and Hayes's campaign manager), two ex–Union generals, and an Iowa congressman. A dozen federal investigators were also dispatched by friendly elements in the Grant administration. Democratic "statesmen," as these observers were called, included a former governor of Georgia and Connecticut's Leverett Saltonstall. They were led by New York newspaperman Manton Marble.

But the problem was at the top of the ticket. Hayes had been a dark horse contender for the Republican nomination. He was only the titular head of the party. On the Democratic side, Tilden was very much the man. Rather than kicking visibly into command mode, Tilden remained implacably cool, calling for calm and to all intents and purposes appearing to trust the system. The Civil War had ended only a dozen years earlier. Now, hotheaded Democratic partisans spoke openly of taking up arms, and Democratic militias drilled on parade grounds around the country. Perhaps Tilden's pacific demeanor was inspired in part by a desire to dampen these sentiments. Also, perhaps his legal background caused him to keep a low profile. Among his various accomplishments was putting Boss Tweed, of the infamous Tammany Hall machine, behind bars. Modern commentators speculate that Tilden thought the contest would end up in the courts, as disputes of all stripes have a tendency to do in the United States. There he expected to carry the day. But first the votes needed to be counted.

Despite the seeming rough parity in forces between the two camps, the Democratic partisans in Florida and elsewhere, perhaps following Tilden's lackluster lead, while vigorously pressing their interest, remained a step or so behind the Republicans. The head of the Republican camp, William Chandler, for instance, toted a satchel stuffed with $10,000 in cash. Thoughtfully, the Grant administration also dispatched an active duty general and several companies of troops to Tallahassee.

The first county whose votes were scrutinized was Alachua, Gainesville being the county seat. Democrats claimed 219 votes had been added after the polls closed. Their story was that the ballot box had been kept by a Republican county chairman who bribed two poll inspectors to certify the additional ballots. After two days examining the issue the Republican board duly ruled there was insufficient reason to countenance the claim, and all Republican votes were chalked up for Hayes. One of the two ex-Union generals threw in the towel. Though twice wounded in the Civil War, Francis Barlow didn't have what it took to stand up to such brazenness. He turned tail and ran back to Brooklyn. Thereafter he was persona non grata to the party. The other Civil War general showed a better public face while privately confiding to his wife that "it was terrible to see the extent to which all classes go in their determination to win." For holding his tongue in public, this ex-serviceman received appointment as territorial governor of New Mexico. In that arena, far from the political turmoil of Washington, Lew Wallace dealt with the likes of William F. Bonny, a.k.a. Billy the Kid, and amused himself penning *Ben Hur* and similar novels.

In the meantime, the 90-odd margin for Tilden transformed into a 924-plus majority for Hayes. To achieve that end, the canvassing board threw out almost two thousand Democratic votes. On December 6, the electors, as prescribed by law, formally cast their votes in the various state capitals. In Tallahassee, the Republican votes were duly recorded and certified by the carpetbagger governor, Stearns. The Democrats were not behindhand, and they produced their own slate of electors in favor of Tilden. The U.S. Senate was controlled by the Republicans, but the Democrats had possession of the House. The Constitution gave the House the role of selecting the president in cases where no candidate received a majority of electoral votes. But before the electoral votes could be acted on in the House, the vote of the electoral college had first to be certified by the president of the U.S. Senate, controlled by Republicans, who were perfectly capable of counting only the Republican electors and proclaiming Hayes president. Backing them up were President Grant and the federal armed forces. In short, the U.S. Congress was at loggerheads. After much wrangling, a fifteen-member commission to settle the matter was agreed upon. The commission was composed of five Democratic legislators, five Republican lawmakers, and five Supreme Court justices. Four of the justices were evenly split between the parties, and the special task of those four justices was to pick the fifth justice, who would be the deciding vote. The odds-on favorite was Justice David Davis, an independent from Illinois. But Democratic state legislators, sensing an opportunity to turn the tide for Tilden, elected him to the U.S. Senate. Davis promptly resigned the Supreme Court—and the presidential quandary. All the remaining jurists were Republican. The one most acceptable to southern Democrats was Joseph Bradley, who had unexpectedly voted to limit the power of Reconstruction. The hapless Democrats picked Bradley. He did as most Gilded Age politician could be sure to do—he went for the home side—and the ultimate result was the swearing in of Rutherford (universally known as Rutherfraud) Hayes.

How does the election of 1876 reflect on the contest in 2000? Both elections were almost complete draws. The country saw the absurd spectacle of the device that was supposed to make a selection in the political arena, the election, being thrown into the political arena for a determination. In both instances, politicians chose the institution that ostensibly was the least political, the Supreme Court, to cast the final ballot. All this is not the same as saying that the politicians actually expected an objective determination. In the case of the imbroglio of 1876, the Democrats tried to manipulate the presumed deciding vote on the commission, Justice Davis, by electing him to the Senate. It is assumed that the Bush team chose the Supreme Court as the final arbiter because of the edge in Republican justices, all of whom — as Bugliosi notes — did indeed rule in Bush's favor. In both cases, despite harsh words by critics from the other political side, the system produced a president without undue civil disorder (and indeed hardly any civil disorder at all, never mind the vitriolic rhetoric). The appearance of the rule of law — though a bit tarnished — was preserved, and the republic stumbled on.

In the introduction, I promised to reveal the true winner of the 2000 race for the presidency in Florida and thereby the nation as determined by the *Miami Herald*. Thanks to Florida's sunshine law, the ballots were open to inspection after the election. The *Miami Herald* employed an identical methodology in an inspection of all "undervotes," those ballots on which the machine count registered no vote for president, about 60,000 ballots. The *Herald*'s team consisted of a reporter and an accountant from a respected firm of CPAs, and an employee of the supervisor of elections in each county. Using the most restrictive standard, that which would allow only for cleanly punched holes, out of the approximately six million votes cast in Florida, Gore won by three votes (9). Had a more permissive standard been employed counting "every pinprick, dimple or hanging chad," Bush would have racked up an additional thousand votes. In short, a recount would most likely have not produced any more satisfactory result, in terms of yielding a clear winner, than what we ended up with. Let us hope, but without any great optimism, that our nation's supervisors of elections and canvassing boards learned something from the drawn-out election of 2000.

## Works Cited and Consulted

Bugliosi, Vincent. *The Betrayal of America: How the Supreme Court Undermined the Constitution and Chose Our President.* New York: Thunder's Mouth Press/Nation Books, 2001.

Dershowitz, Alan. *Supreme Injustice: How the High Court Hijacked Election 2000.* New York: Oxford University Press, 2001.

Kaplan, David A. *The Accidental President: How 143 lawyers, 9 Supreme Court Justices, and 5,963,110 (Give or Take a Few) Floridians Landed George W. Bush in the White House.* New York: Morrow, 2001.

Merzer, Martin. *The Miami Herald Report: Democracy Held Hostage.* New York: St. Martin's Press, 2001.

Morris, Roy, Jr. *Fraud of the Century: Rutherford B. Hayes, Samuel Tilden, and the Stolen Election of 1876.* Waterville, Maine: Thorndike Press, 2003.

Sammon, Bill. *At Any Cost: How Al Gore Tried to Steal the Election.* Washington, D.C.: Regnery, 2001.

# About the Contributors

**Edmondson Asgill** received a Ph.D. from the University of South Florida and holds the rank of professor at Bethune-Cookman University. His research interests are in African, African-American, Caribbean and American literatures.

**Joy M. Banks**, a Florida native, is the catalog librarian at Florida Southern College. She earned a master of library and information science degree at Clarion University of Pennsylvania. She has also published on Florida historical fiction.

**Salena Coller** is an academic librarian at American InterContinental University. She holds an MSLS from the University of South Florida. Her writing interests include American literature, Florida history, information literacy and technology in the classroom.

**Steve Glassman**, MFA/MA, professor of humanities at Embry-Riddle University, has authored or edited twelve books, most dealing with Florida.

**Duncan H. Haynes**, professor emeritus at the University of Miami, received a Ph.D. in molecular biology from the University of Pennsylvania and conducted postdoctoral work at the Max Planck Institute in Goettingen, Germany. He writes South Florida–based mysteries under the pen name Dirk Wyle (www.dirk-wyle.com).

**Keith L. Huneycutt**, professor of English and chair of the Humanities Division at Florida Southern College, earned his Ph.D. from the University of North Carolina at Chapel Hill in 1988. He is a past president of the Florida College English Association. His publications include a co-authored book, *Echoes from a Distant Frontier: The Brown Sisters' Correspondence from Antebellum Florida* (2004), and various articles on Florida literature and history.

**Valerie E. Kasper** is an instructor in English at Saint Leo University. Her interest is African American literature.

**Steven Knapp** is an assistant professor of English at Indian River State College in Fort Pierce, Florida. In 2006, on a grant from Rotary International, he taught English and world history in Peru. His literary interests include G.K. Chesterton and Zora Neale Hurston.

**Sarah M. Mallonee** is an assistant professor of English at Indian River State College. She is currently finishing her dissertation on 19th century Anglo-Irish writers at the University of Florida.

## About the Contributors

**James H. Meredith**, a retired professor of English at the U.S. Air Force Academy, is president of the Ernest Hemingway Foundation and Society, and a member of the board of the F. Scott Fitzgerald Society. His articles, "Hemingway's Band of Brothers: The World War I Veterans in *To Have and Have Not*" and "Who Murdered the Vets?" are forthcoming in *Hemingway's Key West: A Reassessment*.

**Margaret Mishoe** received her Ph.D. in linguistics from the University of South Carolina. She is currently an assistant professor in humanities at Embry Riddle University. Her fields of interest include Southern dialects, in-group language, and diversity issues in language. She is working on a book of creative nonfiction to be titled *Redneck Palaces: Growing Up Poor in the South*.

**Rafael Miguel Montes** is a professor of English at St. Thomas University in Miami, Florida. A graduate of the University of Miami doctoral program in English, he is the author of *Making Places/Haciendo Lugares: Generational Traumas in Contemporary Cuban-American Literature* and has published numerous articles in the field of Cuban studies and popular culture.

**Linda B. Moore** is a composition instructor at the University of West Florida.

**Jeff Morgan**, associate professor of English at Lynn University, is the author of *Sarah Orne Jewett's Feminine Pastoral Vision* and is poetry editor for *Florida English*. He lives in Boynton Beach with his wife, Dana, and son, Colin.

**Michael Perez** is a lecturer in humanities at Embry-Riddle University in Daytona Beach. He earned a master of fine arts degree in creative writing from the University of Houston. Recent poems have appeared in *BLOOM* and *Crab Orchard Review*.

**Tammy Powley** is an assistant professor of English at Indian River State College in Fort Pierce, Florida. She is a graduate of the University of Central Florida, where she earned a Ph.D. in texts and technology. Her academic interests include weblogging and domestic technology, and she regularly writes for the arts and crafts industry.

**Alan Pratt**, Ph.D., is a professor of humanities at Embry-Riddle University in Daytona Beach, the motorsports capital of Florida. He writes about motorcycles, modernism, and meaninglessness. His books include *The Dark Side: Thoughts on the Futility of Life*, *The Critical Response to Andy Warhol*, and *Black Humor: Critical Essays*.

**Kathleen Robinson** is a visiting assistant professor at Eckerd College in St. Petersburg, Florida. She is currently completing her Ph.D. in modern American literature at the University of South Florida in Tampa. Her research interests range from Ernest Hemingway and Rebecca West to trauma and rhetorical theory.

**E. Stone Shiflet** is the writing-across-the-curriculum director for Capella University. She is the board secretary for the Florida College English Association and is actively involved in research on the Florida footprint of both F. Scott Fitzgerald and Ernest Hemingway. She received a Ph.D. from the University of South Florida.

# Index

*Ace Ventura* 140, 141
Achenbach, Joel 134
advertising age 15, 18
African Americans 3, 22, 107, 116, 139–142, 185, 187, 193–199, 261
Air Force Academy 3
Alaska 48, 217, 225
Alcazar Hotel 51, 52, 53
Alexander Springs 101
Allen, Ross 21–22, 30, 230
alligators 5, 11, 17, 25–27, 31–33, 85, 94, 101, 111, 117, 123–128, 131–137, 140, 142, 227, 228, 232, 259
"American Riveria" 205
America's Cup 204
Ames, Fisher 215
*Ammidown* 30, 31
Angelfish Creek 90
Anglos 181
Anheuser-Busch 7, 8, 9, 14, 29
Animal Kingdom 12
anti-assimilation 173
Apollo 1, 163–171
*Apollo 13* 168
Aquatica 9, 12, 17
Archive of the Indies 206
Arizona 67, 122, 217, 225
Army Corps of Engineers 81, 96, 104
Art deco 45, 53, 54, 55, 98, 104, 241
Asgill, Edmondson 3, 185
Ashton, Chas 239, 251
Atlantic Coast 261
Atocha 211–214, 216
*The Autobiography of an Ex-Colored Man* 199

Bacchus, A.E. "Bean" 185, 186, 187, 188, 232
Bacon, Kevin 168
Bahia Honda 89, 90
Bain, Elizabeth M. 162–163, 170
Baker, Carlos 93, 154, 157, 259
Baker, Hezekiah 187
Baldwin, Paul 209
Banana River 65, 160
Baraka, Imamu Amiri 187, 199
Barbour, Thomas 60, 126
Barnes Sound 90
barrier islands 77, 83, 84, 85, 91, 92, 237
Barry, Dave 1, 16, 17, 75, 137
Bartram, William 25, 31, 127

baseball 4, 224, 232
bass fishing 236
Bay of Pigs 175
Beach, William J. 206
Beare, Nikki 215
Beater, Jack 215
Beatty, Bob 188, 190, 193, 199
Behune Cookman University 3, 26, 106, 193
Beirne, Mike 8, 17
Bellavance-Johnson, Marsha 150, 156–157
Belleair Beach 105, 112
Berle, Milton 34
Bernhard, Brendan 116
The Bible 227
Bike Week 236, 238, 240, 243, 244, 247, 248, 250, 251
Biketoberfest 238, 248, 250
Biltmore Hotel 80
*The Birdcage* 34, 36, 38
Biscayne Bay 47, 73, 74, 78, 80, 84, 89–91
bisexuality 40
Bishop, Elizabeth 43, 44
Black, Al 188, 192
Blake, William 196, 199
Blech, Jörg 134–134
Blind Pig 156
Bluebird 240
boating 22, 29, 66, 72–74, 77–82, 86, 88, 92, 93, 94, 133, 140, 164, 203, 210, 218
Boca Ciega Bay 118, 192
Boca Raton 48, 93
*Body Heat* 140, 142, 144, 145
*Body of Evidence* 114
Boey, Valerie 121, 134
Bogart, Humphrey 57, 144, 155, 228
Bogle, Donald 104, 116
Bok Tower 24
Bond, James 139, 185
Bonus March on Washington 154
Boren, Lamar 101
Borges, Luis 178
Boston 151, 184, 199, 218, 222
Botánica el Indio Amazónico 179
Bowers 10, 17
Boynton Beach 55, 56, 229
Braden, Susan 50–53, 56
Bradenton 85, 224
*The Brady Bunch* 165
Bragg, Rick 31

267

The Breakers Hotel 49, 50, 51, 93
*Breakfast at Tiffany's* 42
Brennan, Carlene Fredericka 150, 157
Breslauer, Ken 20, 29, 31
Brevard 60, 75, 160, 161, 163, 165, 166, 170, 171
Bridges, Lloyd 22, 101, 207
Briggs, Amy 68, 75
Brinnin, John 43
Brokaw, Tom 41
Bronfman, Edgar 10, 18
Brontë, Emily 197
Broward 81, 92, 117, 243, 254
Brown, Bob 15, 17, 30–31
Brown, Ed 215, 230
Brown, Thomas 248, 251
Brubaker, "Bru" 105
Buckner, George 191
Buffet, Jimmy 213–215
Bugliosi, Vincent 258, 259, 264
bull shark 118, 129–130, 135–136
Bullock, Penelope 196, 199
Buñuel, Luis 178
Burgess, Robert 215
*Burn Notice* 106, 108, 109, 110, 115
Burnett, Gene 215
Busch Gardens 7, 24, 29, 85
Butler, Joseph A. 134, 192, 193
Butler, Robert 190
buttonwood 90
*By Reef and Trail: Bob Leach's Adventures in Florida* 204

Cabeza de Vaca, Álvar Núñez 216, 228, 230
caiman 124
Caine, Horatio 106–108, 113
Caldicott, David 134
California 6, 17, 22, 46, 77, 99, 100, 106, 107, 114, 115, 138, 140, 159, 165, 184, 217, 225, 234, 237, 242
Calle Ocho 178, 182
Caloosahatchee River 81, 82, 86
Campbell, Sir Malcolm 239–240
Campbell, Mark R. 108, 126, 134
Canada 94, 168, 217
Cancun 231
*Cane* 106, 110, 116
Cape Canaveral 1, 61, 65, 70, 72, 132, 160–164, 167, 171
Cape Kennedy 100
Cape Verde 71–72
*Capitana (El Rubi Segundo)* 206
Capodagli, Bill 17
Capote, Truman 42–44
Captain Kirk 167
Carbonell, Nestor 110
Card Sound 90
The Cardozo 54
Carlson, Charlie 26
Carney, Art 102
carnival 164, 239
Carr, Archie 126

Carrère and Hastings 51–52
Carter 1, 16, 104
Caruso, David 106–107, 115
The Casa Monica 51, 53
*El Castillito* 172
Castro, Fidel 107, 175, 176, 177
Centers for Disease Control 75, 122, 134
Chaflin, Paul 47
*The Challenger* 168, 252
Chesnutt, Charles 188, 195, 199
Chicago 35, 52, 91, 116, 205, 215–216, 218, 232
*Chicago Tribune* 205
China 15, 144, 246
*China Moon* 144
Chinese dragon 124
Choy, Barry 65, 75
Christ of the Deep 90
CIA 108, 175
Ciardi, John 43
Cidre, Cynthia 110
City Walk 9–10, 13
Civil War 21, 30, 33, 57, 95, 127, 149, 153, 155, 160, 193, 194, 232, 262, 263
Clair, Maxine 195, 199
Clark, James 6, 17
Clarke, Gerald 43, 44
Clarke, Joe 196
Clearwater 29, 85
Clewiston 82
coastline 77–78, 84, 85, 91
Cocoa Beach 94, 100, 161–164, 166, 167
*The Cocoanuts* 140
Coconut Grove 78, 80, 91, 178
Coconut Grove Sailing Club 78
*Cocoon* 143
Cole, E.C. 205
Coleridge, Samuel Taylor 21
Coles, David J. 19, 31
Colgate College 231, 232
Coller, Salena 4, 231
*The Columbia* 168
Connecticut 222, 262
contact zones 181
Cook, Geoffrey 193, 199
Cooper, Gordon 161
Coral Gables 32, 46, 80, 177
Coral Gables Waterway 80
Coral Reef Yacht Club 78
coral reefs 83, 88–89, 92
coral snakes 118–119
Cordova Hotel 53
Cormier, Dan 229–230
cottonmouth 122
Cowpens 90
Crane, Louise 43
Crawford, Janie 196, 197
*The Creature from the Black Lagoon* 22
*The Creature Walks Among Us* 22
Crislip, Kathleen 231, 235
Crist, Gov. Charles 139, 192
Crockett, James "Sonny" 103

Index                                                                269

crocodiles 25–26, 118, 124–125, 128, 132
Croker, Frank 239
"Cross My Heart and Hope to Die" 233
Croucher, Sheila L. 173, 184
Cruz-Martínez, A.X. 134
*CSI: Crime Scene Investigation* 106
*CSI: Miami* 106
*CSI: New York* 106
Cuba 3, 103, 104, 110, 116, 140, 141, 142, 145, 152, 157, 172–179, 182–184, 207
Cuban-Americans 103, 177, 182
cultural paralysis 173
Cunanan, Andrew 41–42
Cypress Gardens 20, 22, 23–25, 29–32

Daley, Brian James 131, 135
Daniels, Willie 190–91, 193
Dante Alighieri 217
Davidson, W.C. 21
Davis, Arthur P. 196, 199
Davis, D.P. 205
Davis, David 263, 264
Davis, Susan G. 8, 17
Davis Island Yacht Club 78
Day, Dwayne 171
Daytona Beach 4, 37, 61, 68, 70, 79, 94, 193, 231, 234–251, 256
*Daytona: From the Birth of Speed to the Death of the Man in Black* 238
Daytona 200 240
Daytona 500 238, 242, 249
Deering, James 47, 91
Deggans, Eric 110, 116
Deland, Henry 245
DeMille, Cecil B. 203, 215
De Mott, John S. 235
Dershowitz, Alan 264
Destin 139
DeVries, Janet 56
Dexter, Morgan 110
diaspora 176
Dick, Philip K. 159, 171
Dickinson, Emily 150, 170–171
Didion, Joan 174–178, 181, 184
Ding Darling National Wildlife Refuge 117
dinoflagellate 67–68
Dionysus 232
Discovery Cove 7–8, 13, 28
Disney, Walt 5–23, 29, 31, 34, 36, 37, 44, 115, 138, 157, 161, 164, 212, 216, 219, 236
Disney World 6–7 9–13, 29
Disney's Hollywood Studios 7, 12
Disson, Hamilton 81
*The Divine Comedy* 228
Dodge Charger 238
Doll, Susan 30, 31, 104, 116, 139, 140–145, 233, 235
dolphins 2, 8, 13, 27, 28, 67, 91, 140, 142
Donahue, Troy 199
Douglas, Marjory Stoneman 79, 97, 114
Drye, Willie 154, 157

Duggins, Pat 167, 169, 171
Dunbar, Paul Lawrence 194, 199
Dunlop, Beth 46–48, 56
Duquesne, Calleigh 106

ear amoeba 58, 66, 67
Earnhardt, Dale 99, 242, 245
Eckerd College 3
Eden 30, 100, 226, 227
The Edison Hotel 54
Eglin Air Force Base 164
Eisner, Michael 9
Elizondo, Hector 110
Elliott Key 78, 84, 89, 91
Ellison, Ralph 43
Embry-Riddle Aeornautical University 3–4, 247
*Empty Nest* 99, 114, 115
Enge, Kevin M. 122, 135
*The Enterprise* 168
EPCOT 12
*Esquire* 151–153, 157, 158
estuarine 127
Everglades 2, 21, 33, 47, 48, 50, 58, 59, 62, 79, 80, 81, 86–87, 93, 97–98, 100–101, 111, 125, 126, 132, 133, 139, 144, 175, 193, 236
Everglades City 80, 86
exile 110, 172, 176, 178–179, 182

Faberes, Shelley 233
Faherty, William Barnaby 161–168, 171
Fairchild, David 60–61
Fairchild Tropical Garden 60
Fakahatchee swamp 126
*A Farewell to Arms* 148, 150, 157, 158
Faulkner, William 148, 155
FBI 114, 175
Fears, Mary L. 194, 199
Feast of Flowers 23
Federal Wrecking Act of 1825 203
Fernandez, Susan J. 141–142, 144, 146
*First Men on the Moon* 165
Fisher, Ames, Jr. 90
Fisher, Mel 3, 208–216
Fisher, Rudolf 188, 199
fishing 66, 77, 79, 81–86, 89, 91–92, 94, 95, 127, 141, 147–148, 151, 161, 204, 218, 236, 242
Fitch, Jim 188–189, 199
Fitch, Moe 215
Fitzgerald, F. Scott 152–153
Flagler, Henry 42, 45, 49–53, 56, 89, 91, 93–94, 143–144, 161, 205
Flamingo 86–87, 125, 132
Flekke, Mary M. 30, 31
Fletcher, Alex 188–189, 199
*Flipper* 99–101, 140, 178, 219
Florea, Johnny 215
Florida Bay 65, 84, 87, 88, 90, 125, 132
Florida black racers 122
Florida East Coast Railroad 89, 91, 94

Florida Internal Improvement Fund 209
Florida Keys 44, 59, 66, 73, 77, 79, 84, 87–91, 97, 125, 138, 142, 154–155, 202–203, 206, 210, 212, 215–216
Florida Splendid China 15, 17
Floridaland 29, 31
Flynn, Hal 135
Fontainebleau Hotel 99–100
*Fool's Gold* 214, 216
*For Whom the Bell Tolls* 150
Ford Motor Company 223–224
foreignness 179
Ft. Lauderdale 15, 35, 78, 92–94, 97, 117, 151, 230–235, 243
Ft. Lauderdale Yacht Club 78
Ft. Myers 82
Ft. Pierce 94, 185, 189, 209, 210
Ft. Walton Beach 85
Fort Wilderness 7
Fox, Charles Donald 210, 215
France, William, Jr. 243
France, William, Sr. 239–241, 243–246
Francis, Connie 46, 94, 233, 263
Frick, Olin 206, 208
Frost, Robert 43
Funkshion 38

Gainesville 17, 31, 32, 41, 56, 76, 116, 130, 145, 146, 157, 158, 171, 184, 191, 200, 235, 262
Gale, Kevin 111, 116
García, María Cristina 184
Garvin, Glenn 107, 110, 116
Gasparilla 86, 215
Gatorama 26, 31
Gatorland 19, 20, 25, 26, 27, 31, 32
Gay Days 36, 44
Geerts, B. 64, 75
Geggis, Anne 247–251
Gellhorn, Martha 148, 149
Gemini 163
Genoa 51
Genovese, Peter 31–32
*Gentle Ben* 99, 100, 101, 219
Georgia 35, 62, 77, 82, 94, 120, 124, 134, 202, 222, 237, 262
Gerena-Morales, Rafael 221, 230
Germany 155, 168
Gibson, James 188, 190, 192
Gillingham, James C. 135
Gilpin, Vincent 215
Gingrich, Arnold 151, 152, 158
Glassman, Steve 1, 57, 117, 146, 244, 250–252
Glenn, John 115, 161, 167, 239
Glenn, Scott 161
Glicksberg, Charles 187, 199
Goddard, Paulette 203
*God's Trombones* 194, 199
Goggin, Dr. John M. 209
*Going to Miami: Exiles, Tourists, and Refugees in the New America* 173
Gold Coast 92, 103

Golden, Fran 104–105, 114–116
Golden, Joseph 65–66
Golden Age of television 98
Golden Dragon 209
*The Golden Girls* 99, 114, 115
Goldstone, James 215
Gonzalez, Rick 55–56
Goodnough, Abby 133, 135
Gorin, Janice 146
Goss, James 102, 116, 215
*Governor's Report on Treasure* 209
Grable, Betty 23, 142
Grant, Ulysses 261–263
Grapefruit League 224, 232
Gray, Norris 163, 171
Great Depression 33, 54, 73, 140, 152, 155, 240
Great Hurricane of 1935 147
*Green Hills of Africa* 148
Greenberg, Paul 151, 158
Griggs, Melissa 251
Grissom, Gus 161, 164
Guillemette, Roger 166, 171
Gulf Coast 62, 141, 216, 261
Gulf of Mexico 67, 68, 72, 77, 82, 84, 88, 90, 106, 118, 135
Gulf Stream 68, 71, 72, 83, 88–90, 92, 95
*Gunga Din* 180

Hagman, Larry 100
Hair, Alfred 188–189, 191–192
Haise, Fred 168
Halifax River Yacht Club 78
Hall, Ken 189, 192, 199
Hall, W.A. 204
Hanks, Tom 168
Harbor Branch Oceanographic Institution 94
Harcourt Brace Jovanovich 8
Harding, Brett E. 131, 135
Harlem Renaissance 188, 195
Harley-Davidson 238, 245, 249
Harris, Ed 144, 161
Harris, Katherine 254, 255, 258, 259
Harris, Susan 115
Haug, Jim 249, 251
Havana 72, 91, 153, 172–175, 180, 182, 184
Hawk Channel 89, 90
Haynes, Duncan 77
Hearn, Lafcadio 21, 32
Hedstrom, Oscar 239
Hemingway, Ernest 3, 43, 73, 90, 147–158
Hemingway, Gregory 136, 148, 150
Hemingway, Hadley 150
Hemingway, Pauline 148–150, 157
Hensley, Joe L. 229–230
*Hercules Against the Moon* 165
Hersey, John 43
Heupel, Michelle R. 130, 135
Hiaasen, Carl 1, 180
Hialeah 172–173
Higgins, Cara 151
The Highwaymen 3, 185–193, 198, 199–200

Hiller, Herbert L. 234–235
Hillsborough County 121, 134
Himes, Tommy C. 126, 135
Hinman, Dayle 114
Hinton, Ed 238–239, 240–241, 251
Hirschorn, Michael 113, 116
Hodanish, Stephen 75
Hohauser, Henry 42, 50, 53–54
Holland 168
Hollis, Tim 21–23, 29–32
Holy Land Experience 15, 17
Homestead-Miami Raceway 236
homosexuality 33, 35, 36, 38, 40, 43, 44, 141
*Homosexuality and Citizenship in Florida* 40
Hood, Glenda 192
Howard, Ron 143, 168
Huber, Daniel R. 135
*Huckleberry Finn* 142
Hudnut Perfumes 149
Hudson, L. Frank 216
Hughes, Langston 187, 195, 199
Hulk Hogan 99, 105, 112, 116
Huneycutt, Keith 3, 19
Hunter, Rod 118, 135, 211
hurricanes 1, 3, 42, 58, 59, 63–64, 71, 72, 74–75, 81, 98, 138, 142, 144, 153, 187, 227–228, 259
Hurston, Zora Neale 185, 186, 193–194, 196–200
Hurt, William 140, 144
Huston, John 57

*I Dream of Jeannie* 99, 100, 167, 171, 219
"I Dream of Jeannie Lane" 167
immigrants 19, 85, 145, 183, 228
InBev 14
Indian Key 73, 90
Indian River 4, 65, 94, 160, 161, 185, 186, 217
Indian River Community College 3
Indianapolis Speedway 239
Inez (hurricane) 70, 71
International Fishing Hall of Fame 151
International Game Fish Association 151
International Speedway 241–243, 245, 248
Intracoastal Waterway 50, 70, 78, 84–85, 91–94, 96, 237
Irene Marie Models 42
Iscan, M. Yagar 128, 135
Islands of Adventure 9, 10, 13, 17
Ivan Tors Studios 101

*The Jackie Gleason Show* 42, 102, 219
Jacksonville 25, 35, 37, 70, 78, 82, 91, 94, 98, 139, 189, 194, 232
Jamaica 231
James, Daniel 136
Japan 34
Jardines de Sabatini 47
*Jaws* 130, 139, 140
Jefferson, Thomas 188
Jewfish Creek 90

Jewfish Key 154
Jim Crow laws 180, 186, 194
John F. Kennedy Library 151
Johns Committee 40, 41
Johnson, Don 103, 105
Johnson, James Weldon 185, 193–196, 198–199
Johnson, Lyndon 209
Johnson, Rosamond 194
*Jonah's Gourd Vine* 196, 199
Jones, Jane Anderson 26, 32
Juan Carlos, King 53, 212
Juckett, Gregory 136
Jumperoo 26, 27
Juneteenth 193, 198
Juniper Spring 82
Jupiter 92, 93, 105, 217, 224

Kahn, Chris 75
Kaplan, David 200, 259, 260, 264
*Karenia brevis* 67
Kasper, Valerie 3, 98
Kawasaki 238
Kayemba, Paul 139, 146
Keller, Daniel 9, 17
Kemanjo, Wangero Leewanika 187
Kennedy, John F. 163, 168–169, 176, 252
Kennedy, Sarah 8, 17
Kennedy Space Center 94, 159–160, 163, 170–171, 191, 217
Key Biscayne 78, 84, 89, 91
Key Biscayne Yacht Club 78
Key Largo 57, 72, 89, 90, 132, 144, 228
Key West 1, 3, 34, 37, 42, 43–44, 48, 70–71, 73, 77, 85, 89, 90–91, 99, 111, 147–158, 202–203, 211–214, 216, 243
Killicks, Logan 196
Kinsey, Alfred 233
Kirby, Doug 27, 31
kitsch 179
Klinkenberg, Jeff 192, 200
Knapp, Steven 4, 217–219, 223
Köppen, Wladimir 59
Kramden, Ralph 102
Krome Detention Center 177
Ku Klux Klan 186
Kubinski, Thad 117
Kubrick, Stanley 167

*LA Ink* 112
Labor Day Hurricane of 1935 74
Lake Buena Vista 6
Lake City 26, 31, 193
Lake George 24
Lake Monroe 94, 236
Lake Okeechobee 58, 65, 74, 77, 79, 80, 81–82
Lake Placid 226–227, 230
Lake Wales 24
Lake Worth 93
Lakeland 3, 13, 20, 25, 192, 224
Lane, Nathan 34
Langley, Ricky 136

Lanier, Sidney  21, 202–204, 216
Larsen, Nella  195, 200
*Lassie*  99–101
Latin America  47
Latin Grammys  174
Leesburg  243, 244
Lemmon, Jack  105
LeMoyne, Jacques  126, 127
Leno, Jay  107
Leon County  114, 228, 254
Letterman, David  107, 108
Levin, Henry  235
Lewis, R.L.  188, 191–192
Liberty City  180
*Life on Mars*  174, 178, 179, 184
*Life on the Hyphen*  182, 184
*Light This Candle: The Life and Times of Alan Shepard*  167
Lightner, Otto  52
lightning  58, 61, 62, 63, 66, 69, 70, 75–76, 130
Lignumvitae,  90
Lincoln, Abraham  38, 105, 188, 194
*The Lion's Paw*  82, 97
Little Haiti  180
Little Havana  180, 182
Loggerhead Lane  12, 13, 17
London  45, 75, 95, 112, 184, 216
*Lonely Planet*  7, 10, 11, 13, 17
Long, Nancy Ann Zrinyi  200
Long Key  73
Longboat Key  85
*Lost in Space*  164–165, 171
Louvre (Musée du)  47
Lovell, Jim  168
Lower Matecumbe Key  73, 90, 153, 154
Lucas, George  167
Lurie, Alison  44
Luscombe, Richard  151, 158
Lynch, Charles  134, 164–166, 170–171
Lynn University  3
Lyon, Eugene  216

MacDonald, John D.  93
machismo  177
Madrid  47, 48
Magic Kingdom  5–7, 11–12, 18, 29, 36, 37, 39
*Malecón*  182
Mallonee, Sarah M.  4, 217, 227
Mallory Dock  90
Mallory Square  44
Malone, Vernon  216
Manatee River  85
manatees  2, 67, 85, 90, 94
mangrove  77, 79–80, 83, 86–88, 90, 95, 125, 127, 132
Mann, Michael  105
Marathon  89–90
Marco Island  78–79, 86
Marco Island Yacht Club  78
Maready  25, 32
Marineland  20, 22, 27–28, 32

Marling, Karal Ann  6, 17
Marsh, Bill  231, 233, 235
Marth, Del  139, 146
Martinique  155
Marx Brothers  57
Matanzas Inlet  94
Matheson, Whitney  80, 111, 116
Mathewson, R. Duncan, III  216
McAuliffe, Christa  168–171
McCarthy, Kevin M.  40, 216, 232, 235
McEveety, Vincent  216
McGee, Travis  93
McIver, Stuart  156, 158
McKee, Art  206, 207, 215
McLendon, Roy  148, 150, 158, 192
McLeod-Bethune, Mary  185, 193, 198, 200
McLuhan, Marshall  169, 171
McNeil, Alex  102, 105, 116
Mediterranean Revival  46, 47, 48, 49, 52, 53, 55, 56
*Meet the Fockers*  140, 143
Mel Fisher Maritime Museum  90, 216
Menzer, Joe  241, 251
Mercury  161, 163
Meredith, James  3, 147
Merzer, Martin  264
Mexico  71, 84, 209, 225, 228, 231, 263
Miami  1, 3, 6, 16, 20, 23–24, 26, 28, 30, 31, 32, 34–38, 41, 42, 47–48, 53–56, 60–61, 66, 72–73, 77–81, 83–84, 88, 90–93, 98–116, 123, 125, 127, 139–140, 142, 145, 150–151, 172–184, 205, 207, 211, 215–216, 222, 232, 236, 240, 243, 248, 251, 253, 254, 258, 259, 264
Miami Animal Police  99, 111
Miami Beach  37–38, 41, 54–55, 80, 84, 91, 102–104, 112
Miami-Dade  73, 81, 92, 103, 111, 176, 243, 254
*Miami Ink*  112
*Miami Vice*  100, 106
Michigan  220–224, 227
Mickey Mouse  6, 12, 14, 36, 37, 236
*Midnight Cowboy*  143
Miguel Montes, Rafael  3, 172
Minnie Mouse  12, 164
*Minority Report*  159
Minton, Jim  191–192, 200
Mishoe, Margaret  3, 33
Missouri  34, 44, 148
Mizner, Addison  45, 47–48, 50, 53–54, 56
Molasses Reef  90
Monroe, Gary  186–190, 192, 200
*Monster*  141, 248
*Moon Pilot*  165
Moore, Linda B.  3, 138, 186
Morgan, Harry  110, 155
Morgan, Jeff  3–4, 45, 231
Mormino, Gary  5–7, 17, 19, 21, 23, 24, 27, 29–32
Morris, Roy, Jr.  261, 264
*Morro Castle*  152, 153, 157, 172

Moser Channel 90
Moto Guzzi 238
motorcycles 240, 243, 246, 251
motorsports 4, 236, 237, 238, 239, 240, 241, 244, 246, 247, 248, 249, 250
Mount Holyoke 232
MTV 34, 103
Muir, John 127
Mullane, Mike 169, 170, 171
*Murderball* 112
Myakka River 95

Naegleria 66, 67
Naples 86, 125–126, 224, 226, 236
NASA 3, 98, 100, 160, 163, 165–171
NASCAR 4, 238, 240–246, 248–251
*National Geographic* 26, 75, 157, 209, 210, 212, 213–214, 216
National Public Radio 169
Navarre Beach 139
NCSL Elections Reform Task Force 230
Negro spirituals 195
Neillands, Robin 27, 32
Nelson, Major 167
Nelson, Richard Allen 100–103, 116
*New Masses* 155
New River 93
New Smyrna Speedway 236
New York 17, 26, 31, 32, 41, 43–45, 54, 56, 72, 97, 99, 102–103, 105–106, 116, 133, 135–136, 138, 140, 146, 150–151, 157–158, 166, 171, 184, 199, 200, 204, 215, 216, 218, 220, 222, 229–231, 235, 251, 261, 262, 264
*New York Times* 204
Newton, Harold 186, 187, 188, 190, 192
Niehrling, Henry 60
Noonburg, Greer E. 136
Northerners 217–219, 224, 226
Northrop Aeronautical Institute 165
nurses 99, 114, 115

Oberlin College 232
O'Brien, James 76, 99
O'Brien, Jodie Munro 244, 251
Ocala 20, 23, 82, 101, 119
Ocala National Forest 82, 101
O'Connell, Martin 136
*Of Mules and Men* 196
Ogle, Maureen 149, 154, 158
Ogrosky, Kirk 136
Ohr, Jim 97
Okaloosa 139
Okeechobee 76, 81, 86, 94
Okeechobee Waterway 81, 86, 94
Oklawaha 21
Olbermann, Keith 2
Olds, Ranson E. 238
Olustee 193, 198
O'Neil, Mary Elizabeth 136
Orange Bowl 176
Orlando 5–18, 23, 26–29, 32, 34, 36, 38, 58, 75, 82, 95, 115, 157, 168, 189, 199, 216, 222, 227, 236, 243, 251, 256
Ormond Beach 68, 237–238, 240, 251
Ormond Hotel 238–239
Orr, Catherine 47, 56
Orr, William 142
Osceola 21
O'Shea, John 43
O'Sullivan, Maurice 31–32, 146
Overtown 180

*Packaging Miami* 173
Padron, Justo (Jose) 123
Page, Roby 215, 248, 251
Palacio Real 47
Palazzo Carega 51
Palazzo Pitti 50
Palm Beach 25, 47–49, 54, 56, 74, 81, 92–93, 105, 110, 114, 217, 227, 230, 232, 248, 254, 255, 256–258
Panama City 79, 189, 231, 235, 243
Panhandle 79, 82, 85, 138
Papy, Capt. Frank 97
*Paradise Lost* 139, 144, 173
Paramount Pictures 9, 215
Parente, Audrey 246, 251
Parrish, Henry 132, 136
Parrot Jungle 24, 31
Parsley, Rodney 194
Patricios, Nicholas 54, 56
Patterson, Lundquist 167, 171
Paxton, Bill 168
Peace River 86
Pegram, Cynthia T. 67, 75
Pennekamp Coral Reef State Park 90
Pensacola 61, 70, 77–79, 85, 118, 138, 146
Perez, Lisandro 173, 181–184
Perez, Michael 3, 33
Pérez-Firmat, Gustavo 181–184
Perkins, Maxwell 147–148, 154
Persall, Steve 115–116
Pervos, Stephani 112–113, 116
Pfeiffer, Gustavus Augustus 149
Philadelphia 21, 45, 216, 232
Philcox, Phil 216
Phillips, Louis 101, 116
Phillips, Mark 165, 171
Pillans, R.D. 136
Pinsky, Mark 15
Plant, Henry 45, 53, 56, 143, 205
Plantation Key 90, 206, 207
Polevitzky, Igor B. 5
Ponce de León, Juan 1, 23, 30, 51, 52–53, 94, 98, 138, 141, 201, 205, 227, 228
Ponce Inlet 237
Pope, Dick 23, 24, 29
Port Canaveral 94, 164
Port St. Lucie 224, 226, 229
Porter, A.P. 198, 200, 202
Powley, Tammy 3, 159
Pratt, Alan 4, 236

Prentiss, Paula 233
Presley, Elvis 140, 233
Proctor, Emily 106–107
prostitution 103
Puerto Rico 231
Punnett, Dick 237, 239, 251
"Puppet on a String" 233
Pyle, Rod 163–165, 170, 171
python, Burmese 133–134

Quander, Folami 195
¿Qué Pasa, USA? 99
quinces 177, 178

Rainbow Springs 29
rattlesnakes: canebrake 122; Eastern diamondback 117, 119, 120, 122–123, 132, 134, 242, 245; Pacific Coast 121; pygmy 136
Rawlings, Marjorie Kinnan 22, 142
Ray, Russell 216
Ray, William Carl 21
Real Eight Company 207, 208, 209, 210, 211
Reap the Wild Wind 203, 215–216
Red Badge of Courage 148
red tide 58, 67, 68
Reddick, Ed 209
requiem sharks 129
Reuters 106
Revkin, Andrew C. 133, 136
Revolutionary War 33, 81, 175
Reynolds, Burt 105–106
Reynolds, Christopher 231, 235
Reynolds, Michael S. 143, 148, 158
Rhodes, Captain Rich 97
Rice, Aaron N. 136
Rickenbacker, Eddie 239
Rico, Ricardo 103
Ridgway, Charles 7, 18
Rieff, David 173–174, 181–184
Riehl, Herbert 59–60, 75
The Right Stuff 160–161
Ripley's Believe It or Not 27
The River Rats 206–208
Roach, John 75
Roberts, Livingston 188
Robinson, Katherine 3, 144, 201
Rocket to the Moon 165
Rockledge 165
Rolle, Denys 95
Roosevelt, Eleanor 73, 155, 193
Roosevelt, Franklin D. 154
Rosenthal, Marvin 15
Rosewood 142
Royal Caribbean 164
Rubin, Judy 9, 18
RuPaul 34

Sagal, Boris 235
St. Andrews Yacht Club 78
St. Augustine 26, 27, 32, 51, 52, 53, 60, 61, 79, 94, 95, 141, 149, 232

St. John's County 53
St. Johns River 61, 78, 82, 94, 95
St. Leo University 3
St. Lucie River 81, 94
St. Petersburg 20, 29, 31–32, 76–79, 85, 116, 137, 192, 200, 215–216, 224, 232, 251
St. Petersburg Yacht Club 78
St. Thomas University 3
Salas, Pablo 149
saltwater crocodiles 127
Sammon, Bill 255–256, 258, 264
Samy, Ramar Perumal 123, 136
San Antonio 45
Sanchez, Elda E. 118, 136
Sanford 82, 94, 95, 197
Sanibel Island 82, 86
Santería 179
Sarasota 17, 24, 29, 32, 44, 75, 78–79, 85–86, 97, 116, 137–138, 146, 157, 158, 215–216, 224, 235
Sarasota Bay 85
Sarasota Yacht Club 78
Savage, Carol 32
Sawgrass Mills Mall 15, 18
Scarface 41, 140, 145
Schmalz, Jeffrey 104, 116
Schmid, T.H. 136
Schoeneman, Deborah 30, 32
Schwarzenegger, Gov. Arnold 139
scuba 85, 90, 92, 101–102, 210
sea fans 88, 92, 95
Sea Hunt 22, 30, 32, 99, 101, 207, 215
Seagram Company 10
Seaquarium 28, 31–32, 101
Seaside 139, 143
SeaWorld 6–10, 12–18, 20, 28, 29
Sebring Raceway 236
Second Seminole War 98
Seminoles 21, 22, 25–26, 33, 94, 98, 126–127
Seven Mile Bridge 90
Shamu 3, 8
shark, great white 129, 130
Shark River 86
Shasta 20
Sheldon, Sidney 100, 167
Shelton, Robyn 75
Shepard, Alan 161, 167, 170–171
Shiflet, Stone 3, 147
Shulman, Allan T. 53, 56
Siegel, Wayne 55–56
silver 20–24, 26, 29, 30, 32, 101, 207, 213
Silver Springs 20–24, 26, 29, 30, 32, 101, 207
Simonton, John 149
Simonton Street 149
Simpson, Charles Torrey 60
Sinatra, Frank 178
Sinclair, Gail 156, 157, 158
Six Flags Over Israel 15, 17
six-toed cats 43, 150
Sloppy Joe's 90, 148, 154, 156, 158
Smallwood Store Museum 86

Smiley, Nixon 216
Smith, Ellen 144–145, 146
Smith, Franklin 31, 53
Smith, Jedwin 211, 213, 216
Smith, Stanley K. 225, 230
Smits, Jimmy 110, 116
Smyrna Yacht Club 78
snorkeling 83, 92, 218
snowbirds 217–223, 225–226, 228, 229–230
Solomon, Deborah 145–146
*Some Like It Hot* 141
South Beach, Miami 3, 34, 37–38, 41–42, 45, 53–55, 98, 103–104, 109, 111–112, 116, 143, 174, 178, 180–181
South Carolina 261
South Padre Island 231
Space Coast 159, 160, 161, 163, 164, 165, 166, 167, 169, 170, 171
Spain 22, 33, 45–46, 48, 50–53, 72, 85, 92–95, 98–99, 139, 149, 150, 153, 155, 160, 176–177, 180–182, 201, 204, 206–209, 211–212, 214–216, 227–228, 244
Speedweeks 238, 246
Splash Island 25
Splendid China 15
sponges 87, 88, 92
spring break 141, 231, 234, 235
spring training 232, 233
Sputnik 161, 163, 171
Squier, Ken 241, 242, 251
Stamm, Doug 20, 21, 30, 32
Stapleton, Jay 247, 251
*Star Trek* 159, 167, 168
*Star Trek: The Motion Picture* 167
*Star Wars* 167
Stevens, Wallace 43
Stevenson, Robert Louis 204
Stowe, Harriet Beecher 21
Stowe, Madeleine 144
Strabel, Thelma 203, 216
Strang, Louis 239
Streamline Moderne 55
Strictland, Alice 251
Stuart, Alexander 174, 178–181, 184
sturgeon 118, 133, 135
Sunbelt 217, 218, 220
Sunshine Skyway Bridge 96
Sunshine State 1–7, 19, 26, 34–35, 57, 59, 61, 75, 98, 99, 115–116, 118, 126, 133, 134, 138–139, 142, 145, 146, 163–164, 171, 201, 216, 218–219, 224, 229, 235, 259, 261
*Surfside 6* 99, 219
Suwannee River 132
swamp buggies 236
Swigert, Jack 168

Tallahassee 17, 31, 35, 37, 61, 114, 139, 189, 192, 216, 222, 235, 254, 262–263
Tampa 7, 29, 32, 35, 37, 53, 60–61, 65–66, 70, 74, 85, 116, 121, 189, 202, 214, 216, 221–222, 227, 232, 243

Tarbell, Ida M. 48, 56
Tarpon Springs 85
Tartikoff, Brandon 103
*Tarzan* 22, 27, 98, 139
Taylor, June 37, 137
Taylor, L.B. 216
Tebeau, Charleton 23, 30, 32
*Tell My Horse* 196, 199
Ten Thousand Islands 86
Tennant, Andy 216
Terry Bolea, a.k.a. Hulk Hogan 105
*Their Eyes Were Watching God* 196, 199
Theron, Cherize 141
Thomas, Philip Michael 103
Thompson, Neal 154, 167, 171
Thompson, Robert J. 03, 116
Thompson, Tommy 216
Thompson, William 201, 216
Thornton, Billy Ray 32
*Thunder in Paradise* 105–106
*Thunder Mountain* 9
*Thunderball* 139
Thurman, Howard 185, 193, 198
tidal backwaters 91
Tift, Asa 150
tiger shark 128, 129
Timucuan 25
*To Have and Have Not* 148, 155, 158
Tommy Bartlett's International Deer Ranch 23
tornadoes 63
*Total Recall* 159
Tran, Paula 139, 140, 146
transgender 40
Travel Channel 174
travel narratives 22, 174–176, 204
Treasure Coast 92, 216, 219
treasure hunters 201–213, 214, 215
*Treasure Island* 204
*Treasure of Matecumbe* 212, 216
treasure salvors 211
treasure seekers 201, 216
Trevor-Morris Company 149
Triumph Motorcycles 238
Trogdon, Robert W. 155, 158
Tropicana 163, 164
Truett, Richard 250–251
Tucker, Steve 240–242, 251
Turner, Buffy 216
Twain, Mark 142, 148
"Twelve Hours of Sebring" 236
2000 presidential election 2
*2001: A Space Odyssey* 167
Tyson, Tinothy B. 55–56

United States 1, 2, 15, 27, 33, 45–46, 53, 57–58, 62, 67, 72, 74, 99, 112, 118, 136, 148, 159, 161, 163, 170, 172–173, 201, 203, 208–209, 233–234, 236, 238, 241, 243, 262
Universal Orlando 6, 10, 13
University of Central Florida 13, 17, 168

University of Florida  105, 116, 230
University of West Florida  3
*Urca de Lima*  206, 216
Utopia  228

Vaca Key  90
Vega, Alex  110
Veitch, Kristin  109, 116
vernacular art  187
Vero Beach  59, 70, 94, 224, 234–235
Verrill, A. Hyatt  248, 251
Versace, Gianni  41–42
*Vibrio vulnificus*  131, 135
Viele, John  42, 44, 202, 216
Vizcaya  45, 47, 48, 91
Voight, Jon  143
Volusia  161, 236, 238, 243, 247–248, 252–254, 256–258
Volusia Speedway Park  236
von Braun, Dr. Wernher  161

Wagner, Kip  207–209, 210, 216
Wakulla Springs  22, 139
Walker, Alice  186, 196, 200
Walker, Matty  140, 142, 144
Wannado City  15, 16, 18
water moccasin  122
waterspouts  64, 65, 76
Watkins, Tim  206, 208
Wayne, John  203
Weeki-Wachee  23, 30
Wentz, Laurel  15, 18
Wet 'n' Wild  8, 10
*Where the Boys Are*  141, 233, 234, 235
White, Robb  82, 97
Whiteback  127
Whitehead, John  149, 150
Wiersema, Fred  12, 17

Wilbur, Richard  43
wildfire  68
Wilkinson, Jerry  216
Will, Lawrence  74, 76
Williams, Ester  23
Williams, Robin  34
Williams, Tennessee  43
Williams, Tim  26
Williams, Van  99
Willis, Ken  242, 251
Winsberg, Morton D.  71, 76
Winter Speed Carnival  239
Winton, Alexander  238
Wintz, Cary D.  194, 200
Wolfson, Mitchell  180
Wood, John A.  53
Woodward, Allan R  137
World War II  4, 5, 19, 20, 22, 31–32, 55, 127, 161, 163, 240
World's Most Famous Beach  237, 247
wreckers  202–203, 216
Wright, Bruce  127
Wright, Susan  241, 243, 251
WTVJ of Miami  207
Wuornos, Aileen  114, 141, 248
Wyle, Dirk  3

yachts  78
*The Yearling*  22, 140, 142
Yerkovich, Anthony  103
Yoruba  195
Young, Claiborne  97
YouTube  38, 44, 108

Zaffiro, Eileen  251
Zoglin, Richard  103, 104, 116
Zucco, Tom  137